Tenth Workshop on Noisy User-generated Text (W-NUT 2025)

Albuquerque, New Mexico, USA
3 May 2025

ISBN: 979-8-3313-1932-8

Printed from e-media with permission by:

Curran Associates, Inc.
57 Morehouse Lane
Red Hook, NY 12571

Some format issues inherent in the e-media version may also appear in this print version.

Printed with permission by Curran Associates, Inc. (2026)

For permission requests, please contact the Association for Computational Linguistics
at the address below.

Association for Computational Linguistics
209 N. Eighth Street
Stroudsburg, Pennsylvania 18360

Phone: 1-570-476-8006
Fax: 1-570-476-0860

acl@aclweb.org

Additional copies of this publication are available from:

Curran Associates, Inc.
57 Morehouse Lane
Red Hook, NY 12571 USA
Phone: 845-758-0400
Fax: 845-758-2633
Email: curran@proceedings.com
Web: www.proceedings.com

W-NUT 2025

The Tenth Workshop on Noisy and User-generated Text (W-NUT 2025)

Proceedings of the Workshop

May 3, 2025

Order copies of this and other ACL proceedings from:

Association for Computational Linguistics (ACL)
317 Sidney Baker St. S
Suite 400 - 134
Kerrville, TX 78028
USA
Tel: +1-855-225-1962
acl@aclweb.org

Introduction

The W-NUT 2025 workshop focuses on a core set of natural language processing tasks on top of noisy and user-generated text, such as those found on social media, web forums and online reviews. The internet has democratized content creation leading to an explosion of informal user-generated text, publicly available in electronic format, motivating the need for NLP on noisy text to enable new data analytics applications. We have received a total of 18 main workshop submissions, of which 16 are included in the proceedings. The workshop will be held in hybrid in-person and virtual modes. We have two invited speakers: Su Lin Blodgett and Verena Blaschke, who have generously agreed to share their ongoing research work. We are very thankful to have them in our workshop. We would like to thank the Program Committee members who reviewed the papers, as well as all of the workshop participants for submitting their work.

Organizing Committee

General Chair

JinYeong Bak, Sungkyunkwan University

Program Chair

Hyeju Jang, Indiana University Indianapolis

Co-Organizers

Rob van der Goot, IT University of Copenhagen
Weerayut Buaphet, Vidyasirimedhi Institute of Science and Technology
Alan Ramponi, Fondazione Bruno Kessler
Wei Xu, Georgia Institute of Technology
Alan Ritter, Georgia Institute of Technology

Program Committee

Reviewers

Sweta Agrawal, Hamed Alhoori, Emily Allaway, Antonios Anastasopoulos, Maria Antoniak

Eduardo Blanco

Tommaso Caselli, Paul Cook, Danilo Croce

Micha Elsner

Yoshinari Fujinuma

YeongJun Hwang, Mika Hämäläinen

Kokil Jaidka, Aditya Jain, Chao Jiang, Ishan Jindal

HyunJin Kim, Suyoung Kim, Sachin Kumar

Jaehyeok Lee, Jing Li, Lucy H. Lin, Nikola Ljubešić

Yasuhide Miura, Manuel Montes, W. Graham Mueller

Günter Neumann, Vincent Ng

Naoki Otani

Rahul Raja, Alan Ramponi, Shubhashis Roy Dipta

Iñaki San Vicente, Danae Sanchez Villegas, H. Schwartz, Mirco Schönfeld, Vishal Shah, Vincent Siddons, Dan Simonson, Abhai Pratap Singh, Andreas Spitz

Joel R. Tetreault

Sai P Vallurupalli, Daniel Varab

Xiaojun Wan, Dustin Wright

Mike Zhang

Keynote Talk

Beyond "noisy" text: How (and why) to process dialect data

Verena Blaschke
LMU Munich & MCML
2025-05-03 09:30:00 – Room: **25 - Navajo/23 - Nambe**

Abstract: Processing data from non-standard dialects links two lines of research: creating NLP tools that are robust to "noisy" inputs, and extending the coverage of NLP tools to underserved language communities. In this talk, I will describe ways in which processing dialect data differs from processing standard-language data, and discuss some of the current challenges in dialect NLP research. For instance, I will talk about strategies to mitigate the effect of infelicitous subword tokenization caused by ad-hoc pronunciation spellings. Additionally, I argue that we should not only consider *how* to tackle dialectal variation in NLP, but also *why*. To this end, I will highlight perspectives of some dialect speaker communities on which language technologies should (or should not) be able to process or produce dialectal in- or output.

Bio: Verena Blaschke is a final-year PhD student at LMU Munich. She currently researches NLP for non-standard dialects and other low-resource language varieties, investigating how robust language models are towards language variation (and how to make them more robust). Her research is supervised by Barbara Plank and co-supervised by Hinrich Schütze. She also completed a research internship at Apple where she worked on multilingual NLP, and she previously developed software for machine-assisted historical linguistics at the University of Tübingen.

Keynote Talk

What Can We Learn from Perspectives on Noisy User-Generated Text?

Su Lin Blodgett
Microsoft Research Montréal
2025-05-03 16:00:00 – Room: **25 - Navajo/23 - Nambe**

Abstract: As language technologies become increasingly ubiquitous, research has shown that they struggle with real-world language variation and use. How can we expand the set of perspectives that inform our (and thus our technologies') engagement with such variation and use, and what can we learn by doing so? First, I will describe work on minoritized language varieties: building on work using quantitative methods to illustrate technologies' poor performance for such varieties, in this work we interview speakers of African American Language to better understand their experiences with language technologies and the impacts on them when technologies fail. I will discuss what this means for how we might design and assess language technologies to handle language variation, including the limits of quantitative methods for understanding people's experiences. Second, I will discuss disagreement in people's expectations and preferences—as technologies are increasingly designed to adapt to language variation, how do people think they should behave? I will describe work on natural language generation systems showing that people's expectations can vary widely, highlighting the importance of taking into account people's complex beliefs about language and technology, and raising questions about how to decide what constitute desirable system behaviors, when engaging with real-world language variation and use.

Bio: Su Lin Blodgett is a researcher in the Fairness, Accountability, Transparency, and Ethics (FATE) group at Microsoft Research Montréal. Her research examines the ethical and social implications of language technologies, focusing on the complexities of language and language technologies in their social contexts, and on supporting NLP practitioners in their ethical work. She completed her Ph.D. in computer science at the University of Massachusetts Amherst, where she was supported by the NSF Graduate Research Fellowship, and has been named as one of the 2022 100 Brilliant Women in AI Ethics.

Table of Contents

Program

Saturday, May 3, 2025

09:15 - 09:30	*Opening Remarks*
09:30 - 10:30	*Invited Talk - Verena Blaschke*
10:30 - 11:00	*Break*
11:00 - 12:30	*Presentation - Oral*
12:30 - 14:00	*Lunch and Networking*
14:00 - 15:30	*Presentation - Poster*
15:30 - 16:00	*Break*
16:00 - 17:00	*Invited Talk - Su Lin Blodgett*
17:00 - 17:30	*Best Paper Presentation*
17:30 - 17:40	*Closing*

Towards a Social Media-based Disease Surveillance System for Early Detection of Influenza-like Illnesses: A Twitter Case Study in Wales

Mark Drakesmith*[1] Dimosthenis Antypas*[2] Clare Brown[1]
Jose Camacho-Collados[2] Jiao Song[1]

[1]Communicable Disease Surveillance Centre, Public Health Wales, Cardiff, United Kingdom
{mark.drakesmith,clare.brown5,jiao.song}@wales.nhs.uk

[2]Cardiff NLP, School of Computer Science and Informatics,
Cardiff University, Cardiff, United Kingdom
{antypas,camachocolladosj}@cardiff.ac.uk

Abstract

Social media offers the potential to provide detection of outbreaks or public health incidents faster than traditional reporting mechanisms. In this paper, we developed and tested a pipeline to produce alerts of influenza-like illness (ILI) using Twitter data. Data was collected from the Twitter API, querying keywords referring to ILI symptoms and geolocated to Wales. Tweets that described first-hand descriptions of symptoms (as opposed to non-personal descriptions) were classified using transformer-based language models specialised on social media (BERTweet and TimeLMs), which were trained on a manually labelled dataset matching the above criteria. After gathering this data, weekly tweet counts were applied to the regression-based Noufaily algorithm to identify exceedances throughout 2022. The algorithm was also applied to counts of ILI-related consultations with general practitioners (GPs) for comparison. Exceedance detection applied to the classified tweet counts produced alerts starting four weeks earlier than by using GP consultation data. These results demonstrate the potential to facilitate advanced preparedness for unexpected increases in healthcare burdens.

1 Introduction

Surveillance of symptoms of infectious diseases in the population, also known as syndromic surveillance, is an important public health function to provide warning of an incoming epidemic and prepare healthcare systems for increased demand. Such surveillance systems traditionally rely on clinical data, for example, general practitioner (GP) consultations, ambulance call-outs, sickness-related absences, and access to telephone advice services. Such data sources can be slow due to the reporting mechanisms they rely on.

In recent years, there has been increasing interest in leveraging social media to develop an early warning detection (EWD) system for infectious diseases (Pilipiec et al., 2023; McClymont et al., 2024; Aiello et al., 2019; Joshi et al., 2019). Social media provides a rapid, and high-volume data source, offering the potential to provide reliable detection of a disease outbreak or public health incident faster than traditional reporting mechanisms. Such data sources will enable more rapid and timely response to anticipate increased demand on health services.

1.1 Related Work

A systematic review of methods developed to use social media to facilitate disease surveillance identified 23 papers from as early as 2010 (Pilipiec et al., 2023) (See also (McClymont et al., 2024; Aiello et al., 2019; Joshi et al., 2019). While a wide variety of social media platforms and diseases were the subjects of these studies, the review found Twitter to be the most used social media platform and influenza the most targeted disease. A wide variety of natural language processing methods have been employed to identify health-related posts ranging from simple keyword filtering, to topic modelling and sentiment analysis. Some EWD systems built on these approaches include Epitweetr (Espinosa et al., 2022), The Twitter Health Surveillance (THS) System (Rodríguez-Martínez and Garzón-Alfonso, 2018) and SENTINEL (Şerban et al., 2019).

An issue that has been highlighted (Mollema et al., 2015) is the propensity of health-related posts to be from news, government and political outlets reporting or advising on an ongoing outbreak, rather than more direct accounts from individuals in the community describing their first-hand experiences of symptoms. For a timely and accurate signal reflecting true disease prevalence, it is important to correctly separate the latter from the former. Only a few studies have tried to directly address this issue (Şerban et al., 2019; Mackey et al.; Shen et al., 2020).

*Joint first author

Proceedings of the Tenth Workshop on Noisy and User-generated Text, pages 1–9
May 3, 2025

1.2 Aims

Our main aim is to develop an early detection system that can predict contagious illnesses' outbreaks such as influenza. To this end, we developed a pipeline to ingest Twitter (now known as X) data matching symptom-related keywords, localised to Wales, and classify tweets that describe first-hand accounts of influenza-like illnesses (ILIs), and apply an exceedance detection algorithm, a method to produce alerts of higher-than-expected incidence. We test the method's ability to provide early warning of the recent spike in flu cases in the end of 2022 which was much higher than in the previous years and placed significant demand on the healthcare system. Finally, we compared the performance of the method applied to Twitter data to that applied to general practitioner (GP) consultations for ILIs, a more established syndromic surveillance indicator.

2 Methods

In order to detect potential outbreaks in social media, we primarily rely on Twitter data (Section 2.1) and an automatic NLP-based classification methodology (Section 2.2). Then, we present the GP consultation data we use as a comparison (Section 2.3) and our methodology to identify outbreaks based on data (Section 2.4).

2.1 Data

The Twitter Academic API (Twitter, 2023) was utilised to collect tweets originated from Wales from January 2020 to January 2023. Only tweets in the English and Welsh language were collected.

2.1.1 Geolocation

Due to limitations of Twitter's API (i.e. we could only filter countries by ISO alpha-2 code and there is no one available for Wales) we utilise a map of Wales (`https://datashare.ed.ac.uk/handle/10283/2410?show=full`) and divide it in 34 equal areas which are used as parameters for the "boundary_box" field of the API. In total, 5,278,425 tweets were gathered that certainly originated from the region of Wales.

2.1.2 Keyword matching

In an effort to collect a sufficiently large dataset that can allow us to identify any early signal related to flu outbreaks, we initially identified relevant tweets by applying a filter of 22 relevant keywords during the API call: ('flu', 'ill', 'sick', 'unwell', 'fever', 'cough', 'coughing', 'bug', 'headache', 'hoarseness', 'muscle pain', 'sore throat','high temperature', 'tummy pain', 'covid-19', 'covid', 'covid19', 'coronavirus', 'blocked nose', 'runny rose', 'aches', 'fevery'). Keywords referring to symptoms were principally used, but also keywords referring to 'flu' and 'covid' were included as these are likely to be mentioned in lieu of respiratory symptoms. With geolocation and keyword filtering, 35,724 tweets were retrieved. Counts and overview of the size of the datasets can be found in Figure 1 and Table 1.

2.2 Classification

An important consideration is the identification of first-hand accounts of symptoms being experienced, which are more representative of prevalence of symptoms in the community, as opposed to tweets that provide general advice or discussion about symptoms and illnesses (see Table 2 for examples). We therefore employ a small manual annotation (section 2.2.1) and NLP methods (Section 2.2.2) to classify such tweets. In total, 2,213 tweets were classified as being first-hand accounts, approximately 6% of all retrieved tweets.

2.2.1 Manual Annotation

Aiming to investigate the difficulty of the classification and also to collect data for the training of machine learning models a sample of 121 tweets was also manually annotated by three different coders. This sample was geolocated to the whole UK, to avoid a large overlap with the Wales dataset to serve as an independent training set. Each annotator was asked to annotate tweets as TRUE if the tweet contained descriptions of ILI symptoms from a first-person perspective, and FALSE otherwise. Our results indicate a strong agreement between the coders which achieve an average of 0.68 when considering Cohen's Kappa. Having established a high agreement between the coders, an additional 751 tweets were individually annotated, bringing the total number of gathered tweets to 878[1].

2.2.2 Automatic Classification

There has been a recent influx of new large language models in the NLP field such as OpenAI's GPT-3 and Google's Bard that achieve impressive results on difficult tasks. However, for simpler tasks such as binary text-classification, as in our use case, smaller models fine-tuned for the particular task can achieve similar performances without

[1]Class distribution: 613 FALSE, 265 POSITIVE entries.

Year	Geolocated to Wales	Matching ILI keywords, without classification	Classified as first-hand account of ILI symptoms
2020	1,382,874	13,173	499
2021	1,967,665	14,225	823
2022	1,927,886	8,326	891
Total	5,278,425	35,724	2,213

Table 1: Counts of tweets pulled pulled from the API, with geolocation, keyword matched and classified for first-hand accounts of ILI symptoms. (2022 includes 1st week of 2023)

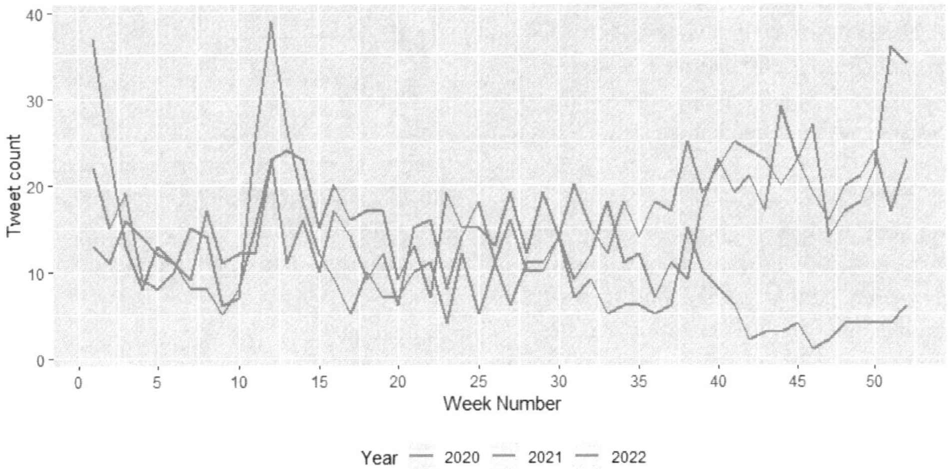

Figure 1: Counts of tweets classified as referring to first-hand accounts of ILI symptoms, geolocated to Wales.

Class	Example
TRUE	"I've never felt so ill. coughing, shivering, aching. Luckily my mom is supplying me with medication, water and soup!"
FALSE	"If you have aches, fever and feel generally unwell, it might be flu. Make sure to rest, drinking plenty of water & take over the counter medicines to ease symptoms."

Table 2: Examples of tweets classified at whether or not they describe first-hand accounts of ILI symptoms.

the need of huge computational resources or paying API services.

Two large pre-trained language models were tested for the classification process: Twitter-RoBERTa (Loureiro et al., 2022) and BERTweet (Nguyen et al., 2020). Both models are based on the RoBERTa (Liu et al., 2019) architecture which in turn is an expansion of BERT (Devlin et al., 2019). RoBERTa models are essentially deep neural networks of 12 layers and utilise techniques such as attention masks (Vaswani et al., 2017) and dynamic masking of tokens during training that allows them to understand language relations and create accurate representations (by mapping words into a high dimension embedding vectors). To achieve this the models are usually trained on large corpora of text. Specifically, BERTweet and Twitter-RoBERTa are pre-trained in a large corpus of tweets, 850 and 124 million tweets respectively, and are tailored for usage in social media context.

These transformer-based language models were selected as: (1) they consistently outperform previous text-classification approaches and adapt well to different domains and (2) since they have been pre-trained on Twitter data, they perform better in social media text data (i.e. short, unstructured text, internet slang, emojis, etc) (Barbieri et al., 2020; Antypas et al., 2023).

Due to the small size of the annotated set, a 5-fold cross-validation method is also applied where the whole dataset is used. We also ensured that distribution of classes in the train and test sets in each fold is the same.

All models used are based on the implementations of the base versions provided by Hugging Face (Wolf et al., 2020) while Ray-Tune (Liaw et al., 2018) was utilised to optimise the models' hyper-parameters (i.e. learning rate, training batch-size, warm-up rate, number of epochs).

To establish the difficulty of the task and better evaluate the performance of the language models, three baseline models were also tested. An SVM classifier based on TFIDF features is tested, along with two frequency-based classifiers (predicting the most frequent and least frequent classes).

2.3 Clinical data

As a comparison to the Twitter data, a more traditional public health indicator was also analysed. Data on weekly counts of GP consultations for influenza-like illnesses (ILI) reported in Wales for the period January 2020 to December 2023 was extracted (Public Health Wales, 2023). A total of 11,152,985 GP consultations for ILIs were recorded for the period of interest. There was a notable surge in ILI-related consultations in towards the end of 2022, peaking in weeks 49-51 (Figure 2)

2.4 Exceedance detection

Exceedance detection (Farrington et al., 1996; Zareie et al., 2023) is an approach used by several public health authorities to identify significantly high incidences of diseases relative to historic baseline data (for example, Kavanagh et al. 2012). Exceedance detection was performed using a modified version of the Farrington algorithm (Noufaily et al., 2013) as implemented in the R package *surveillance* (Salmon et al., 2016). Briefly, the algorithm iteratively fits a quasi-Poisson model to historic data and detect significant deviations in the present data from that predicted by the model. The model was fit to the 2 previous years of data (2020-2021) and exceedance detected for data in the year 2022. Counts were binned into weekly intervals. A window width or 3 weeks and detection threshold of $\alpha = 0.05$ (all other parameters kept to default values).

Exceedance detection was applied to the classified tweet counts. For comparison, the keyword-matched tweet counts (without classification) and the counts of ILI GP consultations were also analysed.

	F1			Accuracy
	FALSE	TRUE	Macro	
BERTweet	**88.44**	74.70	**81.57**	**84.16**
T-RoBERTa	87.30	**74.80**	81.05	83.14
SVM	84.13	33.39	58.76	74.37
Most Frequent	82.23	0.00	41.11	69.82
Least Frequent	0	46.37	23.18	30.18

Table 3: Average F1 scores for each class. The accuracy and mean macro-F1 scores are also reported. The "Most Frequent" baseline indicates a baseline predicting always FALSE, while the "Least Frequent" baseline indicates a baseline predicting always TRUE.

3 Results

In this section, we present both the classification results that are used as basis for our analysis (Section 3.1), and the results of our exceedance detection algorithm based on the classification output (Section 3.2).

3.1 Classification results

When considering the results of the cross-validation classification experiment, the BERTweet model performs slightly better than the Twitter-RoBERTa (T-RoBERTa) one. Table 3 displays the average macro-F1 scores for each class that the two models achieve.

Both models appear to struggle to identify the positive class where their performance drops approximately by 10 ten points in terms of F1 score. In general, tweets that indicate first-person flu symptoms in a more subtle way pose difficulties for the models. For example both *'When you're too ill to watch TV or read a book music is what keeps you sane. Currently listening to Queen. Freddie was the absolute best, without a doubt.'* and *'@user My family had it we were ill for 2 days 7 of us non jabbed... '* are labelled as positive but classified by BERTweet as negative entries. At the same time, negative labelled tweets such as *'@user My partner has had it for 2 feverish nights horrendous coughing, headache, sore eyes but covid negative.'* and *'Is there anyone in this country NOT coughing and spluttering and snotting and just generally feeling yuck¿* which describe symptoms in a more general way are also labelled as positive by BERTweet.

Due to its slightly better performance, the BERTweet classifier was used for subsequent analysis.

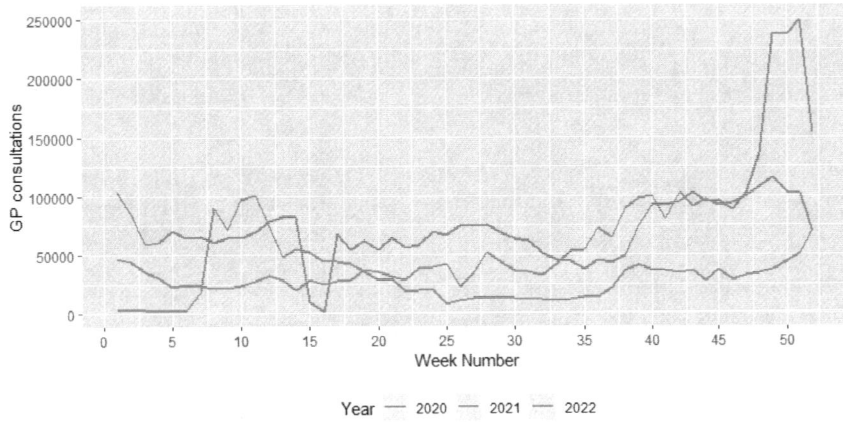

Figure 2: Counts of ILI-related GP consultations between 2020 and 2022

3.2 Exceedance detection

Using the classified tweet counts provided by BERTweet, a cluster of alerts was triggered for weeks 44-46 and 50-52 of 2022 (Figure 3 – see Section 2.4 for more details on how this experiment was performed). For ILI GP consultations, a cluster of alarms were triggered for weeks 48 of 2022, onwards (Figure 5). The classified tweet counts therefore alerted to a significant increase in ILI-related tweets approximately 4 weeks before a corresponding alert was triggered for ILI-related GP consultations. For tweet counts derived from ILI keyword matching without classification, no alerts were triggered (Figure 4).

4 Discussion

This study has demonstrated the utility of using social-media data to provide early exceedance alerts of influenza-like illnesses (ILIs) earlier than routine clinical data. the classified tweet counts produced an exceedance alert 4 weeks lead time on routine clinical data. It can supplement existing evidence for practitioners to assess if a season has started earlier than anticipated or is more extreme than usual, and provide public health authorities a valuable tool to prepare for an incoming surge in demands on the healthcare system.

Furthermore, this study shows the importance of correctly classifying first-hand accounts of symptoms, as matching on ILI-related keywords alone produced counts that are heavily biased by mass media content, not reflective of prevalence of symptoms in the community. We show that tweet counts using keyword matching alone failed to produce any alarms. Despite the fact that the classifier struggles with some particular linguistic patterns and contexts, the classified tweet counts does show a significant increase in tweet counts that coincide with an increase in GP consultations.

4.1 Limitations

A significant issue is the relative scarcity of Twitter users who enable geolocation. Approximately 3% of tweets matching keywords had geolocation enabled. An attempt was made to overcome this by retrieving data without geolocation and estimating location with the *carmen* Python library. This method had its own issues due to the large volume of key-word matching tweets exceeding the available quote of the API, but then very few located to Wales, much fewer than using true geolocation. The resulting performance was poorer.

The exceedance detection method has limitations. It is only useful for detection of exceedance in infections with seasonal trends (e.g. influenza). It can only detect increases higher than on previous years, but does not provide a quantification of the magnitude of the increase. An alternative approach is to use time-series modelling, such as ARIMA, GAM, etc. which do not rely on seasonal behaviour. Further evaluation using non-seasonal outbreaks would be helpful. However a difficulty arises when considering the overlap of symptom profiles between seasonal and non-seasonal diseases (e.g. symptoms of non-seasonal Covid-19 overlap with those of seasonal influenza) and are not easily separated in the data.

A further issue is that the approach to EWD, is that only significant increases, relative to previous years will be detected. An increase in healthcare

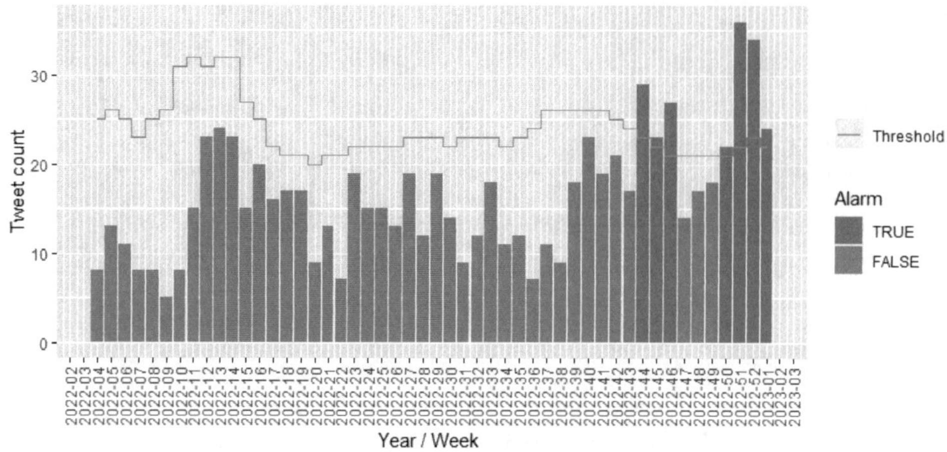

Figure 3: Exceedance detection of weekly tweet counts in 2022, geolocated to Wales, classified as mentioning first-hand accounts of ILI symptoms

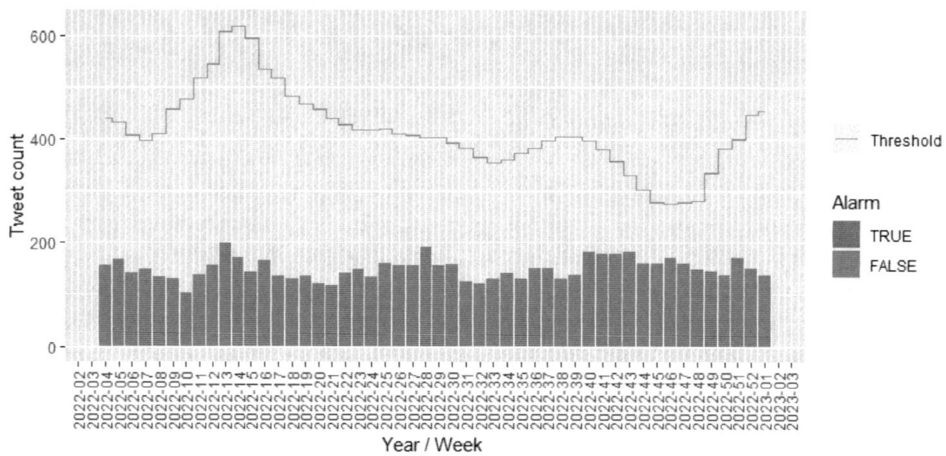

Figure 4: Exceedance detection of weekly tweet counts in 2022, geolocated to Wales, matching ILI keywords, without classification.

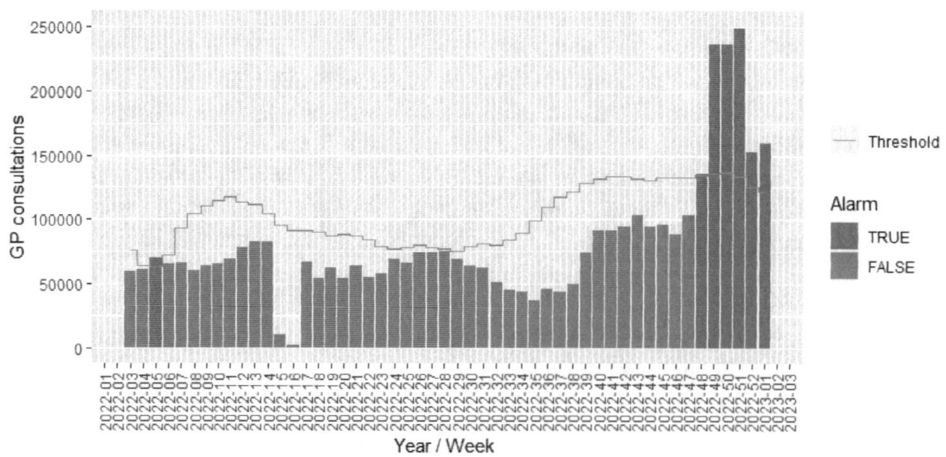

Figure 5: Exceedance detection of ILI-related GP consultations in 2022 in Wales.

burdens may be operationally significant within a given year, even if it is not statistically higher than previous years. The approach however, is useful for detecting increases in healthcare burdens that are unusually early compared to previous years.

The choice of training dataset has potential issues. There may be language differences between Wales and the rest of the UK, either use of Welsh language or Welsh-specific dialects in English specific to Wales, which the training dataset would not capture.

For robust exceedance detection, it is recommended to use 5 years of data to compute the baseline (Noufaily et al., 2013). However due to the API quota limits on how many historic years' data could be retrieved, we could only use 2 years (2020-2021). This makes it difficult to comprehensively evaluate the reliability of the method. A further complication is that these years were significantly impacted by the Covid-19 pandemic. This is likely to lead to significant changes in how people engage with social media compared to normal. As a side note, there is a notable peak in ILI-related tweets around week 12, which would have been at the height of the first wave of the pandemic. With this peak included in the baseline, the threshold for exceedance will be higher than normal during these weeks, resulting in under-detection of exceedance.

While the proposed approach shows promise for providing EWD for infectious diseases, a significant setback occurred with the withdrawal of the free Academic Twitter API in early 2023. This makes this data source much less accessible. This has big implications for research and non-commercial applications such as disease surveillance (Davidson et al., 2023a,b). There are a number of alternative 'microblogging' platforms that have received more attention in the past year, such as Mastodon, Threads, and Bluesky. However, these platforms do not have the same volume of users as Twitter, meaning content relevant for syndromic surveillance will be very sparse. Also, most of these platforms lack an accessible interface to facilitate rapid automated data retrieval. Platforms such as Instagram and TikTok have very large user-bases, but the predominance of image and video-based content makes them unamenable to NLP methods.

More generally, changing patterns in how the public engage with social media should be considered. In recent years concerns about privacy and digital sanctity have driven social media users to be less inclined to publicly share details of their personal well-being. A 2018 survey of social media use in Wales reported only approximately 10% of users shared details of their health on social media, and only a quarter of those were shared publicly (Song et al., 2020). It is expected that this proportion will be lower today. Another study monitored Twitter usage among participants in a flu symptom survey (Daughton et al., 2018). This study found participants rarely tweeted about their symptoms while experiencing them (of 266 symptom-related tweets identified, only 3 were made within 2 weeks of an instance of flu-like symptoms, of which there were 426). If these usage patterns are reflective of the wider population, it will significantly impact on the reliability of social-media as a syndromic surveillance tool.

Digital representativeness is another issue. Social media platforms disproportionately over-represent some demographics over others (Anderson, 2021). In Wales, there was no significant difference in social media use across demographics, although, use of Twitter was lower in more deprived areas (Song et al., 2020). The potential for social media to reach hard-to-reach populations should be considered for distributing important public heath guidance to control the spread of disease.

5 Conclusion

In this paper, we demonstrate that social-media based syndromic surveillance is capable of providing an advance warning of healthcare burdens earlier than traditional syndromic indicators. The results are encouraging and suggest that an adoption of social media indicators to supplement traditional disease surveillance is feasible with current technology. We also demonstrate the importance of NLP-based classification in identifying references to first-hand accounts of symptoms experienced. Nonetheless, validation of these conclusions with larger datasets is warranted. Furthermore, issues around access to social media data, digital representation and changing patterns of social media engagement should be considered when using social media data for syndromic surveillance.

6 Ethics Statement

Twitter data was accessed via the Twitter Academic API (Twitter, 2023) and only aggregated anonymised data is presented. Additionally, all user mentions have been removed from posts. No individual health status data was reported or analysed. Aggregated GP consultation data is openly available from the Public Health Wales ARI GP Consultations dashboard (Public Health Wales, 2023).

7 Competing Interests Statement

All authors have no competing financial interests to declare.

8 Funding Statement

This research was supported by a Public Health Wales Specialist Support Grant. Jose Camacho-Collados was supported by a UKRI Future Leaders Fellowship.

References

Allison E. Aiello, Audrey Renson, and Paul N. Zivich. 2019. Social media- and internet-based disease surveillance for public health. *Annual Review of Public Health*, 41:101–118.

Brooke Auxier and Monica Anderson. 2021. Social Media Use in 2021. *Pew Research Center: Internet, Science & Tech.*

Dimosthenis Antypas, Asahi Ushio, Francesco Barbieri, Leonardo Neves, Kiamehr Rezaee, Luis Espinosa-Anke, Jiaxin Pei, and Jose Camacho-Collados. 2023. SuperTweetEval: A Challenging, Unified and Heterogeneous Benchmark for Social Media NLP Research. In *Findings of the Association for Computational Linguistics: EMNLP 2023*, pages 12590–12607, Singapore. Association for Computational Linguistics.

Francesco Barbieri, Jose Camacho-Collados, Luis Espinosa Anke, and Leonardo Neves. 2020. TweetEval: Unified benchmark and comparative evaluation for tweet classification. In *Findings of the Association for Computational Linguistics: EMNLP 2020*, pages 1644–1650, Online. Association for Computational Linguistics.

Ashlynn R. Daughton, Michael J. Paul, and Rumi Chunara. 2018. What Do People Tweet When They're Sick? A Preliminary Comparison of Symptom Reports and Twitter Timelines. *ICWSM Social Media and Health Workshop.*

Brittany I. Davidson, Joanne Hinds, and Daniel Racek. 2023a. Shifting landscapes of social media data for research. *The Times Higher Education.*

Brittany I. Davidson, Darja Wischerath, Daniel Racek, Douglas A. Parry, Emily Godwin, Joanne Hinds, Dirk van der Linden, Jonathan F. Roscoe, Laura Ayravainen, and Alicia G. Cork. 2023b. Platform-controlled social media APIs threaten open science. *Nature Human Behaviour*, 7(12):2054–2057.

Jacob Devlin, Ming-Wei Chang, Kenton Lee, and Kristina Toutanova. 2019. BERT: Pre-training of deep bidirectional transformers for language understanding. In *Proceedings of the 2019 Conference of the North American Chapter of the Association for Computational Linguistics: Human Language Technologies, Volume 1 (Long and Short Papers)*, pages 4171–4186, Minneapolis, Minnesota. Association for Computational Linguistics.

Laura Espinosa, Ariana Wijermans, Francisco Orchard, Michael Höhle, Thomas Czernichow, Pietro Coletti, Lisa Hermans, Christel Faes, Esther Kissling, and Thomas Mollet. 2022. Epitweetr: Early warning of public health threats using Twitter data. *Eurosurveillance*, 27(39):2200177.

C. P. Farrington, N. J. Andrews, A. D. Beale, and M. A. Catchpole. 1996. A Statistical Algorithm for the Early Detection of Outbreaks of Infectious Disease. *Journal of the Royal Statistical Society. Series A (Statistics in Society)*, 159(3):547–563.

Aditya Joshi, Sarvnaz Karimi, Ross Sparks, Cécile Paris, and C. Raina Macintyre. 2019. Survey of Text-based Epidemic Intelligence: A Computational Linguistics Perspective. *ACM Comput. Surv.*, 52(6):119:1–119:19.

Kimberley Kavanagh, Christopher Robertson, Heather Murdoch, George Crooks, and Jim McMenamin. 2012. Syndromic surveillance of influenza-like illness in Scotland during the influenza A H1N1v pandemic and beyond. *Journal of the Royal Statistical Society. Series A (General)*, 175(4):939–958.

Richard Liaw, Eric Liang, Robert Nishihara, Philipp Moritz, Joseph E Gonzalez, and Ion Stoica. 2018. Tune: A research platform for distributed model selection and training. *arXiv preprint arXiv:1807.05118.*

Yinhan Liu, Myle Ott, Naman Goyal, Jingfei Du, Mandar Joshi, Danqi Chen, Omer Levy, Mike Lewis, Luke Zettlemoyer, and Veselin Stoyanov. 2019. Roberta: A robustly optimized bert pretraining approach. *arXiv preprint arXiv:1907.11692.*

Daniel Loureiro, Francesco Barbieri, Leonardo Neves, Luis Espinosa Anke, and Jose Camacho-collados. 2022. TimeLMs: Diachronic language models from Twitter. In *Proceedings of the 60th Annual Meeting of the Association for Computational Linguistics: System Demonstrations*, pages 251–260, Dublin, Ireland. Association for Computational Linguistics.

Tim Mackey, Vidya Purushothaman, Jiawei Li, Neal Shah, Matthew Nali, Cortni Bardier, Bryan Liang, Mingxiang Cai, and Raphael Cuomo. Machine Learning to Detect Self-Reporting of Symptoms, Testing Access, and Recovery Associated With COVID-19 on Twitter: Retrospective Big Data Infoveillance Study. 6(2):e19509.

Hannah McClymont, Stephen B. Lambert, Ian Barr, Sotiris Vardoulakis, Hilary Bambrick, and Wenbiao

Hu. 2024. Internet-based Surveillance Systems and Infectious Diseases Prediction: An Updated Review of the Last 10 Years and Lessons from the COVID-19 Pandemic. 14(3):645–657.

Liesbeth Mollema, Irene Anhai Harmsen, Emma Broekhuizen, Rutger Clijnk, Hester De Melker, Theo Paulussen, Gerjo Kok, Robert Ruiter, and Enny Das. 2015. Disease Detection or Public Opinion Reflection? Content Analysis of Tweets, Other Social Media, and Online Newspapers During the Measles Outbreak in the Netherlands in 2013. 17(5):e3863.

Dat Quoc Nguyen, Thanh Vu, and Anh Tuan Nguyen. 2020. BERTweet: A pre-trained language model for English Tweets. In *Proceedings of the 2020 Conference on Empirical Methods in Natural Language Processing: System Demonstrations*, pages 9–14, Online. Association for Computational Linguistics.

Angela Noufaily, Doyo G. Enki, Paddy Farrington, Paul Garthwaite, Nick Andrews, and André Charlett. 2013. An improved algorithm for outbreak detection in multiple surveillance systems. *Statistics in Medicine*, 32(7):1206–1222.

Patrick Pilipiec, Isak Samsten, and András Bota. 2023. Surveillance of communicable diseases using social media: A systematic review. 18(2):e0282101.

Public Health Wales. 2023. GP consultations for acute respiritory infections.

Manuel Rodríguez-Martínez and Cristian C Garzón-Alfonso. 2018. Twitter Health Surveillance (THS) System. *Proceedings of the IEEE International Conference on Big Data*, 2018:1647–1654.

Maëlle Salmon, Dirk Schumacher, and Michael Höhle. 2016. Monitoring Count Time Series in R: Aberration Detection in Public Health Surveillance. *Journal of Statistical Software*, 70:1–35.

Cuihua Shen, Anfan Chen, Chen Luo, Jingwen Zhang, Bo Feng, and Wang Liao. 2020. Using Reports of Symptoms and Diagnoses on Social Media to Predict COVID-19 Case Counts in Mainland China: Observational Infoveillance Study. 22(5):e19421.

Jiao Song, Catherine A. Sharp, and Alisha R. Davies. 2020. Population health in a digital age: Patterns in the use of social media in Wales.

Twitter. 2023. Twitter API Accademic Research Access (Web Archive from 07/07/2023).

Ashish Vaswani, Noam Shazeer, Niki Parmar, Jakob Uszkoreit, Llion Jones, Aidan N Gomez, Łukasz Kaiser, and Illia Polosukhin. 2017. Attention is All you Need. In *Advances in Neural Information Processing Systems*, volume 30. Curran Associates, Inc.

Thomas Wolf, Lysandre Debut, Victor Sanh, Julien Chaumond, Clement Delangue, Anthony Moi, Pierric Cistac, Tim Rault, Remi Louf, Morgan Funtowicz, Joe Davison, Sam Shleifer, Patrick von Platen, Clara Ma, Yacine Jernite, Julien Plu, Canwen Xu, Teven Le Scao, Sylvain Gugger, Mariama Drame, Quentin Lhoest, and Alexander Rush. 2020. Transformers: State-of-the-art natural language processing. In *Proceedings of the 2020 Conference on Empirical Methods in Natural Language Processing: System Demonstrations*, pages 38–45, Online. Association for Computational Linguistics.

Bushra Zareie, Jalal Poorolajal, Amin Roshani, and Manoochehr Karami. 2023. Outbreak detection algorithms based on generalized linear model: A review with new practical examples. *BMC Medical Research Methodology*, 23(1):1–16.

Ovidiu Şerban, Nicholas Thapen, Brendan Maginnis, Chris Hankin, and Virginia Foot. 2019. Real-time processing of social media with SENTINEL: A syndromic surveillance system incorporating deep learning for health classification. *Information Processing & Management*, 56(3):1166–1184.

Sentiment Analysis on Video Transcripts: Comparing the Value of Textual and Multimodal Annotations

Quanqi Du, Loic De Langhe, Els Lefever, Véronique Hoste
LT3, Language and Translation Technology Team, Ghent University, Belgium
Groot-Brittanniëlaan 45, 9000 Ghent, Belgium
firstname.lastname@ugent.be

Abstract

This study explores the differences between textual and multimodal sentiment annotations on videos and their impact on transcript-based sentiment modelling. Using the UniC and CH-SIMS datasets which are annotated at both the unimodal and multimodal level, we conducted a statistical analysis and sentiment modelling experiments. Results reveal significant differences between the two annotation types, with textual annotations yielding better performance in sentiment modelling and demonstrating superior generalization ability. These findings highlight the challenges of cross-modality generalization and provide insights for advancing sentiment analysis.

1 Introduction

With the rise of the internet and online platforms, especially the proliferation of social media, user-generated content (UGC) has become widely accessible to the public. UGC appears in various forms and modalities, ranging from online textual movie reviews on platforms like IMDB[1] and Rotten Tomatoes[2], to video blogs (vlogs) in video-sharing platforms such as YouTube[3] and TikTok[4].

UGC holds significant value for companies, marketers and politicians (Van Hee et al., 2014), as it contains sentiment-rich information that can be leveraged to monitor public opinion and support the decision-making process (Wankhade et al., 2022). For instance, sentiment analysis based on tweets has been utilized to model user satisfaction in mobile payments (Kar, 2021) and predict election outcomes (Stefanov et al., 2020).

Sentiment analysis on UGC predominantly focuses on text, partly because textual sentiment modelling is more developed and computationally efficient compared to other modalities, such as audio and video. In contrast, systems capable of automatically understanding the content and sentiment of videos are still in their infancy (Stappen et al., 2021; Wang et al., 2023). Consequently, sentiment analysis of non-textual UGC is often converted to text-based analysis through subtitles or transcripts. For instance, Stappen et al. (2021) investigated the use of video transcripts to capture contextual and emotional information in videos.

A critical question arises when annotating transcripts: Should information from non-textual modalities be considered during annotation? In real-life scenarios, sentiment annotations typically reflect the emotional status across modalities. As a result, some studies incorporate multimodal information into the final annotation (Morency et al., 2011; Pérez-Rosas et al., 2013; Nguyen-The et al., 2022). However, another common approach is to perform annotation solely based on textual information, excluding other modalities to avoid interference (Clavel et al., 2013; Stappen et al., 2021; Bekmanova et al., 2022; Efat et al., 2023). This approach is practical since the input for sentiment modelling is usually text, and annotating textual data is less complex compared to multimodal data.

Both approaches to sentiment annotation have their merits and are often intertwined. In some cases, researchers do not differentiate between them, applying multimodal annotations to textual sentiment modelling under the assumption that sentiment labels across modalities are consistent. However, this assumption does not always hold true. For instance, the text "I love this weather" might be labelled as positive, but when the speaker's tone is sarcastic and they wear a frown, the sentiment might be perceived as negative. Previous studies have shown that emotion labels in multimodal setups do not always align with those derived from textual modalities alone (Ellis et al., 2014; Yu et al., 2020; Du et al., 2023, 2024).

[1]https://www.imdb.com
[2]https://www.rottentomatoes.com
[3]https://www.youtube.com
[4]https://www.tiktok.com

Proceedings of the Tenth Workshop on Noisy and User-generated Text, pages 10–15
May 3, 2025 ©2025 Association for Computational Linguistics

Accurate annotations are crucial for building effective models. However, in the field of sentiment analysis on UGC transcripts, few studies have compared sentiment annotations derived solely from textual information with those incorporating multimodal information, or examined the impact of these differences on sentiment modelling. To address this gap, this paper seeks to answer the following research questions:

1. Do sentiment annotations on video transcripts based solely on textual information differ from those that include information from other modalities? If so, to what extent?

2. How does the inclusion or exclusion of non-textual information in video transcript annotations impact sentiment modelling?

2 Related Studies

A significant portion of sentiment analysis research has traditionally relied on datasets comprising user-generated text. Common sources include social media platforms, such as tweets (Gyanendro Singh et al., 2020), and reviews from domains like products, hotels, and movies (Van et al., 2022; Thakkar et al., 2023). While these studies have provided valuable insights into sentiment classification, they are predominantly focused on textual data.

Recently, sentiment analysis has evolved beyond textual analysis to incorporate other modalities, such as audio and video, giving rise to multimodal sentiment analysis (Wu et al., 2024). This shift reflects the growing prevalence of opinion-sharing in video formats on platforms like YouTube and TikTok (Zadeh et al., 2017; Gandhi et al., 2023), where diverse modalities provide richer contextual information for understanding sentiments.

An essential aspect of multimodal sentiment analysis is the fusion of different modalities (Gandhi et al., 2023; Zhu et al., 2023). Fusion strategies are broadly categorized into two types: early fusion and late fusion. Early fusion, also known as feature-level fusion, integrates features from each modality at the input level, whereas late fusion, or decision-level fusion, combines the outputs of unimodal sentiment analyses to generate the final prediction. Recently, advanced fusion approaches, such as tensor fusion networks (Yan et al., 2022) and dynamic fusion methods (Hu et al., 2022a), have been proposed to enhance performance.

While incorporating non-textual information generally improves the performance of multimodal sentiment analysis, there remains a heavy reliance on textual modalities. This phenomenon, termed *text-predominance*, is evident in studies showing a significant drop in classification accuracy – from approximately 80% to 54% – when textual information is excluded from multimodal models trained on multimodal data (Liu et al., 2022). In contrast, removing audio or visual information results in only a marginal accuracy decline, such as a reduction from 87% to 85% (Hu et al., 2022b), a trend corroborated by Wu et al. (2024).

It seems that we can still rely on textual information despite the availability of other modalities, especially when considering the imbalance of the cost and the improvement when introducing non-textual modalities. However, when we decide to take into consideration only the textual modality of the opinioned videos, which set of annotations should be used, the textual one or the multimodal one, as multimodal labels do not always reflect sentimental states in texts (Yu et al., 2020; Du et al., 2024). In the following, we are going to investigate the differences and influence of the two sets of sentiment annotations.

3 Datasets

The definition of UGC varies across disciplines. In the context of social media, UGC is defined as *any kind of text, data or action performed by online digital systems users, published and disseminated by the same user through independent channels, that incur an expressive or communicative effect either on an individual manner or combined with other contributions from the same or other sources* (Santos, 2022). Based on this definition, we selected two datasets for our study: the UGC dataset UniC (Du et al., 2024), and the non-UGC dataset CH-SIMS (Yu et al., 2020).

UniC is an English audio-visual emotion dataset with independent annotations for each modality (i.e., text, audio, and silent video) as well as overall emotion states of the videos. This UGC dataset comprises nearly 1,000 video clips collected from YouTube, focusing on the topic of *reviews*.

CH-SIMS is a Chinese multimodal sentiment analysis dataset featuring over 2,000 curated video segments with both multimodal and independent unimodal annotations. The videos in CH-SIMS are sourced from movies, TV series, and variety shows, implying that the professional actors in CH-SIMS tend to express emotions more explicitly in all modalities than the non-professionals in UniC. This difference may also influence the sentiment annotations across modalities.

For both datasets, sentiment labels were originally designed as negative, weakly negative, neutral, weakly positive and positive. In this paper, we grouped weakly negative and weakly positive into negative and positive, respectively, for further experiments and analysis.

4 Experiment

4.1 Statistical Analysis

We first analyzed the sentiment distribution across modality setups. As shown in Figure 1, the sentiment distributions in both datasets vary depending on the modality setup. Compared to the multimodal setup, the number of both negative and positive instances decreases in the textual modality, while the number of neutral instances increases. A possible explanation for this trend is that the additional information from audio and visual modalities helps annotators discern sentiment polarities that might otherwise be interpreted as neutral in text-only expressions.

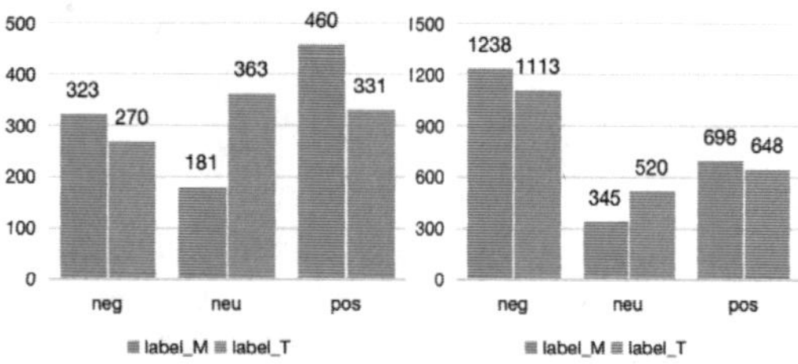

Figure 1: Distribution of textual and multimodal annotations in Unic (left) and CH-SIMS (right).

To evaluate the relationship between annotations across modalities, we conducted significance tests. Chi-Square test results indicate that the relationship between the two types of annotations is statistically significant and not random, with a P-value of 2.49e-98 for UniC and a P-value of 6.80e-235 for CH-SIMS.

To further explore the similarities between the textual and multimodal annotations, we compared the two annotation types. In UniC, 63.69% of instances were assigned the same sentiment annotations across the two modality setups, while in CH-SIMS, this percentage increased to 69.09%. To measure the agreement between the two annotation sets, Cohen's kappa coefficient (Cohen, 1960) was applied. The results show a higher level of agreement in CH-SIMS, with a kappa score of 0.5494, compared to 0.4964 in UniC. These findings highlight a notable difference between the two sets of sentiment annotations, suggesting that the distinctions are not negligible.

The confusion matrices for the two annotation types in both datasets, presented in Figure 2, provide further insights into how sentiment labels change when transitioning between modalities. For example, the inclusion of audio-visual information in UniC led to a shift of approximately 30% of negative and 12% of positive annotations from their textual counterparts. This discrepancy is exemplified in Figure 3, where a video clip is annotated as negative in the text but positive in the multimodal context. The sentiment shift primarily arises from the cheerful tone of voice and the presence of a smile. In contrast, for CH-SIMS, the corresponding shifts were about 15% and 28%, respectively. These results demonstrate the varied impact of multimodal information on sentiment annotations across the two datasets.

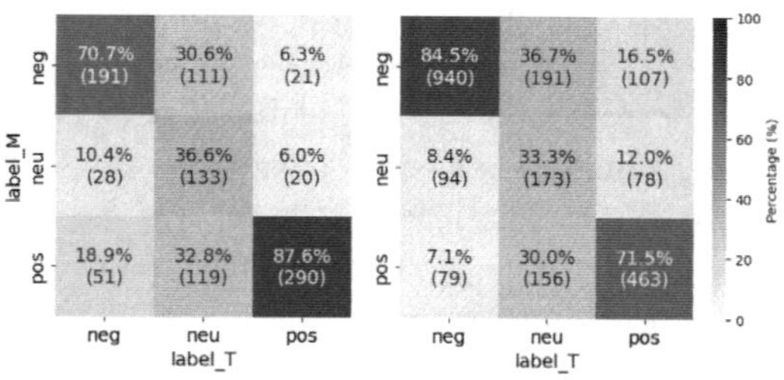

Figure 2: Confusion matrix (Left: UniC; Right: CH-SIMS) of textual and multimodal annotations. The frequency is normalized vertically against the number of textual annotations with different sentiment labels.

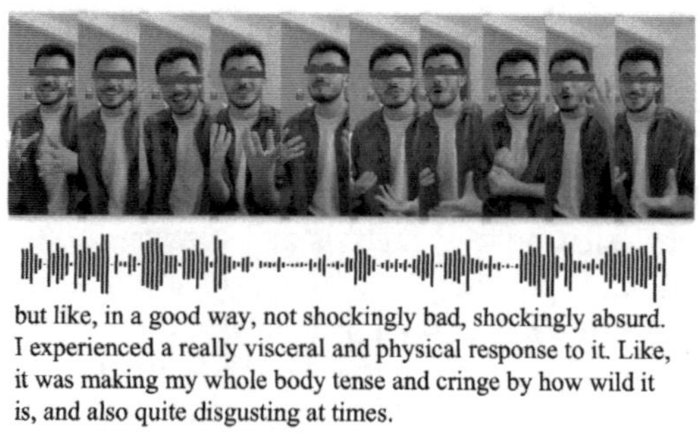

Figure 3: A video clip example from UniC.

	Acc-text		F1-text		Acc-mm		F1-mm	
Training data	mean	SD	mean	SD	mean	SD	mean	SD
UniC-text	74.57	1.57	**74.62**	1.66	54.98	2.14	53.03	1.69
CH-SIMS-text	71.18	0.44	**68.33**	0.95	59.36	1.27	52.60	0.29
UniC-mm	44.67	1.19	38.66	1.36	58.76	1.03	**43.38**	0.86
CH-SIMS-mm	60.70	0.87	**46.15**	2.07	63.03	0.91	45.13	1.22

Table 1: Model performances on test datasets when fine-tuned with textual (text) and multimodal (mm) annotations, respectively, and evaluated against textual (text) and multimodal (mm) annotations, respectively, from UniC and CH-SIMS. Accuracy (ACC) and F1-Macro (F1) are averaged from the results of three experiments. SD stands for standard deviation.

4.2 Sentiment Modelling

To further examine the differences between the two types of sentiment annotation, we applied both in the task of transcript-based sentiment modelling by fine-tuning a RoBERTa-base model (Liu et al., 2019) for UniC and a Chinese RoBERTa model (Cui et al., 2021) for CH-SIMS, respectively. Specifically, all instances from both datasets were shuffled and randomly split in the training, validation and test sets in an 8:1:1 ratio. The models were fine-tuned using a learning rate of 1e-5, and a batch size of 8, and 10 epochs with an early-stopping strategy.

For evaluation, both accuracy and macro F1 scores were used to assess performance across textual and multimodal annotations, providing insights into cross-modality performance and the generalization potential between modality setups. Each fine-tuning experiment was repeated three times with different random seeds, and the averaged results are presented in Table 1.

As shown in Table 1, for both UniC and CH-SIMS, the models fine-tuned with textual annotations performed better when evaluated against textual annotations than against multimodal annotations. This highlights barriers across modalities and significant information loss when transitioning from multimodal data to a single modality for both datasets. Interestingly, while the model performed significantly better on textual annotations from UniC (F1 = 74.57) compared to CH-SIMS (F1 = 68.33), the performance gap narrowed when evaluated against multimodal annotations (F1 = 53.03 for UniC versus F1 = 52.60 for CH-SIMS). This suggests a common limitation in the model's ability to generalize from text to multimodality across both datasets.

The scenario became more complex when multimodal annotations were used for fine-tuning. For both UniC and CH-SIMS, models fine-tuned with multimodal annotations achieved only moderate performance (F1 = 42.38 for UniC and F1 = 45.13 for CH-SIMS), reflecting the limitations of text-based language models in generalizing from textual to multimodality setups. Additionally, the models' performance varied when evaluated against multimodal annotations versus textual annotations. For UniC, the F1 score dropped noticeably from 43.38 to 38.66, while CH-SIMS showed a marginal increase, with the F1 score rising from 45.13 to 46.15. This indicates differing capacities of multimodal annotations to encapsulate information relevant to textual annotations.

More notably, when comparing evaluations against multimodal annotations, models fine-tuned with textual annotations generally outperformed those fine-tuned with multimodal annotations for both datasets. This finding suggests the sentiment generalization ability of textual annotations in text-based language models.

5 Conclusion

This study investigated the differences between sentiment annotations on video transcripts derived from textual and multimodal setups, as well as their impact on transcript-based sentiment modelling.

The statistical analysis revealed a significant difference between the two types of sentiment annotations with absolute similarities less than 70% and kappa scores less than 0.55, highlighting the influence of multimodal information on sentiment labelling in video data. The modelling experiments further demonstrated that text-based annotations outperformed multimodal annotations when evaluated against both textual and multimodal labels. Also, a significant cross-modality performance gap was observed. For instance, the macro F1 score dropped from 74.62 to 53.03 when the evaluation labels shifted from text-based to multimodality for UniC, underscoring the challenges of generalizing sentiment models across different modalities.

For future research, we will investigate the incorporation of additional modalities (e.g., audio and facial expressions) and advanced models (e.g., multimodal fusion models), enabling a more comprehensive and nuanced analysis.

6 Limitations

A notable limitation of this study is the linguistic difference between the datasets: UniC is in English, while CH-SIMS is in Chinese. As a result, the comparison between UGC and non-UGC may be influenced by cross-cultural differences, which were not explicitly addressed in this research. Future studies should consider incorporating datasets from the same linguistic and cultural context to allow for stronger and more nuanced comparisons. Unfortunately, the current availability of datasets limits the feasibility of such an approach.

7 Acknowledgments

This research received funding from the Flemish Government under the Research Program Artificial Intelligence (174K02325). We would also like to thank the anonymous reviewers for their valuable and constructive feedback.

References

Gulmira Bekmanova, Banu Yergesh, Altynbek Sharipbay, and Assel Mukanova. 2022. Emotional speech recognition method based on word transcription. *Sensors*, 22(5):1937.

Chloé Clavel, Gilles Adda, Frederik Cailliau, Martine Garnier-Rizet, Ariane Cavet, Géraldine Chapuis, Sandrine Courcinous, Charlotte Danesi, Anne-Laure Daquo, Myrtille Deldossi, et al. 2013. Spontaneous speech and opinion detection: Mining call-centre transcripts. *Language Resources and Evaluation*, 47:1089–1125.

Jacob Cohen. 1960. A coefficient of agreement for nominal scales. *Educational and Psychological Measurement*, 20(1):37–46.

Yiming Cui, Wanxiang Che, Ting Liu, Bing Qin, and Ziqing Yang. 2021. Pre-training with whole word masking for Chinese BERT. *IEEE/ACM Transactions on Audio, Speech, and Language Processing*, 29:3504–3514.

Quanqi Du, Sofie Labat, Thomas Demeester, and Veronique Hoste. 2023. Unimodalities count as perspectives in multimodal emotion annotation. In *Proceedings of the 2nd Workshop on Perspectivist Approaches to NLP co-located with 26th European Conference on Artificial Intelligence (ECAI 2023)*. CEUR Workshop Proceedings.

Quanqi Du, Sofie Labat, Thomas Demeester, and Veronique Hoste. 2024. UniC: A dataset for emotion analysis of videos with multimodal and unimodal labels. *Research Square preprint doi.org/10.21203/rs.3.rs-4443808/v1*.

Azher Ahmed Efat, Asif Atiq, Abrar Shahriar Abeed, Armanul Momin, and Md Golam Rabiul Alam. 2023. Empoliticon: NLP and ML based approach for context and emotion classification of political speeches from transcripts. *IEEE Access*, 11:54808–54821.

Joseph G Ellis, Brendan Jou, and Shih-Fu Chang. 2014. Why we watch the news: A dataset for exploring sentiment in broadcast video news. In *Proceedings of the 16th International Conference on Multimodal Interaction*, pages 104–111.

Ankita Gandhi, Kinjal Adhvaryu, Soujanya Poria, Erik Cambria, and Amir Hussain. 2023. Multimodal sentiment analysis: A systematic review of history, datasets, multimodal fusion methods, applications, challenges and future directions. *Information Fusion*, 91:424–444.

Loitongbam Gyanendro Singh, Anasua Mitra, and Sanasam Ranbir Singh. 2020. Sentiment analysis of tweets using heterogeneous multi-layer network representation and embedding. In *Proceedings of the 2020 Conference on Empirical Methods in Natural Language Processing (EMNLP)*, pages 8932–8946, Online. Association for Computational Linguistics.

Dou Hu, Xiaolong Hou, Lingwei Wei, Lianxin Jiang, and Yang Mo. 2022a. MM-DFN: Multimodal dynamic fusion network for emotion recognition in conversations. In *ICASSP 2022-2022 IEEE International Conference on Acoustics, Speech and Signal Processing (ICASSP)*, pages 7037–7041. IEEE.

Guimin Hu, Ting-En Lin, Yi Zhao, Guangming Lu, Yuchuan Wu, and Yongbin Li. 2022b. UniMSE: Towards unified multimodal sentiment analysis and emotion recognition. In *Proceedings of the 2022 Conference on Empirical Methods in Natural Language Processing*, pages 7837–7851.

Arpan Kumar Kar. 2021. What affects usage satisfaction in mobile payments? Modelling user generated content to develop the "digital service usage satisfaction model". *Information Systems Frontiers*, 23(5):1341–1361.

Yihe Liu, Ziqi Yuan, Huisheng Mao, Zhiyun Liang, Wanqiuyue Yang, Yuanzhe Qiu, Tie Cheng, Xiaoteng Li, Hua Xu, and Kai Gao. 2022. Make acoustic and visual cues matter: Ch-SIMS v2. 0 dataset and AV-Mixup consistent module. In *Proceedings of the 2022 international conference on multimodal interaction*, pages 247–258.

Yinhan Liu, Myle Ott, Naman Goyal, Jingfei Du, Mandar Joshi, Danqi Chen, Omer Levy, Mike Lewis, Luke Zettlemoyer, and Veselin Stoyanov. 2019. Roberta: A robustly optimized BERT pretraining approach. *arXiv preprint arXiv:1907.11692*.

Louis-Philippe Morency, Rada Mihalcea, and Payal Doshi. 2011. Towards multimodal sentiment analysis: Harvesting opinions from the web. In *Proceedings of the 13th International Conference on Multimodal Interfaces*, pages 169–176.

Maude Nguyen-The, Soufiane Lamghari, Guillaume-Alexandre Bilodeau, and Jan Rockemann. 2022. Leveraging sentiment analysis knowledge to solve emotion detection tasks. In *International Conference on Pattern Recognition*, pages 405–416. Springer.

Verónica Pérez-Rosas, Rada Mihalcea, and Louis-Philippe Morency. 2013. Utterance-level multimodal sentiment analysis. In *Proceedings of the 51st Annual Meeting of the Association for Computational Linguistics (Volume 1: Long Papers)*, pages 973–982.

Marcelo Luis Barbosa dos Santos. 2022. The "so-called" UGC: An updated definition of user-generated content in the age of social media. *Online Information Review*, 46(1):95–113.

Lukas Stappen, Alice Baird, Erik Cambria, and Björn W Schuller. 2021. Sentiment analysis and topic recognition in video transcriptions. *IEEE Intelligent Systems*, 36(2):88–95.

Peter Stefanov, Kareem Darwish, Atanas Atanasov, and Preslav Nakov. 2020. Predicting the topical stance and political leaning of media using tweets. In *Proceedings of the 58th Annual Meeting of the Association for Computational Linguistics*, pages 527–537, Online. Association for Computational Linguistics.

Gaurish Thakkar, Nives Mikelic Preradovic, and Marko Tadić. 2023. Croatian film review dataset (cro-FiReDa): A sentiment annotated dataset of film reviews. In *Proceedings of the 9th Workshop on Slavic Natural Language Processing 2023 (SlavicNLP 2023)*, pages 25–31, Dubrovnik, Croatia. Association for Computational Linguistics.

Thin Dang Van, Hao Duong Ngoc, and Ngan Nguyen Luu-Thuy. 2022. Sentiment analysis in code-mixed Vietnamese-English sentence-level hotel reviews. In *Proceedings of the 36th Pacific Asia Conference on Language, Information and Computation*, pages 54–61, Manila, Philippines. Association for Computational Linguistics.

Cynthia Van Hee, Marjan Van de Kauter, Orphée De Clercq, Els Lefever, and Véronique Hoste. 2014. LT3: Sentiment classification in user-generated content using a rich feature set. In *Proceedings of the 8th International Workshop on Semantic Evaluation (SemEval 2014)*, pages 406–410, Dublin, Ireland. Association for Computational Linguistics.

James Z Wang, Sicheng Zhao, Chenyan Wu, Reginald B Adams, Michelle G Newman, Tal Shafir, and Rachelle Tsachor. 2023. Unlocking the emotional world of visual media: An overview of the science, research, and impact of understanding emotion. *Proceedings of the IEEE*, 111(10):1236–1286.

Mayur Wankhade, Annavarapu Chandra Sekhara Rao, and Chaitanya Kulkarni. 2022. A survey on sentiment analysis methods, applications, and challenges. *Artificial Intelligence Review*, 55(7):5731–5780.

Zehui Wu, Ziwei Gong, Jaywon Koo, and Julia Hirschberg. 2024. Multimodal multi-loss fusion network for sentiment analysis. In *Proceedings of the 2024 Conference of the North American Chapter of the Association for Computational Linguistics: Human Language Technologies (Volume 1: Long Papers)*, pages 3588–3602, Mexico City, Mexico. Association for Computational Linguistics.

Xueming Yan, Haiwei Xue, Shengyi Jiang, and Ziang Liu. 2022. Multimodal sentiment analysis using multi-tensor fusion network with cross-modal modeling. *Applied Artificial Intelligence*, 36(1):2000688.

Wenmeng Yu, Hua Xu, Fanyang Meng, Yilin Zhu, Yixiao Ma, Jiele Wu, Jiyun Zou, and Kaicheng Yang. 2020. CH-SIMS: A Chinese multimodal sentiment analysis dataset with fine-grained annotation of modality. In *Proceedings of the 58th Annual Meeting of the Association for Computational Linguistics*, pages 3718–3727, Online. Association for Computational Linguistics.

Amir Zadeh, Minghai Chen, Soujanya Poria, Erik Cambria, and Louis-Philippe Morency. 2017. Tensor fusion network for multimodal sentiment analysis. In *Proceedings of the 2017 Conference on Empirical Methods in Natural Language Processing*, pages 1103–1114, Copenhagen, Denmark. Association for Computational Linguistics.

Linan Zhu, Zhechao Zhu, Chenwei Zhang, Yifei Xu, and Xiangjie Kong. 2023. Multimodal sentiment analysis based on fusion methods: A survey. *Information Fusion*, 95:306–325.

Restoring Missing Spaces in Scraped Hebrew Social Media

Avi Shmidman,[1,2,†] **Shaltiel Shmidman**[1,‡]
[1]DICTA, Jerusalem, Israel
[2]Bar-Ilan University, Ramat Gan, Israel
[†]avi.shmidman@biu.ac.il
[‡]shaltieltzion@gmail.com

Abstract

A formidable challenge regarding scraped corpora of social media is the omission of spaces, causing pairs of words to be conflated together as one. In order for the text to be properly parsed and analyzed, these missing spaces must be detected and restored. However, it is particularly hard to restore whitespace in languages such as Hebrew which are written without vowels, because a conflated form can often be split into multiple different pairs of valid words. Thus, a simple dictionary lookup is not feasible. In this paper, we present and evaluate a series of neural approaches to restore missing spaces in scraped Hebrew social media. Our best all-around method involved pretraining a new character-based BERT model for Hebrew, and then fine-tuning a space restoration model on top of this new BERT model. This method is blazing fast, high-performing, and open for unrestricted use, providing a practical solution to process huge Hebrew social media corpora with nothing more than a consumer-grade GPU. We release the new BERT model and the fine-tuned space-restoration model to the NLP community.

1 Introduction

Scraped corpora of social media tend to contain many instances of missing spaces, where two or more words have been run together as one. This phenomenon is likely due to the fact that the HTML source of internet pages often encodes different parts of the text in distinct HTML tags, without explicit indication of whether two consecutive tags contain a single word or two separate words. Scraping algorithms exercise various heuristics to decide whether to add a space or not; however, these heuristics do not always succeed. In practice, the NLP researcher is often faced with digital corpora of scraped social media in which a substantial number of lines are corrupted with conflated words. These missing spaces can impair downstream tasks such as parsing, segmentation, and information retrieval. Additionally, when these corpora are used to train language models, the errors are propagated forward into the model. Thus, it is essential to restore missing spaces wherever possible.

The problem of missing spaces is particularly acute in languages such as Hebrew, in which words are generally written as consonants alone. The omission of vowels results in extreme ambiguity, such that a given sequence of letters can generally be interpreted as multiple different words (Tsarfaty et al., 2019). Crucially, this means that when two words are run together, they generally cannot be separated by means of a simple dictionary lookup, because there are multiples ways of splitting the conflated sequence into two valid Hebrew words.

For instance, here is an actual line contained in the Hebrew section of the public OSCAR corpus (Ortiz Suárez et al., 2020): רמת קושיכל אחד יכול ("Level of difficulty Everyone can do it"). The words קושי ("difficulty") and כל ("every") are conflated together in the corpus as a single string. However, there is more than one way to split this string; if we were to apply a dictionary lookup, we could also split it into the two words קו ("line") and שיכל ("transposed"). Another line in the same corpus contains the conflated string קריאהבמה, which can be split into קריאה ("reading") and במה ("in what"), or into קריא ("readable") and הבמה ("the stage"). Hundreds of thousands of additional sentences within the Hebrew portion of the OSCAR corpus are similarly corrupted. Yet, the OSCAR internet crawl is the primary component of virtually all publically-available Hebrew BERT models, including heBERT (Chriqui and Yahav, 2021), AlephBERT (Seker et al., 2022), and AlephBertGimmel (Gueta et al., 2023).

An efficient context-aware method is needed to fix this. In this paper, we present and evaluate a series of neural approaches for the restoration of the missing spaces within social-media corpora.

Proceedings of the Tenth Workshop on Noisy and User-generated Text, pages 16–25

2 Task Definition

We formalize the space-restoration task as follows: given an input string s with characters $c_1 ... c_n$ where $|s| = n$, our goal is to predict a binary label for each c_i, indicating whether a space should appear before the character at that position. This formulation treats the problem as a character-level sequence labeling task, which is particularly suitable for languages like Hebrew where subword boundaries must be handled carefully.

3 Neural Models for Space Restoration

In this study, we develop and evaluate a series of neural models for the restoration of the missing spaces.

3.1 Existing Encoder Models for Hebrew

Existing Hebrew encoder-based models such as mBERT (Devlin et al., 2018), AlephBertGimmel (Gueta et al., 2023), HeRo (Shalumov and Haskey, 2023), and DictaBERT (Shmidman et al., 2024b) are trained with a wordpiece tokenizer, which obscures character-level information and impairs their ability to perform well on character-level labeling tasks. In contrast, TavBERT (Group, 2023) adopts a character-based representation for Hebrew, preserving full granularity over all character positions. TavBERT thus opens the door to the possibility of training an encoder-based model to perform char-level predictions for whitespace restoration.

3.2 A New Character-based Encoder Model

As noted, TavBERT provides a possible basis for training a model to provide character-level predictions for Hebrew words. Nevertheless, at its core, TavBERT was designed with word prediction in mind; accordingly, it was trained with a SpanBERT-style objective, wherein the model is trained to predict a series of consecutive masked characters, rather than just a single character. Indeed, as we will see below (Section 5), fine-tuning TavBERT for this task results in a low-performing model.

Therefore, as part of this study, we pretrain a new character-level BERT model for Hebrew, dubbed `DictaBERT-char`. Our new model is pretrained on the standard BERT masked-language-modeling objective at the character level; that is, it is trained to predict single masked characters, rather than spans or wordpieces. We hypothesize that this will produce a model that is more robustly tuned to the fine-grained requirements of character-level tasks, such as the space-restoration task.[1]

In order to pretrain this new model, we adopt the same essential training setup and corpus used in the training of the Hebrew BERT model DictaBERT, which has been shown to be highly successful on a wide variety of NLP tasks (Shmidman et al., 2024b). We make two key modifications: (1) We use a purely character-level tokenizer to fully capture potential space boundaries, and (2) we set a consistent context length of 2048 throughout training (rather than gradually scaling from 256 to 512), in order to address the lower compression ratio when working at the character level.

The model was trained on a DGX Workstation with 4xA100 40GB GPUs for a total of 31,600 steps. Each step included a batch size of 4,096 examples, where each example had a context length of (up to) 2,048 tokens in order to accommodate the character-level tokenizer. The rest of the parameters, including the training corpus, are the same as DictaBERT, detailed by Shmidman et al. (2024b).

3.3 Decoder-based Models (LLMs)

Generative large language models (LLMs) have demonstrated remarkable capabilities across many NLP tasks, including sequence-to-sequence problems. As these models are generative, we can leverage their ability to generate free-form text to solve char-level tasks such as our space-restoration task. We explore two avenues regarding LLMs.

First, we fine-tune an open-weight LLM. We use Dicta-LM 2.0 (Shmidman et al., 2024a), a 7B parameter LLM continuously trained in Hebrew (based on Mistral-7B (Jiang et al., 2023)). This model is particularly strong regarding Hebrew tasks, as indicated by its position on the Hebrew LLM Leaderboard.[2]

Second, we evaluate a prompt engineering approach with two state-of-the-art proprietary LLMs: GPT-4o and GPT-4o-Mini (OpenAI, 2024).

4 Experimental Setup

4.1 Training Corpus

The training data set was created automatically by augmenting texts and removing spaces randomly.

[1]We release this model to the public on HuggingFace under the CC-BY-4.0 license: `https://huggingface.co/dicta-il/dictabert-char`

[2]`https://huggingface.co/spaces/hebrew-llm-leaderboard/leaderboard`

We start with a collection of 150,000 Hebrew sentences from high-quality Hebrew corpora.[3] Next, in 20% of the sentences, we randomly remove between 1 and 4 spaces.

4.2 Test Corpus

The test data set contains 6,000 sentences, and was created similarly to the training data, with three important caveats:

1. We wish to minimize the likelihood of the models having previously seen any of these sentences. Therefore, we collect the test corpus sentences from the newly-released FineWeb2 corpus (Penedo et al., 2024), after removing any documents that appeared in previous Hebrew corpora (such as OSCAR (Ortiz Suárez et al., 2020) and mC4 (Xue et al., 2021)).

2. In order to focus the evaluation metrics on the ability of the models to handle missing spaces, we removed 1-4 random spaces from each of the sentences in the test corpus.

3. To ensure that the test data reflects real-world challenging cases, we only remove spaces between two words, rather than before or after punctuation marks. Missing spaces next to punctuation can easily be fixed using rule-based methods; the word-conflation errors are where we need a neural model.

We release the test corpus to the NLP community so that future studies can reproduce and compare to the results of this paper.[4]

4.3 Training Details

4.3.1 Training Encoder Models

We train the encoder models on the sequence labeling task described above (Section 2). For each character, the models are fine-tuned to predict a binary label indicating whether a space should appear before it or not.

The BERT encoders generate contextualized character representations, followed by a linear layer that maps these representations to logits. We train by minimizing the cross-entropy loss between the predicted logits and the true labels.

During initial fine-tuning, we observed that the model almost exclusively predicted the negative label, likely due to the the class imbalance (the average sentence had 115 characters but fewer than 4 missing spaces - a ratio of roughly 99:1). To address this, we trained the encoder models only on the 20% of examples where spaces were removed. Within each example, we also downsampled the negative labels, keeping only 10% of the $l_i = 0$ labels, ensuring a more balanced ratio.

The hyperparameters and loss graphs are detailed in Appendix B.

4.3.2 Training The Decoder-based Model

For the decoder-based fine-tuned model, we train on the full training data, where 80% of the examples had no spaces removed. We use a supervised fine-tuning (SFT) approach, similar to instruction tuning in large language models (Zhang et al., 2024).

Each example was formatted as:

```
[SRC] {input sentence} [/SRC]
{output sentence}</s>
```

We compute the loss only on the completion (i.e., the output sentence), ensuring that the model focuses on predicting the correct restoration of spaces. Since most of the training examples already contained correctly spaced text, this setup allowed the model to learn both how to copy well-formed sentences and also how to correct corrupted ones without being biased toward over-inserting spaces.

The hyperparameters and loss graphs are detailed in Appendix C.

During testing, we constrained the model's output by using guided decoding in the inference engine, in order to prevent any alterations other than additional spaces. This allowed for a reliable evaluation of its ability to restore proper spacing, without the need to worry that the generative model might otherwise modify the text.

4.3.3 Prompting General-Purpose LLMs

To craft an ideal prompt, we used OpenAI's o1 model (OpenAI, 2024). We provided the model with a definition of the task as a character-level sequence labeling task, and we emphasized that the prompt should clearly instruct the model to modify only spaces, without altering any other characters. The final prompt can be found in Appendix D.

[3] The sentences are gathered from high-quality Hebrew corpora such as newspapers and ebooks, rather than from scraped social media, to avoid the possibility that these sentences themselves might already be corrupted with missing spaces.

[4] https://huggingface.co/datasets/dicta-il/hebrew-space-restoration-corpus

When testing, we verify that the model's output is "valid", that is, identical to the input except for the addition of spaces. If the model makes any other modifications, we treat the sentence as unchanged, since we cannot reliably evaluate an output that differed beyond spacing adjustments. GPT-4o produced valid outputs 95.2% of the time, while GPT-4o-Mini produced valid outputs only 83.5% of the time.

5 Results

We evaluate each model's ability to accurately restore all missing spaces across the sentences in our test corpus. We compute precision, recall, and F1 score for restoring a space (a positive label). Results are presented in Table 1.

Model	Precision	Recall	F1
Our Model (T=0.5)	90.1%	**99.0%**	.943
Our Model (T=0.9)	97.0%	96.7%	.968
tau/TavBERT	13.0%	13.4%	.131
DictaLM2.0 (FT)	97.5%	97.9%	**.976**
DictaLM2.0-AWQ (FT)	97.2%	97.7%	.974
GPT-4o	**98.9%**	93.6%	.961
GPT-4o-Mini	97.7%	84.5%	.906

Table 1: Performance on the space restoration task, measured in terms of precision, recall, F1 for positive labels (i.e., correctly adding a missing space). For our model we presented results with two different thresholds.

The fine-tuned 7B-parameter decoder model (Dicta-LM 2.0) outperforms the other methods, with our new character-based model not far behind, with both of these models being lightweight enough to run on consumer hardware. Additionally, we evaluate a 4-bit quantized version of the model using AWQ quantization (Lin et al., 2023). This version requires only 5GB of VRAM to run efficiently and performs nearly as well as the full-precision model.

To provide a more realistic view of practical usage, we compared the performance of the 7B models and the encoder model, as shown in Table 2. Both were evaluated on an RTX 4090 GPU; we ran our char-based BERT model using the standard HuggingFace implementation, and we ran the DictaLM model via vLLM.

Our char-based BERT model outputs logit values, which are then transformed using softmax into normalized scores between 0 and 1, allowing us to set a confidence threshold. Based on this, we present a graph of its metrics across different thresholds in Figure 1. Notably, when setting the threshold to 0.9, the F1 score surpasses that of GPT-4o, as shown in Table 1, and is only slightly shy of the F1 score achieved by model based on DictaLM 2.0 model (0.968 vs. 0.976). Furthermore, our char-based BERT model runs nearly 30 times faster than DictaLM2.0 with guidance, making it a highly efficient method for real-world corpora. In Appendix A we present examples of output from the model when run on real-world Hebrew sentences, with a qualitative analysis of its successes and failures.

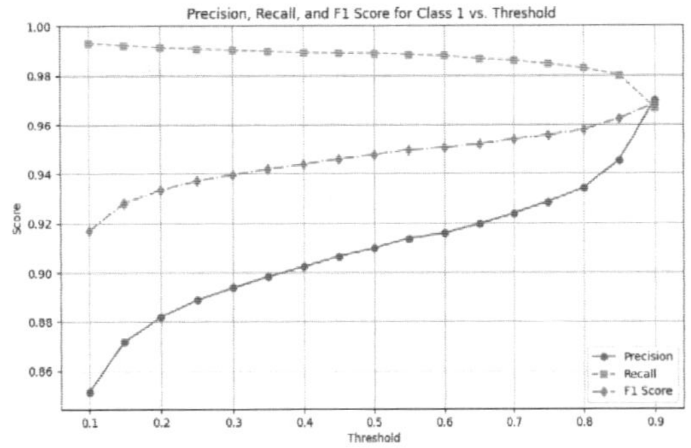

Figure 1: Precision, Recall, and F1 score of our new char-based BERT model across different confidence thresholds, when run on the test set.

Model	Time (s)	Invalid
New char-based Hebrew BERT	23.46	0
DictaLM2.0 (not guided)	616.8	3.6%
DictaLM2.0 (guided)	676.8	0
DictaLM2.0-AWQ (not guided)	437.3	16.9%
DictaLM2.0-AWQ (guided)	1081.5	0

Table 2: Inference time comparison of the models running on 12,000 sentences on an RTX 4090. The "guided"/"not guided" label indicates whether the model was run with or without the guided backend enforcing valid output (i.e., restricting modifications to only adding spaces. This increases runtime since the engine has to construct a new predictions tree for each input). The third column notes the percentage of outputs that were invalid, where the model altered more than just spaces.

6 Conclusion

Almost all of the methods presented here provide decent accuracy on the space restoration task. However, because scraped social media corpora tend to be huge, the decoder-based methods are largely impractical, due to issues of speed (thus for the open Dicta-LM model), or cost (thus regarding the commercial LLM models). Fortunately, the fine-tuned character-BERT model which we presented here provides a practical solution: it is blazing fast, free for unrestricted use, and achieves accuracy which rivals the other methods. We are thus pleased to hereby release this model to the NLP community.

Furthermore, the character-based Hebrew BERT model which we pretrained as part of this project is released here as well, so that NLP researchers can continue to fine-tune it for other character-level NLP tasks as well.

Acknowledgements

This work has been funded by the Israel Science Foundation (Grant No. 2617/22) and by the European Union (ERC, MiDRASH, Project No. 101071829; Principal investigators: Nachum Dershowitz, Tel-Aviv University; Judith Olszowy-Schlanger, EPHE-PSL; Avi Shmidman, Bar-Ilan University, and Daniel Stoekl Ben Ezra, EPHE-PSL), for which we are grateful. Views and opinions expressed are, however, those of the authors only and do not necessarily reflect those of the European Union or the European Research Council Executive Agency. Neither the European Union nor the granting authority can be held responsible for them.

References

Avihay Chriqui and Inbal Yahav. 2021. Hebert & hebemo: a hebrew bert model and a tool for polarity analysis and emotion recognition. *Preprint*, arXiv:2102.01909.

Jacob Devlin, Ming-Wei Chang, Kenton Lee, and Kristina Toutanova. 2018. BERT: pre-training of deep bidirectional transformers for language understanding. *CoRR*, abs/1810.04805.

Tau NLP Group. 2023. Tavbert: Hebrew character-based bert model. Accessed: 2025-01-21.

Eylon Gueta, Avi Shmidman, Shaltiel Shmidman, Cheyn Shmuel Shmidman, Joshua Guedalia, Moshe Koppel, Dan Bareket, Amit Seker, and Reut Tsarfaty. 2023. Large pre-trained models with extra-large vocabularies: A contrastive analysis of hebrew bert models and a new one to outperform them all. *Preprint*, arXiv:2211.15199.

Albert Q. Jiang, Alexandre Sablayrolles, Arthur Mensch, Chris Bamford, Devendra Singh Chaplot, Diego de Las Casas, Florian Bressand, Gianna Lengyel, Guillaume Lample, Lucile Saulnier, Lélio Renard Lavaud, Marie-Anne Lachaux, Pierre Stock, Teven Le Scao, Thibaut Lavril, Thomas Wang, Timothée Lacroix, and William El Sayed. 2023. Mistral 7b. *arXiv preprint*, arXiv:2310.06825.

Ji Lin, Jiaming Tang, Haotian Tang, Shang Yang, Wei-Ming Chen, Wei-Chen Wang, Guangxuan Xiao, Xingyu Dang, Chuang Gan, and Song Han. 2023. AWQ: Activation-aware weight quantization for LLM compression and acceleration. *arXiv preprint arXiv:2306.00978*.

OpenAI. 2024. GPT-4o system card. *arXiv preprint arXiv:2410.21276*.

OpenAI. 2024. OpenAI o1 System Card. *arXiv preprint arXiv:2412.16720*.

Pedro Javier Ortiz Suárez, Laurent Romary, and Benoît Sagot. 2020. A monolingual approach to contextualized word embeddings for mid-resource languages. In *Proceedings of the 58th Annual Meeting of the Association for Computational Linguistics*, pages 1703–1714.

Guilherme Penedo, Hynek Kydlíček, Vinko Sabolčec, Bettina Messmer, Negar Foroutan, Martin Jaggi, Leandro von Werra, and Thomas Wolf. 2024. Fineweb2: A sparkling update with 1000s of languages.

Amit Seker, Elron Bandel, Dan Bareket, Idan Brusilovsky, Refael Greenfeld, and Reut Tsarfaty. 2022. AlephBERT: Language model pre-training and evaluation from sub-word to sentence level. In *Proceedings of the 60th Annual Meeting of the Association for Computational Linguistics (Volume 1: Long Papers)*, pages 46–56, Dublin, Ireland. Association for Computational Linguistics.

Vitaly Shalumov and Harel Haskey. 2023. Hero: Roberta and longformer hebrew language models. *arXiv:2304.11077*.

Shaltiel Shmidman, Avi Shmidman, Amir DN Cohen, and Moshe Koppel. 2024a. Adapting llms to hebrew: Unveiling dictalm 2.0 with enhanced vocabulary and instruction capabilities. *Preprint*, arXiv:2407.07080.

Shaltiel Shmidman, Avi Shmidman, Moshe Koppel, and Reut Tsarfaty. 2024b. MRL parsing without tears: The case of Hebrew. In *Findings of the Association for Computational Linguistics ACL 2024*, pages 4537–4550, Bangkok, Thailand and virtual meeting. Association for Computational Linguistics.

Reut Tsarfaty, Shoval Sadde, Stav Klein, and Amit Seker. 2019. What‘s wrong with Hebrew NLP? and how to make it right. In *Proceedings of the 2019 Conference on Empirical Methods in Natural Language Processing and the 9th International Joint Conference on Natural Language Processing (EMNLP-IJCNLP): System Demonstrations*, pages 259–264, Hong Kong, China. Association for Computational Linguistics.

Linting Xue, Noah Constant, Adam Roberts, Mihir Kale, Rami Al-Rfou, Aditya Siddhant, Aditya Barua, and Colin Raffel. 2021. mT5: A massively multilingual pre-trained text-to-text transformer. In *Proceedings of the 2021 Conference of the North American Chapter of the Association for Computational Linguistics: Human Language Technologies*, pages 483–498, Online. Association for Computational Linguistics.

Shengyu Zhang, Linfeng Dong, Xiaoya Li, Sen Zhang, Xiaofei Sun, Shuhe Wang, Jiwei Li, Runyi Hu, Tianwei Zhang, Fei Wu, and Guoyin Wang. 2024. Instruction tuning for large language models: A survey. *Preprint*, arXiv:2308.10792.

A Appendix: Qualitative Analysis

We survey here a set of representative examples of the successes and failures of the best all-around model presented in the paper (that is, the model based upon the new Hebrew character-based BERT released with this paper), with the threshold set to 0.9 (the optimal threshold, as per Figure 1 in the paper).

All input examples in this section are taken from the publically-available OSCAR internet crawl (Ortiz Suárez et al., 2020).

A.1 Successes

We first present a series of cases where the OSCAR lines are missing one or more spaces and our model successfully restores the spaces in the proper places. These cases demonstrate the strengths and capabilities of the model:

Input:
תשובותהלכתיות – הרבישראליוסףהכהןשיחי' הנדל, רבקהילתחב"דמגדלהעמק.
Output:
תשובות הלכתיות – הרב ישראל יוסף הכהן שיחי' הנדל, רב קהילת חב"ד מגדל העמק.

Input:
משה אליסקבלן מפתח
Output:
משה אליס קבלן מפתח

Input:
פלפלשחורגרוס
Output:
פלפל שחור גרוס

Input:
כדאי לנו מאוד לשים לב לכלל הזה, כי הוא דיחשוב, ואנחנו ממש עשויים לעבור עליו מעת לעת.
Output:
כדאי לנו מאוד לשים לב לכלל הזה, כי הוא די חשוב, ואנחנו ממש עשויים לעבור עליו מעת לעת.

Input:
יש לוודא כי הקבלן יהיה אחראי לתיקון רישום הבית המשותףוהדירות החדשות .
Output:
יש לוודא כי הקבלן יהיה אחראי לתיקון רישום הבית המשותף והדירות החדשות .

Input:
הכולטלוויזיהמוזיקהמחולקולנועתיאטרון
Output:
הכול טלוויזיה מוזיקה מחול קולנוע תיאטרון

Input:
אז תמשיך להצליחואני אמשיך להנות מכך.
Output:
אז תמשיך להצליח ואני אמשיך להנות מכך.

Input:
זמן הכנהשלושת רבעי שעה
Output:
זמן הכנה שלושת רבעי שעה

A.2 Failures

Next, we identify three categories where our model tends to fail:

Failures due to additional typos: When the input text contains additional typographical errors beyond the missing spaces, our model will sometimes attempt to add spaces in the middle of misspelled words words, as in the following examples:

Input: מרסססים את הקציצות בתרסיס שמן.

Output: מרס ס סים את הקציצות בתרסיס שמן.

Input: שיא עונת הדלעויים.

Output: שיא עונת הדל עויים.

Failures due to proper nouns: Our model does not always recognize proper nouns for what they are, and sometimes attempts to divide them into two, especially when one (or both) of the resulting pieces is a common Hebrew word.

Input: גנוקאש היא תכנת החשבונאות הפיננסית המובילה המורשית ברשיון גנו.

Output: גנו קאש היא תכנת החשבונאות הפיננסית המובילה המורשית ברשיון גנו.

Input: ובכל זאת – מדטכניקה היא יעד למיזוג עם חברת האם אילקס מדיקל.

Output: ובכל זאת – מד טכניקה היא יעד למיזוג עם חברת האם אילקס מדיקל.

Input: מרחק מנקודה קודמת: מקדש קיומיזו נמצא במרחק של כ-2.5 קילומטרים משוק נישיקי.

Output: מרחק מנקודה קודמת: מקדש קיומי זו נמצא במרחק של כ-2.5 קילומטרים משוק נישיקי.

Failures due to unusual grammatical suffixes: When the input text contains relatively long words which also contain a relatively rare grammatical suffix, our model is sometimes fooled and attempts to add a space before the grammatical suffix, as in the following examples:

Input: בואו בהמוניכן – יהיה מזגן.

Output: בואו בהמוני כן – יהיה מזגן.

Input: וה' אמר לכם לא תוסיפון לשוב בדרך הזה עוד.

Output: וה' אמר לכם לא תוסיפו ן לשוב בדרך הזה עוד.

In light of these failures, practical use of the model would entail use of additional filters in order to restrain the model from splitting too eagerly. For instance, an NER model could be used to identify proper names in the text, and to restrain the space restoration model from splitting those names. Similarly, in order to avoid the issue with grammatical suffixes, a script could check whether the letters after a word-split form of the few dozen sequences of letters which comprise Hebrew grammatical suffixes; in such cases, it would be wise to ignore the additional space predicted by the model.

B Appendix: Encoder Training Details

The models were fine-tuned on a single NVIDIA A10G GPU. We used a learning rate of $2e-6$, and a batch size of 16. We trained using mixed BF16 precision, with 500 warmup steps (27%). You can view the loss graph from the fine-tuning of both `tau/tavbert-he` and of our new char-based Hebrew BERT model in Figure 2. Total train runtime was 350 seconds for 30,000 training examples.

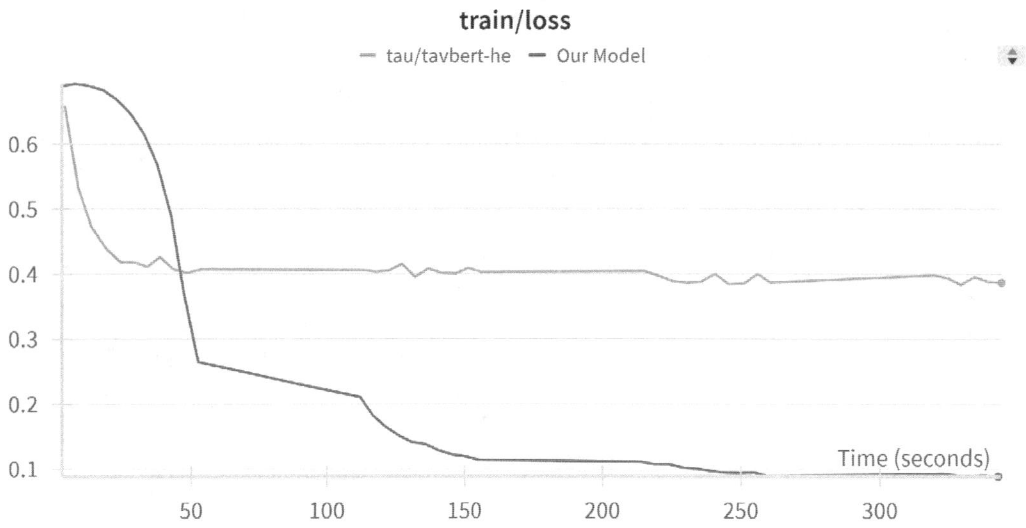

Figure 2: Training loss graph when fine-tuning our new char-based Hebrew BERT model and tau/tavbert-he

C Appendix: Decoder Training Details

The fine-tuning of Dicta-LM 2.0 was done on an NVIDIA-DGX with 4xA100 40GB. The training was done using the HuggingFace TRL library together with DeepSpeed. We set the initial learning rate to 5e-6, with a global batch size of 128 (per device batch size of 4, with 8 gradient accumulation steps). We used the `adamw_8bit` optimizer provided by the bitsandbytes library. Total training time was 110 minutes for 150,000 examples.

D Appendix: Prompt for General Purpose LLMs

Below is the entire prompt used with GPT-4o to complete the missing-spaces task:

```
You are a specialized tool for detecting and correcting missing spaces in Hebrew
↪  text. In the next message, I will provide you with a single Hebrew sentence.
↪  Your task is:

1. Identify any places in the sentence where spaces between words have been omitted.
2. Reinsert these missing spaces so that the sentence becomes correctly spaced.
3. Preserve all other text exactly as it appears in the input. This means:
    • Do not alter any words beyond adding missing spaces.
    • Do not, under any circumstance, add any letters!
    • Do not change or add punctuation.
    • Do not correct spelling or grammar (unless it solely involves inserting
    ↪  spaces).
    • Do not rearrange or remove any words or letters.
```

```
• Do not add or modify diacritics (niqqud).

Your output must be the exact same sentence, in Hebrew, with the only difference
↪ being the addition of the missing spaces. If there are no missing spaces,
↪ return the exact input sentence verbatim.

{input sentence}
```

Identifying and analyzing noisy spelling errors in a second language corpus

Alan Juffs
Department of Linguistics
University of Pittsburgh
juffs@pitt.edu

Ben Naismith
Duolingo and
University of Pittsburgh
ben.naismith@duolingo.com

Abstract

This paper addresses the problem of identifying and analyzing 'noisy' spelling errors in texts written by second language (L2) learners' texts in a written corpus. Using Python, spelling errors were identified in 5774 texts greater than or equal to 66 words (total=1,814,209 words), selected from a corpus of 4.2 million words (Juffs, Han, and Naismith 2020). The statistical analysis used hurdle() models in R, which are appropriate for non-normal, count data, with many zeros.

1 Introduction

The problem of 'noisy data' addressed in this paper is how to automatically identify and analyze spelling errors in texts written by speakers of English as a second language. This issue is important in automated scoring of written texts in high-stakes tests such as the internet based TOEFL (iBT) and Duolingo English Test (DET). Tests such as these use models that include numerous features, and these features may produce different values depending on whether they are considering correctly or incorrectly spelled tokens. Thus, this paper reports on one method of identifying the rate of spelling errors in the written output of learners of English as a second language in an Intensive English Program (IEP; Juffs 2020) over time and addresses the optimal statistical method for measuring those errors. The first languages (L1s) of these learners varied in their orthographies from abjads (Arabic), alphabets (Spanish, Korean), logographic characters (Chinese), and a mix of logographic and syllabaries (Japanese). At the time of data collection, the IEP had three levels of proficiency with approximate equivalent CEFR levels (Common European Framework of Reference; Council of Europe, 2001) as follows: level 3 low-intermediate, CEFR A2-B1; level 4 intermediate, CEFR B1+-B2; and advanced, C1 and above. Therefore, this corpus is representative of the population of IEP students across the USA at the time of data collection between approximately 2007-2012. (We note, however, that international student populations in US IEPs vary somewhat by region and have varied over time from the 1960s until present.)

English spelling poses special challenges because it uses a 'deep' orthography, meaning that the spoken sounds of English do not closely match their written forms and vice-versa. For example, the same sound /i/ is represented by different letters in 'ea' as in 'eat', 'e' as in the first 'e' in 'scene', 'ee' as in 'see', and 'y' as in 'quickly'.

Specifically, our research questions were the following. In terms of the rate of spelling errors in learners' written texts:

1. How can the spelling errors in a (typed) written corpus of 4.2 million words (Juffs, Han, and Naismith 2020) be automatically and accurately identified and calculated using Python?

2. Is there an effect for L1?

3. Is there an effect of proficiency level in the IEP?

4. Is there an interaction between L1 and IEP level?

2 Related Work

Spelling correction has been a long-standing challenge in natural language processing (NLP), with approaches ranging from traditional rule-based methods to modern deep learning models. Early spell checkers relied on edit-distance algorithms such as Damerau-Levenshtein (Damerau 1964, Mitton 1996), often combined with dictionary-based look-ups. However, these early methods

Proceedings of the Tenth Workshop on Noisy and User-generated Text, pages 26–37
May 3, 2025

struggled with errors where a misspelling results in another valid word (e.g., 'form' instead of 'from'). Subsequently, statistical models leveraging n-grams (Brill and Moore 2000) and probabilistic approaches (Carlson and Fette 2007) were introduced, enabling some level of context-aware correction. More recently, deep learning methods have demonstrated superior accuracy by leveraging contextual embeddings (Devlin et al. 2018; Jayanthi, Pruthi, and Neubig 2020).

Among open-access models used for spell checking, *NeuSpell* is trained on diverse datasets and uses contextual embeddings such as BERT and ELMo (Jayanthi, Pruthi, and Neubig 2020). *SymSpell*, though often considered a rule-based system, incorporates bigram look-ups to enhance context awareness, allowing it to resolve some ambiguous cases where single-word spell checkers might fail. Similarly, *JamSpell* incorporates a 3-gram language model to refine corrections based on surrounding words (Ozinov 2019). Unlike deep learning models, which infer spelling corrections from large corpora, *SymSpell* and similar models use a pre-compiled frequency dictionary to determine valid words and generate correction candidates efficiently (Garbe 2021b). The Spell Checker Oriented Word List (SCOWL; Atkinson 2019) is one of the most widely used resources, providing a hierarchical lexicon of words categorized by frequency and linguistic validity. Other resources, such as Hunspell and Aspell, also use wordlist-based approaches, making them highly efficient for misspellings but limited when handling real-word errors (Näther 2020).

For L2 learner errors, the choice of a spelling correction system is particularly important. Rule-based systems offer a more conservative approach, as they avoid over-correcting errors that might be intentional learner choices or non-standard but comprehensible variants (Näther 2020). In contrast, deep learning models, while highly accurate, may introduce unwanted corrections that mistake the intended choices in learners' *interlanguage* (Selinker 1972), particularly when trained on L1-English corpora. Other proprietary systems, such as Google's spell checker and Microsoft's *BingSpell*, remain inaccessible for customization, though they benefit from large-scale user data and adaptive correction mechanisms. Therefore, in settings or applications focusing on learner data, a hybrid approach using open-source tools (e.g., using wordlist-based methods to avoid excessive intervention, supplemented by context-aware models for ambiguous cases) may be the most effective strategy (Bryant et al. 2019; Omelianchuk et al. 2020). In high-stakes English proficiency assessments that implement automated scoring of writing, spelling accuracy is explicitly listed as a dimension of the scoring models (e.g., TOEFL, DET, PTE). However, details about the spelling error identification methods are scarce.

Although the problem of correcting spelling with computers has a long history, as far as we are aware, spelling errors in a second language written corpus in L2 English with various L1s have not been addressed. The Pittsburgh English Language Institute Corpus (PELIC) is unusual in that it contains longitudinal data in addition to a variety of L1s. In addition, the appropriate statistical models for analyzing the rate of errors has not been determined. Applied linguists are not just interested in computational detection and correction, but also in the potential qualitative impact of spelling errors on human graders, along with pedagogical implications.

While the cited on-line spelling checking resources are coded in a variety of computer languages, for applied linguists who work with L2 data, Python is the main programming language, and so Python was used to provide accessibility to such researchers. A complete description of PELIC spelling error identification and correction is provided at a public GitHub repository and Jupyter Notebook (Naismith, Starr, and Bacas 2021), where links include the following resources which were used in this paper:

(1) SCOWL Lists (Atkinson 2019). This website contains English word lists that contain abbreviations, acronyms, British, American and Commonwealth spellings, contractions, and taboo words that can be used in spell checkers. The resource also contains scripts in perl for the creation of tailored lists.

(2) Symspell (Garbe 2021b). *Symspell* is a spelling correction algorithm that only deletes erroneous spellings according to limited specifications. Garbe 2021b claims that it is one million times faster than other models, for example, Norvig, which was 80-90% accurate. This program deals with single words, compounds, and word-segmentation. The website contains code in a variety of programming languages in addition to Python.

Related work in applied second language reading and spelling research has noted that for L2, the challenges of English orthography are compounded by the influence of their L1 writing systems and limited vocabulary size (Hamada and Koda 2008, Humaidan and Martin 2019). An important construct in this domain is *lexical quality* Perfetti and Hart 2002, which established the importance of strong links in the mental lexicon among sound (phonology), orthography, and meaning. Poor links among sounds, graphemes, and semantics in any direction in lexical representations pose problems in both reading comprehension (Perfetti and Stafura 2013) and writing production (Dunlap 2012). Moreover, Baker and Hawn 2022 raise the problem that computer-automated grading may unfairly disadvantage some groups, known as 'algorithmic bias' in education.

Thus, this work is innovative because it is a rare(?) example of explicitly *interdisciplinary* work drawing on computational linguistics in automatic spell-checking and correction, applied statistics, with insights from applied linguistics research on literacy and instruction.

3 Spelling Identification

Spelling errors were identified using the following steps. First, SCOWL was consulted, and a SCOWL file was created and used to decide whether a word in the IEP texts was 'real' or not (SCOWL List for PELIC). All items were included from the lists except the abbreviations dictionary. Words that had previously been considered 'non-words' by dictionaries were added to our list, for example, 'southside', which is a neighborhood of Pittsburgh, 'frisbee', which is a toy/game, and 'onsen', which is a Japanese loanword for 'hot spring'. All hyphenated words were included as real words, forexample, 'prize-winning'. After running the revised dictionary, a list of misspellings with their adjacent words was created, followed by a dictionary of misspelled items. Examples in the dictionary of common misspellings included '*alot', '*becouse', '*sould', etc.

A Python module, Symspell (Garbe 2021a), was used that included the spelling errors and corrections for those errors. Examples, of corrections made are 'beccuase' -> 'because', 'nise' -> 'nice', 'friendlly' -> 'friendly'. Only word and bigram frequencies, but not full sentence context, were considered in resolving the appropriate target. This practice is consistent with other spellcheckers (Hunspell, pyspell, etc.). Thus, following this common practice the accuracy of corrected tokens will not be 100%. Nevertheless, the accuracy was inspected by random sampling and found that where the word is accurately spelled, the checker correctly does nothing 100% of the time (Naismith, Starr, and Bacas 2021), that is, there are no false positives.

An important caveat is that incorrect spellings that are actual words, for example, the pronoun 'him' misspelled as the real word 'hem', are not corrected. Such 'clang associates' (Schmitt and Meara 1997) are not counted as spelling errors in this automated process because it is difficult to automatically identify and correct misspellings that are real words. It might be possible to differentiate clang associates based on part of speech, for example, noun 'hem' vs. pronoun for 'him', or frequency of clang associate based on phonology, for example, 'ship' vs. 'sheep', but these possibilities have not yet been explored. Nevertheless, based on the corrections, it was possible to programmatically count and tally the misspellings in each text in the database. These text-based counts were the basis of the data in the study.

To control for number of errors by text length, the spelling errors were calculated by dividing the number of errors by the number of tokens in each text and multiplying by 100. Because the appropriate statistical analysis requires whole numbers (no decimals), 0.5 was added to the result of all calculations before the number was converted to an integer. Thus, 0.287 errors in a text remains 0, but a score of 0.847 became 1.347, and was converted to the integer 1.

4 Statistical Models

This section addresses the problem of the appropriate statistical model for non-normal count data with many zeros. Models that permit inferential quantitative investigation of count data include the Poisson family of analyses. Zeileis, Kleiber, and Jackman 2008 provide a detailed review of Poisson models that are both suitable and unsuitable for count data such as the spelling error data under consideration. Two points about our spelling error data are relevant here for Poisson analysis. First, standard Poisson analysis for count data is inappropriate for over-dispersed data, that is, data with very large numbers of outliers. Second, these data contain very large numbers of zeros, that is, texts without spelling errors – in fact over 50% for each

L1 and level. In this context, Crawley 2013 (Chapter 14) also raised the problem of high frequency of '0' in count data. Zeileis, Kleiber, and Jackman 2008 recommended the 'hurdle()' procedure for data with these characteristics. The hurdle() procedure is available in the (R package 'pscl') and is discussed in greater detail in the next section.

5 Results

In addition to L1 and level, other available student information that relates to the data includes standardized proficiency scores of a placement test and writing sample on entry to the IEP as well as self-reported biological gender. Neither the placement score nor the writing sample scores correlated at higher than r = -.07 to the number of errors and were therefore not included in any model even though these correlations were reliable at p<.0001 due to the large n sizes. Gender was also non-significant as a predictor.

The percentage of texts with 0 errors are displayed in Table 1 by L1 and level. It can be observed that over 50% of texts by each L1 at each level are error-free. Thus, the data are characterized by many scores of 0. In fact, 4554 of the total 5774 texts (78.7%) had 0 errors, not counting unknown clang associates. The numbers of students contributing data appear in Table 1. The majority of students at each level were Arabic speakers, while the fewest were Spanish speakers. Nevertheless, variability by L1 and level can be observed which makes the analysis important for proficiency assessment. Table 2 reports means and standard

Table 1: Percentage of Texts over 66 words with 0 Spelling Errors and Number of Texts by L1/Level.

	Level 3		Level 4		Level 5	
L1	%errors	Texts	%errors	Texts	%errors	Texts
Arabic	61.2	490	77	1126	85.2	709
Chinese	76.5	260	82.0	677	84.2	431
Japanese	70.0	60	79.1	249	90.3	134
Korean	67.0	276	80.7	685	87.9	404
Spanish	63.6	55	79.7	138	73.3	75

deviations of spelling errors, including texts with 0 errors. For example, the Arabic speakers at level 3 have an average of one error per text in their writing and also standard deviation of 1.52 errors. However, these means mask the fact that many texts by Arabic speaking learners have many more than just one error. The large number of texts reduces the mean but the visualization in Figure 1 shows

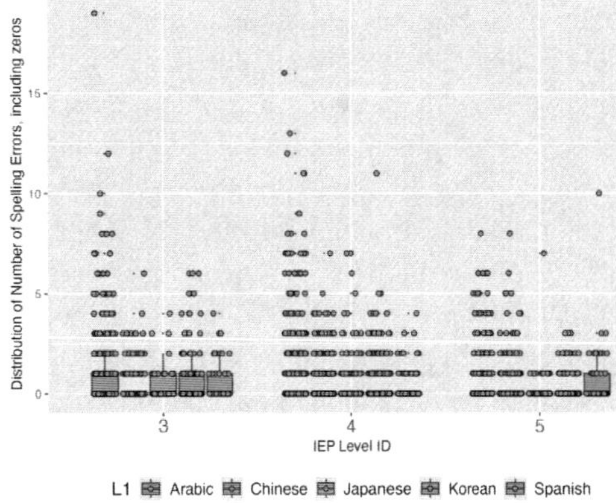

Figure 1: Box Plot Distribution of Errors (including zeros) in the count data by L1 and Level

the variability more clearly. As evident from Table 2, which represents the raw mean errors per student in each language group, and Figure 1, which illustrates the *mean proportion of errors per 100 words for each language group*, there are large numbers of texts with zero errors. The errors that do occur are not normally distributed. Thus, in Figure 1, the red columns represent Arabic-speaking students who at level 3 and level 4 have many more spelling errors per 100 words than other students. The boxplot and outliers show that many more of the Arabic-speaking students' texts had errors, frequently over five in each text as indicated by the circles above the boxes. Based on Zeileis, Kleiber, and Jackman 2008, analyses showed that the data are overdispersed. As Crawley 2013 states, in standard Poisson analyses "it is assumed that residual deviance is equal to the residual degrees of freedom (because the variance and the mean should be the same)". In these spelling data, a standard Poisson model revealed that residual de-

Table 2: Spelling Errors per text by L1 and Level

	Level 3		Level 4		Level 5	
L1	Mean	SD	Mean	SD	Mean	SD
Arabic	1.05	1.52	0.62	1.35	0.42	0.88
Chinese	0.43	0.55	0.28	0.46	0.33	0.56
Japanese	0.42	0.39	0.64	1.48	0.13	0.22
Korean	0.55	0.73	0.30	0.41	0.24	0.40
Spanish	0.76	0.87	0.27	0.33	0.39	0.51

viance was 8422.4 on 5759 degrees of freedom. Overdispersion can sometimes be dealt with using the quasi-Poisson technique. However, both Zeileis, Kleiber, and Jackman 2008 and Hoftstetter et al. 2016 show that a better method is the hurdle() technique. This approach provides regressions for the number of zeros and the count values separately by factor. Thus, one can determine effects of factors both on the number of zero counts and the count data in one model. Recall that all spelling error counts had been adjusted to 'count' integer data, that is whole numbers for analysis. Following Hoftstetter et al. 2016, we evaluated hurdle() and zeroinfl() negative binomial logistical regression models, concluding that the following hurdle() model was optimal: $hnb < -hurdle(PROP3\ L1 * level_id, data = L1FW3LNONA, na.action = na.exclude, dist = "negbin")$.

The results are provided in Table 3, with the statistics for the count data in the left half of the table and those for the texts with zero errors in the right part. In each half of Table 3, the intercept estimates are the log odds of spelling errors compared to zero errors, the other estimates are the log odds of those measures compared to the intercept.

Table 3: Hurdle Model Results

	Count Model (Truncated NegBin)		Zero Hurdle Model (Logit)	
Variable	Estimate	Std. Error	Estimate	Std. Error
Intercept	-1.151	0.891	-0.456	0.092***
L1Chinese	-0.904	0.291**	-0.726	0.173***
L1Japanese	-1.331	0.526*	-0.391	0.296
L1Korean	-0.917	0.251***	-0.253	0.158
L1Spanish	-0.683	0.457	-0.103	0.295
level_id4	-0.075	0.178	-0.752	0.116***
level_id5	-0.224	0.228	-1.293	0.140***
L1Chinese:level_id4	0.193	0.360	0.419	0.212*
L1Japanese:level_id4	0.929	0.600	0.267	0.342
L1Korean:level_id4	0.118	0.326	0.029	0.198
L1Spanish:level_id4	-0.525	0.620	-0.057	0.370
L1Chinese:level_id5	0.478	0.417	0.801	0.242***
L1Japanese:level_id5	0.265	0.813	-0.090	0.429
L1Korean:level_id5	-0.456	0.450	0.023	0.244
L1Spanish:level_id5	0.584	0.649	0.841	0.408*
Log(theta)	-2.376	1.014*		
Significance Codes: *** p<0.001, ** p<0.01, * p<0.05				
Log-likelihood		-4537		
N		5774		

Log odds can be converted to odds using the `exp()` function in R Levshina 2015. These converted odds are in Table 4, Appendix A, in the column Incidence Rate Ratios, produced using the `tab_model()` function. The intercept (reference level) was automatically selected (dummy coded) as Arabic level 3 in both models. This is why 'Arabic' appears nowhere in Table 3. The significance level of the intercept is an estimate of the outcome when the L1 and the level are at their reference levels.

A reliable chi-square statistic for the interaction of L1 and level_id in the model ($df = 16$, LRT = 30.37, $p = 0.016$) revealed that it contains frequencies of errors that are contingent on L1 and level. In addition, compared to an (inappropriate) standard Poisson model, the Akaike Information Criterion (AIC) confirmed that the `hurdle()` model with negative binomial was a better fit. The significant $\log(\theta) = -2.37$, $p = 0.019$ in the count data section in Table 3 also confirmed that these data were overdispersed and that therefore the negative binomial hurdle analytic technique was the appropriate one (cf. [p. 524-525]Hoftstetter).

Unpacking these statistics, Table 3 can be interpreted following [p. 257-266]Levshina) and Hoftstetter et al. 2016. Visualization of the count data in boxplots appears in Figure 1, which included texts with zero errors. The count model (Intercept) shows the odds of a spelling error Arabic, $level3 = Exp(-1.15) = 0.32$, and is not significant compared to zero. This result makes sense because while 39% of texts do contain at least one error, 61% of level 3 Arabic texts are error free. However, the odds of a spelling error by Chinese learners at $level3 = Exp(-0.90449) = 0.40$ is reliably lower than the intercept (see Appendix A). Thus, the odds of Chinese speakers making a spelling error per 100 words at level 3 are reliably 0.4 times lower than Arabic at that level due to the negative estimate. The other L1 data can be similarly interpreted. The odds of a spelling error by Japanese, $level3 = Exp(1.33061) = 0.26$. Thus, the odds of Japanese speakers making an error at level 3 are 0.26 times lower than Arabic at that level. Note the higher variance and lower p value for the Japanese speakers, which reduces the odds compared to the Chinese speakers. The odds of a spelling error by Korean, level 3 speakers is also lower = $Exp(-0.9174) = 0.40$. The odds of a spelling error Spanish, $level3 = Exp(-0.68308) = 0.51$. The co-efficient is also negative. However, the higher variance, lower z, and non-significant p values mean the Spanish level 3 speakers are not statistically different from the Arabic level 3 learners in the count data.

The hurdle model, having selected the count data with a lower limit of 1, then proceeds to model the number of texts by L1 and level with 0 errors, that is, the zero data. For zero hurdle model coefficients, [p. 523]Hoftstetter) state that "the zero model represents the probability of observing a positive count". In this case, the Arabic level 3 intercept with errors is reliable: $Exp(-0.456) = 0.63$, which means the odds of Arabic speakers making a spelling error compared to zero is reliably negative 0.63, with Table 1 showing that 61% of their texts contain no errors. Only the Chinese speakers show a difference from the Arabic speakers' texts being even less likely to make a spelling error at level 3. In this case, Chinese speakers at level 3 are 0.48 times less likely than them to produce text with an error, consistent with the count data. In Table 1, the level 3 columns illustrate this result, showing that 76.5% of Chinese learner texts at level 3 have no spelling errors, which is higher than any other L1 by over 6%. However, the Japanese, Korean, and Spanish speakers are not different from Arabic speakers at level 3.

To the right part of Table 3, in the zero hurdle model, level-id is statistically significant at both level 4 and level 5. This result means that the odds of Arabic speakers' texts having an error decreased significantly at level 4 by 0.47 and at level 5 by 0.27 compared to Arabic level 3.

The Chinese speakers' estimates at level 4 and level 5 compared to the (Intercept) show a reliable difference, except this time in a positive direction. This result means that compared to texts with an error for Arabic levels 4 and 5, the odds of the Chinese level 4 and level 5 learner producing a text with even one error increases by odds of 1.52 and 2.23 respectively. At level 5, the Spanish speakers also reliably increase the odds of making an error by 2.32 compared to the intercept, with only 73% of their texts at level 5 being error-free. No other comparisons with Arabic-speakers' level 3 in the model are reliable.[1]

6 Discussion

The differences by L1 are statistically reliable according to the chi square test on the entire model. Thus, while spelling mistakes by all IEP learners with access to spell-checkers in word processing software are relatively low, they are noticeably and reliably different by L1. Moreover, it is important to note that overall the learners improved in their accuracy over time.

Returning to the research questions, the results first demonstrated an effect for L1. When a text contains errors, Arabic-speaking learners make more spelling errors than Chinese-speaking, Japanese-speaking, and Korean-speaking (but not Spanish-speaking) learners at level 3, but these differences disappear at levels 4 and 5. Regarding texts with 0 errors, the pattern is similar, but the odds of Chinese-speaking learners making an error remains somewhat higher at level 4 and level 5 compared to level 3 Arabic speakers. Thus, there is an interesting interaction and difference between the Arabic-speaking and Chinese-speaking learners such that Arabic speakers decrease their proportion of errors in texts, while Chinese speakers seem to be more stable compared to the Arabic-speaking learners. Taken together, a cautious interpretation of these results suggests the most reliable difference is between the Arabic-speaking in contrast to the Chinese-speaking learners as there are differences between these groups in both the count and zero hurdle models. While Japanese-speaking, and Korean-speaking learners at level 3 differ from Arabic speaking learners producing texts with fewer errors, the zero model showed no differences among these three L1s. The Spanish speakers make errors at a statistically similar rate to the Arabic speakers.

Second, as to the effect of level of IEP at 4 and 5, we can see that for texts with errors there is no effect. This means that the rate of errors in texts varies little across levels overall. However, numbers of texts with zero errors increases from level 3 to level 4 and remains steady at level 5. We may infer that use of the spell-checker with word processing skills improved along with knowledge of orthography, and especially for the Arabic-speaking learners.

Third, interactions exist in the rate of errors among Arabic-speaking learners. A decrease occurred from level 3 to level 4, but not for other L1s, indicated by the interaction of level for level 4 with numbers of zero error texts. In addition, for the zero-count data, Chinese speakers showed an interaction at levels 4 and 5, indicating that the number of zero error texts remained more constant compared to Arabic level 3. Figure 1 shows that

[1] It is possible to make multiple pairwise comparisons by changing the reference level from Arabic to other L1s. However, given the limited number of errors and the similar means and dispersion statistics in Table 2 and Figure 1, it is unlikely that other pairwise comparisons would be reliable. One possibility was the very low Japanese error rate at level 3 is different from L1s other than Arabic. Overall, Japanese speakers are reliably less likely make an error, but Arabic speakers' odds of errors increase consistent with the model in which they are the reference level.

errors by Chinese speakers at levels 4 and 5 remain higher, while other L1 error rates declined.

To some extent, this outcome is reassuring for automated scoring of many features, for example those related to lexical sophistication (vanHout and Vermeer 2007), because automated measures of lexical sophistication, for example, Advanced Guiraud (Daller, Turlik, and Weir 2013), based on word-processed texts will not unduly penalize one group at intermediate and high-intermediate levels, for example, Arabic-speaking learners, by excluding misspelled low-frequency words, that is, words with a frequency band higher than 2000 at a higher rate than other L1s. This possibility had been suggested by Naismith, Han, et al. 2018 but now seems to be less of a concern based on this analysis. This confidence is possible due to the low number of statistically significant differences among the groups and the low numbers of errors per text overall. The group most at risk would be the Arabic level 3 learners, who made the most errors. Specifically, automatic scoring of lexical sophistication measures derived from frequencies of lemmas in an external corpus will not be affected by learners losing credit for too many misspelled words above the 2k frequency band at intermediate levels and above.

However, Arabic-speaking learners' errors may be salient to human raters compared to other L1 groups. This impression arises from the visualization of the data, even if it is not statistically robust, because of the numbers of texts that contain outlier tallies of spelling mistakes. Although the L1 effect is only statistically reliable at level 3, the tendency is very noticeable on a qualitative level at levels 4 and 5 also. Such a pattern of errors could cause human raters to negatively perceive Arabic speakers' writing, when only 61.2% of their texts at level 3 are error free compared to Chinese speakers' 76.5%. Thus, in high stakes testing where *both* human and computer-based automatic scoring are deployed, spelling errors have spelling errors have the potential to create bias against one group, even though those learners 'know' the items in question.

Moreover, these spelling errors (even when using word processing software), and the evidence from the reading studies cited in the introduction, are indicative of wider problems with lexical quality Perfetti and Stafura 2013 at the low-intermediate level (level 3). Thus, these data support interventions with spelling for all L1s, perhaps especially at the low-intermediate stage at the early stages of learning. When spellcheckers highlight many words – including proper names not frequent in English – it may be difficult for learners to guess which words are misspelled and, perhaps more importantly, which ones are the correct replacements. In fact, due to the saliency of spelling errors reported previously by Dunlap 2012 in student transcriptions of their own speech, one IEP instituted a dictation component as part of its curriculum to address lexical quality. This decision is given additional support by these data and other studies such as those reported in Humaidan and Martin 2019.

7 Qualitative Review of 'Noisy' Errors

This section provides a qualitative review of the type and frequency of orthography mistakes in these word-processed data to complement the quantitative analysis based on automatic tagging in the previous section. This review provides additional insights into these 'noisy' data that vary by L1 and proficiency. The process through which this was done was that the first author, an experienced English as a second language teacher, reviewed all the spelling errors in the texts. Thus, the list is not exhaustive but provides some indication of the challenges that learners face. The mistakes fall generally into four categories: (i) mistakes many learners make with frequent words; (ii) errors across L1s with the use of English spelling conventions; (iii) those forms influenced by L1 morpho-phonology; (iv) forms flagged as errors even though they are correct, for example, the (now sadly outdated) blend 'Brangelina' or abbreviations, for example, NHK, CBS (Japanese and US TV stations), and RMB (= Renminbi, the Chinese currency).

In the first category, regardless of L1 and level, many learners made mistakes with some *frequent* words, for example, 'because' (the range of misspellings of this word is very large) and 'studying', with the 'y' plus 'ing' creating uncertainty. Errors flagged due to spelling conventions of English double consonants were also frequent across learners both at morphological boundaries, for example, *writting, *eightteen, *eatting, vs. *regreting, and within words, for example, *recomendation, *profesion vs. *bussiness. Unsurprisingly, given the different double consonant spelling rules in Spanish, Spanish-speaking learners made many errors with double consonants.

Second, errors influenced by L1 morpho-phonology seemed especially frequent at level 3. Caution is in order as some could be simply 'typos', and others of these errors could be spacing problems that are influenced by English chunks (e.g., many learners made a mistake with *alot) or reduced stress on functors such as indefinite articles. However, Arabic speakers seemed to produce more with pronouns such as *iowe, and *idid, in addition to more frequent lack of spacing between indefinite articles and nouns (e.g., *anest and *abeach). In addition, trilled /r/ pronunciation could plausibly have produced *bearrd. Omitted vowels by Arabic speakers at the lower levels are also quite frequent, even in common words, but especially with liquids /l/ and /r/, for example, *evry and *evrybady, but also other words *amrica and *cmfortable. Such omission may be attributed to the influence of the abjad orthography, which only marks some vowels in Arabic and which also affects reading L2 reading in English (Martin and Juffs 2021). Because Arabic lacks the phoneme /p/, there is also an occasional, predictable voicing error in orthographic 'p' vs. 'b' (e.g., *laptob).

For Chinese speakers, it is possible to identify errors due to syllable structure constraints in Mandarin, which disallows consonant clusters (some possible with glides) in onsets and permits only alveolar and velar nasals in syllable final position. Potential examples of such influence include epenthesis (e.g., *samalled = 'smelled' and *sipricy = 'spicy') and what one could term metathesis *firiend 'friend' and *porblem 'problem'. In general, Chinese, Japanese (e.g., *toraditional 'traditional'), and Korean speakers (e.g., *zebara 'zebra') seemed more likely to insert a vowel compared to the Arabic speakers from the examples reviewed in the data. However, such qualitative observation would need to be quantitatively confirmed with inferential statistical analysis.

Finally, all L1s showed influence of vowel quality pronunciation on spelling, especially the [ae] as in 'cat' vs. [ɛ] in 'ketchup', for example, Korean level 3, *trevel = 'travel' and Korean level 4 *demage = 'damage' shows vowel raising from [ae] to [ɛ] in learners' phonological representations of these words. (We note that a merger between these two sounds may be occuring in some English varieties in Australia and in the northern cities of the USA near the Great Lakes.) Schwa [ə] in unstressed syllables also caused learners to have problems in identifying the correct grapheme, for example, Chinese level 4 *mechine = 'machine' and Arabic level 5 *sentance = 'sentence'. Some diphthongs (e.g., [ej] for Japanese *fervorite = 'favorite') also posed challenges, but less so.

The impression from this review of specific errors is that the influence of L1 morpho-phonology on spelling accuracy was more evident at level 3. This finding suggests that because learners do not control the pronunciation of the word, it is harder for them to evaluate choices provided by the spell-checker. This difficulty is due to their own representation of meaning to sound, being influenced by L1 phonology, is stronger than the link from meaning to orthography. Thus, this qualitative review suggests a possible developmental trajectory of orthographic accuracy from influence of L1 pronunciation on spelling accuracy at lower proficiency progressing to greater challenges based on proper nouns, abbreviations, and longer, less familiar technical words at the higher levels. Such an impression requires careful review of the whole data set to be supported quantitatively and faces the challenge of reconstructing the source of each error, which is a non-trivial task.

It is worth re-emphasizing that a limitation to this analysis is that we do not account for 'clang' effects in the spelling data (e.g., *sees, *case, and *scene for a target such a 'cease') which we found in responses to prompts in reading vocabulary test data (Heilman et al. 2010) or 'hem' vs. 'him', which actually occurred in the corpus. Automated spelling correction cannot correct words that are actually in the dictionary without further refinement of the correction algorithms. It is possible that were clang effects included in the analysis as spelling errors, the results would be different.

8 Conclusion

This paper considered the problem of identifying and measuring orthographic errors in a written IEP corpus by five different groups of L1 speakers across three levels of proficiency. Python coding enabled the identification and enumeration of errors. Using statistical models for overdispersed count data, the findings are that at the low-intermediate level, Arabic speakers make errors at a significantly higher rate per text than peers from some, but not all, L1 groups at the same level of proficiency. These L1 differences are reduced at intermediate and high-intermediate/advanced levels, with Chinese-speaking learners changing somewhat less than other groups in the proportion of texts with spelling errors. Gender was not found to be significant, perhaps because so many of the Arabic-speaking learners were male and hence it is difficult to tease apart this factor from L1 influence. The statistical models did not demonstrate important differences in the groups in spelling errors at higher proficiency levels, which should be seen as a positive outcome for automatic assessment. However, the large numbers of errors by Arabic L1 students in some texts could create a perception that they are worse than other L1 groups, when in fact they are not at levels 4 and 5.

9 Directions for Further Research

Future research might develop automatic coding to identify learner errors based on L1 phonological influence at lower levels of proficiency to confirm the qualitative examples identified in this paper and which are well known to English teachers, for example, confusion among 'ship', 'sheep', 'sip', and 'seep', which involves knowledge of contrasts between tense vs. lax vowels and alveolar vs. post-alveolar fricatives. The results also suggest that many low-intermediate students could benefit from targeted spelling instruction to improve lexical quality. Instructional interventions can be created to determine if instruction makes a difference in speeding up the progress and accuracy of learners. This instruction would not only improve spelling, but also reading comprehension through improved lexical access during text processing (e.g., Hopp 2016). It might also help students make the *correct choices* when choosing the appropriate form in spell-checking and potentially improve their grades for mechanics in tests that grade for that component. Therefore, these data support the call in Humaidan and Martin 2019 for an additional pedagogical intervention in orthographic skills that would improve not only writing but also reading competencies.

Finally, spell-checkers might be made more tolerant of common non-English words, acronyms, and abbreviations, which would further reduce false positives of 'errors' in students' writing.

Acknowledgments

None of this work could have been carried out without the help and guidance of Dr. Na-Rae Han. In addition, we are grateful to our undergraduate research assistants Eva Bacas, Guiseppe Livorno, John Starr, and Sean Steinle. This work was supported by the National Science Foundation for their grant via the Pittsburgh Science of Learning Center, funded award number SBE-0836012. (Previously NSF award number SBE-0354420) and the Social Sciences and Humanities Research Council of Canada.

References

Atkinson, Kevin (2019). *SCOWL: Spell Checker Oriented Word Lists*. Retrieved from http://wordlist.aspell.net.

Baker, Ryan and Aaron Hawn (2022). "Algorithmic Bias in Education". In: *International Journal of Algorithmic Bias in Education* 32, pp. 1052–1092. DOI: 10.1007/s40593-021-00285-9.

Brill, Eric and Robert C. Moore (2000). "An improved error model for noisy channel spelling correction". In: *Proceedings of the 38th Annual Meeting on Association for Computational Linguistics*, pp. 286–293. DOI: 10.3115/1075218.1075255.

Bryant, Christopher et al. (2019). "The BEA-2019 shared task on grammatical error correction". In: *Proceedings of the Fourteenth Workshop on Innovative Use of NLP for Building Educational Applications*, pp. 52–75. DOI: 10.18653/v1/W19-4406.

Carlson, Andrew and Ian Fette (2007). "Memory-based context-sensitive spelling correction at web scale". In: *Sixth International Conference on Machine Learning and Applications (ICMLA 2007)*, pp. 166–171. DOI: 10.1109/ICMLA.2007.50.

Crawley, Michael J (2013). *The R Book*. Chichester, West Sussex: Wiley. DOI: https://onlinelibrary.wiley.com/doi/book/10.1002/9781118448908.

Daller, Michael, John Turlik, and Iain Weir (2013). "Vocabulary acquisition and the learning curve". In: *Vocabulary Knowledge: Human ratings and automated measures*. Ed. by Scott Jarvis and Michael Daller. Amsterdam: John Benjamins, pp. 185–218. DOI: https://doi.org/10.1075/sibil.47.

Damerau, Frederick J. (1964). "A technique for computer detection and correction of spelling errors". In: *Communications of the ACM* 7.3, pp. 171–176. DOI: https://doi.org/10.1145/363958.363994.

Devlin, Jacob et al. (2018). "BERT: Pre-training of deep bidirectional transformers for language understanding". In: *Proceedings of NAACL-HLT 2019*. DOI: 10.18653/v1/N19-1423.

Dunlap, Susan (2012). "Orthographic quality in English as a second language". Thesis. DOI: http://d-scholarship.pitt.edu/13614/.

Garbe, Wolfe (2021a). *https://github.com/wolfgarbe/symspell*. Computer Program. DOI: URL : https://github.com/wolfgarbe/symspell.

– (2021b). *SymSpell: 1 million times faster spelling correction & fuzzy search*. Retrieved from https://github.com/wolfgarbe/symspell.

Hamada, Megumi and Keiko Koda (2008). "Influence of first language orthographic experience on second language decoding and word learning". In: *Language Learning* 38.1, pp. 1–31. DOI: 10.1111/j.1467-9922.2007.00433.x.

Heilman, Michael et al. (2010). "Personalization of reading passages improves vocabulary acquisition". In: *International Journal in Artificial Intelligence in Education* 20.1, pp. 73–98. DOI: 10.3233/JAI-2010-0003.

Hoftstetter, Hedwig et al. (2016). "Modeling Caries Experience: Advantages of the Use of the Hurdle Model". In: *Caries Research* 50. DOI: 10.1159/000448197.

Hopp, Holger (2016). "The timing of lexical and syntactic processes in second language sentence comprehension". In: *Applied Psycholinguistics* 37.5, pp. 1253–1280. DOI: 10.1017/S0142716415000569.

Humaidan, Abdulsamad Y and Katherine I Martin (2019). "Instructor-generated Orthographic Assessments in Intensive English Classes". In: *Handbook of Research on Assessment Literacy and Teacher-Made Testing in the Language Classroom*. Ed. by Eddy White and Thomas Delaney. Hershey, PA: IGI Global, pp. 204–243. ISBN: 9781522569879. DOI: 10.4018/978-1-5225-6986-2.ch011.

Jayanthi, Shardul M., Danish Pruthi, and Graham Neubig (2020). "NeuSpell: A neural spelling correction toolkit". In: *Proceedings of the 2020 EMNLP (Systems Demonstrations)*, pp. 158–164. DOI: 10.18653/v1/2020.emnlp-demos.21].

Juffs, Alan (2020). *Aspects of Language Development in an Intensive English Program*. Routledge Studies in Applied Linguistics. New York: Taylor and Francis. DOI: 10.4324/9781315170190.

Juffs, Alan, Na-Rae Han, and Ben Naismith (2020). *The University of Pittsburgh English Language Institute Corpus (PELIC)*. Online Database. DOI: 10.5281/zenodo.3991977.

Levshina, Natalia (2015). *How to do Linguistics with R*. Amsterdam: Benjamins. DOI: https://doi.org/10.1075/z.195.

Martin, Katherine I and Alan Juffs (2021). "Eye-tracking as a window into assembled phonology in native and non-native reading". In: *Journal of Second Language Studies* 4.1, pp. 66–96. DOI: https://benjamins.com/catalog/jsls.19026.mar.

Mitton, Roger (1996). "Spellchecking by Computer". In: *Journal of the Simplified Spelling Society* 20.1, pp. 4–11. DOI: www.spellingsociety.org/uploaded_journals/j20-journal.pdf.

Naismith, Ben, Na-Rae Han, et al. (2018). "Accurate Measurement of Lexical Sophistication with Reference to ESL Learner Data". In: *Proceedings of the 11th International Conference on Educational Data Mining*. Ed. by Kristy Elizabeth Boyer and Michael Yudelson, pp. 259–265. DOI: http://educationaldatamining.org/EDM2018/.

Naismith, Ben, John Starr, and Eva Bacas (2021). *PELIC Spelling*. Online Database. URL: https://github.com/ELI-Data-Mining-Group/PELIC-spelling.

Näther, Marius (2020). "An in-depth comparison of 14 spelling correction tools on a common benchmark". In: *Proceedings of the 12th Conference on Language Resources and Evaluation (LREC 2020)*, pp. 1849–1857. DOI: https://aclanthology.org/2020.lrec-1.228/.

Omelianchuk, Kostiantyn et al. (2020). "GECToR – Grammatical Error Correction: Tag, not rewrite". In: *Proceedings of the Fifteenth Workshop on Innovative Use of NLP for Building Educational Applications*, pp. 163–170. DOI: 10.18653/v1/2020.bea-1.16.

Ozinov, Filipp (2019). *JamSpell*. Retrieved from https://github.com/bakwc/JamSpell. Online Resource.

Perfetti, Charles and Lesley Hart (2002). "The lexical quality hypothesis". In: *Precursors of functional literacy*. Ed. by Ludo Verhoeven, Carsten Elbro, and Pieter Reitsma. 11th ed. Studies in

Language and Literacy. Amsterdam: John Benjamins, pp. 189–214. DOI: 10.1075/swll.11.14per.

Perfetti, Charles and Josepeh Stafura (2013). "Word knowledge in a theory of reading comprehension". In: *Scientific Studies of Reading* 18.1, pp. 22–37. DOI: 10.1080/10888438.2013.827687.

Schmitt, Norbert and Paul M Meara (1997). "Researching vocabulary through a word knowledge framework: word associations and verbal suffixes". In: *Studies in Second Language Acquisition* 19, pp. 17–36. DOI: https://doi.org/10.1017/S0272263197001022.

Selinker, Larry (1972). "Interlanguage". In: *International Review of Applied Linguistics* 10, pp. 209–231. DOI: https://doi.org/10.1515/iral.1972.10.1-4.209.

vanHout, Roland and Anne Vermeer (2007). "Comparing measures of lexical richness". In: *Modelling and Assessing Vocabulary Knowledge*. Ed. by Helmut Daller, James Milton, and Jeanine Treffers-Daller. Cambridge: Cambridge University Press, pp. 93–115. DOI: https://doi.org/10.1017/CBO9780511667268.

Zeileis, Achim, Christian Kleiber, and Simon Jackman (2008). "Regression Models for Count Data in R". In: *Journal of Statistical Software* 27.8, pp. 1–25. DOI: https://www.jstatsoft.org/article/view/v027i08.

A Appendix A. Table of Effects in hurdle() model[2]

Table 4: Effects in hurdle() model

Predictors	*Incidence Rate Ratios*	*CI*	*p*
Count Model			
(Intercept)	0.32	0.06 – 1.81	0.197
L1 [Chinese]	0.40	0.23 – 0.72	**0.002**
L1 [Japanese]	0.26	0.09 – 0.74	**0.011**
L1 [Korean]	0.40	0.24 – 0.65	**<0.001**
L1 [Spanish]	0.51	0.21 – 1.24	0.135
level_id [4]	0.93	0.65 – 1.32	0.675
level_id [5]	0.80	0.51 – 1.25	0.326
L1 [Chinese] * level_id [4]	1.21	0.60 – 2.46	0.591
L1 [Japanese] * level_id [4]	2.53	0.78 – 8.21	0.121
L1 [Korean] * level_id [4]	1.13	0.59 – 2.13	0.717
L1 [Spanish] * level_id [4]	0.59	0.18 – 1.99	0.397
L1 [Chinese] * level_id [5]	1.61	0.71 – 3.65	0.251
L1 [Japanese] * level_id [5]	1.30	0.27 – 6.41	0.744
L1 [Korean] * level_id [5]	0.63	0.26 – 1.53	0.311
L1 [Spanish] * level_id [5]	1.79	0.50 – 6.40	0.369
Zero-Inflated Model			
(Intercept)	0.63	0.53 – 0.76	**<0.001**
L1 [Chinese]	0.48	0.34 – 0.68	**<0.001**
L1 [Japanese]	0.68	0.38 – 1.21	0.187
L1 [Korean]	0.78	0.57 – 1.06	0.109
L1 [Spanish]	0.90	0.51 – 1.61	0.726
level_id [4]	0.47	0.38 – 0.59	**<0.001**
level_id [5]	0.27	0.21 – 0.36	**<0.001**
L1 [Chinese] * level_id [4]	1.52	1.00 – 2.30	**0.048**
L1 [Japanese] * level_id [4]	1.31	0.67 – 2.56	0.435
L1 [Korean] * level_id [4]	1.03	0.70 – 1.52	0.884
L1 [Spanish] * level_id [4]	0.94	0.46 – 1.95	0.878
L1 [Chinese] * level_id [5]	2.23	1.39 – 3.58	**0.001**
L1 [Japanese] * level_id [5]	0.91	0.39 – 2.12	0.834
L1 [Korean] * level_id [5]	1.02	0.63 – 1.65	0.926
L1 [Spanish] * level_id [5]	2.32	1.04 – 5.16	**0.039**
Observations	5774		
R^2 / R^2 adjusted	0.040 / 0.038		

[2]Variance explained in Poisson/hurdle() models, which are special types of logistic regression, is difficult to interpret. The table of results from the model in Appendix A includes an R^2 statistic that suggests that just 3.8% of the variance in the entire model (count and zero) is accounted for by the factors of L1 and level. This result is unsurprising given that 78.7% of texts in the entire sample are error free.

Automatic normalization of noisy technical reports with an LLM: What effects on a downstream task?

Mariame Maarouf[1,2,3] and **Ludovic Tanguy**[1]
[1] CLLE: CNRS & University of Toulouse, France
[2] Centre National d'Études Spatiales (CNES)
[3] MeetSYS
mariame.maarouf@univ-tlse2.fr
ludovic.tanguy@univ-tlse2.fr

Abstract

This study explores the automatic normalization of noisy and highly technical anomaly reports by an LLM. Different prompts are tested to instruct the LLM to clean the text without changing the structure, vocabulary or specialized lexicon. The evaluation of this task is made in two steps. First, the Character Error Rate (CER) is calculated to assess the changes made compared to a gold standard on a small sample. Second, an automatic sequence labeling task is performed on the original and on the corrected datasets with a transformer-based classifier. If some configurations of LLM and prompts can reach satisfying CER scores, the sequence labeling task shows that the normalization has a small negative impact on performance.

1 Introduction

This study focuses on the automatic cleaning of technical and noisy texts and its impact on an automatic fine-grained semantic labeling task. The goal is to assess the capacity of a generative LLM to automatically rectify noise phenomenons in technical texts that are going to be automatically processed afterwards.

The dataset used in this work is composed of French written anomaly reports during Ariane 5 rocket maintenance operations. These types of maintenance records have proven to be not only filled with words from a technical specialized lexicon, but also extremely noisy (text in uppercase, missing accents, spelling errors and misuse of punctuation) (Bikaun et al., 2024b). As such, we chose to explore the cleaning of the noise by an automatic rectification task performed by prompting a generic pretrained large language model (LLM). Three different LLMs were evaluated, with four different prompts covering different levels of information. A first intrinsic evaluation compared the output of the LLM compared to a gold standard. A second, extrinsic evaluation consisted in measuring the performance of an automatic sequence labeling task. We compare the same classifier when trained and applied to the corrected versus original of the annotated data. The results of the automatic semantic labeling allow us to determine whether these corrections are beneficial to the fine-grain semantic analysis of those texts.

This article is organized as follows. Section 2 is a short review of related work on noise in technical text data. In section 3, we present the dataset of French anomaly reports and the methods used to correct the noise. The results of the intrinsic evaluation are presented in Section 4 and the sequence labelling task and its results are presented in Section 5.

2 Related work

Reporting anomalies is a common procedure in the space and aviation domain, as it is encouraged and has become part of the general culture among professionals. Numerous studies have been conducted on using NLP (Natural Language Processing) on aviation anomaly reports showing that a number of different techniques can be of use in the treatment of such texts (Yang and Huang, 2023), ranging from text classification to information retrieval (Tanguy et al., 2016), (Persing and Ng, 2009). The same kind of anomaly reports dataset used in this work, focusing on maintenance operations on Ariane 5 rockets, has already been the object of NLP experiments in Kurela et al. (2020); Galand et al. (2018) but with other objectives (assessing risk level) and based on a coarser grain text analysis. Maintenance reports have also been shown to be particularly noisy and technical texts (Bikaun et al., 2024b) (Akhbardeh et al., 2020), and thus are difficult to process by the usual NLP pipelines conceived for (and from) standardized texts (Brundage et al., 2021), (Dima et al., 2021).

Proceedings of the Tenth Workshop on Noisy and User-generated Text, pages 38–44
May 3, 2025

Several studies have already explored ways to clean this type of texts, from rule-based approaches (Hodkiewicz and Ho, 2016) to lexical normalization techniques (Bikaun et al., 2024a). The use of generative LLMs for correction has also been studied, for post-OCR noisy texts in Thomas et al. (2024) and Zhang et al. (2024) and seems to provide better error reduction rates. Bolding et al. (2023) has also shown promising results in the use of an LLM to clean noisy texts while preserving their semantic integrity. Wang et al. (2024) confirm these results, but also shows that the performance of the LLM varies according to the type of noise and that some models have a better ability to perform this task.

3 Corpus, noise and automatic normalization

Our dataset contains 1050 anomaly reports written in French in an industrial setting. This sample was randomly extracted from a much larger database with tens of thousands similar items. These reports are produced systematically every time an irregularity (however trivial) is encountered by an operator in a critical environment. As can be seen in Table 1, a report consists of a short description of a problem (average length = 19.3 words per report) filled with acronyms, components identifiers and specialized lexicon, mostly in telegraphic-like speech, as can be expected in a workplace communication between professionals (Falzon, 1987). But different noise phenomenons are also commonly found: the text is mostly in uppercase, accents are absent, punctuation and spacing is not respected, and some spelling errors can be found. These phenomenons can be explained by a number of factors related to the conditions in which these texts are typed and formatted. The goal of this study is to test if normalizing the text without reformulating or changing the meaning of the text is possible and beneficial to its analysis. The usual preprocessing techniques have proven to be of limited efficiency on this kind of texts, and run the risk of losing too much information (Brundage et al., 2021). For example, an attempt at POS-tagging on our dataset with *Stanza* (Qi et al., 2020) resulted in a 20% error rate.

For this experiment, we selected three small-sized quantized LLMs that could be run locally on a workstation (a constraint due to the confidentiality of the target data), able to process French and which reach state-of-the-art performance in generic benchmarks: *Meta-Llama-3.1-8B-Instruct*, *Meta-Llama-3-8B-Instruct* (Dubey et al., 2024) and *Mistral-7B-Instruct-v0.3* (Jiang et al., 2023). For each model, four different prompts were defined with incrementally additional information. The first one included only the context of creation of this dataset (i.e. operators reporting anomalies during the maintenance of a rocket) and the requested task (i.e. remove the noise phenomenons without altering the meaning). In the second prompt we added the goal of this operation : to prepare the text for further processing by a non-specified NLP program. For the third one, a list of the different expected types of noise to rectify was given. And finally, in the fourth prompt, two reports and their rectified versions were given as examples (few-shot prompting) (*cf.* Appendix A). As is commonly recommended in such cases, all four prompts were written in standard English, with the explicit indication that the source and target texts are in French (Jin et al., 2024). LLM temperature was set to zero, resulting in deterministic outputs and thus not requiring several runs.

4 Intrinsic evaluation of the correction

For a first evaluation of the results, the Character Error Rate (CER) was calculated on a gold standard of 15 manually normalized reports by the authors. A selection of reports were chosen randomly and 15 were selected to get a representation of all the different noise phenomenons. The correction process is not trivial as each word needs to be corrected, at least by putting the correct case back, decisions have to be made regarding abbreviations and punctuation, some words can be ambiguous due to the lack of accents... Table 2 gives the average CER score for the original and each prompting of the LLMs. The scores of the three different LLMs are close, the variations rely on the prompts. As expected, the first two prompts (with less developed instructions) give high error rates, close to the original reports score, which shows a lot of differences with the gold standard. The indication of a post-processing goal in the second prompt did not improve the results and even seems to have worsened it. However, the addition of the list of phenomenons to consider lead to significant improvement. The insertion of examples in the prompt was not efficient though, and even costed a few points to the results, except for Mistral.

Description of the anomaly
PONT 150 KN :DEFAUTS D'ISOLEMENT SUR LES MOTEURS SUIVANTS :MO12 : DIRECTION GV ===>2,8MohmMO13/14 : DIRECTION MV/PV ===>2,6Mohm ET 1,5MohmMO9 : LEVAGE GV ===>4,7MohmMO6/8 : TRANSLATION MV/PV ===> 4,5Mohm ET 2,3MohmNORME : ISOLEMENT MINI > 5 Mohm
DEGRADATION BETON DESSUS CARNEAUX :1) DESSUS CARNEAU EAP2.JPG2) DESSUS CARNEAU NORD 1.JPG AFFAISEMENT GENERAL3) DESSUS CARNEAU NORD.JPG

Table 1: Examples of anomaly reports

Dataset	Character Error Rate
Original Reports	0.43
Llama 3 prompt 1	0.32
Llama 3 prompt 2	0.35
Llama 3 prompt 3	**0.06**
Llama 3 prompt 4	**0.08**
Llama 3.1 prompt 1	0.35
Llama 3.1 prompt 2	0.34
Llama 3.1 prompt 3	0.10
Llama 3.1 prompt 4	**0.08**
Mistral prompt 1	0.28
Mistral prompt 2	0.39
Mistral prompt 3	**0.07**
Mistral prompt 4	**0.07**

Table 2: CER of the automatic rectification

Dataset	Output	CER
Original report	SYNTHESE HSY062 A OFF ATTENDU A ON.	0.35
Gold report	Synthèse HSY062 à OFF attendue à ON.	
Llama3 prompt 1	Synthèse HSY062 : À l'occasion de l'arrêt attendu à bord.	0.47
Llama3 prompt 2	Synthèse HSY062 : Analyse d'anomalie - À l'occasion de l'offre attendue à ce moment-là.	0.64
Llama3 prompt 3	Synthèse HSy062 : À off attendu à on.	0.20
Llama3 prompt 4	Synthèse HSY062 à off attendu à on.	0.13

Table 3: Examples of correction

The examples in Table 3 show one report and its rectification proposed by Llama 3 according to the different prompts. The text to correct was "SYNTHESE HSY062 A OFF ATTENDU A ON." (tr. "Synthesis HSYP62 on OFF expected on ON"). In this particular report, the expected corrections were limited: put back the lowercase and put back the accents on "Synthèse" and the two occurrences of "à". As already stated, the two first prompts produced less accurate corrections. In this case (which is an extreme one) the output contains additional words and substantial changes in meaning (tr. "on the occasion of the stop expected on board" for prompt 1 and "Anomaly analysis - On the occasion of the offer expected at this moment" for prompt 2). This behavior may even be considered as an hallucination. Their respective CER scores are 0.47 for prompt 1 and 0.64 for prompt 2. Prompts 3 and 4 got almost perfect results, although they respectively obtained 0.2 and 0.13 CER. In prompt 3, the punctuation ":" was added, which could be considered acceptable, and one of the acronym letter was put in lowercase. For both of the prompts, "on" and "off" were put in lowercase, which is not the case for the gold but can hardly be considered a mistake. This first intrinsic evaluation allowed us to identify a subset of promising configurations: we arbitrarily consider for the extrinsic evaluation the 5 which obtained a CER of less than 0.1 (indicated in boldface in Table 2).

5 Evaluation on a downstream task

The second experiment conducted in this study consists in an automatic annotation of the 6 datasets (the original reports and the five datasets with a low CER) through a sequence labeling task. The original reports dataset was manually annotated based on a twelve-class typology of sequences. These classes are related to the main type of technical problem reported (i.e. "leakage", "malfunction", "missing component"...). The annotated text segments are lexical markers (cues) of the class ("leak", "leaking", "absence", "missing", "not present"...). The annotation was performed by three linguists. The inter-annotator agreement between the linguists and a field expert was measured with a *gamma* score (Mathet et al., 2015) of 0.63. In the first example in Table 1, the trigger is "DEFAUT" (tr. "DEFECT") and in the second one, "DEGRADATION". Over the 1050 reports, a total of 1406 segments were identified (1114 are used for training, 292 for testing, with an unbalanced distribution of categories). Several fine-tuned transformer-based token classifiers[1] were tested for this task on the original reports dataset with no preprocessing other than folding the whole text in lowercase. The two models that gave the best results for the original corpus on a token-level evaluation were *bert-base-multilingual-uncased* (Devlin et al.,

[1]Hyper-parameters: learning-rate = $1e-5$, epoch = 20

Classifier	bert-base-multilingual-uncased			camembert-large		
Dataset	Precision	Recall	F-score	Precision	Recall	F-score
Original reports	0.72	0.77	**0.74**	0.71	0.79	**0.74**
Llama 3 prompt 3 (list)	0.60	0.67	0.64	0.66	0.78	**0.71**
Llama 3 prompt 4 (examples)	0.63	0.73	**0.68**	0.58	0.74	0.65
Llama 3.1 prompt 4 (examples)	0.58	0.66	0.62	0.64	0.77	**0.70**
Mistral prompt 3 (list)	0.57	0.66	0.62	0.63	0.73	**0.68**
Mistral prompt 4 (examples)	0.62	0.67	0.64	0.62	0.74	**0.68**

Table 4: Sequence labeling classifier scores

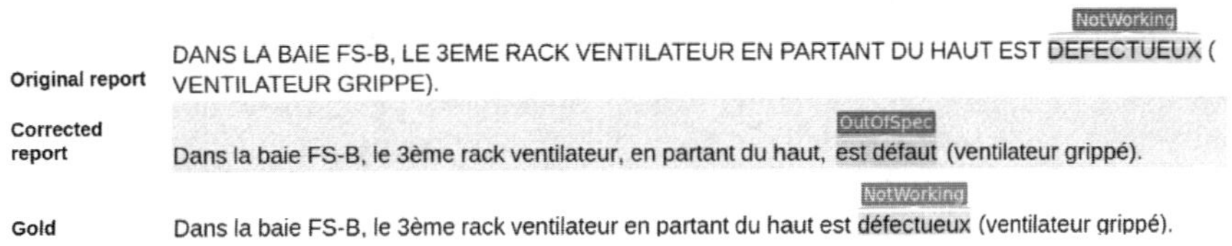

Figure 1: Example of automatic correction impacting the annotation

2019) and *camembert-large* (Martin et al., 2020) with respectively 0.68 and 0.67 macro-average F1. However, given the nature of the manual annotation task, the precise segment boundaries may vary without meaningful differences. As such, to get a more accurate view of the scores, the "nervaluate" metric was used, and especially the "entity-type" measure[2] to compute a labeled sequence based evaluation. This measure considers that a sequence which overlap the gold data is a true positive if the type (class) is correct. For the two selected models *bert-base-multilingual-uncased* and *camembert-large*, the entity-type macro-average F1 are both 0.74 (Table 4). Given the tight results, we selected these two classifier configurations to perform the automatic labeling on the corrected datasets.

To reverberate the manual annotation from the original reports to the corrected reports, adjustments had to be done. To that effect, the corresponding offsets of the target sequence in the corrected versions were determined based on the output of the GNU wdiff utility[3], with local homothety transformations for adapting to insertions and deletions. The sequence labeling task was then re-evaluated, using the five corrected versions of both the training and test sets, without any other preprocessing except using the lowercase for *bert-base-multilingual-uncased.*

The results of the automatic sequence labeling shown in Table 4 indicate that the rectification did not increase the scores (best F1 scores in boldface). Instead, they show slightly lower scores for the best two configurations, with 0.71 and 0.70 F1 against 0.74 attained with the original reports dataset. The *camembert-large* classifier obtains overall better results on the rectified data. Potential reasons to this would be that the model has been trained specifically for French language and as such is able to handle the accents, whereas *bert-base-multilingual-uncased*'s tokenizer strips them. Moreover, this BERT model is uncased, which was not an issue for the original reports that were all in uppercase, but for the rectified datasets, the case issues have been corrected. As such, *camembert-large* benefits from more precise and less ambiguous formulations. The decrease of the overall scores also implies a loss of semantic information during the normalization process that impacts the performance of the labeling task.

6 Conclusion

In this study, we have demonstrated that the automatic correction of a technical and noisy text with an LLM produces mitigated results. The scores given by the CER seemed satisfactory enough to assume an efficient correction of the noise, at the condition that the LLM is accurately prompted (context, goal of the normalization and list of phenomenons to correct). However, the results of the sequence labeling task do not confirm this hypothesis. Some semantic information may be lost and lead to a negative impact on the sequence labeling task. In the example in Figure 1, we can see a case where the LLM overcorrected and modified a critical word. The word "DEFECTUEUX" (tr. "defective") was replaced by "défaut" (tr. "defect"). In

[2]https://www.davidsbatista.net/blog/2018/05/09/Named_Entity_Evaluation/

[3]https://www.gnu.org/software/wdiff/

the reports, "defect/défaut" is often found and used with the meaning of "problem" or "inadequacy". As such, it has been manually labeled most of the time with the label "Out of specification". It differs from "defectueux/ defective" which means that a component is not functioning, thus labeled with "Not working". In this example, by changing this particular word, the LLM has modified the meaning of the sentence and even its correctness (in this case "est défaut" is nor grammatically accurate, nor attested in the corpus). The classifier applied on the rectified text thus incorrectly labels "est défaut" as "Out of specification", while the original text get a correct label of "Not Working" for "DEFECTUEUX". To conclude, we can say that the use of transformers models on noisy and technical data seems to be quite robust and able to cope with such a corpus, addressing the main types of noise. However, the noise itself does not seem to bear the difficulty of the sequence labeling task given the score obtained on the normalized dataset close to the score of the original reports dataset.

Acknowledgments

The authors would like to thank the CNES and MeetSYS for funding this work and providing the corpus and expertise required for this study.

Experiments presented in this paper were carried out using the OCCIDATA platform that is administered by IRIT and supported by CNRS and University of Toulouse (`https://occidata.irit.fr`).

References

Farhad Akhbardeh, Travis Desell, and Marcos Zampieri. 2020. MaintNet: A collaborative open-source library for predictive maintenance language resources. In *Proceedings of the 28th International Conference on Computational Linguistics: System Demonstrations*, pages 7–11, Barcelona, Spain (Online). International Committee on Computational Linguistics (ICCL).

Tyler Bikaun, Melinda Hodkiewicz, and Wei Liu. 2024a. MaintNorm: A corpus and benchmark model for lexical normalisation and masking of industrial maintenance short text. In *Proceedings of the Ninth Workshop on Noisy and User-generated Text (W-NUT 2024)*, pages 68–78, San Ġiljan, Malta. Association for Computational Linguistics.

Tyler K. Bikaun, Tim French, Michael Stewart, Wei Liu, and Melinda Hodkiewicz. 2024b. MaintIE: A fine-grained annotation schema and benchmark for information extraction from maintenance short texts. In *Proceedings of the 2024 Joint International Conference on Computational Linguistics, Language Resources and Evaluation (LREC-COLING 2024)*, pages 10939–10951, Torino, Italia. ELRA and ICCL.

Quinten Bolding, Baohao Liao, Brandon Denis, Jun Luo, and Christof Monz. 2023. Ask language model to clean your noisy translation data. In *Findings of the Association for Computational Linguistics: EMNLP 2023*, pages 3215–3236, Singapore. Association for Computational Linguistics.

Michael P. Brundage, Thurston Sexton, Melinda Hodkiewicz, Alden Dima, and Sarah Lukens. 2021. Technical language processing: Unlocking maintenance knowledge. *Manufacturing Letters*, 27:42–46.

Jacob Devlin, Ming-Wei Chang, Kenton Lee, and Kristina Toutanova. 2019. Bert: Pre-training of deep bidirectional transformers for language understanding. *Preprint*, arXiv:1810.04805.

Alden Dima, Sarah Lukens, Melinda Hodkiewicz, Thurston Sexton, and Michael P. Brundage. 2021. Adapting natural language processing for technical text. *Applied AI Letters*, 2(3):e33.

Abhimanyu Dubey, Abhinav Jauhri, Abhinav Pandey, Abhishek Kadian, Ahmad Al-Dahle, Aiesha Letman, Akhil Mathur, Alan Schelten, Amy Yang, Angela Fan, Anirudh Goyal, Anthony Hartshorn, Aobo Yang, Archi Mitra, Archie Sravankumar, Artem Korenev, Arthur Hinsvark, Arun Rao, Aston Zhang, and Aurelien Rodriguez. 2024. The llama 3 herd of models. *Preprint*, arXiv:2407.21783.

Pierre Falzon. 1987. Langages opératifs et compréhension opérative. *Le Travail Humain*, n°50:281–286.

Loïc Galand, Michal Kurela, and Horacio Romero Clavijo. 2018. Techniques de TAL pour la recherche des "signaux faibles" et catégorisation des risques dans le REX SDF des lanceurs spatiaux. In *Congrès Lambda Mu 21, " Maîtrise des risques et transformation numérique : opportunités et menaces "*, Reims, France.

Melinda Hodkiewicz and Mark Ho. 2016. Cleaning historical maintenance work order data for reliability analysis. *Journal of Quality in Maintenance Engineering*, 22:146–163.

Albert Q. Jiang, Alexandre Sablayrolles, Arthur Mensch, Chris Bamford, Devendra Singh Chaplot, Diego de las Casas, Florian Bressand, Gianna Lengyel, Guillaume Lample, Lucile Saulnier, Lélio Renard Lavaud, Marie-Anne Lachaux, Pierre Stock, Teven Le Scao, Thibaut Lavril, Thomas Wang, Timothée Lacroix, and William El Sayed. 2023. Mistral 7b. *Preprint*, arXiv:2310.06825.

Yiqiao Jin, Mohit Chandra, Gaurav Verma, Yibo Hu, Munmun De Choudhury, and Srijan Kumar. 2024. Better to ask in english: Cross-lingual evaluation of large language models for healthcare queries. In *Proceedings of the ACM Web Conference 2024*, WWW '24, page 2627–2638, New York, NY, USA. Association for Computing Machinery.

Michal Kurela, Mathilde Bacqué, and Remi Laurent. 2020. Classification automatique des faits techniques pour la conformité des lanceurs spatiaux. In *Congrès Lambda Mu 22 " Les risques au cœur des transitions " (e-congrès) - 22e Congrès de Maîtrise des Risques et de Sûreté de Fonctionnement, Institut pour la Maîtrise des Risques*, Le Havre (e-congrès), France.

Louis Martin, Benjamin Muller, Pedro Javier Ortiz Suárez, Yoann Dupont, Laurent Romary, Éric de la Clergerie, Djamé Seddah, and Benoît Sagot. 2020. CamemBERT: a tasty French language model. In *Proceedings of the 58th Annual Meeting of the Association for Computational Linguistics*, pages 7203–7219, Online. Association for Computational Linguistics.

Yann Mathet, Antoine Widlöcher, and Jean-Philippe Métivier. 2015. The Unified and Holistic Method Gamma (γ) for Inter-Annotator Agreement Measure and Alignment. *Computational Linguistics*, 41(3):437–479.

Isaac Persing and Vincent Ng. 2009. Semi-supervised cause identification from aviation safety reports. In *Proceedings of the Joint Conference of the 47th Annual Meeting of the ACL and the 4th International Joint Conference on Natural Language Processing of the AFNLP*, pages 843–851, Suntec, Singapore. Association for Computational Linguistics.

Peng Qi, Yuhao Zhang, Yuhui Zhang, Jason Bolton, and Christopher Manning. 2020. Stanza: A python natural language processing toolkit for many human languages. In *Association for Computational Linguistics (ACL) System Demonstrations*, pages 101–108.

Ludovic Tanguy, Nikola Tulechki, Assaf Urieli, Eric Hermann, and Céline Raynal. 2016. Natural language processing for aviation safety reports: From classification to interactive analysis. *Computers in Industry*, 78:80–95.

Alan Thomas, Robert Gaizauskas, and Haiping Lu. 2024. Leveraging LLMs for post-OCR correction of historical newspapers. In *Proceedings of the Third Workshop on Language Technologies for Historical and Ancient Languages (LT4HALA) @ LREC-COLING-2024*, pages 116–121, Torino, Italia. ELRA and ICCL.

Bin Wang, Chengwei Wei, Zhengyuan Liu, Geyu Lin, and Nancy F. Chen. 2024. Resilience of large language models for noisy instructions. In *Findings of the Association for Computational Linguistics: EMNLP 2024*, pages 11939–11950, Miami, Florida, USA. Association for Computational Linguistics.

Chuyang Yang and Chenyu Huang. 2023. Natural language processing (nlp) in aviation safety: Systematic review of research and outlook into the future. *Aerospace*, 10(7):600.

James Zhang, Wouter Haverals, Mary Naydan, and Brian W. Kernighan. 2024. Post-ocr correction with openai's gpt models on challenging english prosody texts. In *Proceedings of the ACM Symposium on Document Engineering 2024*, DocEng '24, New York, NY, USA. Association for Computing Machinery.

A Prompts

Included in prompt version	Text
1,2,3,4	You are a trained linguist working with maintenance operators. Your task is to correct sentences written in French by these operators. These texts describe problems occurring during the maintenance of a rocket. You are correcting these texts because they contain a lot of noise. You must write a standardized version of these texts without modifying, reformulating, or changing any words. Do not alter the vocabulary.
2,3,4	You need to clean these text because they will be automatically processed afterward.
3,4	Here is a list of the different phenomenons to correct you may encounter : - missing spaces and punctuation - mispelled words - the whole text in uppercase - missing accents. Even if you encounter an unfamiliar word, keep it as it is. When displaying your answer, write only the corrected version of the sentence without adding line breaks, additional information, explanations, or notes.
4	Here are two examples. The text "CORROSION LEGERE SUR OVM50005CORROSION PLUS IMPORTANTE SUR OVM5006 (VANNE ALIM PISCINE)" becomes "Corrosion légère sur OVM50005. Corrosion plus importante du OVM5006 (vanne ALIM piscine)." The text "POULIE DE RENVOI SUR CAISSSON LBS LH2 GRIPPEE SUR SON AXE." becomes "Poulie de renvoi sur caisson LBS LH2 grippée sur son axe.".
1,2,3,4	Here is the text to rectify: [text inserted]

We're Calling an Intervention: Exploring Fundamental Hurdles in Adapting Language Models to Nonstandard Text

Aarohi Srivastava and **David Chiang**
Computer Science and Engineering
University of Notre Dame
Notre Dame, IN, USA
{asrivas2, dchiang} @nd.edu

Abstract

We present a suite of experiments that allow us to understand the underlying challenges of language model adaptation to nonstandard text. We do so by designing *interventions* that approximate core features of user-generated text and their interactions with existing biases of language models. Applying our interventions during language model adaptation to nonstandard text variations, we gain important insights into when such adaptation is successful, as well as the aspects of text variation and noise that are particularly difficult for language models to handle. For instance, on text with character-level variation, out-of-the-box performance improves even with a few additional training examples but approaches a plateau, suggesting that more data is not the solution. In contrast, on text with variation involving new words or meanings, far more data is needed, but it leads to a massive breakthrough in performance. Our findings reveal that existing models lack the necessary infrastructure to handle diverse forms of nonstandard text, guiding the development of more resilient language modeling techniques. We make the code for our interventions, which can be applied to any English text data, publicly available.

1 Introduction

Nonstandard text is all around us. Whether a user adopts a regional dialect, follows different spelling conventions, or uses culturally-specific vocabulary, encountering text variation in most day-to-day NLP use cases is inevitable (Blodgett et al., 2016; Huang et al., 2020). Yet, recent work continues to find large gaps in performance between standard and nonstandard text and speech (Kantharuban et al., 2023; Faisal et al., 2024), and efforts to reduce this gap are typically case-, variety-, or task-dependent (Held et al., 2023; Joshi et al., 2024). The distinction between standard and nonstandard text is often contextual. In written English, *going to* is standard, while *gonna* or *gunna* is nonstandard. Likewise, *I am not* (standard) contrasts with *I ain't* (nonstandard). Similarly, *color* (American English) vs. *colour* (British English) reflects orthographic variation. Whether deploying a large-scale system for diverse users or working towards language model personalization, it is important to understand the challenges of adapting a language model to different varieties. Specifically, how can we improve a model's performance in a new domain (in this case, a new variety) by leveraging knowledge from an existing one (i.e., the standard one)?

This is tricky; it is difficult to tease apart the interactions between the complex and intertwined features that comprise linguistic variation, and the black-box nature of language models makes it even more difficult to do so. But we can reach some firmer conclusions if, on the one hand, we can devise ways of controlling different levels of text variation, and, on the other hand, we study the structure of the model (as opposed to its parameter values). We find that the model structure itself induces biases towards the standard variety of a language, and it does so in different ways at different levels of linguistic structure.

Current language models like BERT (Devlin et al., 2019) and GPT (Radford et al., 2019) are actually a hybrid of two models: a frequency-based subword tokenizer and a Transformer-based encoder or decoder. The tokenizer determines subword units, and the Transformer embeds the subwords into a vector space where it operates on the vectors. Frequent words are often kept together as a single token, while infrequent words are often broken up into several shorter-length tokens. When both the tokenizer and the Transformer are biased towards standard text, a rigid relationship develops between tokens and their vector representations. Small changes to the token sequence (e.g., resulting from spelling variation) can break the model's ability to understand it properly (Kumar et al., 2020; Soper et al.,

Proceedings of the Tenth Workshop on Noisy and User-generated Text, pages 45–56
May 3, 2025

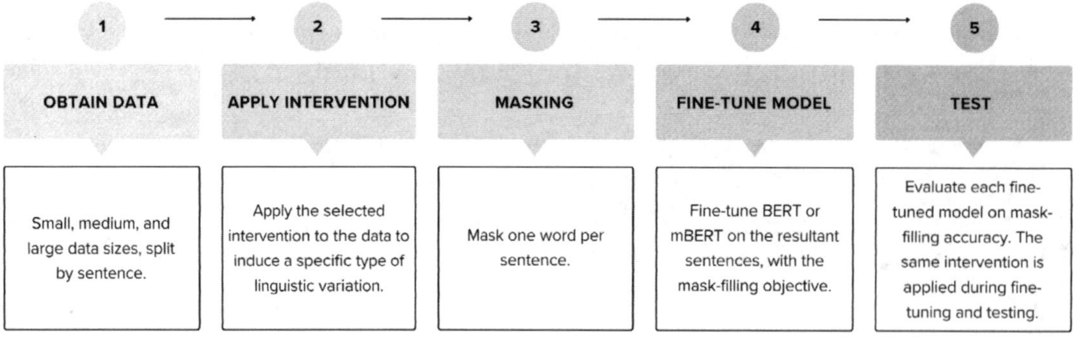

Figure 1: A sketch of our train/test pipeline.

2021; Blaschke et al., 2023; Srivastava and Chiang, 2023a; Chai et al., 2024). See the example below, where $\overset{\text{tok}}{\rightsquigarrow}$ denotes tokenization:

$$\text{coffee} \overset{\text{tok}}{\rightsquigarrow} \text{coffee}$$
$$\text{cofee} \overset{\text{tok}}{\rightsquigarrow} \text{co, fe, e}$$

While the model would associate the token *coffee* with the appropriate word, one misspelling in the input means the model must figure out that the token sequence *co, fe, e* refers to the same thing as *coffee*, which is certainly not trivial. Moreover, since the subword tokenizer of a pre-trained model cannot be modified without large-scale retraining, such issues can typically only be addressed through model adaptation methods (e.g., fine-tuning). However, because this approach does not resolve the underlying problem, it is crucial to explore the challenges and success cases in adapting language models to different forms of nonstandard text.

To this end, we develop synthetic manipulations that exploit our knowledge of what happens when a Transformer-based language model interacts with nonstandard text. Our experiments isolate data-related factors that can play a role in language model adaptation (e.g., type, amount, and composition of training data), and we assemble a suite of nine interventions to synthetically induce tokenization and embedding disruption, grounded in traits of user-generated text and at different levels of linguistic structure (e.g., orthographic, morphological, lexical), in controlled settings. We make the code for these interventions publicly available.[1] Our experiments (outlined in Figure 1) evaluate and stress-test BERT's ability to adapt to various types of nonstandard text under different conditions. Our findings inform important questions about the fundamental hurdles of adapting language models to nonstandard text:

- Language models adapt more effectively to lexical variation at the subword and multi-subword levels (e.g., new words, word senses, and meanings) during fine-tuning but struggle with within-subword variation (e.g., character-level changes, unconventional spellings).
- When handling lexical variation, greater data availability is vital for successful knowledge transfer. Multilingual models are also more helpful in such cases.
- In contrast, for text with character-level variation (within-subword changes), increasing data offers limited benefits. Instead, achieving robustness likely requires alternative solutions. Monolingual models outperform multilingual ones in such cases.

2 Related Work

As larger language models with new capabilities emerge, engaging with nonstandard text (e.g., dialects, language varieties, noisy text) – a hallmark of content generated by today's diverse user base – remains a challenge. Language models are not robust to noisy text, plummeting in performance when faced with seemingly simple issues like misspellings, typos, and grammatical errors, even though such issues naturally arise in almost any use case (Kumar et al., 2020; Yin et al., 2020; Aspillaga et al., 2020). These limitations have been documented even in large models. For instance, Pagnoni et al. (2024) find that Llama 3 and 3.1 perform poorly in robustness tests involving character-level noise, and Chai et al. (2024) highlight the sensitivity of large language models to character-level variations.

Improving model performance on nonstandard text is not trivial. For instance, Faisal et al. (2024)

[1] `https://github.com/aarsri/interventions-linguistic-variation`

document a persistent performance gap between standard and dialectal text, even after in-variety fine-tuning. Approaches to increasing robustness to linguistic variation, though often successful, tend to be highly dependent on the language variety and task, typically requiring data for each dialect in question (Held et al., 2023) and exposing differences in performance across tasks and varieties (Srivastava and Chiang, 2023b). Given the vast, unpredictable nature of user-generated text, which often involves multiple types of linguistic variation at once, these challenges become even more pronounced. Thus, it is essential to take a step back and develop a deeper understanding of why such adaptation remains difficult and what is needed to facilitate effective learning.

Past work has explored challenges of cross-lingual transfer (Philippy et al., 2023). For instance, Wu et al. (2023) investigate three key factors – embedding space disruption, tokenization changes, and word order changes – by transforming GLUE datasets to induce each type of shift. They find that while language models can adapt to tokenization and word order changes, they struggle to recover from embedding space disruption (e.g., learning new alignments). Similar conclusions are drawn by Deshpande et al. (2022) and Jain et al. (2022); Deshpande et al. (2022) highlight the importance of subword overlap and token embedding alignment for successful knowledge transfer, while Jain et al. (2022) suggest leveraging word alignment and dictionary matching techniques. Building on these findings, our experiments examine core features of nonstandard text and explore their interactions with these modeling challenges.

3 Levels of Text Variation

Variation is a natural response to the productive nature of language. It can be observed at all levels of linguistic reasoning (Haber, 1976; Geeraerts et al., 1994): character-level change (e.g., spelling, abbreviation, orthography), morphological and syntactic variation (i.e., word and sentence structure), lexical and semantic variation (new word senses and meanings), and variation in style and tone, often related to language-external sociopolitical factors. Style and tone variation operate at a higher level of reasoning, integrating features from the first three categories. Viewing user-generated text in terms of these core features elucidates the challenges language models face in adapting to its variability.

When dealing with nonstandard text, we encounter infrequent strings far more often, which inherently challenges existing biases of language models and impacts downstream performance. The tokenizer produces longer sequences of tokens comprised of shorter subwords, a phenomenon called *oversegmentation* (Soper et al., 2021; Srivastava and Chiang, 2023a). Shorter subwords can appear in many more contexts and take on different meanings each time, a phenomenon called *subword replacement* (Srivastava and Chiang, 2023a). Even in the case of new word senses/meanings, for which the token sequence may not change as much, the model would lack the relevant knowledge.

Drawing on documented features of user-generated text, we have devised a suite of 9 interventions that operate at different levels of linguistic structure. We apply these interventions to all text used in our experiments. The interventions fall into four categories: character-level change, subword boundary manipulation, morphological variation, and lexical variation. All the interventions require the model to learn to map between standard (seen) and nonstandard (rare or unseen) text for effective knowledge transfer. However, differences in how the interventions affect tokenization can influence the difficulty of learning these mappings during fine-tuning. For this reason, the interventions are designed to cause a fair amount of disruption, with some acting as stress tests. All of our data and experiments are in English, but the algorithmic nature of many of our interventions can be extended to other languages.

3.1 Character-Level Change

Character-level change can arise for several reasons, including phonological influences (e.g., accent, sound change), new methods of writing (e.g., social media), and typological errors (Condorelli and Rutkowska, 2023). We include two interventions under this category; the first is a reflection of phonological variation, and the second is more of a stress test.

1. **IPA**: Letters corresponding to consonants on the IPA chart that form a minimal feature pair (voiced vs. unvoiced) are swapped. For example, *p* and *b*, which differ only in the voicing feature but share the same place and manner of articulation, are swapped. Changes to consonants are a hallmark of modern English orthographic variation, particularly observed on social media (Eisenstein, 2015; Ilbury, 2020).

For instance, such variations are prevalent in corpora of noisy text like MultiLexNorm (Van Der Goot et al., 2021); examples include dese/these, dey/they, smyle/smile, and sadest/saddest.

$$\text{boots} \overset{\text{IPA}}{\rightsquigarrow} \text{poodz} \overset{\text{tok}}{\rightsquigarrow} \text{p, ood, z}$$

2. **Shift**: A Caesar cipher is applied to the letters of the alphabet: $a \rightarrow b, b \rightarrow c, ..., z \rightarrow a$. This intervention is the most extreme form of orthographic change, in which every alphabetic symbol is renamed. It roughly approximates situations where a language variety uses a different alphabet than the standard variety or where social media trends using symbols that resemble letters. **Shift** serves as a stress test, as well as a means of comparison to milder interventions like **IPA**.

$$\text{boots} \overset{\text{Shift}}{\rightsquigarrow} \text{cpput} \overset{\text{tok}}{\rightsquigarrow} \text{c, pp, ut}$$

While orthographic changes like the ones above would ordinarily only require us to learn to map one character to another (or one spelling of a word to another, as in texting abbreviations), the structure imposed by the model makes this task more complex. As exemplified above, adapting to this category of variation would require the model to learn a one-to-many mapping from a single token to a list of tokens.

3.2 Subword Boundaries

As demonstrated above, linguistic variation often results in changes to subword token boundaries, which triggers a domino effect and ultimately results in lower quality contextual embeddings assigned to nonstandard text by the model (Kumar et al., 2020; Soper et al., 2021). Because of this, we include three interventions that overtly manipulate subword boundaries, two of which preserve the original spelling of the word and only split tokens. Successful adaptation would once again involve learning a one-to-many mapping, but with more of the surface level appearance (i.e., spelling) intact. Examples like "ammmazing" (amazing) in MultiLexNorm (Van Der Goot et al., 2021) resemble this situation.

1. **Reg**: Subword regularization using the MaxMatch Dropout (Hiraoka, 2022) method for BERT's WordPiece algorithm is applied with a dropout of 0.5. This means 50% of the subword vocabulary is randomly dropped with each tokenization call.

$$\text{boots} \overset{\text{tok}}{\rightsquigarrow} \text{boots}$$
$$\text{boots} \overset{\text{Reg}}{\rightsquigarrow} \text{boot, s}$$

2. **Char**: Subword regularization using the MaxMatch Dropout (Hiraoka, 2022) method for WordPiece is applied with a dropout of 1, meaning each letter of a word is its own token.

$$\text{boots} \overset{\text{Char}}{\rightsquigarrow} \text{b, o, o, t, s}$$

3. **Pig**: Words are converted to Pig Latin, in which the word-initial consonant(s) is moved to the end, and a suffix (*ay* or *yay*) is added. For example, *pig latin* becomes *igpay atinlay*.

$$\text{boots} \overset{\text{Pig}}{\rightsquigarrow} \text{ootsbay} \overset{\text{tok}}{\rightsquigarrow} \text{o, ots, bay}$$

3.3 Morphological Variation

In English, morphological variation can occur in inflectional or derivational affixes (Neef, 2009; Zanuttini and Horn, 2014). Inflectional endings are morphemes with grammatical functions that typically change grammatical features like part of speech and number (e.g., plural *-s*). This is a type of morphosyntactic variation, which relates to grammatical acceptability and is often highly stigmatized – some utterances may be grammatical in one variety and not in the standard, or vice versa. In contrast, derivational affixes are used to change the meaning of a word, which may or may not also change its part of speech. Unlike inflectional endings, which are a functional category, derivational affixes have much more room for variation.

1. **–End**: Using MorphyNet (Batsuren et al., 2021), inflectional endings are dropped from words that have them.

$$\text{boots} \overset{\text{–End}}{\rightsquigarrow} \text{boot} \overset{\text{tok}}{\rightsquigarrow} \text{boot}$$

2. **Affix**: Using MorphyNet (Batsuren et al., 2021), derivational prefixes and suffixes are mapped cyclically. For instance, *non-* becomes *ab-*, *ab-* becomes *pre-*, etc. *Nonsense* is now *absense* (not "absence"), *absence* is now *presence*, and so on. In this way, we tinker with part of a word but change its whole meaning.

$$\text{nonsense} \overset{\text{Affix}}{\rightsquigarrow} \text{absense} \overset{\text{tok}}{\rightsquigarrow} \text{a, bs, ense}$$

Because the lemma is preserved in these cases, learning the appropriate knowledge will require a mix of recovering token mappings and transferring existing knowledge about the meaning of the word from the lemma.

There are several examples of morphosyntactic variation found in user-generated text (Zanuttini and Horn, 2014). A common feature in MultiLexNorm (Van Der Goot et al., 2021) seems to be informal contractions (e.g., "imma," "finna," "tryna," "hella"). Because these forms have lower preservation of the lemma, the model may also see them as new words, bringing us to the final category: lexical variation.

3.4 Lexical Variation

Word-level variation can be just that – a new word introduced to refer to a specific, perhaps novel, referent, or to be used in a new context. But lexical variation can often introduce semantic variation; the typical process being that a word's senses expand and eventually shift to the new meaning, through specialization, generalization, or subjectification (Kakharova, 2021; Geeraerts et al., 2024). Such occurrences are extremely common on social media and in colloquial settings.

1. **Hyp**: Exemplifying specialization, through which a word's range of reference narrows, words with hyponyms found in WordNet (Princeton University, 2010) are replaced by their hyponym.

$$\text{boot} \overset{\text{Hyp}}{\rightsquigarrow} \text{buskin} \overset{\text{tok}}{\rightsquigarrow} \text{bus, kin}$$

2. **Ant**: Exemplifying subjectification, through which a word's meaning becomes more positive (ameliorization) or negative (pejorization), words with antonyms found in WordNet (Princeton University, 2010) are replaced by their antonym.

$$\text{nice} \overset{\text{Ant}}{\rightsquigarrow} \text{nasty}$$

With the lexical interventions, the model must learn to map between contextual meanings of seen words. Variation is at the subword or multi-subword level.

3.5 Interventions in Action

Through these four categories of interventions, we are able to examine a range of underlying factors in modeling and adaptation capability for nonstandard text, from tokenization-specific issues (character-level change and subword boundaries), to token-embedding relationships (morphological variation), to contextual representation shift (lexical variation). Moreover, within each category, we include milder, more realistic interventions (e.g., **IPA**) and stress tests (e.g., **Shift**). Our experiments reveal whether a model has a chance at recovering each type of mapping during fine-tuning, and under which data-related conditions.

Size	Sentences	Word Count Quartiles			
		Average	P_{25}	P_{50}	P_{75}
S	264	19.9	10	18	26
M	2641	18.5	10	16	24
L	26415	18.4	10	16	24

Table 1: Sentence and word count statistics (25th, 50th, and 75th percentiles) for each data split.

4 Data Preparation

To compare the model's ability to adapt to each synthetic variety, we fine-tune and test it with the mask-filling objective on text with the appropriate intervention applied. We provide a sketch of our train/test pipeline in Figure 1. All of our data is sourced from Wikicorpus (Reese et al., 2010) to reduce external effects of choice of data. We reserve half the Wikicorpus articles for fine-tuning and half for testing. These are separated into sentences using the sentence tokenizer from NLTK (Loper and Bird, 2002). In our experiments, a *word* is any string that satisfies Python's isalpha function and is an element of NLTK word tokenizer's output. Sentences with 0 or 1 words are eliminated.

When fine-tuning, we vary the amount of data used. Each split is a fixed set of sentences sampled from the fine-tuning articles. The number of sentences in each split covers three orders of magnitude. We report statistics in Table 1 on sentence length (measured by number of *words*) for each split to demonstrate that they are comparable in this regard. In addition to varying the data size and intervention, we also vary the composition of the fine-tuning data. It could be *mixed*, meaning the intervention is only applied to half the sentences, or *full*, meaning the intervention is applied to all sentences.

Fine-tuning typically focuses on adapting a model to a specific task, making it challenging to simultaneously adapt the model to a new language variety. Task-specific factors can also complicate this process, especially in experiments involving disrupted text. For example, some tasks, like intent classification, rely on identifying key words in the input, while others, like sentiment analysis, require an overall understanding of the sentence, and more linguistically complex tasks, such as linguistic acceptability, demand deeper grammatical reasoning. These variations create a complex interaction between handling perturbed text and meeting the requirements of each task, potentially introducing bias into the experiment. To avoid these complications, we select mask-filling as our fine-tuning task. Mask-filling aligns with the models' pre-training objective, allowing fine-tuning resources to focus exclusively on adapting to the new language variety without interference from task-specific factors.

Our masking policy during fine-tuning is as follows. One *word* per sentence is randomly selected to be masked. We practice whole-word masking, meaning the model could be asked to fill one or more consecutive mask tokens, given the number of subword tokens that comprise the masked word. Depending on the word to be masked, it is possible the intervention does not actually change that word. While this is natural for fine-tuning, to make sure the comparison during testing is fair, we mandate that the word masked at test time is actually modified by all nine interventions. This filtering yields a test set of 931 sentences sampled from the testing articles. For each sentence, the same word is masked in all interventions/tests for consistency.

5 Experiments

There are four axes of variation in our experiments: *amount* of fine-tuning data (small, medium, large), *composition* of fine-tuning data (50% (mixed) or 100% (full) of sentences are noised), *intervention* to be applied (9 total), and *multilinguality* (monolingual or multilingual pre-trained model). We use BERT-base-cased[2] (BERT) as the monolingual English model, and BERT-base-multilingual-cased[3] (mBERT) as the multilingual model. We do not include character-level models like CharacterBERT (El Boukkouri et al., 2020) and CANINE (Clark et al., 2022) in our experiments; unlike BERT and mBERT, they cannot be used out-of-the-box for mask-filling and would not yield comparable results. For larger models, it is often unclear whether success stems from pre-training exposure, parameter-based knowledge retention, or true adaptation (our focus). Using BERT, we minimize such confounds.

For each possible combination of the four axes of variation, a pre-trained model is fine-tuned on the corresponding data with the masked language modeling objective. As described in Section 4, one word per sentence is masked (whole word masking), and the fine-tuning objective is to fill the masked token(s) with the tokens of the original word.

We use Low-Rank Adaptation (LoRA, Hu et al. (2021)) for parameter-efficient fine-tuning, which adapts the attention weights of each Transformer encoder layer and freezes all other parameters. We follow Hu et al.'s guidelines for hyperparameter choice, using the AdamW optimizer (Loshchilov and Hutter, 2018) with a linear scheduler, LoRA rank of 8, and LoRA scaling factor α of 8. We use learning rate $7 \cdot 10^{-4}$ for the small data amount and $5 \cdot 10^{-4}$ for the medium and large data amounts. On an NVIDIA A10 Tensor Core GPU, fine-tuning takes 12 seconds/epoch for the small data amount, 2 minutes/epoch for the medium data amount, and 18 minutes/epoch for the large data amount. LoRA was chosen over standard fine-tuning for two key reasons: (1) standard fine-tuning is highly susceptible to distribution shift issues, and (2) LoRA provides greater control over where learning occurs (in encoder parameters associated with attention).

We measure performance with three metrics: from most to least strict, exact match, 1-best, and 5-best accuracy. Exact match accuracy measures for how many masked words each token of the word is predicted correctly, divided by the test set size. 1-best accuracy measures the total number of masked tokens filled correctly (by the top probability prediction) divided by the total number of masked tokens in the test set. Similarly, 5-best accuracy measures the total number of masked tokens whose top five predictions include the correct answer, divided by the total number of masked tokens in the test set. The 1-best accuracy metric provides the best summary of the results Table 2; we include results using the other two metrics in Tables 5 and 6.

6 Results

The main 1-best results for our experiments are found in Table 2, and the normalized scores are reported in Table 3. Additional results using the other metrics are included in Tables 4-6. We reiterate the categories of interventions (see Section 3) below:

- Character-Level Change: **IPA**, **Shift**
- Subword Boundary Variation: **Reg**, **Char**, **Pig**
- Morphological Variation: **−End**, **Affix**
- Lexical Variation: **Hyp**, **Ant**

6.1 Baselines: We need an intervention!

We include a baseline row for each model (data amount 0), in which the pre-trained model, without any additional fine-tuning, is tested on each inter-

[2] https://huggingface.co/bert-base-cased
[3] https://huggingface.co/bert-base-multilingual-cased

vention. We also include a baseline intervention *None*, in which the models are evaluated on the original text without any intervention applied.

As expected, monolingual BERT is better out-of-the-box at the mask-filling task on English Wikipedia text. Fine-tuning without any intervention results in overfitting – an expected outcome, as the model has already been trained on the same task with similar data. Thus, we also include relative performance – each baseline score in Table 2 is normalized by the corresponding *None* performance and expressed as a percentage in Table 3. Out-of-the-box performance (data amount 0) is extremely low across the board, demonstrating that our experiments will provide clear findings as BERT cannot already solve these tasks.

6.2 Mixed vs. Full Composition: What is needed to learn new mappings?

The knowledge transfer that takes place when adapting a model to a new variety of the language is akin to learning how to map elements of the standard variety to the new one. One of the varied parameters of our experiments is whether the fine-tuning data is mixed (intervention is only applied to 50% of sentences) or full (intervention is applied to all sentences). Sometimes, we might expect model learning to benefit from seeing both standard and nonstandard versions of text during fine-tuning, while other times, this only makes learning the appropriate patterns more difficult.

Our results indicate that the latter holds true when dealing with linguistic variation; average performance (not including baseline scores) is about 4.2 points, or 36%, higher, with the full composition (Table 2) rather than the mixed composition (Table 4). Performance with full composition is also higher when comparing averages for each intervention category, so the mixed composition does not provide an advantage for any type of variation tested. Because of this difference in performance, we refer only to the full composition results when discussing and analyzing the remaining factors below.

6.3 Data Size: When is more data needed?

Across our experiments, particularly looking at the normalized performance relative to the baseline intervention scores (Table 3), more fine-tuning data helps. At the same time, the utility of adding more fine-tuning data differs depending on the type of mapping needed for a class of interventions.

When it comes to the orthographic interventions (**IPA**, **Shift**) and **−End**, the input sequence is affected by tokenization-related issues (i.e., oversegmentation and subword replacement), and the model must learn one-to-many mappings between tokens during fine-tuning for successful knowledge transfer. In this case, simply fine-tuning, even on the small or medium data amounts, results in a big improvement, but further improvements are much smaller. While fine-tuning helps, it is not sufficient to fully recover the mapping due to the model's inability to draw on sub-atomic knowledge (i.e., within-subword character-level information).

Subword boundary manipulation still involves the issues of oversegmentation, but the closeness in spelling may result in a stronger association by the model between the contextual representations of pre- and post-intervention versions of the same words. When adapting to the synthetic varieties with subword boundary manipulation, performance improves gradually as more data is added.

Strikingly, there is an apparent breakthrough effect when fine-tuning with the largest data size for the lexical interventions (**Hyp**, **Ant**) and **Affix**. While the performance attained is comparatively low for the small and medium data sizes, there is a massive jump when the large data size is used for fine-tuning. This is most clearly observed in the exact-match performance (Table 5) for BERT and the relative performance for mBERT, which nears or exceeds 100% in these three tasks. These tasks require relearning the usage of words in new contexts. Mapping word-level information (i.e., new spellings) as well as contextual meaning evidently requires much more data, but when the data requirement is satisfied, the model is capable of recovering (multi-) subword level information.

6.4 Monolingual vs. Multilingual: Which type of knowledge is more helpful?

For the most part, the average performance (not including baseline performance) is extremely close between BERT and mBERT. Notably, mBERT provides a substantial advantage for adapting to variation in meaning (**Affix**, **Hyp**, and **Ant**), providing a 20% boost in absolute scores (Table 2) and a 74% relative improvement in normalized scores (Table 3). Because mBERT is trained on several languages, it is likely not as rigid in terms of relating words to specific meanings/contexts, providing an advantage here.

		Interventions									
Model	Data	None	IPA	Shift	Reg	Char	Pig	−End	Affix	Hyp	Ant
BERT	0	58.8	2.6	2.3	7.0	5.4	9.3	1.5	0.1	0.1	0.2
	S	52.4	3.4	5.6	9.0	12.2	15.3	32.3	0.3	2.0	2.6
	M	48.6	15.3	8.7	12.7	16.1	14.8	28.9	14.5	9.5	19.1
	L	47.7	18.8	9.5	11.6	26.5	23.1	37.6	35.7	29.6	29.6
mBERT	0	42.0	2.6	2.2	5.1	6.4	13.8	2.6	1.7	1.7	1.1
	S	38.8	10.4	4.4	4.7	11.6	13.6	23.1	1.7	5.2	7.1
	M	31.6	12.1	3.7	12.1	20.5	16.7	30.5	18.8	17.6	19.7
	L	34.4	13.2	5.2	11.1	29.7	21.3	30.0	41.7	28.9	33.6

Table 2: 1-best accuracy results (single run) for all experiments with the full data composition using the base version of the model. Data amount 0 denotes the out-of-the-box baseline performance compared to fine-tuning with the small (S), medium (M), or large (L) data sizes.

		Interventions									
Model	Data	None	IPA	Shift	Reg	Char	Pig	−End	Affix	Hyp	Ant
BERT	0	100.0	4.4	3.8	11.9	9.2	15.7	2.6	0.2	0.1	0.3
	S	100.0	6.5	10.8	17.2	23.3	29.2	61.7	0.5	3.8	4.9
	M	100.0	31.5	18.0	26.1	33.1	30.5	59.4	29.8	19.6	39.3
	L	100.0	39.4	19.9	24.4	55.4	48.3	78.8	74.9	62.0	62.1
mBERT	0	100.0	6.1	5.3	12.1	15.1	32.8	6.2	4.1	4.0	2.5
	S	100.0	26.9	11.4	12.1	30.0	35.2	59.6	4.3	13.3	18.3
	M	100.0	38.4	11.6	38.1	64.9	52.9	96.4	59.5	55.5	62.4
	L	100.0	38.4	15.0	32.2	86.2	61.8	87.0	120.9	83.9	97.6

Table 3: Relative performance (single run) normalized by the baseline (*None*), as percentages using the base version of the model. Data amount 0 denotes the out-of-the-box baseline performance compared to fine-tuning with the small (S), medium (M), or large (L) data sizes.

6.5 Implications for User-Generated Text

Our interventions provide insights into how language models adapt to the diverse noise patterns in user-generated text. We examine cases where token sequences are disrupted but meaning is preserved (e.g., character-level changes) and those where meanings shift with minimal impact on tokenization (e.g., lexical variation), as well as intermediate cases like subword boundary manipulation.

Our findings show that models struggle to process variations within subwords. Given the prevalence of character-level changes in user-generated text, particularly on social media, fine-tuning on additional data alone is insufficient for robust adaptation. This poses challenges for NLP applications in these domains, especially when users prefer to retain their stylistic choices rather than conform to standardized text. At the same time, we find that with sufficient data, models can learn certain morphological and lexical variations, making it possible to adapt to new words, slang, and evolving usage patterns. However, given the diversity of user-generated content, some phenomena may be too sparse for effective learning, highlighting the need for more targeted approaches beyond data scaling.

7 Conclusion

We introduce a suite of interventions that synthetically modify English text to analyze interactions between features of nonstandard and user-generated text with underlying biases of language models. Our experiments isolate data-related factors that can contribute to language model adaptation, revealing critical insights into the limitations of adapting language models to nonstandard text. We explore several cases, ranging from character-level changes that over-segment the token sequence to lexical variations that alter contextual representations. Some interventions require learning one-to-many mappings within subwords, while others demand associations across multiple subwords.

Our findings highlight key adaptation challenges. BERT-like models struggle to adapt to character-level changes, even with additional data, but can successfully handle lexical shifts and new word senses with enough exposure to relevant fine-tuning data. Notably, interventions involving affix changes and antonym substitutions achieve performance comparable to or exceeding mBERT baselines. This suggests that while models can effectively learn word-to-word mappings, structural constraints hinder their ability to process finer-grained variations within subwords or at the character level. These limitations arise from how tokens are segmented and represented within the model, restricting its ability to capture within-subword (sub-atomic) variations.

Ultimately, while current models adjust well to meaning-related variations given enough data, they struggle with fine-grained structural disruptions, where constituents are smaller than a subword (e.g., character-level). Despite the prevalence of such variation (e.g., social media), current language models lack the capability to facilitate the required flexibility between tokens and embeddings for straightforward adaptation methods like fine-tuning, unless the relevant knowledge is already incorporated during pre-training. This underscores the need for more flexible tokenization and modeling approaches, especially for handling the complexities of user-generated text and enabling the model to effectively capture within-subword (e.g., character-level) information.

Limitations

While our experiments explored numerous possibilities within the scope of our study, they are certainly not exhaustive. We recognized the vast array of potential variations and interventions that could be considered and aimed to curate a feasible selection that still offered a diverse representation of linguistic challenges and adaptation scenarios. Beyond the selection of interventions to design, it would be valuable to expand the scope of experiments in the other dimensions, as well: languages, data sizes, and models.

For instance, our interventions and experiments were developed and executed in English. While narrowing down the language dimension allowed us to develop the highly controlled experiments needed for this study, it also means insights are missing for languages in which the character-, subword-, and word-level paradigm used in this work may not apply in the same way. Examples include languages with richer morphology (e.g., Turkic languages) and languages for which characters correspond to syllables, words, or concepts (e.g., Sino-Tibetan languages). Similarly, while the code for the interventions can largely be extended to other Indo-European languages, it would require more modification before it could be used for other language families.

Furthermore, while our choices for the small, medium, and large data sizes are informed by runtime and typical fine-tuning data sizes in NLP work, some of our results point to trends as data size increases. As a result, it would be valuable to extend these tables to see an even bigger picture as data size continues to increase. In addition, while we used LoRA for model adaptation in this study, there are other approaches that could be explored to better understand the nuances of parameter-efficient fine-tuning.

Finally, our work focuses on the widely-used BERT, which is an Encoder-only language model of relatively small size. While the small size is beneficial for our study, as it assures us that the model has not already seen the intervention tasks during pre-training, diversity in the type of model (e.g., encoder-decoder, decoder-only, LLMs) can help paint a bigger picture for our results and their implications in a wider range of settings.

References

Carlos Aspillaga, Andrés Carvallo, and Vladimir Araujo. 2020. Stress test evaluation of Transformer-based models in natural language understanding tasks. In *Proc. LREC*, pages 1882–1894.

Khuyagbaatar Batsuren, Gábor Bella, and Fausto Giunchiglia. 2021. MorphyNet: a large multilingual database of derivational and inflectional morphology. In *Proc. SIGMORPHON*, pages 39–48.

Verena Blaschke, Hinrich Schütze, and Barbara Plank. 2023. Does manipulating tokenization aid cross-lingual transfer? A study on POS tagging for non-standardized languages. In *Proc. VarDial*, pages 40–54.

Su Lin Blodgett, Lisa Green, and Brendan O'Connor. 2016. Demographic dialectal variation in social media: A case study of African-American English. In *Proc. EMNLP*, pages 1119–1130.

Yekun Chai, Yewei Fang, Qiwei Peng, and Xuhong Li. 2024. Tokenization falling short: On subword robustness in large language models. In *Findings of the ACL: EMNLP*, pages 1582–1599.

Jonathan H Clark, Dan Garrette, Iulia Turc, and John Wieting. 2022. CANINE: Pre-training an efficient tokenization-free encoder for language representation. *Transactions of the Association for Computational Linguistics*, 10:73–91.

Marco Condorelli and Hanna Rutkowska. 2023. *The Cambridge Handbook of Historical Orthography*. Cambridge University Press.

Ameet Deshpande, Partha Talukdar, and Karthik Narasimhan. 2022. When is BERT multilingual? isolating crucial ingredients for cross-lingual transfer. In *Proc. NAACL HLT*, pages 3610–3623.

Jacob Devlin, Ming-Wei Chang, Kenton Lee, and Kristina Toutanova. 2019. BERT: Pre-training of deep bidirectional transformers for language understanding. In *Proc. NAACL-HLT*, pages 4171–4186.

Jacob Eisenstein. 2015. Systematic patterning in phonologically-motivated orthographic variation. *Journal of Sociolinguistics*, 19(2):161–188.

Hicham El Boukkouri, Olivier Ferret, Thomas Lavergne, Hiroshi Noji, Pierre Zweigenbaum, and Jun'ichi Tsujii. 2020. CharacterBERT: Reconciling ELMo and BERT for word-level open-vocabulary representations from characters. In *Proc. ICLR*, pages 6903–6915.

Fahim Faisal, Orevaoghene Ahia, Aarohi Srivastava, Kabir Ahuja, David Chiang, Yulia Tsvetkov, and Antonios Anastasopoulos. 2024. DIALECTBENCH: An NLP benchmark for dialects, varieties, and closely-related languages. In *Proc. ACL*, pages 14412–14454.

Dirk Geeraerts, Stefan Grondelaers, and Peter Bakema. 1994. *The structure of lexical variation: Meaning, naming, and context*. 5. Walter de Gruyter.

Dirk Geeraerts, Dirk Speelman, Kris Heylen, Mariana Montes, Stefano De Pascale, Karlien Franco, and Michael Lang. 2024. *Lexical Variation and Change: A Distributional Semantic Approach*. Oxford University Press.

Lyn R. Haber. 1976. Leaped and leapt: A theoretical account of linguistic variation. *Foundations of Language*, pages 211–238.

William Held, Caleb Ziems, and Diyi Yang. 2023. TADA: Task agnostic dialect adapters for English. In *Findings of the ACL*, pages 813–824.

Tatsuya Hiraoka. 2022. MaxMatch-Dropout: Subword regularization for WordPiece. In *Proc. ICLR*, pages 4864–4872.

Edward J. Hu, Phillip Wallis, Zeyuan Allen-Zhu, Yuanzhi Li, Shean Wang, Lu Wang, Weizhu Chen, et al. 2021. LoRA: Low-rank adaptation of large language models. In *Proc. ICLR*.

Minlie Huang, Xiaoyan Zhu, and Jianfeng Gao. 2020. Challenges in building intelligent open-domain dialog systems. *ACM Transactions on Information Systems (TOIS)*, 38(3):1–32.

Christian Ilbury. 2020. "Sassy Queens": Stylistic orthographic variation in Twitter and the enregisterment of AAVE. *Journal of Sociolinguistics*, 24(2):245–264.

Neel Jain, John Kirchenbauer, Jonas Geiping, and Tom Goldstein. 2022. How to do a vocab swap? A study of embedding replacement for pre-trained transformers.

Aditya Joshi, Raj Dabre, Diptesh Kanojia, Zhuang Li, Haolan Zhan, Gholamreza Haffari, and Doris Dippold. 2024. Natural language processing for dialects of a language: A survey. *ACM Computing Surveys*.

Nilufar Nuridinovna Kakharova. 2021. On the nature of linguistic variation and its types. *Asian Journal of Research in Social Sciences and Humanities*, 11(11):507–510.

Anjali Kantharuban, Ivan Vulić, and Anna Korhonen. 2023. Quantifying the dialect gap and its correlates across languages. In *Findings of the ACL: EMNLP*, pages 7226–7245.

Ankit Kumar, Piyush Makhija, and Anuj Gupta. 2020. Noisy text data: Achilles' heel of BERT. In *Proc. W-NUT*, pages 16–21.

Edward Loper and Steven Bird. 2002. NLTK: The natural language toolkit. In *Proc. ACL-02 Workshop on Effective Tools and Methodologies for Teaching Natural Language Processing and Computational Linguistics*, pages 63–70.

Ilya Loshchilov and Frank Hutter. 2018. Decoupled weight decay regularization. In *Proceedings of the International Conference on Learning Representations (ICLR)*.

Martin Neef. 2009. Morphological variation: A declarative approach. In *Describing and Modeling Variation in Grammar*, pages 117–133. Mouton de Gruyter Berlin.

Artidoro Pagnoni, Ram Pasunuru, Pedro Rodriguez, John Nguyen, Benjamin Muller, Margaret Li, Chunting Zhou, Lili Yu, Jason Weston, Luke Zettlemoyer, et al. 2024. Byte latent transformer: Patches scale better than tokens. *arXiv preprint arXiv:2412.09871*.

Fred Philippy, Siwen Guo, and Shohreh Haddadan. 2023. Towards a common understanding of contributing factors for cross-lingual transfer in multilingual language models: A review. In *Proc. ACL*.

Princeton University. 2010. About WordNet.

Alec Radford, Jeffrey Wu, Rewon Child, David Luan, Dario Amodei, Ilya Sutskever, et al. 2019. Language models are unsupervised multitask learners.

Samuel Reese, Gemma Boleda, Montse Cuadros, Lluís Padró, and German Rigau. 2010. Wikicorpus: A word-sense disambiguated multilingual Wikipedia corpus. In *Proc. LREC*.

Elizabeth Soper, Stanley Fujimoto, and Yen-Yun Yu. 2021. BART for post-correction of OCR newspaper text. In *Proc. W-NUT*, pages 284–290.

Aarohi Srivastava and David Chiang. 2023a. BERTwich: Extending BERT's capabilities to model dialectal and noisy text. In *Findings of the ACL: EMNLP*, pages 15510–15521.

Aarohi Srivastava and David Chiang. 2023b. Fine-tuning BERT with character-level noise for zero-shot transfer to dialects and closely-related languages. In *Proc. VarDial*, pages 152–162.

Rob Van Der Goot, Alan Ramponi, Arkaitz Zubiaga, Barbara Plank, Benjamin Muller, Iñaki San Vicente Roncal, Nikola Ljubešic, Özlem Çetinoğlu, Rahmad Mahendra, Talha Çolakoglu, et al. 2021. MultiLexNorm: A shared task on multilingual lexical normalization. In *Proc. W-NUT*, pages 493–509. Association for Computational Linguistics.

Zhengxuan Wu, Alex Tamkin, and Isabel Papadimitriou. 2023. Oolong: Investigating what makes transfer learning hard with controlled studies. In *Proc. EMNLP*, pages 3280–3289.

Fan Yin, Quanyu Long, Tao Meng, and Kai-Wei Chang. 2020. On the robustness of language encoders against grammatical errors. In *Proc. ACL*.

Raffaella Zanuttini and Laurence Horn. 2014. *Microsyntactic Variation in North American English*. Oxford University Press.

A Appendix

		Interventions									
Model	**Data**	**None**	**IPA**	**Shift**	**Reg**	**Char**	**Pig**	**−End**	**Affix**	**Hyp**	**Ant**
BERT	0	58.8	2.6	2.3	6.9	5.4	9.3	1.5	0.1	0.1	0.2
	S	52.4	2.4	5.9	11.0	11.7	17.4	18.5	0.8	0.6	0.8
	M	48.6	7.5	8.3	12.5	13.1	16.3	26.7	10.6	8.3	3.0
	L	47.7	14.4	8.3	12.0	19.9	20.3	15.1	25.5	17.0	19.7
mBERT	0	42.0	2.6	2.2	5.1	6.4	13.8	2.6	1.7	1.7	1.1
	S	38.8	10.5	1.5	7.4	12.3	10.1	5.2	4.2	1.3	6.8
	M	31.6	9.3	4.8	12.8	14.1	16.2	7.6	24.0	9.7	8.5
	L	34.4	14.7	6.8	13.0	16.4	16.9	11.9	29.5	25.3	22.8

Table 4: 1-best accuracy results (single run) for all experiments with the mixed data composition using the base version of the model. Data amount 0 denotes the out-of-the-box baseline performance compared to fine-tuning with the small (S), medium (M), or large (L) data sizes.

		Interventions									
Model	**Data**	**None**	**IPA**	**Shift**	**Reg**	**Char**	**Pig**	**−End**	**Affix**	**Hyp**	**Ant**
BERT	0	62.0	0.1	0.0	12.1	0.0	0.0	1.6	0.1	0.0	0.2
	S	55.1	0.3	0.0	9.9	0.5	0.0	34.2	0.1	1.8	3.2
	M	51.3	2.4	2.3	12.5	1.2	0.2	30.7	3.2	10.1	18.1
	L	50.3	9.8	2.2	10.2	7.3	7.5	39.0	25.2	31.2	31.5
mBERT	0	44.8	1.2	0.9	6.8	0.9	1.4	2.9	0.5	1.7	0.8
	S	40.7	1.2	0.4	1.8	0.8	0.9	25.5	0.4	7.0	10.4
	M	33.6	2.7	0.2	9.9	8.1	2.8	33.3	9.0	13.5	17.1
	L	37.0	5.3	0.8	8.5	8.9	7.7	32.2	31.0	27.7	30.5

Table 5: Exact match accuracy results (single run) for all experiments with the full data composition using the base version of the model. Data amount 0 denotes the out-of-the-box baseline performance compared to fine-tuning with the small (S), medium (M), or large (L) data sizes.

		Interventions									
Model	**Data**	**None**	**IPA**	**Shift**	**Reg**	**Char**	**Pig**	**−End**	**Affix**	**Hyp**	**Ant**
BERT	0	77.0	10.5	10.0	13.9	26.4	23.9	21.5	2.2	1.2	0.5
	S	74.3	17.1	17.3	23.5	46.6	33.1	47.1	2.0	6.9	8.5
	M	74.9	29.3	28.3	27.9	55.6	40.2	46.6	31.7	23.8	31.0
	L	62.6	35.2	33.5	27.6	60.0	51.8	55.8	52.6	45.2	45.9
mBERT	0	64.1	6.9	8.6	14.3	25.3	27.4	21.5	4.1	2.6	2.3
	S	63.5	21.2	14.3	15.4	44.9	32.8	36.9	5.5	11.2	16.1
	M	61.6	24.9	14.4	29.3	55.2	35.2	46.9	31.2	32.5	36.6
	L	49.0	25.2	19.3	23.7	62.4	44.7	43.7	56.8	44.7	47.7

Table 6: 5-best accuracy results (single run) for all experiments with the full data composition using the base version of the model. Data amount 0 denotes the out-of-the-box baseline performance compared to fine-tuning with the small (S), medium (M), or large (L) data sizes.

On-Device LLMs for Home Assistant: Dual Role in Intent Detection and Response Generation

Rune Birkmose* **Nathan Mørkeberg Reece*** **Esben Hofstedt Norvin***
Johannes Bjerva **Mike Zhang†**
Aalborg University, Denmark
*{rbirkm20, nreece20, enorvi20}@student.aau.dk †jjz@cs.aau.dk

Abstract

This paper investigates whether Large Language Models (LLMs), fine-tuned on synthetic but domain-representative data, can perform the twofold task of (i) slot and intent detection and (ii) natural language response generation for a smart home assistant, while running solely on resource-limited, CPU-only edge hardware. We fine-tune LLMs to produce both JSON action calls and text responses. Our experiments show that 16-bit and 8-bit quantized variants preserve high accuracy on slot and intent detection and maintain strong semantic coherence in generated text, while the 4-bit model, while retaining generative fluency, suffers a noticeable drop in device-service classification accuracy. Further evaluations on noisy human (non-synthetic) prompts and out-of-domain intents confirm the models' generalization ability, obtaining around 80–86% accuracy. While the average inference time is 5–6 seconds per query—acceptable for one-shot commands but suboptimal for multi-turn dialogue—our results affirm that an on-device LLM can effectively unify command interpretation and flexible response generation for home automation without relying on specialized hardware.

1 Introduction

Smart home technologies and IoT devices have proliferated in recent years, with an expected rise from 16.6 billion to 18.8 billion connected devices by the end of 2024 (IoT Analytics, 2024). Major providers like Amazon, Google, and Apple typically handle speech recognition and intent detection on cloud servers, which raises user concerns about privacy, data ownership, and reliance on proprietary ecosystems (BBC News, 2025). Conventional solutions for home assistants often rely on specialized, domain-specific classifiers for slot and intent detection (SID), paired with templated system responses. While these approaches can be efficient, they can also be rigid, sometimes requiring precisely phrased user inputs and yielding repetitive or unpersonalized answers.

Recent developments in on-device computing—coupled with improvements in model compression and quantization (Liang et al., 2021; Gholami et al., 2022; Lang et al., 2024)—have paved the way for smaller yet still capable language models to run on commodity hardware. These models offer privacy benefits and allow customizable local inference with reduced latency. However, deploying a capable model under strict memory and computational constraints remains challenging. Large-scale Transformer-based language models (Vaswani et al., 2017), and especially LLMs (Touvron et al., 2023; Dubey et al., 2024; Bai et al., 2023; Yang et al., 2024; Groeneveld et al., 2024), have demonstrated remarkable proficiency in tasks ranging from question answering to text generation (Arora et al., 2024; Yin et al., 2024), yet typically demand substantial hardware resources, restricting them to cloud-based services or large compute clusters.

This paper explores whether a smaller, fine-tuned LLM can provide two capabilities essential to a home assistant—accurate recognition of *what* users want (i.e., slot and intent detection), and *natural* textual responses—while running entirely on an edge device with limited CPU and memory. By unifying these tasks into one end-to-end system, we eliminate the need for separate domain-specific classification modules and templated responses, focusing on efficiency, robust language understanding, and strict correctness in JSON action output.

Additionally, we move away from classic SID datasets and other general spoken language understanding benchmarks. Instead, we investigate whether LLMs can be directly applied to digital assistant software. To this end, we take the open-

*The authors contributed equally to this work.

Proceedings of the Tenth Workshop on Noisy and User-generated Text, pages 57–67
May 3, 2025 ©2025 Association for Computational Linguistics

source Home Assistant software[1] as our gold standard for evaluation, targeting real-world device-service pairs and actionable JSON outputs.

Contributions. Our contributions can be summarized as follows:[2] ① We show that a 0.5B LLM can be fine-tuned to already jointly handle SID *and* response generation with high accuracy. ② By quantizing the model (from 16-bit to 8-bit and 4-bit), we quantify trade-offs between memory usage, accuracy, and generative fluency on CPU-only edge hardware. ③ We evaluate the approach on synthetic data, human queries, and out-of-domain tasks, confirming robust generalization.

2 Related Work

Slot and Intent Detection. Traditional approaches to spoken language understanding (SLU) often treat SID separately using domain-specific classification or sequence tagging approaches (Zhang and Wang, 2016; Wang et al., 2018; Weld et al., 2022; Qin et al., 2021; Pham et al., 2023). More recent transformer-based solutions unify both tasks, leveraging contextual embeddings to improve performance (Castellucci et al., 2019; van der Goot et al., 2021; Stoica et al., 2021; Arora et al., 2024) with models like BERT (Devlin et al., 2019). However, many of these solutions still presume tailored sequence labeling datasets or full-size transformer backends. Our work aligns with the shift to more expressive transformer models for SLU, but we push inference to a local environment while also adding dynamic text generation.

Running LLMs on Edge Devices. While training large-scale LLMs remains computationally expensive, numerous works explore strategies for *deploying* them on edge hardware. Haris et al. (2024) propose FPGA-based accelerators to reduce memory overhead for LLM inference. Zhang et al. (2024) distribute an LLM across multiple low-power devices to increase throughput. An empirical footprint study by Dhar et al. (2024) shows that even 7B-parameter models can strain embedded hardware if not sufficiently compressed. Our approach uses a much smaller LLM (0.5B–1.5B parameters) plus weight quantization, showing that near-commodity devices with 8GB RAM can handle both intent classification and text generation if the domain is sufficiently specialized.

[1] `https://github.com/home-assistant/core`

[2] We release all our code and models at `https://github.com/Run396/P9`.

Partition	Train	Test	Total
Classification	23,372	5,843	29,215
LLM	33,361	2,435	35,796

Table 1: **Aggregated Train/Test Splits.** For the classification baseline, 20% of the original training set was used as test data (after removing multi-intent samples). The LLM used the full synthetic data; 2,435 remain as test.

3 Methodology

Our goal is to integrate two core functionalities of a home assistant into a single model:

- **Slot and Intent Detection:** The model outputs a valid JSON object that maps to a desired service (intent) and device (slot) pair:

```
{"service": "light.turn_on",
  "device": "light.living_room",
  "assistant": "Sure, turning on
    on the living room light."}
```

- **Natural Language Generation:** The model also produces a textual response confirming or elaborating on its action, as can be seen in the example above. The text can then be propagated to, e.g., a text-to-speech model.

Traditional classifiers only handle device-service classification and do not produce any text. For user-facing text, the baseline approach would rely on templated responses.

3.1 Data and Pre-processing

To the best of our knowledge, there is no existing human-curated dataset specifically for the Home Assistant software. Thus, we rely on synthetic data. We use a publicly available synthetic dataset (acon96, 2024), which consists of 35,840 synthetic examples designed to mimic Home Assistant commands. Each instance consists of:

- A **User Prompt:** e.g., *"Turn on the kitchen light"*, *"Set the thermostat to 22 degrees"*.
- One **Valid JSON Action**, containing the `service` and `device` fields corresponding to Home Assistant calls.
- A **Natural Language Response:** e.g., a paraphrase or affirmation of the action taken.

Model	Accuracy	BERTScore
Baselines		
SVC Classifier		
Service	76.6	—
Device	45.4	—
DistilBERT		
Service	98.8	—
Device	47.9	—
Qwen2.5-0.5B (16-bit)	98.8	0.84
Qwen2.5-0.5B (8-bit)	98.4	0.79
Qwen2.5-0.5B (4-bit)	81.7	0.88
Qwen2.5-1.5B (16-bit)	96.9	0.84
Qwen2.5-1.5B (8-bit)	96.5	0.83
Qwen2.5-1.5B (4-bit)	90.7	0.82

Table 2: **Slot/Intent Detection and NLG Results on Synthetic Test Data.** Accuracy is based on exact JSON match. BERTScore measures semantic similarity of the generated text vs. gold reference.

Model	CPU	T/Q (s)	Load (s)
Baselines			
SVC Classifier	4	<1	—
DistilBERT	4	<1	—
Qwen2.5-0.5B (16-bit)	4	6.25	±3.2
Qwen2.5-1.5B (16-bit)	4	10.81	±5.6
Qwen2.5-0.5B (8-bit)	4	5.50	±3.2
Qwen2.5-1.5B (8-bit)	4	10.32	±5.6
Qwen2.5-0.5B (16-bit)	2	8.49	±5.6
Qwen2.5-1.5B (16-bit)	2	17.72	±5.6
Qwen2.5-0.5B (8-bit)	2	7.89	±5.6
Qwen2.5-1.5B (8-bit)	2	16.11	±5.6

Table 3: **Computation Time.** Mean time per query (T/Q) across 500 samples under different CPU core counts and quantization levels. Load time is model initialization.

A full example can be found in Figure 1 (Appendix A). We stratify the dataset, maintaining the inherent imbalance (some device types and services appear more frequently). There are 38 service labels and 858 device labels. We split into training and test sets as shown in Table 1. The final training set for the LLM includes ~33k examples, and we set aside 2,435 synthetic samples for evaluation. Note that for the classification-based baselines, we split up the train and test set to separately predict `service` and `device` instead of as one prediction, ending up with double the test data (5,843 samples; excluding multi-intent examples). The input consists of only the user message and leave the system message out. A more detailed distribution of the data can be found in Table 6 (Appendix B).

3.2 Models

Baseline Classifiers. We train a Linear SVC from Scikit-Learn (Pedregosa et al., 2011) on TF-IDF features of the user prompt. The classifier outputs a concatenated device-service pair, which is then wrapped in JSON. Additionally, we fine-tune DistilBERT (Sanh et al., 2019) for classification. We use the transformers library (Wolf et al., 2020) for fine-tuning. We train for 1 epoch using a learning rate of 3×10^{-4} with the AdamW optimizer, and a batch size of 64 on a NVIDIA A10 (24GB) GPUs. Both models have no generative capability, so user-facing text is templated.

Small Large Language Models. We train using a chat-style format with user–assistant pairs. We primarily use the Qwen2.5-0.5B-Instruct model and the Qwen2.5-1.5B-Instruct (Yang et al., 2024). We fine-tune both models for one epoch with a batch size of 4, using the AdamW optimizer at a learning rate of 2×10^{-5} with a cosine scheduler. The maximum sequence length is set to 2,048 tokens. We use the HuggingFace Transformers library (Wolf et al., 2020) for training on NVIDIA L4 (24 GB) GPUs.

Quantization. After fine-tuning and having the original 16-bit model, we produce two quantized versions of each model: NF8 and NF4 (Dettmers et al., 2024), using bitsandbytes.[3] This allows us to compare accuracy, generative quality, and inference speed under varying memory constraints.

3.3 Evaluation

Slot-Intent Detection Accuracy. SID must be correct with near-exact string matching, as JSON calls are consumed downstream by the home automation system. We thus parse the model output for the `service` and `device` fields; if they match the gold annotation exactly, it is counted as correct. Any mismatch or invalid JSON results in an error.

For the classification task, instead, we separately predict `service` and `device` using the same classification model and take the average accuracy.

Text Generation Quality. For the natural language responses using the LLMs, we compare each generated response to the reference using BERTScore (Zhang et al., 2020).

[3]See `https://github.com/bitsandbytes-foundation/bitsandbytes`. We also use double quantization.

Model	Accuracy	BERTScore
Qwen2.5-0.5B	80.0	0.76
Qwen2.5-1.5B	86.7	0.74

Table 4: **Results Out-of-Domain Queries.** Accuracy and BERTScore over 60 OOD samples.

Model	Accuracy	BERTScore
Qwen2.5-0.5B	84.0	0.68
Qwen2.5-1.5B	86.4	0.66

Table 5: **Results Human-Generated Queries.** Accuracy and BERTScore over 81 real-user queries.

Inference Environment. We simulate a CPU-only setup on an 8 GB RAM device with up to four CPU cores. We measure average inference time on a 500-sample subset, varying both quantization level and the number of CPU cores.

4 Results

4.1 Slot and Intent Detection

Table 2 shows the SID performance of both the 0.5B and 1.5B LLMs under various quantization levels, alongside the baseline SVC and DistilBERT. For the 0.5B model, the 16-bit and 8-bit variants reach near-perfect accuracy ($\sim$ 99%). The 4-bit version drops to 81.7%, which is still better than the the SVC baseline (average 61.0% accuracy) and DistilBERT baseline (average 73.4% accuracy).

Interestingly, for the larger 1.5B model, the 16-bit and 8-bit variants achieve 96.9% and 96.5% accuracy, respectively, while the 4-bit version gets 90.7%. Thus, while the smaller 0.5B model actually yields higher raw accuracy in-domain, the 1.5B model remains competitive and in some out-of-domain tests (next section) performs better.

4.2 Natural Language Generation

Although the 4-bit models suffer in SID accuracy, Table 2 shows that the 0.5B 4-bit variant has the highest BERTScore (0.88). This indicates that while it may misclassify device/service fields, the generative text can still be fluent and semantically close to the target. Meanwhile, the 8-bit versions drop in BERTScore for the 0.5B model (0.79) and remain steady for the 1.5B model (0.83). Qualitative samples show that small changes in quantization can shift the style and lexical choices of the generated text.

4.3 Inference Time and Memory

Table 3 summarizes the inference speed across model size, quantization, and CPU core settings. The 8-bit model is only slightly faster than the 16-bit model (5.5 s vs. 6.25 s on 4 cores for the 0.5B). Doubling CPU cores from 2 to 4 reduces latency roughly by half. The 1.5B model takes longer (up to 10–17 s per query), which may be borderline for real-time usage in multi-turn dialogues.

4.4 Out-of-Domain Intents

In Table 4, we evaluate 60 OOD queries that mention either novel device types or services not appearing in the training set. The 0.5B model scores 80.0% accuracy vs. 86.7% for the 1.5B model, with BERTScores of 0.76 and 0.74 respectively. The results suggest that the 1.5B model generalizes somewhat better to unfamiliar domains, though both degrade compared to in-domain performance.

4.5 Human Prompts

Finally, we tested each model on 81 human-written prompts. Ten participants (ages 23–69) contributed typical commands they would issue to a home assistant, including incomplete or ambiguous phrasing. Table 5 shows that the 0.5B model achieves 84.0% accuracy, whereas the 1.5B model is slightly higher at 86.4%. BERTScores are around 0.66–0.68. The gap vs. synthetic data reflects real-user queries with more variation and noisy data.

5 Discussion

Despite near-perfect performance on the synthetic test set, Table 4 and 5 reveal a drop to 80–86% accuracy in real or out-of-domain queries. This discrepancy likely stems from the difficulty of handling spontaneous human phrasing, missing location or device details, and genuinely novel device types. Still, the results surpass the SVC and DistilBERT baseline.

Interestingly, while the 4-bit model can generate fluent natural language responses (often scoring the highest BERTScore in the 0.5B case), its classification accuracy suffers. This underscores that quantizing a model to extreme levels can degrade structured predictions more than open-ended text generation.

Regarding speed, the 1.5B model yields consistent accuracy gains on OOD data but also increases inference time by up to 2–3×. For single-turn commands, 5–6 seconds per query might be acceptable, but multi-turn dialogue would require faster or more efficient strategies. Future work may explore parameter-efficient fine-tuning, context truncation, or advanced quantization (e.g., 8-bit + partial 4-bit layering) to reduce inference times.

6 Conclusion

We present that LLMs can simultaneously perform SID and natural language response generation for a home automation domain. Experiments on an 8GB RAM, CPU-only environment show that 8-bit quantization largely preserves in-domain accuracy (up to 99%) and strong text fluency, while 4-bit introduces significant classification errors despite retaining good generative capability. We further demonstrate promising generalization to human-written prompts and out-of-domain tasks, with accuracy around 80–86%. However, per-query inference times of 5–6 seconds indicate that LLM-based assistants, as implemented here, are not yet ideal for fast multi-turn dialogues on edge devices. Future work can refine these models for faster, more memory-efficient inference, enabling privacy-preserving yet flexible home automation assistants.

Limitations

Our use of synthetic data may limit the diversity of user prompts; while we partially mitigated this with human-written queries, data coverage remains a challenge. The model also relies on structurally valid JSON output. Real-world usage may need fallback logic to handle malformed or incomplete responses. Moreover, we focus on a single domain (home automation); scaling to broader or open-ended tasks likely requires larger models and may degrade performance under CPU-only constraints.

Ethical Considerations

We do not foresee any major ethical issues with this work. The primary domain is home automation, and the dataset is synthetic or user-provided under informed consent. Nonetheless, deploying generative models in user-facing applications requires caution regarding hallucinated or incorrect responses, as well as user data privacy.

Acknowledgments

MZ and JB are supported by the research grant (VIL57392) from VILLUM FONDEN.

References

acon96. 2024. Home Assistant Requests Dataset. `https://huggingface.co/datasets/acon96/Home-Assistant-Requests`. Accessed: 2025.

Gaurav Arora, Shreya Jain, and Srujana Merugu. 2024. Intent detection in the age of llms. *arXiv preprint arXiv:2410.01627*.

Jinze Bai, Shuai Bai, Yunfei Chu, Zeyu Cui, Kai Dang, Xiaodong Deng, Yang Fan, Wenbin Ge, Yu Han, Fei Huang, et al. 2023. Qwen technical report. *ArXiv preprint*, abs/2309.16609.

BBC News. 2025. Apple to pay $95m to settle siri 'listening' lawsuit.

Giuseppe Castellucci, Valentina Bellomaria, Andrea Favalli, and Raniero Romagnoli. 2019. Multi-lingual intent detection and slot filling in a joint bert-based model. *arXiv preprint arXiv:1907.02884*.

Tim Dettmers, Artidoro Pagnoni, Ari Holtzman, and Luke Zettlemoyer. 2024. Qlora: Efficient finetuning of quantized llms. *Advances in Neural Information Processing Systems*, 36.

Jacob Devlin, Ming-Wei Chang, Kenton Lee, and Kristina Toutanova. 2019. BERT: Pre-training of deep bidirectional transformers for language understanding. In *Proceedings of the 2019 Conference of the North American Chapter of the Association for Computational Linguistics: Human Language Technologies, Volume 1 (Long and Short Papers)*, pages 4171–4186, Minneapolis, Minnesota. Association for Computational Linguistics.

Nobel Dhar, Bobin Deng, Dan Lo, Xiaofeng Wu, Liang Zhao, and Kun Suo. 2024. An empirical analysis and resource footprint study of deploying large language models on edge devices. *Proceedings of the ACM*.

Abhimanyu Dubey, Abhinav Jauhri, Abhinav Pandey, Abhishek Kadian, Ahmad Al-Dahle, Aiesha Letman, Akhil Mathur, Alan Schelten, Amy Yang, Angela Fan, et al. 2024. The llama 3 herd of models. *ArXiv preprint*, abs/2407.21783.

Amir Gholami, Sehoon Kim, Zhen Dong, Zhewei Yao, Michael W Mahoney, and Kurt Keutzer. 2022. A survey of quantization methods for efficient neural network inference. In *Low-Power Computer Vision*, pages 291–326. Chapman and Hall/CRC.

Dirk Groeneveld, Iz Beltagy, Evan Walsh, Akshita Bhagia, Rodney Kinney, Oyvind Tafjord, Ananya Jha, Hamish Ivison, Ian Magnusson, Yizhong Wang, Shane Arora, David Atkinson, Russell Authur, Khyathi Chandu, Arman Cohan, Jennifer Dumas, Yanai Elazar, Yuling Gu, Jack Hessel, Tushar Khot, William Merrill, Jacob Morrison, Niklas Muennighoff, Aakanksha Naik, Crystal Nam, Matthew Peters, Valentina Pyatkin, Abhilasha Ravichander, Dustin Schwenk, Saurabh Shah, William Smith,

Emma Strubell, Nishant Subramani, Mitchell Wortsman, Pradeep Dasigi, Nathan Lambert, Kyle Richardson, Luke Zettlemoyer, Jesse Dodge, Kyle Lo, Luca Soldaini, Noah Smith, and Hannaneh Hajishirzi. 2024. OLMo: Accelerating the science of language models. In *Proceedings of the 62nd Annual Meeting of the Association for Computational Linguistics (Volume 1: Long Papers)*, pages 15789–15809, Bangkok, Thailand. Association for Computational Linguistics.

Jude Haris, Rappy Saha, Wenhao Hu, and José Cano. 2024. Designing efficient llm accelerators for edge devices. *arXiv preprint arXiv:2408.00462*.

IoT Analytics. 2024. Number of Connected IoT Devices. `https://iot-analytics.com/number-connected-iot-devices/`. Accessed: 2024-10-16.

Jiedong Lang, Zhehao Guo, and Shuyu Huang. 2024. A comprehensive study on quantization techniques for large language models. *arXiv preprint arXiv:2411.02530*.

Tailin Liang, John Glossner, Lei Wang, Shaobo Shi, and Xiaotong Zhang. 2021. Pruning and quantization for deep neural network acceleration: A survey. *Neurocomputing*, 461:370–403.

Fabian Pedregosa, Gaël Varoquaux, Alexandre Gramfort, Vincent Michel, Bertrand Thirion, Olivier Grisel, Mathieu Blondel, Peter Prettenhofer, Ron Weiss, Vincent Dubourg, et al. 2011. Scikit-learn: Machine learning in python. *the Journal of machine Learning research*, 12:2825–2830.

Thinh Pham, Chi Tran, and Dat Quoc Nguyen. 2023. MISCA: A joint model for multiple intent detection and slot filling with intent-slot co-attention. In *Findings of the Association for Computational Linguistics: EMNLP 2023*, pages 12641–12650, Singapore. Association for Computational Linguistics.

Libo Qin, Tianbao Xie, Wanxiang Che, and Ting Liu. 2021. A survey on spoken language understanding: Recent advances and new frontiers. *arXiv preprint arXiv:2103.03095*.

Victor Sanh, Lysandre Debut, Julien Chaumond, and Thomas Wolf. 2019. Distilbert, a distilled version of bert: smaller, faster, cheaper and lighter. *arXiv preprint arXiv:1910.01108*.

Anda Stoica, Tibor Kadar, Camelia Lemnaru, Rodica Potolea, and Mihaela Dînşoreanu. 2021. Intent detection and slot filling with capsule net architectures for a romanian home assistant. *Sensors*, 21(4):1230.

Hugo Touvron, Louis Martin, Kevin Stone, Peter Albert, Amjad Almahairi, Yasmine Babaei, Nikolay Bashlykov, Soumya Batra, Prajjwal Bhargava, Shruti Bhosale, et al. 2023. Llama 2: Open foundation and fine-tuned chat models. *ArXiv preprint*, abs/2307.09288.

Rob van der Goot, Ibrahim Sharaf, Aizhan Imankulova, Ahmet Üstün, Marija Stepanović, Alan Ramponi, Siti Oryza Khairunnisa, Mamoru Komachi, and Barbara Plank. 2021. From masked language modeling to translation: Non-English auxiliary tasks improve zero-shot spoken language understanding. In *Proceedings of the 2021 Conference of the North American Chapter of the Association for Computational Linguistics: Human Language Technologies*, pages 2479–2497, Online. Association for Computational Linguistics.

A Vaswani, N Shazeer, N Parmar, J Uszkoreit, L Jones, A Gomez, L Kaiser, and I Polosukhin. 2017. Attention is All You Need. In *Advances in Neural Information Processing Systems (NIPS)*.

Yu Wang, Yilin Shen, and Hongxia Jin. 2018. A bi-model based RNN semantic frame parsing model for intent detection and slot filling. In *Proceedings of the 2018 Conference of the North American Chapter of the Association for Computational Linguistics: Human Language Technologies, Volume 2 (Short Papers)*, pages 309–314, New Orleans, Louisiana. Association for Computational Linguistics.

Henry Weld, Xiaoqi Huang, Siqu Long, Josiah Poon, and Soyeon Caren Han. 2022. A survey of joint intent detection and slot filling models in natural language understanding. *ACM Computing Surveys*, 55(8):1–38.

Thomas Wolf, Lysandre Debut, Victor Sanh, Julien Chaumond, Clement Delangue, Anthony Moi, Pierric Cistac, Tim Rault, Remi Louf, Morgan Funtowicz, Joe Davison, Sam Shleifer, Patrick von Platen, Clara Ma, Yacine Jernite, Julien Plu, Canwen Xu, Teven Le Scao, Sylvain Gugger, Mariama Drame, Quentin Lhoest, and Alexander Rush. 2020. Transformers: State-of-the-art natural language processing. In *Proceedings of the 2020 Conference on Empirical Methods in Natural Language Processing: System Demonstrations*, pages 38–45, Online. Association for Computational Linguistics.

An Yang, Baosong Yang, and Beichen Zhang. 2024. Qwen2.5 Technical Report. *arXiv preprint arXiv:2412.15115*.

Shangjian Yin, Peijie Huang, Yuhong Xu, Haojing Huang, and Jiatian Chen. 2024. Do large language models understand multi-intent spoken language? *arXiv preprint arXiv:2403.04481*.

Mingjin Zhang, Jiannong Cao, Xiaoming Shen, and Zeyang Cui. 2024. Edgeshard: Efficient llm inference via collaborative edge computing. *arXiv preprint arXiv:2405.14371*.

Tianyi Zhang, Varsha Kishore, Felix Wu, Kilian Q. Weinberger, and Yoav Artzi. 2020. BERTScore: Evaluating text generation with BERT. In *International Conference on Learning Representations*.

Xiaodong Zhang and Houfeng Wang. 2016. A joint model of intent determination and slot filling for spoken language understanding. In *Proceedings of the International Joint Conference on Artificial Intelligence (IJCAI)*, volume 16, pages 2993–2999.

A Data Examples

We show a data example in Figure 1.

```
[
    {
      "from": "system",
      "value": "You are 'Al', a helpful AI Assistant that controls the devices in
      a house. Complete the following task as instructed or answer the following
      question with the information provided only.\nServices: cover.close_cover(),
      cover.open_cover(), cover.stop_cover(), cover.toggle(), lock.lock(),
      lock.unlock(), media_player.media_next_track(), media_player.media_pause(),
      media_player.media_play(), media_player.media_play_pause(),
      media_player.media_previous_track(), media_player.media_stop(),
      media_player.toggle(), media_player.turn_off(), media_player.turn_on(),
      media_player.volume_down(), media_player.volume_mute(),
      media_player.volume_up(), switch.toggle(), switch.turn_off(),
      switch.turn_on(), timer.cancel(), timer.pause(), timer.start(duration),
      vacuum.pause(), vacuum.return_to_base(), vacuum.start(), vacuum.stop()
      Devices: media_player.harman_kardon_aura 'Harman Kardon Glass Speaker'
      = standby; vol=0.88\ntimer.kitchen_oven 'Kitchen oven timer' =
      active\nlock.office_cabinet 'Office cabinet lock' = unlocked
      cover.master_bedroom 'Master Bedroom' = closed
      vacuum.hallway_neato 'Hallway path cleaner' = docked
      switch.basement_lights 'Basement Lights Switch' = off"
    },
    {
      "from": "user",
      "value": "reverse the master bedroom blinds"
    },
    {
      "from": "assistant",
      "value": "switching Master Bedroom state as requested\n
      ```homeassistant
         {
          \"service\": \"cover.toggle\",
          \"target_device\": \"cover.master_bedroom\"
        }
      ```"
    }
]
```

Figure 1: **Data Example.** In the figure, we show a data example from the acon96 (2024) dataset.

B Data Distribution Detailed

We show a more detailed distribution of the dataset in Table 6.

Class	Total Dataset	Test
climate.set_fan_mode	1080	0
climate.set_humidity	1080	0
climate.set_hvac_mode	1080	0
climate.set_temperature	1000	0
cover.close	385	35
cover.open	395	40
cover.stop	320	25
cover.toggle	365	25
fan.decrease_speed	360	60
fan.increase_speed	300	40
fan.toggle	390	85
fan.turn_off	390	70
fan.turn_on	405	60
light.toggle	450	90
light.turn_off	2535	600
light.turn_on	11940	150
lock.lock	200	125
lock.unlock	185	125
media_player.media_next_track	55	25
media_player.media_pause	55	25
media_player.media_play	70	25
media_player.media_previous_track	55	25
media_player.media_stop	55	25
media_player.turn_off	25	25
media_player.turn_on	40	40
media_player.volume_down	65	35
media_player.volume_mute	60	30
media_player.volume_up	85	40
switch.toggle	250	50
switch.turn_off	500	175
switch.turn_on	540	165
timer.cancel	600	0
timer.start	600	0
todo.add_item	1560	0
vacuum.pause	15	0
vacuum.return_to_base	150	0
vacuum.start	370	220
vacuum.stop	15	0

Table 6: **Detailed Class Distribution Service.** Total Dataset vs. LLM Test Subset

Applying Transformer Architectures to Detect Cynical Comments in Spanish Social Media

Samuel González-López
Tecnológico Nacional/Nogales
Nogales, Sonora, México
samuel.gl@nogales.tecnm.mx

Steven Bethard
University of Arizona
Tucson, Arizona, USA
bethard@email.arizona.edu

Rogelio Platt-Molina
Tecnológico Nacional/Nogales
Nogales, Sonora, México
m22340761@nogales.tecnm.mx

Francisca Cecilia Encinas Orozco
Universidad de Sonora
Nogales, Sonora, México
cecilia.encinasorozco@unison.mx

Abstract

Detecting cynical comments in online communication poses a significant challenge in human-computer interaction, especially given the massive proliferation of discussions on platforms like YouTube. These comments often include offensive or disruptive patterns, such as sarcasm, negative feelings, specific reasons, and an attitude of being right. To address this problem, we present a web platform for the Spanish language that has been developed and leverages natural language processing and machine learning techniques. The platform detects comments and provides valuable information to users by focusing on analyzing comments. The core models are based on pre-trained architectures, including BETO, SpanBERTa, Multilingual BERT, RoBERTuito, and BERT, enabling robust detection of cynical comments. Our platform was trained and tested with Spanish comments from car analysis channels on YouTube. The results show that models achieve performance above 0.8 F1 for all types of cynical comments in the text classification task but achieve lower performance (around 0.6-0.7 F1) for the more arduous token classification task.

1 Introduction

The exponential growth of social networks has created an environment where cynical comments, such as sarcasm, negative sentiments, and dogmatic attitudes, can significantly impact discussions and public perception. In this work, we have focused on negative comments that could generate dysfunctional behaviors among social media users. Cynical behavior is a negative attitude with a broad or specific focus and comprises cognitive, affective, and behavioral components. Cynicism refers to customers' disbelief of companies or the market due to customers' perception of dishonesty and integrity on the seller's part (Indibara et al., 2023). Also, cynicism can generate feelings of betrayal and deception, leading to anger and the desire to stop purchasing products or services from the source that generates their anger (Chylinski and Chu, 2010). In this work, we have focused our efforts on the following elements: sarcasm, negative feelings, specific reasons, and attitude toward being right.

- **Sarcasm** includes mocking, biting, and cruel irony that offends or mistreats someone. Detecting sarcasm in online conversations is complex due to its subjective and contextual nature. What may be evident to a human being may be challenging to a machine. Failure to identify sarcasm can lead to misunderstandings, disagreements, and loss in quality of the online interaction (Gibbs, 2000).
- **Negative Feelings** are where users reflect negatively on a product, usually in a subjective way, influenced by their personal experiences.
- **Specific reasons** are when users identify particular aspects or components of a product, as long as the comment contains negative sentiment, sarcasm, or attitude of being right—for instance, seating comfort linked to a comment with sarcastic content.
- The **Attitude of being right** is where users express their rejection of the product and, in contrast, assert their correctness.

Such expressions come in many forms, written by users who have directly experienced the products they are commenting on and by users who have yet to consume or use the product being discussed. The automotive industry is relevant to emerging

Proceedings of the Tenth Workshop on Noisy and User-generated Text, pages 68–77
May 3, 2025 ©2025 Association for Computational Linguistics

economies (Stone and Cabrera, 2024), consumer decision-making, and the strong influence of online opinions on brand perceptions, which impacts the sales of automotive brands. By focusing on this specific domain, we seek to identify linguistic and expressive patterns characteristic of cynicism in digital communication. Furthermore, this analysis has broader implications, as the methods developed can be applied to other datasets involving product reviews, services, or online content, allowing for a better understanding of the impact of negative emotions on public opinion.

The contributions of our research are as follows:

- We collected and annotated 3705 comments in Spanish from the YouTube platform, achieving kappa of 0.841, 0.834, 0.859, and 0.752 for negative feelings, specific reasons, attitude of being right and sarcasm, respectively.
- We explore detecting cynical comments both as a token classification task and as a text classification task.
- We compare various pre-trained models to be fine-tuned for this task, including SpanBERTa, BETO, Multilingual BERT, and RoBERTuito.
- We implemented a web platform that automatically analyzes video comments using the trained models, and allows users to view each comment's predictions from each of the four models. Our models are hosted on the Hugging Face Platform.

Figure 1 shows examples of the elements analyzed in our platform. Each comment is shown in the language of study, Spanish, with its English translation.

2 Related work

Cynical comments are related to negative aspect and are specific elements that characterize the dark side of consumers of products or services. The closest related work are tasks on irony and sarcasm.

Although both irony and cynicism are close because of the negativity of the content, cynicism can be understood as an extreme form of irony, in which criticism is not only insinuated but used to challenge morality and social conventions openly (Räwel, 2007). For irony detection, AlMazrua et al. (2022) created an annota d corpus of tweets with 8089 positive texts in the Arabic language. The Fleiss's Kappa agreement value was 0.54, a moderate level. This work uses machine learning and deep learning models and reports a 0.68 accuracy with the SVM algorithm. One of the challenges in this work was detecting implicit phrases as part of the irony. Maladry et al. (2022) annotate a corpus of 5566 tweets for the Dutch language, with 2783 labeled as irony. This work reported for a binary classification task a 78.98% for implicit irony and 78.88% for explicit and implicit sentiment. The SVM model performed better than the BERT model. Irony has also been approached with CNNs and Embeddings (FastText, Word2vec) (Ghanem et al., 2020). This study analyzed monolingual and multilingual architectures in three languages, with the monolingual configuration performing better. A second approach, RCNN-RoBERTa, consisting of a pre-trained RoBERTa transformer followed by bidirectional long-term memory (BiLSTM), achieved 0.80 F1 on the SemEval-2018 dataset and 0.78 F1 on the Reddit Politics dataset (Potamias et al., 2020). In a binary classification task performed on Spanish variants for Irony detection (Ortega-Bueno et al., 2019), different representation approaches, such as word embeddings (Word2Vec, FastText) and N-grams, were presented. Our research used contextual transformer representations (BETO, SpanBERTa, RoBERTuito).

Sarcasm detection has received recent NLP research, particularly within sentiment analysis, as sarcasm often leads to misinterpretations of the intended sentiment. Early models relied on traditional machine learning techniques, such as Support Vector Machines (SVM), which utilized handcrafted features like word frequency and sentiment polarity to detect sarcasm (Băroiu and Trăușan-Matu, 2022). However, these methods needed help to capture sarcasm's subtleties and context-dependent nature. Recent advancements have led to the adoption of deep learning models, including Long-Short-Term Memory (LSTM) networks and Bidirectional Encoder Representations from Transformers (BERT), which have improved performance. These models can better understand the context in which sarcasm occurs, such as hyperbole, tone, or contrast between expectations and reality(Zhou, 2023). For instance, models like Cascade use context-driven approaches to capture sarcasm more accurately by analyzing dialogues on platforms like Reddit (Hazarika et al., 2018).

Further developments have seen the rise of multimodal approaches that incorporate both text and audio and visual data, which enhance detection accuracy by providing additional cues like facial expres-

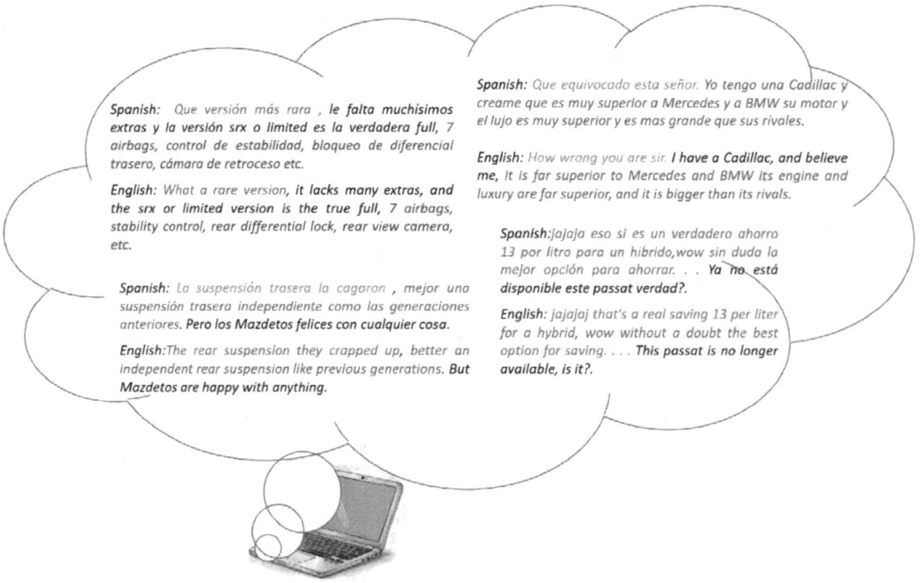

Figure 1: Examples of cynical comments: purple corresponds to Specific Reason expression; green refers to Negative Feeling; blue corresponds to Attitude to being right cynical comments; orange corresponds to Sarcasm.

sions or intonation. Ensemble learning techniques, combining multiple models, have also improved performance in sarcasm detection by leveraging the strengths of different algorithms (Lemmens et al., 2020). Despite these advances, challenges remain, especially when identifying sarcasm in short texts (e.g., tweets) or highly nuanced expressions (Son et al., 2019). Future research will likely focus on improving model robustness in such environments and integrating more sophisticated contextual understanding (Khodak et al., 2018).

The use of AI for detecting cynicism also intersects with ethical concerns. Algorithms designed to filter harmful content sometimes over-censor, inadvertently suppressing freedom of speech by removing comments that are not genuinely harmful but might be misinterpreted by the model (Dietrich, 2024); this delicate balance between moderating harmful content and preserving free expression is a continuing challenge for AI developers. Recent work explores sentiment prediction in online communities, where AI models attempt to predict the likelihood of cynical comments based on previous patterns of behaviors (Kumar and Bhushan, 2023). While promising, these predictive models are still in the early stages and require more refinement to effectively capture the nuances of negative emotional expression. Artificial intelligence has come a long way in detecting explicitly harmful content in social networks, however, it is still difficult to accurately identify cynical negative sentiments.

3 Dataset

Our corpus was constructed in several stages. First, Spanish-language YouTube channels were selected, primarily from Latin America and focusing on new car reviews, and their video comments were downloaded. These comments were then filtered to include only those with at least ten words and five likes, ensuring sufficient text for cynicism analysis and focusing on relevant discussion. This initial filtering resulted in 3705 comments. Two human annotators independently tagged the filtered comments, freely identifying text segments containing any elements analyzed in this study. To prepare them for this task, we developed a comprehensive visual guide, including: an introduction to consumer cynicism and cynical comments: Examples of different types of cynical comments; Visual examples demonstrating the annotation process, using color coding to mark the text. The annotators, a computer science master's student, and a computer science professor, also received a description of the research context and an explanatory video. To ensure consistent annotation, a calibration stage was conducted using 50 comments from the initial pool (which were subsequently excluded from the final corpus). Inter-annotator agreement was measured by checking if one annotator's marked text segment was contained within the other's. A 90%

Cynical expressions	Count	Kappa
Negative Feelings	644	0.834
Specific Reasons	381	0.859
Attitude of being right	605	0.752
Suspicions	155	0.550
Sarcasm	256	0.841

Table 1: Dataset of Cynical Comments.

overlap was considered a match. Comments with less than 90% overlap were deemed disagreements and were excluded from the final labeled corpus, which consisted of 2041 comments. Finally, comments tagged as "Suspicions" were also excluded from the experiments due to their scarcity. Table 1 details the results of the collection.

4 Methodology

We consider two tasks for detecting cynical comments. For token classification, we use the standard inside-out-inside format for token-by-token classification. For text classification, we assigned a label to each YouTube comment as positive for a class if any part of the comment was annotated for that class and as negative if no part of the comment was annotated for that class.

We explored several pre-trained models as potential candidates for fine-tuning and subsequent evaluation on our dataset:

BETO[1] (Cañete et al., 2020) was trained following the BERT paradigm (Devlin et al., 2019), but only on Spanish documents. It is similar in size to bert-based-multilingual-cased.

SpanBERTa[2] was trained following the RoBERTa paradigm (Liu et al., 2019), but trained on 18 GB of OSCAR's Spanish corpus. It is similar in size to BERT-Base.

mBERT[3] was trained on the concatenation of monolingual Wikipedia corpora from 104 languages. Even though mBERT was trained on separate monolingual corpora without a specific multilingual training objective, it still exhibits impressive performance on a variety of multilingual tasks (Pires et al., 2019).

We further investigate a model that was specifically trained for hate speech detection. This model, which is designed to identify expressions of negativity and hostility, could potentially be directly applied to our cynicism corpus without requiring additional fine-tuning:

RoBERTuito[4] is based on the RoBERTa model architecture and the BETO tokenizer (Pérez et al., 2022). It was trained on 622M tweets in Spanish from 432k users for hate speech detection, sentiment and emotion analysis, and irony detection.

For token classification evaluation, a 10-fold cross-validation method was performed. For each cynical comment, the following BERT models were run: SpanBERTa, mBERT, and BETO. The parameters with the best performance were: 160 epochs, $3 \times 10\text{-}5$ of the learning rate, and a batch size of 16. The number of epochs during the fine-tuning was 20, 80, 160, and 200. The batch was computed with 16 and 32 sizes.

For text classification evaluation, training (75%), validation (12.5%), and test (12.5%) collections were constructed. For each cynical comment, the following models were run: mBERT (fine-tuned on our annotated data) and pysentimiento/robertuito (not fine-tuned on our data). We fine-tuned only mBERT because, as will be seen in the results section, there were minimal differences between mBERT and the other pre-trained models. The mBERT parameters with the best performance were: 10 epochs and a batch size of 16. However, the number of epochs during the fine-tuning was 10 and 20. EarlyStopping was also included.

After the experimentation, the best-performing models were deployed to the HuggingFace model hub, and we proceeded with the implementation of a web platform. The objective was to create an online platform where the user only places the link to the YouTube video, and the analysis is performed automatically. The framework is illustrated in Figure 2. The extraction and data processing models are executed every time a new YouTube link needs to be analyzed. The YouTube comments are extracted with Python using the "youtubecommentdownloader" API. The comments are then subjected to a cleaning, tokenization, and preprocessing process using Python. The TensorFlow models are used in the web platform through the HuggingFace API, which allows models to make predictions using the resources of that platform.

5 Results

Table 2 shows detailed results of the token classification task. The first token (B) of specific reasons

[1] https://github.com/dccuchile/beto
[2] https://github.com/chriskhanhtran/spanish-bert
[3] https://github.com/google-research/bert/

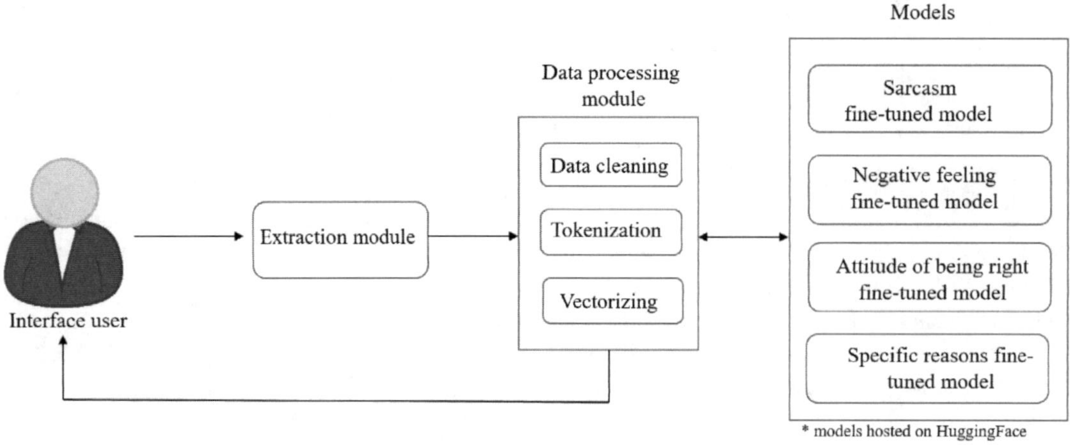

Figure 2: Framework for the implementation of the platform, "CODISCO".

		B			I			O		
Cynicism	Model	Precision	Recall	F1	Precision	Recall	F1	Precision	Recall	F1
NF	SpanBERTa	0.689	0.715	0.705	0.656	0.657	0.660	0.741	0.740	0.737
NF	BETO	0.670	0.688	0.674	0.674	0.644	0.665	0.750	0.766	0.745
NF	mBERT	0.666	0.683	0.673	0.668	0.636	0.646	0.736	0.765	0.747
SR	SpanBERTa	0.505	0.590	0.544	0.706	0.806	0.745	0.576	0.468	0.488
SR	BETO	0.507	0.642	0.565	0.742	0.841	0.778	0.612	0.470	0.500
SR	mBERT	0.510	0.575	0.538	0.711	0.816	0.749	0.610	0.480	0.502
AR	SpanBERTa	0.593	0.720	0.666	0.745	0.868	0.800	0.620	0.421	0.497
AR	BETO	0.593	0.720	0.666	0.745	0.868	0.800	0.620	0.422	0.497
AR	mBERT	0.602	0.717	0.682	0.770	0.862	0.775	0.637	0.477	0.547
SC	SpanBERTa	0.558	0.679	0.612	0.578	0.706	0.635	0.581	0.382	0.461
SC	BETO	0.558	0.685	0.615	0.580	0.745	0.665	0.620	0.383	0.473
SC	mBERT	0.567	0.676	0.616	0.572	0.770	0.656	0.610	0.438	0.509

Table 2: Detailed results on treating cynicism detection as a token classification task, for negative feelings (NF), specific reasons (SR), attitude of being right (AR), and sarcasm (SC).

were the most difficult for models to detect, with models achieving around 0.538 F1, while the inner tokens (I) of attitude of being right were the easiest, with models achieving around 0.800 F1. The different transformer models performed roughly similarly, with all F1s between comparable models within 0.04 F1 of each other. We can see that the high F1 values are distributed between the BETO and the SpanBERTa models. Sarcasm and specific reasons obtained the lowest F1 values. One possibility for this behavior was the corpus size. We can observe that tokens with label (I) for the SR and AR elements are better results than those with label (B).

Tables 3 and 4 show overall results for the token classification task (using a macro-average over the B/I/O labels) and the text classification task, respectively. As with the detailed token classifica-

Cynicism	Model	Precision	Recall	F1
Token classification task				
NF	SpanBERTa	0.697	0.703	0.696
NF	BETO	0.694	0.700	0.693
NF	mBERT	0.691	0.695	0.690
SR	SpanBERTa	0.598	0.622	0.592
SR	BETO	0.621	0.650	0.614
SR	mBERT	0.610	0.625	0.597
AR	SpanBERTa	0.625	0.668	0.648
AR	BETO	0.653	0.668	0.649
AR	mBERT	0.668	0.685	0.670
SC	SpanBERTa	0.572	0.589	0.569
SC	BETO	0.586	0.604	0.584
SC	mBERT	0.583	0.628	0.594

Table 3: Overall results of cynical comment detection as a token classification task, for negative feelings (NF), specific reasons (SR), attitude of being right (AR), and Sarcasm (SC).

Cyn.	Model	Precision	Recall	F1
	Text classification task			
NF	mBERT (fine-tuned)	0.902	0.948	0.925
NF	RoBERTuito (not fine-tuned)	0.620	0.731	0.671
SR	mBERT (fine-tuned)	0.912	0.981	0.945
SR	RoBERTuito (not fine-tuned)	0.500	0.128	0.204
AR	mBERT (fine-tuned)	0.728	0.981	0.849
AR	RoBERTuito (not fine-tuned)	0.461	0.089	0.150
SC	mBERT (fine-tuned)	0.678	0.928	0.783
SC	RoBERTuito (not fine-tuned)	0.416	0.075	0.127

Table 4: Overall results for detecting cynicism, as a text classification task, for negative feelings (NF), specific reasons (SR), and attitude of being right (AR).

tion results, we see that there are only small differences between the different pre-trained models when fine-tuned for token classification, with SpanBERTa being slightly higher on negative feelings, BETO being slightly higher on specific reasons, and mBERT being slightly higher on attitude of being right. The hardest cynicism type to detect in a token classification task is specific reasons, while the easiest is negative feelings.

Table 4 shows that cynicism detection is easier as text classification than as token classification, with the mBERT text classifier achieving > 0.8 F1 for all cynicism types. Applying RoBERTuito without fine-tuning to this text classification task results in lower performance than our fine-tuned models, as expected. However, the fact that RoBERTuito is able to achieve 0.671 F1 on negative feeling detection without any fine-tuning on our corpus indicates that there is significant overlap between hate speech detection and negative feeling detection.

6 CODISCO Platform Interface

We evaluated several BERT-based architectures, of which three have been trained on Spanish corpora (SpanBERTa, BETO and RoBERTuito) and one was trained on multiple languages (mBERT). Our prior research suggested that models tuned for the Spanish language would obtain the best results (Gonzalez-Lopez and Bethard, 2023). However, on the current dataset, mBERT, SpanBERTa, and BETO all performed similarly. For implementing the platform we thus arbitrarily selected BETO.

We have named our platform CODISCO[5], after its acronym in Spanish (Spanish: Comportamientos Disfuncionales de los Consumidores). The APIs generated by the HuggingFace platform are the following:

- Negative Feelings HuggingFace Model
- Specific Reasons HuggingFace Model
- Attitude of being right HuggingFace Model
- Sarcasm HuggingFace Model

Figure 3 shows graphs of the results of the analysis of the comments, together with a word cloud. Figure 4 shows the percentages of each comment in detail.

As previously defined in section 4, we wanted to make the interface as easy to use as possible. So, we decided to develop a single screen where the input and output processing are performed when the user enters the internet address of a YouTube video.

6.1 Platform Output Graphics

6.1.1 Results

This section shows a global summary of the platform's analysis results: the video's title, the total number of comments extracted, and a detailed summary of the analysis results, including the number of comments classified in each evaluated characteristic (sarcasm, negative sentiments, specific reasons, and attitude of being right). This overview provides a clear perspective of the scope and nature of the comments detected in the video.

6.1.2 Bar Graph

The bar chart visualizes the number of comments classified as sarcastic versus those without sarcasm. This graphical representation allows us to quickly identify the prevalence of sarcasm in the analyzed data set. It is a valuable tool for understanding the extent of this dysfunctional behavior in the extracted comments.

6.1.3 Word Cloud

The word cloud below highlights the most frequent words found in comments classified as cynical. This visualization helps to identify linguistic patterns and recurring themes in comments containing cynicism, providing additional insights into the nature of the content analyzed. The words with the largest size in the cloud appear most frequently in this type of comment.

[5] https://www.youtube.com/watch?v=3m9I81EnLrg

Figure 3: Output of the analysis with General Results, Bar Graph, and Word Cloud.

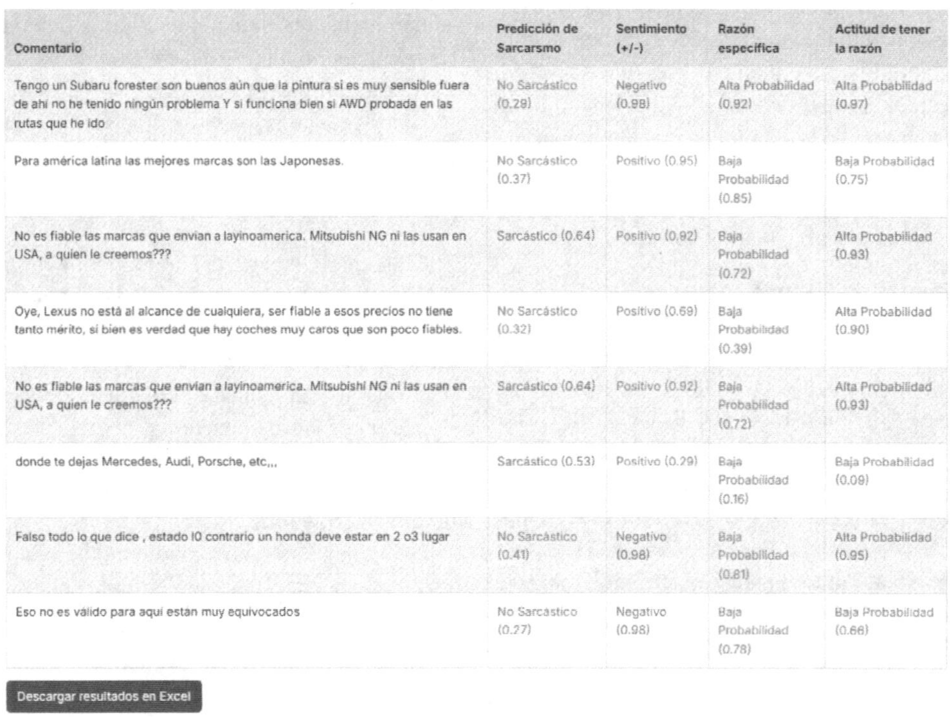

Comentario	Predicción de Sarcarsmo	Sentimiento (+/-)	Razón especifica	Actitud de tener la razón
Tengo un Subaru forester son buenos aún que la pintura si es muy sensible fuera de ahi no he tenido ningún problema Y si funciona bien si AWD probada en las rutas que he ido	No Sarcástico (0.29)	Negativo (0.98)	Alta Probabilidad (0.92)	Alta Probabilidad (0.97)
Para américa latina las mejores marcas son las Japonesas.	No Sarcástico (0.37)	Positivo (0.95)	Baja Probabilidad (0.85)	Baja Probabilidad (0.75)
No es fiable las marcas que envian a layinoamerica. Mitsubishi NG ni las usan en USA, a quien le creemos???	Sarcástico (0.64)	Positivo (0.92)	Baja Probabilidad (0.72)	Alta Probabilidad (0.93)
Oye, Lexus no está al alcance de cualquiera, ser fiable a esos precios no tiene tanto mérito, si bien es verdad que hay coches muy caros que son poco fiables.	No Sarcástico (0.32)	Positivo (0.69)	Baja Probabilidad (0.39)	Alta Probabilidad (0.90)
No es fiable las marcas que envian a layinoamerica. Mitsubishi NG ni las usan en USA, a quien le creemos???	Sarcástico (0.64)	Positivo (0.92)	Baja Probabilidad (0.72)	Alta Probabilidad (0.93)
donde te dejas Mercedes, Audi, Porsche, etc,,,	Sarcástico (0.53)	Positivo (0.29)	Baja Probabilidad (0.16)	Baja Probabilidad (0.09)
Falso todo lo que dice , estado l0 contrario un honda deve estar en 2 o3 lugar	No Sarcástico (0.41)	Negativo (0.98)	Baja Probabilidad (0.81)	Alta Probabilidad (0.95)
Eso no es valido para aqui estan muy equivocados	No Sarcástico (0.27)	Negativo (0.98)	Baja Probabilidad (0.78)	Baja Probabilidad (0.66)

Figure 4: Detailed Output of each Comment with its Value obtained in each Category.

6.2 Usability Survey for CODISCO

We performed a survey of 40 users of the CODISCO platform. Most users found the platform responsive and effective. The scale used for the questions was 1 to 10, with 10 being a positive result. The usability survey questions were:

1. How easy was it for you to understand how to use this interface on your first attempt?
2. Did you find the interface visually appealing?
3. How satisfied are you with the response and speed of the interface?
4. How long did it take you to complete your task using this interface?
5. How intuitive did you find the functions available in the interface?

Figure 5 shows the results. The colors in the graph correspond to the five questions asked to the users, the x-axis corresponds to the users who answered the survey, and the y-axis shows the scale used.

Some users reported problems when using the platform on mobile devices, citing difficulties with the devices, mentioning difficulties with the side menu "categories", and visualization problems. This aspect is critical as it affects the user experience and usability of the platform in mobile contexts. The speed of the interface needs improvement since it obtained low values with respect to the rest of the questions. This could have been caused by the speed of the university internet since those who used the platform and answered the survey were students from school computers. The results allowed us to make improvements to the platform.

7 Discussion

The results obtained in the experiment show that it is possible to detect the four types of cynical comments in Spanish with reasonable reliability. However, we found some points for reflection. Regarding the two tasks analyzed, we found that the performance was higher for the easier text classification task and lower for the more difficult token classification task. However, token classification is closer to the goal of this work, which is to detect exactly which part of the comment represents the cynical comment. It may be helpful to investigate two-stage approaches, in which text classification is first used to identify the general region of cynical comments, and token classification is then used to delineate specific sentences.

For comments labeled as negative feelings, the beginnings of utterances (B) were the easiest to identify, probably because they often begin with terms used to describe dissatisfaction. For comments labeled as specific reasons and attitudes of being right, the middle of utterances (I) were the easiest to identify, probably because these types of cynicism include car-specific terms that might be easier to identify. Future work could investigate whether joint learning of these models could help better establish the boundaries of the different types of cynical comments.

Experiments with RoBERTuito highlight that simply using a trained model for hate speech detection will not provide a solution for detecting cynical comments, even in the related category of negative sentiment: an adjusted RoBERTuito achieves only 0.671 F1, whereas an adjusted mBERT achieves 0.925 F1. Nevertheless, these results indicate some overlap between the two tasks, and the detection of cynical comments could benefit from the hate speech detection models, for example, by using the predictions of the hate speech model as features in the cynical comment detection model.

8 Conclusions

The analysis of cynical comments is crucial, as the sentiments and opinions of vocal customers can significantly influence decisions. Even cynical comments may induce undesirable behavior in other people. We annotated a corpus with four types of cynical comments: negative feelings, specific reasons, an attitude of being right, and sarcasm. We trained models on this corpus for text and token classification tasks.

Our results demonstrate the feasibility of training models to detect cynical comments accurately in this domain. We envision our work as a foundational step toward technologies that can quantify the level of cynicism in YouTube videos. Such analyses could empower companies to position their products strategically based on consumer perceptions. Our implementation with pre-trained models in Spanish represents a substantial advancement in comment moderation on platforms like YouTube. However, areas for improvement include expanding the corpus to encompass more dialectal variations and enhancing the model's robustness in ambiguous contexts. We plan to fine-tune the model

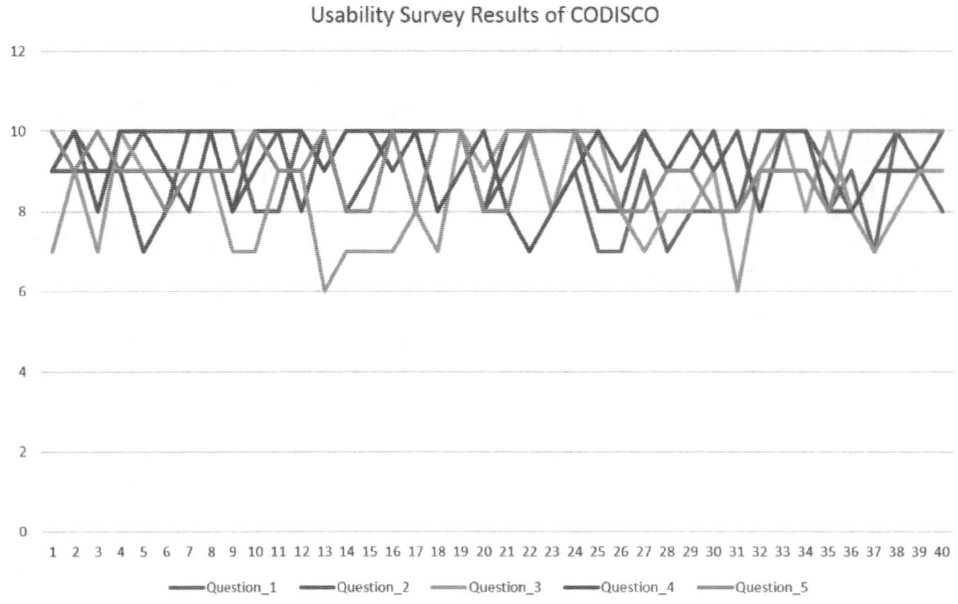

Figure 5: Usability Survey for CODISCO.

with a complementary corpus for future work. The platform has the potential to be adapted for other languages and applications beyond comment moderation, such as sentiment analysis or fake news detection.

Limitations

First, the exclusive focus on the Spanish language restricts the direct generalization of the results to other languages. While Spanish is a global language with many speakers, it is essential to recognize that the linguistic resources and language models available for Spanish do not yet reach the same scale and sophistication as those available for English. This disparity in resource availability could influence the performance and accuracy of the models evaluated in this study. In addition, specific linguistic features distinctive to Spanish, such as its richer morphology and flexible syntax, might require specific adaptations and adjustments to the language models to achieve optimal performance. Second, this study is limited to models with modest computational requirements and precludes evaluating the potential performance of the larger and more advanced language models currently available. The choice of models with modest computational requirements is justified by the need to ensure the reproducibility and accessibility of the research, allowing other researchers to replicate and extend the results obtained. The scientific community should interpret the results presented in this study in the context of the models used. It should not be considered an exhaustive evaluation of the potential of natural language processing in Spanish.

References

Halah AlMazrua, Najla AlHazzani, Amaal AlDawod, Lama AlAwlaqi, Noura AlReshoudi, Hend Al-Khalifa, and Luluh AlDhubayi. 2022. Sa'7r: A saudi dialect irony dataset. In *Proceedinsg of the 5th Workshop on Open-Source Arabic Corpora and Processing Tools with Shared Tasks on Qur'an QA and Fine-Grained Hate Speech Detection*, pages 60–70, Marseille, France. European Language Resources Association.

Alexandru-Costin Băroiu and Ștefan Trăușan-Matu. 2022. Automatic sarcasm detection: Systematic literature review. *Information*, 13(8).

José Cañete, Gabriel Chaperon, Rodrigo Fuentes, Jou-Hui Ho, Hojin Kang, and Jorge Pérez. 2020. Spanish pre-trained bert model and evaluation data. In *PML4DC at ICLR 2020*.

M. Chylinski and A. Chu. 2010. Consumer cynicism: antecedents and consequences. *European Journal of Marketing*, 44(6):796–837.

Jacob Devlin, Ming-Wei Chang, Kenton Lee, and Kristina Toutanova. 2019. BERT: Pre-training of deep bidirectional transformers for language understanding. In *Proceedings of the 2019 Conference of the North American Chapter of the Association for*

Computational Linguistics: Human Language Technologies, Volume 1 (Long and Short Papers), pages 4171–4186, Minneapolis, Minnesota. Association for Computational Linguistics.

Frank Dietrich. 2024. Ai-based removal of hate speech from digital social networks: chances and risks for freedom of expression. *AI and Ethics*.

Bilal Ghanem, Jihen Karoui, Farah Benamara, Paolo Rosso, and Véronique Moriceau. 2020. Irony detection in a multilingual context. In *Advances in Information Retrieval*, pages 141–149, Cham. Springer International Publishing.

Raymond W. Gibbs. 2000. Irony in talk among friends. *Metaphor and Symbol*, 15(1-2):5–27.

Samuel Gonzalez-Lopez and Steven Bethard. 2023. Transformer-based cynical expression detection in a corpus of Spanish YouTube reviews. In *Proceedings of the 13th Workshop on Computational Approaches to Subjectivity, Sentiment, & Social Media Analysis*, pages 194–201, Toronto, Canada. Association for Computational Linguistics.

Devamanyu Hazarika, Soujanya Poria, Sruthi Gorantla, Erik Cambria, Roger Zimmermann, and Rada Mihalcea. 2018. CASCADE: Contextual sarcasm detection in online discussion forums. In *Proceedings of the 27th International Conference on Computational Linguistics*, pages 1837–1848, Santa Fe, New Mexico, USA. Association for Computational Linguistics.

Indirah Indibara, Deepa Halder, and Sanjeev Varshney. 2023. Consumer cynicism: Interdisciplinary hybrid review and research agenda. *International Journal of Consumer Studies*, 47(6):2724–2746.

Mikhail Khodak, Nikunj Saunshi, and Kiran Vodrahalli. 2018. A large self-annotated corpus for sarcasm. In *Proceedings of the Eleventh International Conference on Language Resources and Evaluation (LREC 2018)*, Miyazaki, Japan. European Language Resources Association (ELRA).

Ankit Kumar and Bharat Bhushan. 2023. Ai driven sentiment analysis for social media data. In *2023 International Conference on Computing, Communication, and Intelligent Systems (ICCCIS)*, pages 1201–1206.

Jens Lemmens, Ben Burtenshaw, Ehsan Lotfi, Ilia Markov, and Walter Daelemans. 2020. Sarcasm detection using an ensemble approach. In *Proceedings of the Second Workshop on Figurative Language Processing*, pages 264–269, Online. Association for Computational Linguistics.

Yinhan Liu, Myle Ott, Naman Goyal, Jingfei Du, Mandar Joshi, Danqi Chen, Omer Levy, Mike Lewis, Luke Zettlemoyer, and Veselin Stoyanov. 2019. Roberta: A robustly optimized bert pretraining approach. *Preprint*, arXiv:1907.11692.

Aaron Maladry, Els Lefever, Cynthia Van Hee, and Veronique Hoste. 2022. Irony detection for Dutch: a venture into the implicit. In *Proceedings of the 12th Workshop on Computational Approaches to Subjectivity, Sentiment & Social Media Analysis*, pages 172–181, Dublin, Ireland. Association for Computational Linguistics.

Reynier Ortega-Bueno, Francisco Range, Delia Irazu Hernandez Farias, Paolo Rosso, Manuel Montes y Gomez, and Jose E. Medina-Pagola. 2019. Overview of the task on irony detection in spanish variants.

Juan Manuel Pérez, Damián Ariel Furman, Laura Alonso Alemany, and Franco M. Luque. 2022. RoBERTuito: a pre-trained language model for social media text in Spanish. In *Proceedings of the Thirteenth Language Resources and Evaluation Conference*, pages 7235–7243, Marseille, France. European Language Resources Association.

Telmo Pires, Eva Schlinger, and Dan Garrette. 2019. How multilingual is multilingual BERT? In *Proceedings of the 57th Annual Meeting of the Association for Computational Linguistics*, pages 4996–5001, Florence, Italy. Association for Computational Linguistics.

R.A. Potamias, G. Siolas, and A. Stafylopatis. 2020. A transformer-based approach to irony and sarcasm detection. *Neural Computing and Applications*, pages 1433 – 3058.

Jörg Räwel. 2007. The Relationship between Irony, Sarcasm and Cynicism. *Z Literaturwiss Linguistik*, 37:142–153.

Le Hoang Son, Akshi Kumar, Saurabh Raj Sangwan, Anshika Arora, Anand Nayyar, and Mohamed Abdel-Basset. 2019. Sarcasm detection using soft attention-based bidirectional long short-term memory model with convolution network. *IEEE Access*, 7:23319–23328.

Vladimir Márquez Stone and Seyka Verónica Sandoval Cabrera. 2024. Effects of Automation on Mexican Automotive Employment: 2013–2022. *The Indian Journal of Labour Economics*, 67(3):661–680.

Juliann Zhou. 2023. An evaluation of state-of-the-art large language models for sarcasm detection. *Preprint*, arXiv:2312.03706.

Prompt Guided Diffusion for Controllable Text Generation

Mohaddeseh Mirbeygi and **Hamid Beigy**
Department of Computer Engineering
Sharif University of Technology
Tehran, Iran
m.mirbeygi@sharif.edu and beigy@sharif.edu

Abstract

Text generation under control, or producing linguistically coherent and contextually relevant text, has seen tremendous progress thanks to methods based on PPLM, FUDGE, and diffusion-based models. Yet current state-of-the-art models tend to balance control fidelity with fluency. In addition, classifier-guided strategies (e.g., PPLM) can be predicted in gradient updates providing less coherent text. In contrast, autoregressive-based approaches (e.g., FUDGE) rely on inflexible generation patterns that limit creativity. Recent diffusion methods demonstrate superior performance in iteration and diversity, but indirect methods often fail to introduce sufficient ways to inject task-associated knowledge, leading to the need for many different complex classifier modules during both training and inference. To address this, we introduce a prompt-guided diffusion framework that seamlessly incorporates structured prompts into the diffusion steps, providing precise and flexible control of the generated text. Each prompt combines a target attribute (for example, a sentiment tag), an example corresponding to that label (for example, a positive review), and a slot for the generated sentence. By encoding such prompts using large pre-trained models (such as BART) and integrating these prompts through cross-attention into the diffusion dynamics, our model achieves new state-of-the-art performance on a variety of tasks ranging from IMDB for sentiment, AG-News for topic, and E2E for structured-output to text.

1 Introduction

Text generation: a computational paradigm for producing meaningful written content with coherence, often fueled by NLP models. Its uses include chatbots, content generation systems, machine translation, and other areas. Controllability in text generation concerns the ability to control the outputs for desired characteristics — including tone, style, length, or topic based on predefined criteria or user preference. This is usually done through all sorts of means, from prompt engineering to fine-tuning or control tokens. Unconstrained generation, on the other hand, refers to cases where the generated content deviates from the requirements, resulting in out-of-topic content. Such deviations (known informally as use performance error) are common due to the inherently random nature of sampling or subtle modeling of user intention, additional work is often needed in production to find a satisfactory balance between controllability and creativity in the model.

NLP tasks related to text generation generally relate to a generation task where models attempt to create a set of coherent, meaningful strings from some input, based on generative architectures. Researchers have developed various types of generative strategies. Generative Adversarial Networks (GANs) compete against a discriminator to generate text samples. EBMs work by defining an energy function across the text data, with the model trained to produce lower energy for valid samples and higher energy for invalid samples. This allows for a flexible way to enforce constraints during the generation process. Flow-based models produce exact likelihoods by invertible mapping from simple probability distributions to complex ones, giving much more control. Diffusion models progressively synthesize outputs, denoising random noise through multiple probabilistic steps, yielding stable and high-quality results. These paradigms together illustrate the spectrum of mechanisms for text generation by arranging different trade-offs between controllability, diversity, and fidelity. This paper focuses on the application of diffusion models to the task of text generation.

1.1 Diffusion Model

The diffusion model consists of a Markov chain of unobservable quantities. It begins with an initial

Proceedings of the Tenth Workshop on Noisy and User-generated Text, pages 78–84
May 3, 2025 ©2025 Association for Computational Linguistics

data point x_0 and incrementally corrupts it with Gaussian noise until x_T, according to the posterior $q(x_{0:T} \mid x_0)$. The variables $x_0, \ldots, x_T$ have the same dimensionality as x_0. The main objective is to model the distribution $p_\theta(x_{t-1} \mid x_t)$ for the reverse (denoising) process Ho et al. (2020).

Forward and reverse processes are two key components of a diffusion model. The forward process gradually corrupts data with random noise until it is practically indistinguishable from pure noise. Then the reverse phase tries to reconstruct the original data, learning to deduce how to remove the noise step by step. In the forward process, the transitions in the Markov chain are described by a conditional Gaussian. The generative distribution can be expressed as 1.

$$q(x_{1:T}|x_0) = \prod_{t=1}^{T} q(x_t|x_{t-1}) = \prod_{t=1}^{T} \mathcal{N}\left(x_t; \sqrt{1-\beta_t}x_{t-1}, \beta_t I\right) \quad (1)$$

where every β (fixed or learnable) controls the variance. As the time T becomes larger, the second assumption states that x_T approaches Gaussian noise.

The model learns the reverse path during training to sample data from random noise $p(x_T) = \mathcal{N}(x_T; 0, I)$ and thereby learns $p_\theta(x_{0:T})$ as in equation 2.

$$p_\theta(x_{0:T}) = p(x_T) \prod_{t=1}^{T} p_\theta(x_{t-1}|x_t) = p(x_T) \prod_{t=1}^{T} \mathcal{N}\left(x_{t-1}; \mu_\theta(x_t, t), \sum_\theta(x_t, t)\right) \quad (2)$$

In this Markov chain, we model the dependence on time of the reverse distribution by 3.

$$p_\theta(x_{t-1}|x_t) = \mathcal{N}\left(x_{t-1}; \mu_\theta(x_t, t), \sum\nolimits_\theta(x_t, t)\right) \quad (3)$$

The training aims to maximize the likelihood, which is mathematically equivalent to minimizing the negative log-likelihood by equation 4.

$$E[-logp_\theta(x_0)] \leq E_q[-log\frac{p_\theta(x_{0:T})}{q(x_{1:T}|x_0)}] = L_{vlb} \quad (4)$$

The KL divergence for Gaussians means that the losses at every step (Equations 5 to 8, above) can be expressed in KL terms. Therefore, the total loss is the sum across the chain:

$$L_{vlb} = \sum_{k=0}^{T} L_k \quad (5)$$

$$L_0 = -\log p_\theta(x_0|x_1) \quad (6)$$

$$L_{t-1} = D_{KL}(q(x_{t-1}|x_t, x_0)||p_\theta(x_{t-1}|x_t)) \quad (7)$$

$$L_T = D_{KL}(q(x_T|x_0)||p(x_T)) \quad (8)$$

2 Related Work

Several studies focused on the adaptation of diffusion models originally developed for image generation to the discrete textual domain (Li et al., 2022; Austin et al., 2021). They provide novel methods to approach the problem of continuous diffusion processes versus discrete tokens. Some studies directly construct diffusion as defined in the discrete space and others map the discrete tokens into a continuous representation where standard diffusion pipelines can work (Austin et al., 2021; Chen et al., 2022). Savinov et al. (2021) shows how iterative denoising autoencoders can be placed in a diffusion context and how repeated denoising steps approximate the generative capacity of diffusion. Such approaches can serve as a complement to the widespread autoregressive models held typical for text generation, enabling improvements in controllability, diversity, and sophisticated dependency modeling.

These lines of research also investigate how to use or outgrow diffusion-based text generation. Diffusion-LM Li et al. (2022), which focuses on controlling attributes of generated text, e.g., sentiment domain. Gong et al. (2022) leverages diffusion models for seq2seq tasks like translation, indicating their generality. In summary, this line of work broadens the applicability of diffusion models beyond the domain of continuous data, paving new pathways into how discrete textual outputs can be generated and conditioned.

Diffusion-LM Li et al. (2022) proposes a new paradigm for text generation by utilizing the iterative refinement framework of diffusion models, which has been traditionally used in the setting of continuous data, directly on text tokens. Rather than single-pass autoregressive generations, Diffusion-LM improves the text in multiple passes, potentially leading to greater flexibility and variability in its outputs. This approach trains a token-level denoiser, allowing the approach to modify specific attributes (sentiment, length, etc.) at inference without needing additional retraining.

D3PM Austin et al. (2021) presents a method for diffusion on structured discrete data (e.g. text, categorical data). In this technique, a forward corruption process preserves structural relations, and a reverse denoising process restores the corrupted data in iterations by learning a structured probability form. This approach aims to go beyond the limitations of traditional sequential text generation formats, enabling novel forms of discrete data modeling.

SUNDAE Savinov et al. (2021) proposed a new model of text generation combining the structured representation power of denoising autoencoders with a particular set of step-unrolling techniques in modeling the sequential dependency of text. Next, while standard DAEs generate text in a single step, this framework replays the generation process over an extended range, advising the denoising process on how to convert an embedding with noise into intelligible text. Step Unrolling: This allows the model to learn to incorporate more information about longer context dependencies while enforcing a schism between the input and output of the model, resulting in better-generated text.

There are, however, other utilitarian efforts that use encoder-decoder architectures, with latent representations, with a strong application-oriented motivation. Liu et al. (2024) establishes a generalized view of diffusion, which can be applied to data across continuous or discrete domains since both the encoder and decoder may be tailored. Tan et al. (2023) presents an encoder-decoder breakup for text diffusion, specifically comprising a spiral interplay structure that expands generational high quality, whilst letting knowledge waft from their encoder to its decoder (throughout the diffusion levels).

These papers cover various techniques for further improving text generation using diffusion models by generally combining PLMs, latent spaces, and novel training or sampling techniques. Several of them focus on the synergy between diffusion and PLM. The proposed approach, Ou and Jian (2024) suggests a "linguistic easy-first schedule" to guide the process of diffusion in leveraging linguistic knowledge and PLMs to make the model generate simpler linguistic structures first.

Many studies explored the combination of diffusion with large pre-trained language models (PLMs). Ou and Jian (2024) introduce a "linguistic easy-first schedule" that borrows from linguistic knowledge and leverages PLMs so that simpler patterns first appear in diffusion-based text generation. Chen et al. (2023a) present a resource-frugal diffusion language model with soft-masked noise, which strikes an equilibrium by preserving essential linguistic elements.

The domains where diffusion models can be applied include paraphrasing Zou et al. (2024), dialog systems Xiang et al. (2024), recommendation engines Li et al. (2023), code generation Singh et al. (2023), topic modeling Xu et al. (2023), event argument extraction Luo and Xu (2023), comment generation Liu et al. (2023), style transfer Horvitz et al. (2024), Lyu et al. (2023), key phrase extraction Luo et al. (2023), translation Chen et al. (2023b), poetry generation Hu et al. (2024), text detoxification Floto et al. (2023), empathetic dialog Bi et al. (2023), entity recognition Shen et al. (2023), text summarization Zhang et al. (2023), text inference Yuan et al. (2024), and conversation controllable Chen and Yang (2023).

3 The Proposed Method

Prompt diffusion is an emerging key mechanism for generative modeling, providing a simple yet powerful way to condition outputs of a diffusion model with standard language prompts. While diffusion models have been shown to be powerful samplers (from images to audio to text), achieving explicit, fine-grained control has remained a challenge Nichol and Dhariwal (2021). This is what makes direct control over the generative process and steering it toward certain outputs complex.

To address this problem, diffusion strategies based on prompts condition the diffusion model on text descriptions (i.e., "prompts") that describe the desired properties and guide the generative process of the model. Essentially, a big pre-training language model, e.g. BART, is applied to these textual prompts to turn them into vector representations that contain the prompt's semantic content. These representations are then fed into the denoising network, often using concatenation methods, guiding concerning the prompt during each step of the denoising process.

One particular type of structured prompt uses the target property, such as a sentiment or topic, along with a randomly selected in-class example (to prevent data overlap or leakage), then leaves a blank for the new sentence. Our diffusion model, which is based on a transformer, manages the noisy text embeddings with cross-attention conditioning on the embeddings of prompt processed by BART (or any other similar encoder). This design is shown in figure 1.

Several advantages come with prompt-based diffusion. First, it is highly controllable Sridhar and Vasconcelos (2024): with meticulously engineered prompts, one can dictate the style, content, or other types of attributes, allowing for highly constrained creative output Zhong et al. (2024). Second, it offers versatility: a single pre-trained diffusion model can be used on many tasks by simply changing a prompt instead of fine-tuning each model for each new objective. It is extremely cost-efficient. Third, it offers great potential for few-shot or in-context learning, allowing the model to infer instructions from a few examples Du et al. (2024).

But writing good prompts is not trivial: badly written prompts give bad results, and the encoding of prompts also takes time to generate. Complex prompts may raise challenges as well in terms of coherence. Despite that, prompt-based diffusion is an appealing method, as it provides extensive user-driven guidance combined with the powerful generative capability of extensive diffusion models.

Our system combines a large language model and diffusion for conditional text generation. We adopt a prompt-learning paradigm that concatenates the condition label (e.g., sentiment) with a relevant example review to form a textual prompt. Subsequently, this prompt is encoded (e.g., with BART), bringing about embeddings that guide the diffusion process. The diffusion model is trained to predict the noise added at each time step, effectively modeling the reverse diffusion. Therefore, at inference time, random noise is iteratively converted into meaningful embeddings based on the guidance of the prompt.

So those final embeddings get passed through a BART decoder, benefiting from the pre-trained autoregressive decoding to produce reasonable text. This pipeline elegantly resolves the shortcomings of a completely embedding-based decoding (which can be compelled to revert to rough nearest-neighbor lookups) and produces high-quality text outputs. The prompt method informs the output using the desired condition in the prompt but also dictates the context with the example text, which

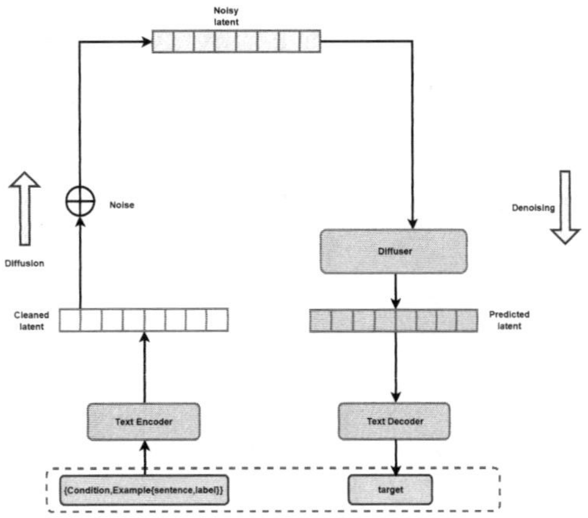

Figure 1: Our Proposed Method

provides a granular steer for what you would want to get as output. By leveraging the strengths of a sizable, pre-trained encoder-decoder (BART) and a purpose-built diffusion model, the components are tailored for their tasks, yielding robust performance on conditional text generation tasks.

4 Experimantal results

We evaluate our approach on three benchmark datasets: IMDB (50,000 movie reviews for sentiment analysis) Maas et al. (2011), AG News (120,000 news articles across four topics: World, Sports, Business, and Sci/Tech) Zhang et al. (2015), and E2E (a data-to-text dataset which involves restaurant descriptions using structured attribute-value pairs) Novikova et al. (2017). Each dataset poses different challenges: IMDB for sentiment polarity, AG News for topic coherence, and E2E for structured semantic fidelity.

Our diffusion training involves two steps: a forward phase where the text embeddings are gradually contaminated with Gaussian noise across T=1000 time steps, and a reverse phase, during which a trained model denoises the signal to reconstruct the data. In the forward step, x_0 progressively transforms into x_T according to a noise schedule $\beta_t = 0.9$, ending with a nearly random noise state (Equation 1). The model is trained to predict the noise at each time t concerning the variational bound (Equation 4), estimating $p_\theta(x_{t-1} \mid x_t)$. Diffusion-based generators instantiate text through a multi-step, iterative denoising process, allowing fine-grained modifications during intermediate steps to satisfy conditions such as syntactic or stylistic properties instead of generating the text token-by-token as in autoregressive models. This iterative routine stabilizes training and provides more robust controllability than single-pass methods.

Our experiments were conducted using the E2E dataset, and the results showed that the proposed method outperformed other approaches. Table 1 lists three generation tasks we experimented with: semantic content, parts-of-speech (POS), and length.

For the semantic content task, we supplied a field (e.g., rating) and provided a value (e.g., 5 stars) to compute a sentence that would accurately personify the relationship between the field and value provided, and the ground truth for the same being the exact match of the 'value'. For the parts-of-speech task, we generated a sequence of POS tags to the model (e.g., Pronoun Verb Determiner Noun) and asked it to output a word sequence of the same length such that the POS tags were aligned with the target according to an oracle POS tagger. Success was measured using word-level exact matches. For the length task, we defined a desired length between 10 and 40 and produced a sequence of up to ±2 the target length.

We also conduct experiments on IMDb and AG-News, assessing their quality using metrics such as BLEU, ROUGH, and BERTScore as shown in table 2.

The numerical results in Table 1 clearly show that PromptDiffusion outperforms all prior controllable text generation methods on all features evaluated: accuracy of semantic content, accuracy of part-of-speech, and text length. In semantic content, PromptDiffusion also delivers high accuracy of 83% outperforming the previous leading methods including Masked DiffusionLM + BERT (82.9%) and DiffusionLEF + BERT (82.4%), without sacrificing the low-perplexity (2.30) and thus fluency. And while achieving 92.5% in part-of-speech accuracy, PromptDiffusion outperforms all other diffusion models and has the lowest perplexity, at 4.7, which means it generates syntactically more coherent outputs.

Table 2 reveals that PromptDiffusion outperforms not only PPLM and FUDGE but also DiffusionLM on the IMDB (sentiment control) and AG News (topic control) datasets in terms of generation quality. In extensive evaluation, of the IMDB dataset, PromptDiffusion achieves BLEU-4 of 10, ROUGE-L of 30, and BERT-Score of 92, outperforming DiffusionLM and GPT-2 by a large margin. This indicates that PromptDiffusion yields semantically more aligned and fluent text while better-preserving intent. These findings further underpin that PromptDiffusion provides a tradeoff between controllability, fluency, and quality, thus is a strong competitive to prior generation methods reaping benefits from traditional structured pre-trained models (e.g. GPT-2), and because it also surpasses them in some tasks in text generation.

Diffusion models give controllable text generation more flexibility and come with significantly more advantages than autoregressive, VAE, or GAN-based approaches. While autoregressive models like GPT predict following a static, token-by-token order, diffusion models slowly guide latent representations through many iterations. Such progressive denoising lends itself well to making subtle tweaks to fit our constraints, such as syntax, length, or style. Diffusion models manage to strike the right balance between accuracy and creativity in comparison to classifier-guided techniques like PPLM, which tend to generate unintelligible outputs owing to erratic updates of gradients, or VAEs that in most cases hit a wall when it comes to diversity. Diffusion models achieve a balance for generation by inserting structured prompts (e.g. target attributes) into continuous input via cross-attention mechanisms without losing fluency.

5 Conclusion

In this work, we propose a prompt-guided diffusion framework for controllable text generation that mitigates critical limitations of the existing methods in balancing precision and fluency. Our method integrates structured prompts that combine target conditions and in-class examples into the diffusion process, achieving fine-grained control over attributes such as sentiment, topic, and adherence to structured data. Dynamic sampling of examples during training ensures robustness to intra-class diversity. Future work might investigate hybrid models that combine the proposed prompt-guided diffusion either with the retrieval-augmented generation or few-shot learning, as well as an extension to multimodal tasks. Such a framework advances the frontier of controllable text generation by bridging human intention with generative AI through intuitive prompting and thus offers a flexible and scalable solution for real-world deployment.

	semantic content		part of speech		length	
	Acc	Perp	Acc	Perp	Acc	Perp
PPLM	9.9	5.32	-	-	-	-
FUDGE	69.9	2.83	27	7.96	46.9	3.11
DiffusionLM	81.2	2.55	90	5.16	99.9	2.16
DiffusionLM + Bert	77.4	2.68	86.2	5.43	99.9	2.68
Masked DiffusionLM + Bert	82.9	2.30	92.9	4.78	100	2.08
DiffusionLEF	81.7	2.46	91.2	5.09	99.9	2.14
DiffusionLEF + Bert	82.4	2.32	92.4	4.82	**100**	2.10
PromptDiffusion	**83**	**2.30**	**92.5**	**4.7**	99.9	**2**

Table 1: results on E2E dataset for controllable generation

	IMDB			AG News		
	BLEU-4	ROUGE-L	Bert-Score	BLEU-4	ROUGE-L	Bert-Score
PPLM	1.6	19	41	2	20	43
FUDGE	1.8	20	43	2.1	22	46
DiffusionLM	7	28	89	7.5	29	90
PromptDiffusion	**10**	**30**	**92**	**11**	**31**	**91**
GPT2	6.1	26	88	6.8	27	89

Table 2: results on IMDB and AGnews

References

Jacob Austin, Daniel D Johnson, Jonathan Ho, Daniel Tarlow, and Rianne Van Den Berg. 2021. Structured denoising diffusion models in discrete state-spaces. *Advances in Neural Information Processing Systems*, 34:17981–17993.

Guanqun Bi, Lei Shen, Yanan Cao, Meng Chen, Yuqiang Xie, Zheng Lin, and Xiaodong He. 2023. Diffusemp: A diffusion model-based framework with multi-grained control for empathetic response generation. *arXiv preprint arXiv:2306.01657*.

Jiaao Chen and Diyi Yang. 2023. Controllable conversation generation with conversation structures via diffusion models. In *Findings of the Association for Computational Linguistics: ACL 2023*, pages 7238–7251.

Jiaao Chen, Aston Zhang, Mu Li, Alex Smola, and Diyi Yang. 2023a. A cheaper and better diffusion language model with soft-masked noise. *arXiv preprint arXiv:2304.04746*.

Linyao Chen, Aosong Feng, Boming Yang, and Zihui Li. 2023b. Xdlm: Cross-lingual diffusion language model for machine translation. *arXiv preprint arXiv:2307.13560*.

Ting Chen, Ruixiang Zhang, and Geoffrey Hinton. 2022. Analog bits: Generating discrete data using diffusion models with self-conditioning. *arXiv preprint arXiv:2208.04202*.

Yingjun Du, Gaowen Liu, Yuzhang Shang, Yuguang Yao, Ramana Kompella, and Cees GM Snoek. 2024. Prompt diffusion robustifies any-modality prompt learning. *arXiv preprint arXiv:2410.20164*.

Griffin Floto, Mohammad Mahdi Abdollah Pour, Parsa Farinneya, Zhenwei Tang, Ali Pesaranghader, Manasa Bharadwaj, and Scott Sanner. 2023. Diffudetox: A mixed diffusion model for text detoxification. *arXiv preprint arXiv:2306.08505*.

Shansan Gong, Mukai Li, Jiangtao Feng, Zhiyong Wu, and LingPeng Kong. 2022. Diffuseq: Sequence to sequence text generation with diffusion models. *arXiv preprint arXiv:2210.08933*.

Jonathan Ho, Ajay Jain, and Pieter Abbeel. 2020. Denoising diffusion probabilistic models. *Advances in neural information processing systems*, 33:6840–6851.

Zachary Horvitz, Ajay Patel, Chris Callison-Burch, Zhou Yu, and Kathleen McKeown. 2024. Paraguide: Guided diffusion paraphrasers for plug-and-play textual style transfer. In *Proceedings of the AAAI Conference on Artificial Intelligence*, volume 38, pages 18216–18224.

Zhiyuan Hu, Chumin Liu, Yue Feng, Anh Tuan Luu, and Bryan Hooi. 2024. Poetrydiffusion: Towards joint semantic and metrical manipulation in poetry generation. In *Proceedings of the AAAI Conference on Artificial Intelligence*, volume 38, pages 18279–18288.

Ling Li, Shaohua Li, Winda Marantika, Alex C Kot, and Huijing Zhan. 2023. Diffusion-exr: Controllable review generation for explainable recommendation via diffusion models. *arXiv preprint arXiv:2312.15490*.

Xiang Li, John Thickstun, Ishaan Gulrajani, Percy S Liang, and Tatsunori B Hashimoto. 2022. Diffusion-lm improves controllable text generation. *Advances in Neural Information Processing Systems*, 35:4328–4343.

Guangyi Liu, Yu Wang, Zeyu Feng, Qiyu Wu, Liping Tang, Yuan Gao, Zhen Li, Shuguang Cui, Julian McAuley, Eric P Xing, et al. 2024. Generating, reconstructing, and representing discrete and continuous data: Generalized diffusion with learnable encoding-decoding. *arXiv preprint arXiv:2402.19009*.

Jiamiao Liu, Pengsen Cheng, Jinqiao Dai, and Jiayong Liu. 2023. Diffucom: A novel diffusion model for comment generation. *Knowledge-Based Systems*, 281:111069.

Lei Luo and Yajing Xu. 2023. Context-aware prompt for generation-based event argument extraction with diffusion models. In *Proceedings of the 32nd ACM International Conference on Information and Knowledge Management*, pages 1717–1725.

Yuanzhen Luo, Qingyu Zhou, and Feng Zhou. 2023. Enhancing phrase representation by information bottleneck guided text diffusion process for keyphrase extraction. *arXiv preprint arXiv:2308.08739*.

Yiwei Lyu, Tiange Luo, Jiacheng Shi, Todd C Hollon, and Honglak Lee. 2023. Fine-grained text style transfer with diffusion-based language models. *arXiv preprint arXiv:2305.19512*.

Andrew L. Maas, Raymond E. Daly, Peter T. Pham, Dan Huang, Andrew Y. Ng, and Christopher Potts. 2011. Learning word vectors for sentiment analysis. In *Proceedings of the 49th Annual Meeting of the Association for Computational Linguistics: Human Language Technologies*, pages 142–150, Portland, Oregon, USA. Association for Computational Linguistics.

Alexander Quinn Nichol and Prafulla Dhariwal. 2021. Improved denoising diffusion probabilistic models. In *International conference on machine learning*, pages 8162–8171. PMLR.

Jekaterina Novikova, Ondřej Dušek, and Verena Rieser. 2017. The E2E dataset: New challenges for end-to-end generation. In *Proceedings of the 18th Annual SIGdial Meeting on Discourse and Dialogue*, pages 201–206, Saarbrücken, Germany. Association for Computational Linguistics.

Yimin Ou and Ping Jian. 2024. Effective integration of text diffusion and pre-trained language models with linguistic easy-first schedule. In *Proceedings of the 2024 Joint International Conference on Computational Linguistics, Language Resources and Evaluation (LREC-COLING 2024)*, pages 5551–5561.

Nikolay Savinov, Junyoung Chung, Mikolaj Binkowski, Erich Elsen, and Aaron van den Oord. 2021. Step-unrolled denoising autoencoders for text generation. *arXiv preprint arXiv:2112.06749*.

Yongliang Shen, Kaitao Song, Xu Tan, Dongsheng Li, Weiming Lu, and Yueting Zhuang. 2023. Diffusionner: Boundary diffusion for named entity recognition. *arXiv preprint arXiv:2305.13298*.

Mukul Singh, José Cambronero, Sumit Gulwani, Vu Le, Carina Negreanu, and Gust Verbruggen. 2023. Codefusion: A pre-trained diffusion model for code generation. *arXiv preprint arXiv:2310.17680*.

Deepak Sridhar and Nuno Vasconcelos. 2024. Prompt sliders for fine-grained control, editing and erasing of concepts in diffusion models. *arXiv preprint arXiv:2409.16535*.

Chao-Hong Tan, Jia-Chen Gu, and Zhen-Hua Ling. 2023. Diffusia: A spiral interaction architecture for encoder-decoder text diffusion. *arXiv preprint arXiv:2305.11517*.

Jianxiang Xiang, Zhenhua Liu, Haodong Liu, Yin Bai, Jia Cheng, and Wenliang Chen. 2024. Diffusiondialog: A diffusion model for diverse dialog generation with latent space. *arXiv preprint arXiv:2404.06760*.

Weijie Xu, Wenxiang Hu, Fanyou Wu, and Srinivasan Sengamedu. 2023. Detime: Diffusion-enhanced topic modeling using encoder-decoder based llm. *arXiv preprint arXiv:2310.15296*.

Shilong Yuan, Wei Yuan, Hongzhi Yin, and Tieke He. 2024. Roic-dm: Robust text inference and classification via diffusion model. *arXiv preprint arXiv:2401.03514*.

Haopeng Zhang, Xiao Liu, and Jiawei Zhang. 2023. Diffusum: Generation enhanced extractive summarization with diffusion. *arXiv preprint arXiv:2305.01735*.

Xiang Zhang, Junbo Zhao, and Yann LeCun. 2015. Character-level convolutional networks for text classification. *Advances in neural information processing systems*, 28.

Linhao Zhong, Yan Hong, Wentao Chen, Binglin Zhou, Yiyi Zhang, Jianfu Zhang, and Liqing Zhang. 2024. User-friendly customized generation with multi-modal prompts. *arXiv preprint arXiv:2405.16501*.

Wei Zou, Ziyuan Zhuang, Shujian Huang, Jia Liu, and Jiajun Chen. 2024. Enforcing paraphrase generation via controllable latent diffusion. *arXiv preprint arXiv:2404.08938*.

FaBERT: Pre-training BERT on Persian Blogs

Mostafa Masumi[◊†], Seyed Soroush Majd[◊], Mehrnoush Shamsfard[◊], and Hamid Beigy[†]

[◊]Computer Science and Engineering Department, Shahid Beheshti University
[◊]*s.majd@mail.sbu.ac.ir, m-shams@sbu.ac.ir*
[†]Computer Engineering Department, Sharif University of Technology
[†]*{m.masumi, beigy}@sharif.edu*

Abstract

We introduce FaBERT, a Persian BERT-base model pre-trained on the HmBlogs corpus, encompassing both informal and formal Persian texts. FaBERT is designed to excel in traditional Natural Language Understanding (NLU) tasks, addressing the intricacies of diverse sentence structures and linguistic styles prevalent in the Persian language. In our comprehensive evaluation of FaBERT on 12 datasets in various downstream tasks, encompassing Sentiment Analysis (SA), Named Entity Recognition (NER), Natural Language Inference (NLI), Question Answering (QA), and Question Paraphrasing (QP), it consistently demonstrated improved performance, all achieved within a compact model size. The findings highlight the importance of utilizing diverse corpora, such as HmBlogs, to enhance the performance of language models like BERT in Persian Natural Language Processing (NLP) applications. FaBERT is openly accessible at `https://huggingface.co/sbunlp/fabert`.

1 Introduction

Recently, we've seen the rise of sophisticated language models like BERT (Devlin et al., 2019), transforming the understanding of languages, including Persian. Whether designed for multiple languages or specifically for Persian, these models have been employed across various applications in Persian Natural Language Processing (NLP). Their training encompassed a diverse range of textual sources, including websites like Wikipedia and social media platforms such as Twitter, as well as news articles and academic journals.

More recently, Large Language Models (LLMs) with a substantial increase in parameters have significantly reshaped the landscape of NLP, excelling in a myriad of tasks. Despite their significant contributions, finely-tuned LMs such as BERT still demonstrate robust performance, achieving comparable results or, in many cases, even outperforming LLMs in traditional Natural Language Understanding (NLU) tasks, including Natural Language Inference (NLI), Sentiment Analysis, Text Classification, and Question Answering (QA) (Yang et al., 2023). Encoder-only models like BERT remain the workhorses of practical language processing, with applications ranging from content moderation to information retrieval systems.

Additionally, LLMs often come with the drawback of slower response times and increased latency compared to smaller models. Moreover, the use of LLMs typically demands advanced hardware, creating accessibility challenges for many users. Privacy concerns may also emerge when employing LLMs online. Notably, encoder models like BERT have found crucial roles in supporting LLM deployments, serving as efficient filters for content safety (Ji et al., 2024), performing rapid document retrieval in RAG systems (Lewis et al., 2020), and enabling cost-effective preprocessing of large-scale data (Penedo et al., 2024). Their compact size and efficient architecture make them particularly suitable for edge devices and mobile applications, where computational resources and power consumption are constrained.

Recent studies (Nguyen et al., 2020; Abdelali et al., 2021) highlight the value of incorporating informal text into training corpora, as it improves a model's ability to handle colloquial language and social media content, leading to better performance on diverse linguistic tasks.

Our motivation is to develop FaBERT, a Persian BERT model exclusively pre-trained on Persian blogs, to enhance performance in traditional NLU tasks and enable efficient processing of both formal and informal texts in the language. Blogs, which have not previously been utilized for pre-

Proceedings of the Tenth Workshop on Noisy and User-generated Text, pages 85–96
May 3, 2025

training Persian LMs, serve as a rich source of colloquial language with flexible sentence structures, idiomatic expressions, and informal lexicons inherent in everyday Persian communication. While recent models have demonstrated commendable capabilities, there still remains room for improvement, particularly in tasks involving informal Persian text. Blog content includes diverse and evolving language variations such as cultural references, informal lexicons, and slang in Persian, which have been user-generated across different demographics over a long period, contributing to FaBERT's robust performance.

Our findings reveal that pre-training on the HmBlogs corpus from Persian blogs enhances the model's performance, leading to state-of-the-art results across various downstream tasks. The main contributions of this paper are:

1. Pre-training a BERT-base model on Persian blog texts in the HmBlogs corpus and making it publicly accessible.

2. Evaluating the model's performance on 12 datasets in various downstream tasks, including sentiment analysis, irony detection, natural language inference, question paraphrasing, named entity recognition, and question answering.

The subsequent sections of the paper are structured as follows: Section 2 provides an introduction and comparison of various BERT models employed for Persian NLP. Section 3 delves into the details of our corpus, model, and its pre-training procedure. Section 4 compares FaBERT's performance in downstream tasks with other models. Finally, Section 5 concludes the paper by summarizing our findings.

2 Related Work

BERT that stands as Bidirectional Encoder Representations from Transformers, has demonstrated its exceptional abilities across a wide range of natural language understanding tasks. Unlike traditional language models that process text in a unidirectional manner (left-to-right or right-to-left), BERT considers both the left and right context of words.

BERT's pre-training involved two training objectives: Masked Language Modeling (MLM) and Next Sentence Prediction (NSP). MLM randomly masks words in a sentence, and the model learns to predict the missing words based on context, enhancing its ability to grasp the semantic meaning and relationships between words within sentences. On the other hand, in the NSP task, the model has to predict whether sentence B logically succeeds sentence A. MLM and NSP are designed for the model to learn a language representation, which can then be used to extract features for downstream tasks. Continuing the discussion, we will present a selection of Persian-language BERT models.

The most well-known Persian language model is ParsBERT (Farahani et al., 2021). It was pre-trained using both MLM and NSP tasks, utilizing a training corpus collected from 8 different sources. ParsBERT has become the preferred choice for Persian NLP tasks, thanks to its outstanding performance.

AriaBERT (Ghafouri et al., 2023) is another Persian language model that follows RoBERTa's enhancements (Liu et al., 2019) and utilizes Byte-Pair Encoding tokenizer. Its diverse training dataset, exceeding 32 gigabytes, includes conversational, formal, and hybrid texts.

Additionally, many Multilingual Language Models have been released since, and few of them include Persian. Multilingual BERT, also known as mBERT, was introduced by Devlin et al. (2019). It was trained with NSP and MLM tasks on the Wikipedia pages of 104 languages with a shared word-piece vocabulary. mBERT has shown impressive zero-shot cross-lingual transfer and is effective in utilizing task-specific annotations from one language for fine-tuning and evaluation in another. Although mBERT has shown solid performance across different languages, monolingual BERT models outperform mBERT in most downstream tasks.

Similarly, XLM-R (Conneau et al., 2019), an extension of the RoBERTa model by Facebook AI, is designed for cross-lingual understanding. This model was pre-trained with the MLM objective on a vast corpus comprising more than 2 terabytes of text from 100 languages and outperformed mBERT in many downstream tasks.

The models previously reviewed adhere to the architecture introduced by the original BERT-base model, featuring 12 layers and 12 attention heads. While maintaining this consistency, there are variations in vocabulary size among these models.

A larger vocabulary facilitates the capture of more unique tokens and their relationships, but it comes at the expense of an increased number of parameters. This, in turn, necessitates more extensive training data for learning embeddings. Conversely, smaller vocabularies may struggle to capture all the details of language, potentially causing information and context to be lost. An instance is found in the multilingual model mBERT, which supports 100 different languages with a vocabulary size of only 100,000. Despite the broad language coverage, this choice leads to a limited set of tokens for each language. Consequently, sentences are transformed into a greater number of tokens, potentially exceeding the maximum supported sequence length and resulting in the loss of information. Table 1 summarizes the vocabulary size and number of parameters for each model under consideration.

Model	Vocabulary Size (K)	# of Parameters (M)
BERT (English)	30	109
mBERT	105	167
XLM-R	250	278
ParsBERT	100	162
AriaBERT	60	132
FaBERT	50	124

Table 1: Vocabulary Size and Parameter Count of Persian BERT Models

3 Methodology

3.1 Training Corpus

The selection of an appropriate training corpus is a pivotal element in the pre-training of a language model. For this effort, we utilized the HmBlogs corpus (Khansari and Shamsfard, 2021), a collection of 20 million posts of Persian blogs over 15 years. HmBlogs includes more than 6.8 billion tokens, covering a wide range of topics, genres, and writing styles, including both formal and informal texts together.

To ensure high-quality pre-training, a series of pre-processing steps were performed on the corpus. Many posts written in the Persian alphabet were erroneously identified as Persian despite not being in the Persian language. This confusion arises from the Persian alphabet's resemblance to the alphabets of other languages like Arabic and Kurdish. Additionally, some other posts had typographical errors, very rare words, or the excessive use of local dialects. Therefore, a post-discriminator was implemented to filter out these improper and noisy posts.

Cleaning documents in Persian poses another challenge due to the presence of non-standard characters[1]. These characters look identical to Persian characters, but their different codes can cause problems during pre-training. Some Persian blogs may also use decorative characters to make the text visually appealing. Such characters were standardized to ensure uniform representation and avoid potential discrepancies. Additionally, words with repetitive characters were corrected.

3.2 Pre-training Procedure

We trained a BERT model following the architecture proposed by Devlin et al. (2019). Our BERT-base model, FaBERT, adheres to the original BERT-base architecture, consisting of 12 hidden layers, each with 12 self-attention heads.

We opted for the WordPiece tokenizer over alternatives such as BPE, as prior evidence indicates no performance improvement (Geiping and Goldstein, 2023), and with a conservative stance, we set the vocabulary size to 50,000 tokens. This decision aimed at finding a balance between capturing linguistic details and managing the computational demands associated with larger vocabularies. It's essential to note that Persian text includes half spaces, a feature absent in English. Consequently, the FaBERT tokenizer has been adapted to handle this feature, ensuring appropriate representation of texts during pre-training and fine-tuning.

The total number of parameters for FaBERT is 124 million. In comparison to other Persian and multilingual base models outlined in Table 1, FaBERT is more compact with fewer parameters.

During pre-training, each input consisted of one or more sentences sampled contiguously from a single document. The samples were of varying lengths to help the model effectively learn the positional encodings.

We implemented dynamic masking, inspired by the methodology introduced by Liu et al. (2019), and omitted the Next Sentence Prediction task from our pre-training process, as it was demonstrated to have no discernible positive impact on performance. The masking rate for dynamic masking was set to 15%. We also utilized the whole word masking approach for enhanced performance. Unlike traditional MLM, which randomly masks individual tokens in a sentence, whole word masking involves

[1]For instance, Arabic 'ي' and 'ك' are occasionally substituted for Persian 'ی' and 'ک'.

Hyperparameter	Value	Hyperparameter	Value
Batch Size	32	Total Steps	18 Million
Optimizer	Adam	Warmup Steps	1.8 Million
Learning Rate	6e-5	Precision Format	TF32
Weight Decay	0.01	Dropout	0.1

Table 2: Pre-training Hyperparameters

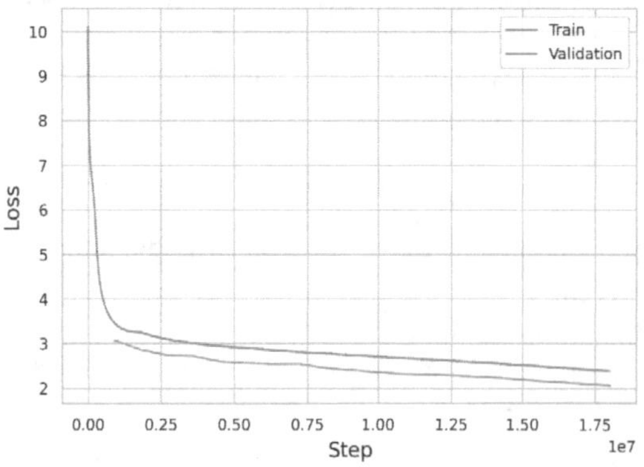

Figure 1: Train and Validation MLM loss in pre-training

masking entire words. Table 2 details the hyperparameters used in the pre-training process.

The training was conducted on a single Nvidia A100 40GB GPU, spanning a duration of 400 hours. The training data was split into 99% for training and 1% for validation. The final validation perplexity achieved was 7.76, and the train and validation loss plot is presented in Figure 1.

4 Experiments and Results

In this section, we assess the FaBERT model across four different categories of downstream tasks. For NLI and Question Paraphrasing, sentence pairs are processed to generate labels based on their relationship. In NER, entities within single input sentences are labeled at the token level. Sentiment Analysis and Irony Detection involve processing individual sentences and assigning corresponding labels. In Question Answering, models utilize a given question and the provided paragraph to generate token-level spans for answers.

For each task, we fine-tuned FaBERT and compared its performance to other state-of-the-art models, such as ParsBERT (Farahani et al., 2021), AriaBERT (Ghafouri et al., 2023), and multilingual models like mBERT (Devlin et al., 2019) and XLM-R (Conneau et al., 2019). Lastly, we analyze the effectiveness of FaBERT's tokenizer and compare it with other BERT models.

To ensure a fair comparison, all models were fine-tuned on the same datasets using consistent train/validation/test splits. For each model and dataset pair, we performed a grid search over hyperparameters, selecting the configuration that achieved the best validation score. The scores reported in this paper correspond to the test set results obtained under these optimal conditions. Details of the grid search ranges and dataset splits are provided in Appendix A.

4.1 Natural Language Inference and Question Paraphrasing

In this section, we analyze FaBERT's ability to understand logical and semantic relationships between sentences, focusing on tasks like Natural NLI and Question Paraphrasing. We assess its performance using the Farstail (Amirkhani et al., 2023), SBU-NLI (Rahimi and ShamsFard, 2024), and ParsiNLU Question Paraphrasing (Khashabi et al., 2021) datasets.

FarsTail

The FarsTail NLI dataset is sourced from multiple-choice questions from various subjects, specifically collected from Iranian university exams. Each of these questions became the basis for generating NLI instances with three different relationships: Entailment, Contradiction, and Neutral.

SBU-NLI

SBU-NLI is another dataset containing sentence pairs categorized into three labels: Entailment, Contradiction, and Neutral. This data is gathered from various sources to create a balanced dataset.

ParsiNLU Question Paraphrasing

This task involves determining the relationship between pairs of questions, specifically classifying whether they are paraphrases. The dataset is created through two means: first, by mining questions from Google auto-complete and Persian discussion forums, and second, by translating the QQP dataset with Google Translate API. As a result, some questions are presented in an informal fashion.

As observed in Table 3, FaBERT demonstrates a +1% improvement in F1 for FarsTail, comparable performance to mBERT in SBU-NLI, and a +2.88% F1 score in the informal ParsiNLU Question Paraphrasing dataset.

4.2 Named Entity Recognition

In this section, we assess the efficacy of FaBERT in NER, a commonly employed intermediate task that

Model	FarsTail	SBU-NLI	Parsi-NLU QP
ParsBERT	82.52	58.41	77.60
mBERT	83.42	66.38	79.48
XLM-R	83.50	58.85	79.74
AriaBERT	76.39	52.81	78.86
FaBERT	**84.45**	**66.65**	**82.62**

Table 3: Performance Comparison in NLI and Question Paraphrasing

Model	ParsTwiner	PEYMA	MultiCoNER v2
ParsBERT	81.13	91.24	**58.09**
mBERT	75.60	87.84	51.04
XLM-R	79.50	90.91	51.47
AriaBERT	78.53	89.76	54.00
FaBERT	**82.22**	**91.39**	57.92

Table 4: Performance Comparison in Named Entity Recognition

facilitates information extraction and entity identification within textual data. Our assessment leveraged formal and informal datasets, including ParsTwiNER (Aghajani et al., 2021), PEYMA (Shahshahani et al., 2018), and MultiCoNER v2 (Fetahu et al., 2023). The comparison of different models for each entity type is detailed in Appendix B.

ParsTwiNER

The ParsTwiNER offers a NER dataset gathered from 7632 tweets collected from the Persian Twitter accounts, offering diverse informal Persian content. Annotation by experts in natural language processing resulted in 24061 named entities across categories such as persons, organizations, locations, events, groups, and nations.

PEYMA

The PEYMA NER dataset, derived from formal text extracted from ten news websites, classifies words into different categories, encompassing persons, locations, organizations, time, date, and more. PEYMA is known as a key asset for training and evaluating NER systems in the Persian language.

MultiCoNER v2

Initially introduced as a part of SemEval task in 2022, MultiCoNER is a multilingual NER dataset crafted to address contemporary challenges in NER, such as low-context scenarios, syntactically complex entities like movie titles, and long-tail entity distributions. The enhanced version of this dataset was used in the following year as part of the SemEval 2023 task. This version, known as MultiCoNER v2, expanded these challenges by adding fine-grained entities and inserting noise in the input text. Gathered from Wikidata and Wikipedia, the dataset spans 12 languages, with Persian being the focus of our evaluations.

The evaluation metrics used include micro-F1 for PEYMA and ParsTwiNER datasets, and macro-F1 for MultiCoNER v2. Table 4 provides a detailed overview of scores achieved by each model. Across the board, all models demonstrated comparable performance in the PEYMA dataset. However, FaBERT model exhibited a slight improvement by achieving a +1.09% increase in F1 score for the informal ParsTwiNER dataset. In the MultiCoNER v2 dataset, both FaBERT and ParsBERT outperformed other models. In general FaBERT and ParsBERT seem to be great options for applications involving NER.

4.3 Sentiment Analysis and Irony Detection

In this section, we assess FaBERT's performance in classifying expressions. We employed DeepSentiPers (Sharami et al., 2020), MirasOpinion (Asli et al., 2020), and MirasIrony (Golazizian et al., 2020) datasets for evaluation.

DeepSentiPers

The DeepSentiPers dataset comprises 9,000 customer reviews of Digikala, an Iranian E-commerce platform. Originally, each sentence's polarity was annotated using a 5-class label set $E = \{-2, -1, 0, +1, +2\}$, representing sentiments from very displeased to delighted. However, our investigation revealed inconsistencies, particularly between the -1 and -2 categories for negative sentiments and the +1 and +2 categories for positive sentiments. Recognizing the overlap between these closely related labels, we opted for a simplified 3-class labeling approach, classifying sentiments as negative, neutral, or positive.

MirasOpinion

MirasOpinion, the largest Persian Sentiment dataset, comprises 93,000 reviews gathered from the Digikala platform. Through crowdsourcing, each review was labeled as Positive, Neutral, or Negative. This dataset was included in the SPARROW, a benchmark for sociopragmatic meaning understanding. Participating in the SPARROW benchmark (Zhang et al., 2023) allowed us to assess FaBERT against various language models.

MirasIrony

MirasIrony, a 2-labeled dataset designed for irony detection, encompasses 4,339 manually labeled Persian tweets. In this dataset, tweets exhibiting a disparity between their literal meaning and sentiment were labeled as positive, while those lacking this characteristic were labeled as negative. Similar to MirasOpinion, we assessed the performance of models on MirasIrony using the SPARROW benchmark.

Model	DeepSentiPers	MirasOpinion	MirasIrony
ParsBERT	74.94	86.73	71.08
mBERT	72.95	84.40	74.48
XLM-R	79.00	84.92	**75.51**
AriaBERT	75.09	85.56	73.80
FaBERT	**79.85**	**87.51**	74.82

Table 5: Performance Comparison in Sentiment Analysis and Irony Detection

Macro averaged F1 score serves as the evaluation metric for DeepSentiPers and MirasOpinion, while Accuracy is employed for MirasIrony. As presented in Table 5, FaBERT achieved the highest scores in sentiment analysis for both DeepSentiPers and MirasOpinion. For irony detection in the MirasIrony dataset, XLM-R outperforms other models, securing the leading position with a score of 75.51%. FaBERT demonstrated notable performance as well, securing the second spot with 74.82% accuracy. Through the SPARROW benchmark leaderboard, other models can be compared with FaBERT on MirasOpinion[2] and MirasIrony[3] tasks.

4.4 Question Answering

To evaluate the question-answering capabilities of FaBERT, our experiments encompassed three datasets: ParsiNLU Reading Comprehension (Khashabi et al., 2021), PQuad (Darvishi et al., 2023), and PCoQA (Hemati et al., 2023). Each dataset is briefly introduced in the following sections. Table 6 summarizes the performance of different models on each dataset.

[2]https://sparrow.dlnlp.ai/sentiment-2020-ashrafi-fas.taskshow

[3]https://sparrow.dlnlp.ai/irony-2020-golazizian-fas.taskshow

ParsiNLU Reading Comprehension Dataset

Reading Comprehension is one of the tasks introduced in the ParsiNLU benchmark and involves extracting a substring from a given context paragraph to answer a specific question. In order to create this dataset, they used Google's Autocomplete API to mine questions deemed popular by users. Starting with a seed set of questions, they repeatedly queried previous questions to expand on the set and add more sophisticated ones. After filtering out invalid questions, native annotators then chose the pertinent text span from relevant paragraphs that provided the answer to each question.

The evaluation of models on this dataset involves comparing the answers generated by the models to the provided ground truth answers. The main metrics used are the F1 score, which measures the overlap between the predicted and ground truth answers, and the exact match (EM) score, which checks if the predicted answers exactly match the ground truth answers. FaBERT scored +6.24% higher in F1 compared to other models in the ParsiNLU Reading Comprehension task.

PQuAD: A Persian question answering dataset

PQuAD is a large-scale, human-annotated question-answering dataset for the Persian language. It contains 80,000 questions based on passages extracted from Persian Wikipedia articles. The questions and their corresponding answers were generated through a crowdsourcing process, where crowdworkers were presented with passages and tasked with crafting questions and corresponding answers based on the provided content. Inspired by the structure of SQuAD 2.0 (Rajpurkar et al., 2018), PQuAD designates 25% of its questions as unanswerable, adding extra complexity to the dataset and enhancing the evaluative challenge.

In this dataset, in addition to F1 and EM scores, the evaluation can be broken down into subsets of questions that have answers (HasAns) and those that do not have answers (NoAns). By considering these metrics, the performance of different models can be compared and analyzed to determine their effectiveness in answering questions or abstaining from answering. The authors also provided an estimation of human performance by asking a group of crowdworkers to answer a subset of questions. Both FaBERT and XLM-R demonstrate remarkable capabilities in question answering, achieving a comparable F1 score performance. However, XLM-R slightly outperforms FaBERT in this aspect.

Model	ParsiNLU		PQuAD					PCoQA				
	Exact Match	F1	Exact Match	F1	HasAns EM	HasAns F1	NoAns	Exact Match	F1	HEQ-Q	HEQ-M	NoAns
ParsBERT	22.10	44.89	74.41	86.89	68.97	85.34	91.79	31.17	50.96	41.07	0.81	48.83
mBERT	26.31	49.63	73.68	86.71	67.52	84.66	**93.26**	26.89	46.11	36.94	1.63	31.62
XLM-R	21.92	42.55	**75.16**	**87.60**	69.79	86.13	92.26	34.52	51.12	44.81	0.81	54.88
AriaBERT	16.49	37.98	69.70	82.71	63.61	80.71	89.08	22.68	41.37	32.89	0	40.93
FaBERT	**33.33**	**55.87**	75.04	87.34	**70.33**	**86.50**	90.02	**35.85**	**53.51**	**45.36**	**2.45**	**61.39**
Human	-	-	80.3	88.3	74.9	85.6	96.80	85.5	86.97	-	-	-

Table 6: Performance Comparison in Question Answering

PCoQA: Persian Conversational Question Answering Dataset

PCoQA is the first dataset designed for answering conversational questions in Persian. It comprises 870 dialogs and over 9,000 question-answer pairs sourced from Wikipedia articles. In this task, contextually connected questions are posed about a given document, and models are required to respond by extracting relevant information from given paragraphs. This dataset provides a suitable context for assessing the model's performance in Persian conversational question answering, similar to the English dataset CoQA (Reddy et al., 2019).

For the PCoQA dataset, in addition to F1 and EM scores, two variants of human equivalence score (HEQ) are suggested by the authors. HEQ-Q measures the percentage of questions for which system F1 exceeds or matches human F1, and HEQ-M quantifies the number of dialogs for which the model achieves a better overall performance compared to the human. FaBERT outperformed other models with +2.39% higher F1 score, handling both answerable and unanswerable questions well. Additionally, the PCoQA dataset proves to be challenging, with all models scoring noticeably lower than humans.

4.5 Vocabulary Impact on Input Length

To evaluate the impact of FaBERT's chosen vocabulary size on its effective maximum input length, a comparative analysis was conducted across datasets with longer sentences, including MirasOpinion, FarsTail, ParsiNLU Reading Comprehension, and PQuAD. The objective was to examine how different tokenizers, including the one trained for FaBERT, influence the number of tokens in each input sentence.

Table 7 provides a summary of median token counts across the aforementioned datasets. Both multilingual models faced challenges due to the lack of sufficient Persian tokens in their vocabularies, potentially impacting their performance on longer inputs due to loss of information. ParsBERT's tokenizer yields the most compact sequences, closely followed by FaBERT. An interesting observation arises in the PQuAD dataset, where ParsBERT outperforms, likely attributed to PQuAD's reliance on Wikipedia, a significant component of ParsBERT's pre-training data.

Overall, FaBERT's tokenizer, despite having a vocabulary size half that of ParsBERT, demonstrated a comparable level of compression. The detailed boxplots for each dataset are available in Appendix C.

Tokenizer	MirasOpinion	FarsTail	ParsiNLU RC	PQuAD
ParsBERT	27	58	113.5	160
mBERT	44	85	165	235
XLM-R	34	74	142.5	210
AriaBERT	28	66	130	207
FaBERT	28	62	119.5	189

Table 7: Median Token Count Yielded by Different Tokenizers

5 Conclusion

In this paper, we pre-trained FaBERT, a BERT-base model from scratch exclusively on the diverse HmBlogs corpus, consisting solely of raw texts from Persian blogs. Notably, our model's smaller vocabulary size resulted in a more compact overall size compared to competitors. FaBERT performed exceptionally well in 12 different datasets, outperforming competitors in nine of them. In the remaining tasks where it did not secure the top position, it consistently ranked among the top performers, closely following the highest-performing model.

Our results indicate that texts with diverse writing styles, both formal and informal, found in Persian blogs can significantly contribute to the high-quality pre-training of language models, including BERT. The effectiveness of the Hmblogs corpus in the performance of our BERT model in downstream tasks demonstrates its potential for being used in pre-training both language models and large language models alongside other relevant Persian corpora. This success aligns with the broader trend in NLP where encoder-only models continue to prove their value, particularly in scenarios requiring efficient processing of large-scale text data while maintaining high performance standards.

The practical advantages of our approach – combining the efficiency of BERT's architecture with rich, diverse training data – position FaBERT as a valuable tool for Persian NLP applications, especially in resource-constrained environments where larger models may be impractical. This work not only advances Persian language processing capabilities but also reinforces the continuing relevance of carefully designed encoder models in the evolving landscape of natural language processing.

Limitations

Biases As FaBERT is trained exclusively on blog data, it inherits potential demographic and sociolinguistic biases present in Persian online communities.

Technical Constraints FaBERT, like other BERT-based architectures, is limited by the standard 512-token sequence length, which impacts its ability to process longer documents or capture long-range dependencies. While our analysis in Section 4.5 shows that FaBERT's tokenizer achieves good compression for Persian text, this architectural constraint remains a challenge. Recent innovations in transformer models have successfully addressed long-context limitations (Zhang et al., 2024), and these advancements could be adapted to Persian NLP tasks in future research.

Embedding Capabilities The Persian NLP landscape faces a scarcity of datasets and benchmarks for training and evaluating text embeddings. Although contrastive learning has demonstrated success in producing high-quality sentence embeddings for other languages, the absence of Persian-specific parallel texts and semantic similarity datasets limits progress in developing such models for Persian. This gap needs to be addressed, given the increasing importance of dense retrievers and semantic search in NLP. Future efforts should prioritize creating resources tailored for Persian sentence embeddings to advance applications such as information retrieval and semantic similarity.

References

Ahmed Abdelali, Sabit Hassan, Hamdy Mubarak, Kareem Darwish, and Younes Samih. 2021. Pre-training bert on arabic tweets: Practical considerations.

MohammadMahdi Aghajani, AliAkbar Badri, and Hamid Beigy. 2021. ParsTwiNER: A corpus for named entity recognition at informal persian. In *Proceedings of the Seventh Workshop on Noisy User-generated Text (W-NUT 2021)*, pages 131–136.

Hossein Amirkhani, Mohammad AzariJafari, Soroush Faridan-Jahromi, Zeinab Kouhkan, Zohreh Pourjafari, and Azadeh Amirak. 2023. FarsTail: A persian natural language inference dataset. *Soft Computing*, pages 1–13.

Seyed Arad Ashrafi Asli, Behnam Sabeti, Zahra Majdabadi, Preni Golazizian, Reza Fahmi, and Omid Momenzadeh. 2020. Optimizing annotation effort using active learning strategies: A sentiment analysis case study in persian. In *Proceedings of the Twelfth Language Resources and Evaluation Conference*, pages 2855–2861.

Alexis Conneau, Kartikay Khandelwal, Naman Goyal, Vishrav Chaudhary, Guillaume Wenzek, Francisco Guzmán, Edouard Grave, Myle Ott, Luke Zettlemoyer, and Veselin Stoyanov. 2019. Unsupervised cross-lingual representation learning at scale. *arXiv preprint arXiv:1911.02116*.

Kasra Darvishi, Newsha Shahbodaghkhan, Zahra Abbasiantaeb, and Saeedeh Momtazi. 2023. PQuAD: A persian question answering dataset. *Computer Speech & Language*, 80:101486.

Jacob Devlin, Ming-Wei Chang, Kenton Lee, and Kristina Toutanova. 2019. BERT: Pre-training of deep bidirectional transformers for language understanding. In *Proceedings of the 2019 Conference of the North American Chapter of the Association for Computational Linguistics: Human Language Technologies, Volume 1 (Long and Short Papers)*, pages 4171–4186, Minneapolis, Minnesota. Association for Computational Linguistics.

Mehrdad Farahani, Mohammad Gharachorloo, Marzieh Farahani, and Mohammad Manthouri. 2021. Pars-Bert: Transformer-based model for persian language understanding. *Neural Processing Letters*, 53:3831–3847.

Besnik Fetahu, Zhiyu Chen, Sudipta Kar, Oleg Rokhlenko, and Shervin Malmasi. 2023. Multi-CoNER v2: A large multilingual dataset for fine-grained and noisy named entity recognition. *arXiv preprint arXiv:2310.13213*.

Jonas Geiping and Tom Goldstein. 2023. Cramming: Training a language model on a single gpu in one day. In *International Conference on Machine Learning*, pages 11117–11143. PMLR.

Arash Ghafouri, Mohammad Amin Abbasi, and Hassan Naderi. 2023. AriaBERT: A pre-trained persian bert model for natural language understanding.

Preni Golazizian, Behnam Sabeti, Seyed Arad Ashrafi Asli, Zahra Majdabadi, Omid Momenzadeh, and Reza Fahmi. 2020. Irony detection in persian language: A transfer learning approach using emoji prediction. In *Proceedings of the Twelfth Language Resources and Evaluation Conference*, pages 2839–2845.

Hamed Hematian Hemati, Atousa Toghyani, Atena Souri, Sayed Hesam Alavian, Hossein Sameti, and Hamid Beigy. 2023. PCoQA: Persian conversational question answering dataset. *arXiv preprint arXiv:2312.04362*.

Jiaming Ji, Mickel Liu, Josef Dai, Xuehai Pan, Chi Zhang, Ce Bian, Boyuan Chen, Ruiyang Sun, Yizhou Wang, and Yaodong Yang. 2024. Beavertails: Towards improved safety alignment of llm via a human-preference dataset. *Advances in Neural Information Processing Systems*, 36.

Hamzeh Motahari Khansari and Mehrnoush Shamsfard. 2021. HmBlogs: A big general persian corpus. *arXiv preprint arXiv:2111.02362*.

Daniel Khashabi, Arman Cohan, Siamak Shakeri, Pedram Hosseini, Pouya Pezeshkpour, Malihe Alikhani, Moin Aminnaseri, Marzieh Bitaab, Faeze Brahman, Sarik Ghazarian, et al. 2021. ParsiNLU: A suite of language understanding challenges for persian. *Transactions of the Association for Computational Linguistics*, 9:1147–1162.

Patrick Lewis, Ethan Perez, Aleksandra Piktus, Fabio Petroni, Vladimir Karpukhin, Naman Goyal, Heinrich Küttler, Mike Lewis, Wen-tau Yih, Tim Rocktäschel, et al. 2020. Retrieval-augmented generation for knowledge-intensive nlp tasks. *Advances in Neural Information Processing Systems*, 33:9459–9474.

Yinhan Liu, Myle Ott, Naman Goyal, Jingfei Du, Mandar Joshi, Danqi Chen, Omer Levy, Mike Lewis, Luke Zettlemoyer, and Veselin Stoyanov. 2019. Roberta: A robustly optimized bert pretraining approach. *arXiv preprint arXiv:1907.11692*.

Dat Quoc Nguyen, Thanh Vu, and Anh Tuan Nguyen. 2020. BERTweet: A pre-trained language model for English tweets. In *Proceedings of the 2020 Conference on Empirical Methods in Natural Language Processing: System Demonstrations*, pages 9–14, Online. Association for Computational Linguistics.

Guilherme Penedo, Hynek Kydlíček, Anton Lozhkov, Margaret Mitchell, Colin Raffel, Leandro Von Werra, Thomas Wolf, et al. 2024. The fineweb datasets: Decanting the web for the finest text data at scale. *arXiv preprint arXiv:2406.17557*.

Zeinab Rahimi and Mehrnoush ShamsFard. 2024. A knowledge-based approach for recognizing textual entailments with a focus on causality and contradiction. *Available at SSRN 4526759*.

Pranav Rajpurkar, Robin Jia, and Percy Liang. 2018. Know what you don't know: Unanswerable questions for squad. *arXiv preprint arXiv:1806.03822*.

Siva Reddy, Danqi Chen, and Christopher D Manning. 2019. Coqa: A conversational question answering challenge. *Transactions of the Association for Computational Linguistics*, 7:249–266.

Mahsa Sadat Shahshahani, Mahdi Mohseni, Azadeh Shakery, and Heshaam Faili. 2018. PEYMA: A tagged corpus for persian named entities. *arXiv preprint arXiv:1801.09936*.

Javad PourMostafa Roshan Sharami, Parsa Abbasi Sarabestani, and Seyed Abolghasem Mirroshandel. 2020. Deepsentipers: Novel deep learning models trained over proposed augmented persian sentiment corpus. *arXiv preprint arXiv:2004.05328*.

Jingfeng Yang, Hongye Jin, Ruixiang Tang, Xiaotian Han, Qizhang Feng, Haoming Jiang, Bing Yin, and Xia Hu. 2023. Harnessing the power of llms in practice: A survey on chatgpt and beyond. *arXiv preprint arXiv:2304.13712*.

Chiyu Zhang, Khai Duy Doan, Qisheng Liao, and Muhammad Abdul-Mageed. 2023. The skipped beat: A study of sociopragmatic understanding in llms for 64 languages. *arXiv preprint arXiv:2310.14557*.

Xin Zhang, Yanzhao Zhang, Dingkun Long, Wen Xie, Ziqi Dai, Jialong Tang, Huan Lin, Baosong Yang, Pengjun Xie, Fei Huang, et al. 2024. mgte: Generalized long-context text representation and reranking models for multilingual text retrieval. In *Proceedings of the 2024 Conference on Empirical Methods in Natural Language Processing: Industry Track*, pages 1393–1412.

Appendix For "FaBERT: Pre-training BERT on Persian Blogs"

A Fine-tuning Hyperparameters

The hyperparameters employed for fine-tuning the models on each dataset, along with the respective train/validation/test split sizes, are outlined in Table 8. For the ParsiNLU benchmark, we adhered to the predefined hyperparameters in the ParsiNLU source code.

B Detailed NER Results

Tables 9, 10, and 11 present F1 scores for entities in PEYMA, MultiCoNER v2, and ParsTwiNER datasets, providing a model comparison for each entity. For instance, In MultiCoNER v2, FaBERT excels in recognizing medical entities, and ParsBERT is better at identifying creative works.

C Tokenizer Comparison Figures

Figures 2, 3, 4, and 5 illustrate the distribution of token counts for each model's tokenizer across the following datasets: PQuAD, ParsiNLU Reading Comprehension, MirasOpinion, and FarsTail. These boxplots provide a visual representation of the variation in token counts for each model.

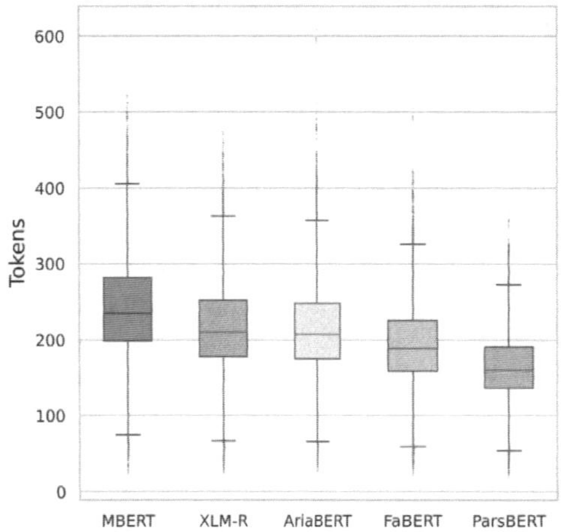

Figure 2: Token count distribution across tokenizers for the PQuAD dataset

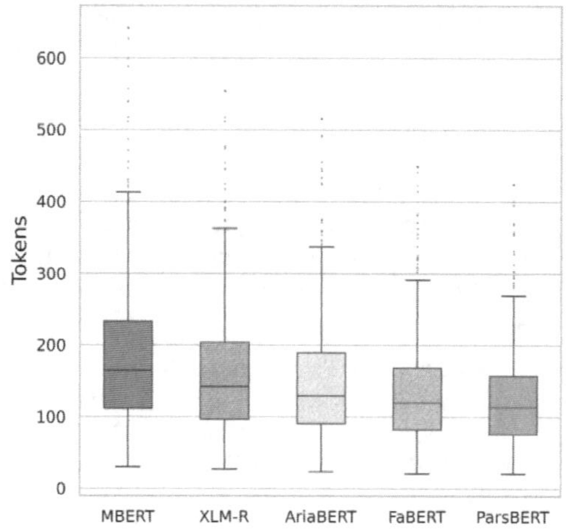

Figure 3: Token count distribution across model tokenizers for the ParsiNLU Reading Comprehension dataset

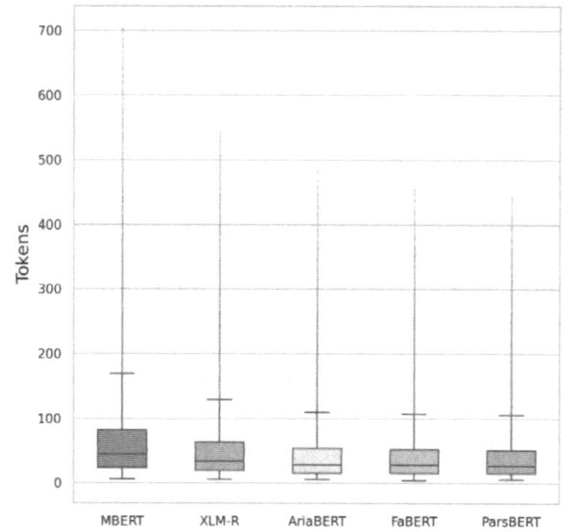

Figure 4: Token count distribution across tokenizers for the MirasOpinion dataset

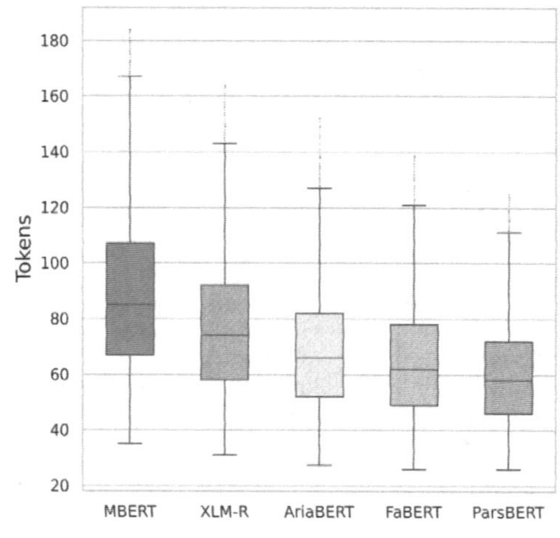

Figure 5: Token count distribution across tokenizers for the FarsTail dataset

Datasets	Train	Validation	Test	Number of Labels	Metrics	Learning Rate	Batch Size	Epochs	Warmup
DeepSentiPers	6320	703	1854	3	Macro F1	2e-5, 3e-5, 5e-5	8,16	3, 7	0, 0.2
MirasOpinion	75094	9387	9387	3	Macro F1	2e-5, 3e-5, 5e-5	8,16	1	0, 0.2
MirasIrony	2352	295	294	2	Accuracy	2e-5, 3e-5, 5e-5	8,16	3, 5	0, 0.2
PQuAD	63994	7976	8002	-	Micro F1	2e-5, 3e-5, 5e-5	8,16	2	0, 0.2
PCoQA	6319	1354	1354	-	Micro F1	3e-5, 5e-5	8,16	3, 7	0, 0.2
ParsiNLU RC	600	125	575	-	Micro F1	3e-5, 5e-5	4	3, 7	0
SBU-NLI	3248	361	401	3	Micro F1	2e-5, 3e-5, 5e-5	8,16	3, 7	0, 0.2
FarsTail	7266	1564	1537	3	Micro F1	2e-5, 3e-5, 5e-5	8,16	3, 7	0, 0.2
ParsiNLU QP	1830	898	1916	2	Micro F1	3e-5, 5e-5	8,16	3, 7	0
PEYMA	8029	926	1027	-	Macro F1	2e-5, 3e-5, 5e-5	8,16	3, 7	0, 0.2
MultiCoNER v2	16321	855	219168	-	Micro F1	2e-5, 3e-5, 5e-5	8,16	3, 7	0, 0.2
ParsTwiNER	6418	447	304	-	Micro F1	2e-5, 3e-5, 5e-5	8,16	3, 7	0, 0.2

Table 8: Dataset Split Sizes and Fine-Tuning Hyperparameters

Entity Type	FaBERT	ParsBERT	AriaBERT	mBERT	XLM-R	Support
Date	89.16	85.65	85.11	84.56	86.73	208
Location	91.95	91.73	91.46	90.25	92.42	595
Currency	94.34	94.34	83.64	90.57	96.15	26
Organization	88.24	89.37	86.38	84.83	87.25	667
Percent	98.63	98.63	93.33	97.14	94.74	36
Person	95.45	95.29	94.6	90.1	95.75	434
Time	96.97	91.43	96.97	76.47	94.12	16
Micro Average	91.39	91.24	89.76	87.84	90.91	1982
Macro Average	93.53	92.35	90.21	87.7	92.45	1982
Weighted Average	91.37	91.23	89.75	87.81	90.92	1982

Table 9: Comparison of F1 Scores for Each Entity Type in PEYMA

Entity Type	FaBERT	ParsBERT	AriaBERT	mBERT	XLM-R	Support
Event	0.5714	0.4444	0.4118	0.4865	0.2308	14
Location	0.8281	0.8414	0.7991	0.7802	0.8088	221
Nation	0.9	0.7385	0.7246	0.7123	0.7397	30
Organization	0.7364	0.6966	0.6691	0.6462	0.7126	129
Person	0.9344	0.8893	0.8745	0.8216	0.8629	244
Political Group	0.6364	0.6667	0.7442	0.7	0.8	22
Micro Average	0.8222	0.8113	0.7853	0.756	0.795	660
Macro Average	0.7301	0.7128	0.7039	0.6911	0.6925	660
Weighted Average	0.8238	0.8119	0.7881	0.7573	0.7943	660

Table 10: Comparison of F1 Scores for Each Entity Type in ParsTwiNER

Entity Type	FaBERT	ParsBERT	AriaBERT	mBERT	XLM-R	Support
AerospaceManufacturer	0.7325	0.7127	0.7196	0.6269	0.638	1030
ORG	0.5809	0.5832	0.5348	0.5479	0.5325	18532
MusicalGRP	0.6282	0.6597	0.59	0.613	0.5954	4668
PrivateCorp	0.3822	0.4033	0.3851	0.2605	0.1749	148
CarManufacturer	0.6511	0.7031	0.6631	0.6291	0.6147	2085
PublicCorp	0.6109	0.6377	0.5819	0.5439	0.562	5926
SportsGRP	0.8159	0.8174	0.8012	0.8046	0.7949	6418
Medication/Vaccine	0.7067	0.6837	0.6342	0.6324	0.6582	4405
MedicalProcedure	0.6307	0.5965	0.5592	0.4904	0.5471	2132
AnatomicalStructure	0.6079	0.5827	0.5151	0.4824	0.4978	3940
Symptom	0.5656	0.5368	0.4671	0.4217	0.4109	821
Disease	0.646	0.6256	0.5737	0.5264	0.5652	3989
Artist	0.7384	0.7347	0.6936	0.7122	0.7155	51617
Politician	0.5786	0.6056	0.534	0.5213	0.5141	19760
Scientist	0.3328	0.3669	0.2952	0.2615	0.2625	3278
SportsManager	0.606	0.6232	0.5376	0.4332	0.4494	3009
Athlete	0.5796	0.5992	0.5356	0.5119	0.5357	12551
Cleric	0.5707	0.5535	0.4875	0.4627	0.4332	4526
OtherPER	0.4254	0.4225	0.3544	0.3647	0.3449	21127
Clothing	0.3912	0.3375	0.3293	0.2054	0.2716	239
Drink	0.5244	0.5683	0.5483	0.4646	0.5041	631
Food	0.6063	0.5971	0.574	0.4788	0.5591	3580
Vehicle	0.5388	0.5388	0.5171	0.4659	0.4952	2865
OtherPROD	0.5851	0.5843	0.5453	0.5109	0.5233	10897
ArtWork	0.0919	0.1085	0.1057	0.1077	0.0691	100
WrittenWork	0.5561	0.5541	0.5028	0.5006	0.5079	13530
VisualWork	0.7447	0.7463	0.7095	0.7445	0.7523	25054
Software	0.6448	0.6586	0.5991	0.5913	0.5911	8058
MusicalWork	0.5408	0.5714	0.5239	0.5492	0.545	6292
Facility	0.5673	0.5671	0.5283	0.5317	0.5347	11393
Station	0.7997	0.7863	0.7812	0.784	0.781	2532
HumanSettlement	0.7608	0.7676	0.7517	0.7658	0.7647	55741
OtherLOC	0.37	0.3348	0.3413	0.2965	0.2376	1241
Micro Average	0.6451	0.6517	0.6081	0.6108	0.6145	312115
Macro Average	0.5792	0.5809	0.54	0.5104	0.5147	312115
Weighted Average	0.6491	0.6531	0.6101	0.6111	0.6131	312115

Table 11: Comparison of F1 Scores for Each Entity Type in MultiCoNER v2

Automatically Generating Chinese Homophone Words to Probe Machine Translation Estimation Systems

Shenbin Qian, Constantin Orăsan, Diptesh Kanojia and Félix do Carmo

Centre for Translation Studies and Institute for People-Centred AI,
University of Surrey, United Kingdom
{s.qian, c.orasan, d.kanojia, f.docarmo}@surrey.ac.uk

Abstract

Evaluating machine translation (MT) of user-generated content (UGC) involves unique challenges such as checking whether the nuance of emotions from the source are preserved in the target text. Recent studies have proposed emotion-related datasets, frameworks and models to automatically evaluate MT quality of Chinese UGC, without relying on reference translations. However, whether these models are robust to the challenge of preserving emotional nuances has been left largely unexplored. To address this gap, we introduce a novel method inspired by information theory which generates challenging Chinese homophone words related to emotions, by leveraging the concept of *self-information*. Our approach generates homophones that were observed to cause translation errors in emotion preservation, and exposes vulnerabilities in MT systems and their evaluation methods when tackling emotional UGC. We evaluate the efficacy of our method using human evaluation for the quality of these generated homophones, and compare it with an existing one, showing that our method achieves higher correlation with human judgments. The generated Chinese homophones, along with their manual translations, are utilized to generate perturbations and to probe the robustness of existing quality evaluation models, including models trained using multi-task learning, fine-tuned variants of multilingual language models, as well as large language models (LLMs). Our results indicate that LLMs with larger size exhibit higher stability and robustness to such perturbations. We release[1] our data and code for reproducibility and further research.

1 Introduction

Machine translation (MT) of Chinese-English news articles has been claimed to achieve human parity in recent years (Hassan et al., 2018). However, research on machine translation of user-generated content (UGC) like tweets has revealed additional challenges including problems with handling slang, emotion, and literary devices like sarcasm and euphemisms (Saadany et al., 2023), as shown in the example translated by ChatGPT[2] and Google Translate in Figure 1. Evaluating MT quality of such texts has become a challenging and urgent task for the improvement their translation quality (Qian et al., 2024c).

Traditional ways of evaluating MT quality involve metrics such as BLEU (Papineni et al., 2002), BLEURT (Sellam et al., 2020) or BERTScore (Zhang et al., 2019) to compare the MT output with one or several reference translations. When references are unavailable, quality estimation (QE) methods are often used to predict scores which approximate human evaluation (Specia et al., 2018). One approach for QE is fine-tuning multilingual pre-trained language models (PTLMs) using human evaluation scores. Frameworks like Multi-dimensional Quality Metrics (MQM) (Lommel et al., 2014), an error-based evaluation scheme, are commonly employed to obtain the human evaluation scores for this purpose.

For machine translation of UGC, Qian et al. (2023) recruited professional translators to evaluate translations of a Chinese UGC dataset using Google Translate, based on an MQM-adapted framework. They found that homophone slang words used by netizens are the most common cause of errors in the translation of emotions. They proposed different types of QE models based on fine-tuning, multi-task learning (MTL) and large language models (LLMs) for automatic evaluation (Qian et al., 2024c,b) and claimed that their models achieved state-of-the-art performance in evaluating MT quality of UGC. In this paper, we investigate whether their models are robust enough to cope with newly generated homophones or human-

[1] `https://github.com/surrey-nlp/homo_gen`

[2] Using `https://chatgpt.com/` in December 2024.

Proceedings of the Tenth Workshop on Noisy and User-generated Text, pages 97–107
May 3, 2025

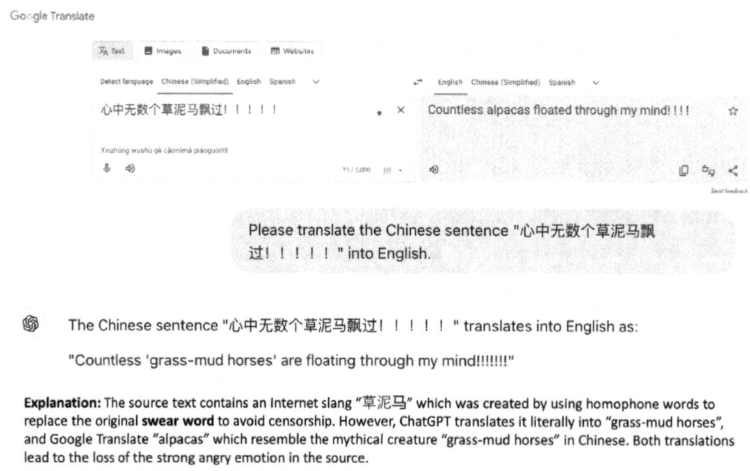

Figure 1: An example of the challenges for translating Chinese UGC

improved translations.

In this regard, we propose a method to automatically generate Chinese homophone words to probe the robustness of these QE systems towards new homophone words and human-improved translations. Our contributions can be summarized as follows:

- We leverage *self-information* in information theory for the generation of Chinese homophones that can be used to replace the original word to create new slang, as a novel method.
- We compare the proposed method with an existing one using *percentile score*. We evaluate the two methods based on human evaluation and show that our approach achieves a higher correlation with it.
- We utilize generated homophone words and human-improved translations as perturbed examples to probe existing QE models. Our analysis reveals that larger LLMs exhibit greater stability and robustness to our perturbations.

The rest of the paper is organized as follows: Section 2 reviews related work on quality evaluation of UGC and Chinese homophone words. Section 3 introduces the main dataset used in this study. Section 4 details the existing generation approach, our proposed method, and the human evaluation and perturbation methods. Section 5 presents and discusses the results of these evaluations. Section 6 concludes the study and outlines future directions, while Section 7 addresses limitations and ethical considerations.

2 Related Work

Section 2.1 provides an overview of related work on the evaluation of UGC translation, and Section 2.2 explores studies focused on Chinese UGC and the generation of homophones.

2.1 Evaluation of UGC Translation

Despite the tremendous improvement of translation quality since the use of neural machine translation, MT systems still struggle when translating emotion-loaded UGC such as tweets. Saadany et al. (2023) analyzed machine translation of tweets for 6 language pairs and found that hashtags, slang, and non-standard orthography are the most prominent causes of translation errors. Different from the language pairs covered by Saadany et al. (2023), Qian et al. (2023) analyzed the English translation of Chinese microblog texts. They found that about 50% of their data have translation errors in emotion preservation and about 41% are major and critical errors. Among the causes of errors, emotion-carrying slang that contains homophones is the most frequent cause.

To take errors in emotion into consideration during evaluation, Saadany et al. (2021) proposed a sentiment-aware measure for evaluating sentiment transfer by MT systems. Using human evaluation data based on MQM, Qian et al. (2024c,b) trained and proposed a series of QE models that can automatically assess MT quality in terms of emotion preservation. They fine-tuned and continued fine-tuned multilingual PTLMs based on TransQuest (Ranasinghe et al., 2020) and COMET (Rei et al., 2020; Stewart et al., 2020; Rei et al., 2022), two commonly-used QE frameworks. They also utilized the Nash (Navon et al., 2022) and Aligned (Senushkin et al., 2023) MTL losses to train models that can perform sentence- and word-level QE concurrently. With the recent advancement of LLMs, Qian et al. (2024b) proposed to prompt and parameter-efficiently fine-tune LLMs for quality estimation of emotion-loaded UGC. They claimed to achieve state-of-the-art results using LLMs for evaluation. However, none of these papers answered the question: *Are these models robust to new homophone slang words?* For this purpose, we propose a method to automatically generate homophone words to test the robustness of their systems.

2.2 Chinese Homophone Words

There have been extensive debates about what a word is in Chinese in both natural language processing and linguistic studies, as Chinese does not have a clear delimiter for word boundaries like spaces in English. Researchers have tried to define words in Chinese from different perspectives. Di Sciullo and Williams (1987) defines the concept of 'word' as the 'listedness' characteristic of lexical items, but the 'listedness' criterion fails to include many Chinese words created recently. In Chinese, usually characters, not words, are listed in lexical dictionaries. Another common way of characterizing the notion of 'word' is to use semantic criteria which define a word as the smallest standalone unit that carries meaning. However, reducing concepts of a word to their semantic primitives is an extremely difficult task (Packard, 2000). From a morphological perspective, a word can be defined as the output of word-formation rules in the language (Di Sciullo and Williams, 1987). As morphological objects are an important construct for Chinese, lots of word-like entities derived using word-formation rules but are not defined by other criteria, can be included as words by this definition. A huge amount of Internet slang created by netizens using word-formation rules such as homophone substitution can be seen as words under this definition.

Homophone substitution refers to the method which uses words or characters pronounced alike but spelt or written differently, and having different meanings from the original word or character (Meng, 2011), as explained in the example "尼玛" in § 4.1. It is extensively used in many fields in China, such as toponymy or anthroponymy (Kałużyńska, 2018), as there are so many homophones in Chinese, given it is a tonal language. Although there are studies working on this particular linguistic phenomenon (Meng, 2011; Chu and Ruthrof, 2017; Kałużyńska, 2018), to the best of our knowledge, only Hiruncharoenvate et al. (2015) have proposed a method to automatically generate homophones using percentile scores (see § 4.1 for more details). In order to explore how to generate homophone words that are more likely to be used by netizens, we propose to use *self-information* (Shannon, 1948) based on the log probability from language models. We compare our method with the existing one via human evaluation, and utilize those generated homophones as perturbations to test the robustness of QE systems proposed by Qian et al. (2024c,b).

3 Data

We used the Human Annotated Dataset for Quality Assessment of Emotion Translation (HADQAET)[3] from Qian et al. (2023) to sample UGC that contains Chinese homophone slang for automatic generation. HADQAET was chosen because, 1) its source texts contain many homophone slang; 2) it has quality evaluation data such as QE scores for the MT texts, error words related to emotion preservation and reference translations, and 3) there are QE systems trained on it (explained in § 4.3).

The source texts of HADQAET originated from the dataset released by the *Evaluation of Weibo Emotion Classification Technology on the Ninth China National Conference on Social Media Processing* (SMP2020-EWECT). It originally has a size of 34,768 instances. Each instance is a tweet-like text segment in Chinese, which was manually annotated with one of the six emotion labels, *i.e.*, *anger*, *joy*, *sadness*, *surprise*, *fear* and *neutral* (Guo et al., 2021). Qian et al. (2023) randomly kept 5,538 instances and used Google Translate to translate them to English. To evaluate translation quality for emotion preservation, they proposed an emotion-related MQM framework and recruited two professional translators to annotate errors and their corresponding severity. Words/characters in both source and target that cause errors were highlighted for error analysis. In addition, they hired a translation company to post-edit the MT output to get reference translations (Qian et al., 2024a). More details about HADQAET can be found in Qian et al. (2023).

We tokenized the source texts using *jieba* (Sun,

[3] `https://github.com/surrey-nlp/HADQAET`

Homophone Slang Causing Errors	Human Translation	Frequencies
尼玛(nima)	(f**k) your mother	60
特么(tama)	what's the f**k	51
卧槽(wocao)	f**k	22
草泥马(caonima)	f**k your mother	22
劳资(laozi)	I	12
In total	/	167

Table 1: Homophone slang words that cause translation errors and their frequencies in HADQAET.

2013) and extracted the words that were highlighted as causes of error. Following Qian et al. (2023), we made a frequency list of these error words and picked those that contain homophone slang with a frequency higher than 10, under the supervision of a Chinese native speaker. This produced a list of 5 homophone slang words (as shown in Table 1) that are most likely to cause translation errors. They were used in this paper to generate homophones that can be used interchangeably in the original source text. We selected the instances (167 in total) containing the 5 homophone slang words from HADQAET, including the source, MT outputs, evaluation data and reference translations to probe trained QE systems and test how robust they are. Methods for homophone generation are presented in § 4.1. Methods to create perturbed data for robustness test are described in § 4.4.

4 Methodology

This section presents our methodology for homophone generation and the evaluation of generated homophones in § 4.1 and § 4.2, respectively. QE models for robustness test as well as the perturbation methods are elaborated in § 4.3 and § 4.4.

4.1 Homophone Generation

Algorithm 1 Homophone generation

Input: W : words for which to generate homophone
Output: $\tilde{W}$: homophones of W
Candidate: C : a set of character combinations that might be $\tilde{W}$, *i.e.* $\tilde{W} \in C$
Corpus: D : dictionary of character frequency in Weibo
For w_i in W **do**
  $w_{iroot} \leftarrow Latinize(w_i)$
  $C_{w_i} = \{Concat(DeLatinize(c^j_{w_i})\ for\ c^j_{w_i}\ in\ w_{iroot})\}$
  Optional: $C_{w_i} \leftarrow$ filter C_{w_i} by D
  $\tilde{W} \leftarrow pick(C_{w_i})$
End for
Return $\tilde{W}$

The method to generate homophone words is shown in Algorithm 1. Since Chinese is a logographic language, we need to Latinize Chinese words into alphabets to get their pronunciation. For example, we can convert the slang "尼玛" (see Table 1 for its meaning) into "nima" using *Pinyin*, a system to transcribe Mandarin Chinese sounds into Latin alphabets. The Latinized words such as "nima", which are the root sounds/words (denoted as w_{iroot}) of the original words, can correspond to many different Chinese written words[4]. We can easily generate numerous different character combinations that bear the same or similar sounds (with different tones) using the root sounds. However, many of them may not make sense and are unlikely to be used in real-world scenarios. We call them candidates (denoted as C_{w_i}) of our final output. We introduced a $pick()$ function explained in the following subsections to select those that are more likely to be used by netizens.

Generation of Candidates After Latinization, we get the root sound of each Chinese character in the original word, *i.e.*, $c^j_{w_i}$. We gathered all Chinese characters (logographs) of the same root sound (Latin alphabets) by using the Chinese character dictionary in *jieba* for de-Latinization. A simple concatenation of each character in the same word can lead to a set of candidates, C_{w_i}. For example, the slang word "尼玛" has two characters, "尼" *ni* and "玛" *ma*, and each has a long list of homophone characters such as "你" or "泥" for *ni* and "吗" or "嘛" for *ma*. To reduce the number of candidates, we first created a dictionary (denoted as D) of character frequency using the full SMP2020-EWECT corpus. Then we selected character combinations whose frequency are higher than 100 to filter out those infrequent words. This resulted in a set of 172 candidates (34.4 for each) of the 5 selected homophone slang that frequently cause translation errors in emotion preservation.

Picking Candidates by Percentile Score We used the method proposed by Hiruncharoenvate et al. (2015) as our baseline to pick candidates, which is explained in Algorithm 2. For each candidate h in the set C_{w_i}, we summed up the frequency of each character c^i_h in candidate/hypothesis h, using the frequency dictionary D. We ranked them by the aggregate frequency F_h in an ascending order for each of the 5 selected slang words. The percentile score $P_{score^{w_i}}$ can be computed by dividing

[4]The root sound has four different tones. Each corresponds to many different characters/words.

the index of a candidate in $C_{w_i sorted}$ by the number of candidates in it and multiplying 100. The output homophone words can be generated by picking the top k samples.

Algorithm 2 Picking candidates by percentile score

Input: C : sets of candidates for w_i in W
Output: $\tilde{W}$: generated homophones
Corpus: D : dictionary of character frequency in Weibo
For h in C_{w_i} **do**
  $F_h = \sum_{i=1}^{N} freq(c_h^i)$ for c_h^i in h, where $c_h^i \in D$
End for
$C_{w_i sorted} \leftarrow$ sort C_{w_i} by F_h
$P_{score^{w_i}} = \{\frac{index}{length(C_{w_i sorted})} * 100\ for\ index\ in\ C_{w_i sorted}\}$
$\tilde{W} \leftarrow P_{score^{w_i}}[1:k]$
Return $\tilde{W}$

Picking Candidates by Self-information We propose to pick candidates by self-information as shown in Equation 1, where $P(x)$ is the probability of an event x (a word in the candidates in our case) and $I(x)$ is the self-information, which quantifies how informative an event is. Our assumption is that the generated word should be informative and unique, and at the same time not infrequent. We employed language models including the Chinese RoBERTa (Cui et al., 2020) and the Qwen1.5 series (1.8B, 4B and 7B) models (Qwen Team, 2024) to get the log probability for our candidates.

$$I(x) = -\log_2(P(x)) \quad (1)$$

4.2 Evaluation of Homophone Words

We recruited two annotators who are frequent users of the Chinese microblogging platform, *Weibo* to rate the 172 generated homophone words from 1 to 5. A score of 5 means the generated homophone can completely replace the one in the original text. A score of 1 means it can not replace the original one at all. A score of 3 is somewhere in between, meaning that the generated homophone can replace the original one, but it may take time for some readers to accept such usage.

The human evaluation was carried out in two scenarios: with (given the source microblog text) and without context (given the generated homophone along with its original word) to test if context is a factor that influences the effectiveness of the generated homophones.

We used the Spearman correlation score (Spearman, 1904) to measure how the percentile and the self-information scores are correlated with the human rated scores to compare between the two methods. We also computed the Spearman correlation score between the scores of the two human annotators for references (see § 5.1 for results).

To provide a quantitative complement to human evaluation, we fine-tuned the Chinese RoBERTa$_{large}$ model (Cui et al., 2020) on the SMP2020-EWECT dataset, creating an emotion classifier that achieved a macro F1 score of 0.95. Manual validation of 100 random samples confirmed the classifier's reliability, yielding an F1 score of 0.90. We then used this classifier to assess whether the predicted emotion labels remained consistent when original homophone slang was replaced with our generated homophone words.

4.3 QE Models for Robustness Test

Since models proposed by Qian et al. (2024c,b) were all trained on HADQAET, we selected two fine-tuned (FT) models based on TransQuest and COMETKIWI (Rei et al., 2022) respectively, one continued fine-tuned (CFT) model based on TransQuest, two MTL models based on the Nash loss, and two instruction-tuned LLMs including Mixtral-8x7B (Jiang et al., 2024) and Deepseek-67B[5], as well as two parameter-efficiently fine-tuned LLMs using QLoRA (Dettmers et al., 2023), *i.e.*, FT-Yi-34B and FT-Deepseek-67B. They were selected to test how robust QE models are in terms of the newly generated homophone slang words.

4.4 Perturbation Methods

We propose two perturbation methods to test the robustness of the selected QE models.

4.4.1 Method 1: Robustness to Homophones

Method 1 is to test the robustness of the QE models to our generated homophones, which were among the most frequent causes of translation errors.

We selected the 167 instances from HADQAET that contain the 5 slang words in the source and replaced them with top 5 generated homophone words in human evaluation (see Table 8 in Appendix A). Everything else remained unchanged. This led to 5 groups of the 167 instances, namely, **M1G1** to **M1G5**[6]. The QE scores produced by the selected models for the 5 groups should be more or less the same as the scores of the original source-MT group, namely, **G0**, if the models are robust.

[5]https://www.deepseek.com/

[6]G1 to G5 are in a ranked order based on human evaluation.

We compared the Spearman and Pearson's correlation scores among the groups for evaluation.

4.4.2 Method 2: Robustness to Improved Translations

Method 2 is to test the robustness of the QE models to translations of improved quality.

We asked a professional translator to correct only the translation of the homophone slang in the MT output for these 167 instances to form a perturbation group, *i.e.*, **M2G1**. We also replaced the entire MT output with a human reference translation for the selected instances to form another perturbation group, *i.e.*, **M2G2**. M2G1 and M2G2 are used to compare with **G0** to see the increase of QE scores, since theoretically better translations should have higher QE scores.

We calculated the percentage of the instances that see an increase of QE scores produced by the selected models to evaluate their robustness to translations of improved quality.

5 Results and Discussion

This section presents and discusses the results of evaluation of our generated homophone words as well as the results of our perturbation methods.

5.1 Evaluation of Generated Homophones

We conducted human evaluation of the generated homophone words under two scenarios: **with** and **without** context. Results are displayed in Tables 2 and 3, respectively.

Methods	Annotator 1	Annotator 2	Avg
I using Chinese RoBERTa	0.1257	0.1205	0.1304
I using Qwen1.5-1.8B	0.1957	0.1938	0.1952
I using Qwen1.5-4B	0.2251	0.2040	0.2215
I using Qwen1.5-7B	**0.2799**	**0.2300**	**0.2647**
Percentile score	-0.0220	-0.1219	-0.0877

Table 2: Spearman correlation scores of self-formation (I) obtained on the Chinese RoBERTa, Qwen1.5 series models and the percentile score with scores annotated **with** context by Annotator 1, 2 and their average.

With Context We can see from Table 2 that the Spearman correlation scores of the percentile score method are extremely low for scores of both annotators and the average score. Our self-information method improves the correlation with human annotators remarkably. This is particularly obvious when we used larger models to get the log probability, since Spearman correlation scores increase steadily when larger models are used.

We also computed the Spearman correlation score between the two annotators as a reference to human-level correlation. Spearman correlation for the human rated scores is 0.6441, which is still higher than our method using self-information.

Methods	Annotator 1	Annotator 2	Avg
I using Chinese RoBERTa	0.2050	0.3160	0.3018
I using Qwen1.5-1.8B	0.1837	0.3475	0.2867
I using Qwen1.5-4B	0.2197	0.3550	0.3156
I using Qwen1.5-7B	**0.2379**	**0.3743**	**0.3286**
Percentile score	0.0867	0.1516	0.1537

Table 3: Spearman correlation scores of self-formation (I) obtained on the Chinese RoBERTa, Qwen1.5 series models and the percentile scores with scores annotated **without** context by Annotator 1, 2 and their average.

Group	Precision	Recall	F1 Score	Same Label
M1G1	0.8892	0.8862	0.8675	0.8863
M1G2	0.8976	0.9042	0.8904	0.9042
M1G3	0.8618	0.8802	0.8634	0.8802
M1G4	0.8192	0.8802	0.8480	0.8802
M1G5	0.8860	0.8862	0.8764	0.8862

Table 4: Precision, recall, F1 score and percentage of instances that have the same label (same label) compared with the original human-annotated emotion label.

Without Context Table 3 re-affirms our results in Table 2: the self-information method obvious surpasses the percentile score method in Spearman correlation for all language models.

The Spearman score for the human rated scores without context is 0.6367, which is similar to that of with context, but is closer to our self-information method (0.3286), compared with the evaluation with context (0.6441 *vs* 0.2647). This may be because Chinese is a context-dependent language (Stallings, 1975) and adding context to the generated homophone words might have an impact on the understanding of their individual meaning.

Emotion Label after Replacement We predicted the emotion label of the 167 instances that have been replaced with the 5 generated homophone words in M1G1 to M1G5 in § 4.4.1. Results are shown in Table 4.

Table 4 indicates that the F1 scores of all groups are very close to the human validated score (0.90) of the emotion classifier. Close to 90% of the instances remain the same emotion label as that of the original source text before homophone replacement. This indicates that our generated homophone

Groups	FT-COMETKIWI		FT-TransQuest		CFT-TransQuest		MTL-XLM-V$_{base}$		MTL-XLM-R$_{large}$	
	ρ	r	ρ	r	ρ	r	ρ	r	ρ	r
G0	0.2617	0.3211	0.2518	0.2954	0.2853	0.3219	0.2179	0.2139	0.1958	0.1841
M1G1	-3.59%	-6.13%	+5.79%	+2.51%	-8.55%	-7.21%	-1.83%	+5.03%	-2.30%	-95.88%
M1G2	-0.50%	-4.05%	+8.21%	+6.43%	-5.06%	-4.90%	+13.58%	+10.26%	-2.76%	-22.98%
M1G3	+2.94%	+1.99%	+0.77%	+2.20%	-9.46%	-6.40%	+1.29%	-3.23%	-5.61%	+1.30%
M1G4	+5.85%	+3.21%	+7.17%	+9.62%	-16.57%	-13.37%	+11.92%	+6.79%	-2.20%	+1.09%
M1G5	+1.34%	-3.45%	+9.99%	+7.74%	-14.09%	-12.84%	+0.09%	+4.67%	+0.82%	-49.17%

Table 5: Spearman ρ and Pearson's r correlation scores of the perturbation groups in Method 1 on fine-tuned COMETKIWI (FT-COMETKIWI), TransQuest (FT-TransQuest) and continued fine-tuned TransQuest (CFT-TransQuest) models, and MTL models based on XLM-V$_{base}$ and XLM-R$_{large}$. The values for M1G1–M1G5 are percentage changes compared to G0. Original values can be found in Table 9 in Appendix A.

Groups	Mixtral 8x7B		Deepseek-67B		FT-Yi-34B		FT-Deepseek-67B	
	ρ	r	ρ	r	ρ	r	ρ	r
G0	0.1886	0.1984	0.2073	0.1338	0.3413	0.3485	0.2802	0.2469
M1G1	-51.73%	-131.45%	-8.39%	-34.39%	+21.09%	+21.18%	-17.20%	+11.62%
M1G2	-59.97%	-131.45%	-26.04%	-54.52%	-23.22%	-22.85%	-4.43%	-1.01%
M1G3	-71.46%	-58.79%	-4.63%	+7.70%	-14.47%	-12.51%	-6.53%	+12.60%
M1G4	-60.18%	-84.36%	-56.35%	-96.49%	-16.86%	-18.94%	+25.91%	+55.24%
M1G5	-35.41%	-131.35%	-37.83%	+0.30%	-44.92%	-36.41%	+5.71%	+33.86%

Table 6: Spearman ρ and Pearson's r correlation scores of the perturbation groups in Method 1 on LLMs and fine-tuned (FT) LLMs as listed in Section 4.3. For M1G1–M1G5, values are expressed as percentage changes relative to G0. Original values can be found in Table 10 in Appendix A.

words evaluated by human annotators are reliable in terms of predicting the emotion labels.

5.2 Results of Perturbation Methods

Method 1 Tables 5 and 6 show the results of our perturbation Method 1, *i.e.*, whether QE models trained by Qian et al. (2024c,b) are robust or stable to the generated homophone words, which are most frequent in causing translation errors.

Table 5 presents results obtained on fine-tuned (FT) COMETKIWI, fine-tuned (FT) TransQuest and continued fine-tuned (CFT) TransQuest models as well as MTL models based on XLM-V$_{base}$ (Liang et al., 2023) and XLM-R$_{large}$ (Conneau et al., 2020). In each model, **G0** serves as a baseline or reference, but we also assess how stable the scores remain across **M1G1** to **M1G5** by reporting how much the score has changed in relation to G0 in percentages. For instance, if an M1G1 correlation score deviates greatly from G0 or from the adjacent group M1G2, we consider that "fluctuation". We can see from the table that Spearman correlation scores of M1G1-M1G5 for MTL models, especially MTL-XLM-R$_{large}$, fluctuate less than those of the FT or CFT models. This indicates that they are relatively more stable in predicting QE scores when tested with the generated homophone words.

Table 6 shows results obtained on LLMs, including prompting LLMs for quality evaluation and fine-tuning (FT) LLMs as quality evaluators. We observe that using LLMs for QE is less stable in terms of score prediction. When we replace the original slang with our generated ones in the source, the correlation scores tend to fluctuate more than those of fine-tuned or MTL models. Among these LLMs, larger models seem to be better at generating consistent QE scores than smaller ones, since Spearman scores of Deekseek-67B or its fine-tuned version fluctuate less than those of Mixtral 8x7B and FT-Yi-34B among the perturbation groups.

Models	M2G1 (%)	M2G2 (%)
FT-COMETKIWI	23.35	53.29
FT-TransQuest	45.86	56.35
CFT-TransQuest	33.15	45.30
MTL-XLM-V$_{base}$	49.72	35.91
MTL-XLM-R$_{large}$	75.69	67.40
Mixtral 8x7B	67.40	63.54
Deepseek-67B	56.91	74.03
FT-Yi-34B	85.64	83.98
FT-Deepseek-67B	81.77	89.50

Table 7: Percentage of instances that see a QE score increase after the MT output was improved as described in Method 2.

Method 2 Table 7 displays the percentage of instances that see an increase of the predicted QE scores after replacing the MT output with improved translations.

Since MT outputs in M2G2 were replaced with reference translations, the percentage of instances that have increased predicted scores should be higher than those of M2G1, where only translation of the homophone slang was corrected. Comparing between the two groups, we find that for fine-tuned COMETKIWI and TransQuest models, though the percentages are usually lower than 50%, they are higher in M2G2 than in M2G1. Whereas for MTL models, the percentages of instances that have increased scores in M2G2 are lower than those of M2G1, indicating that they are less robust towards improved translations. For LLMs, larger models such as Deepseek-67B and its fine-tuned version see an increase of the percentage of the instances that have increased scores for M2G2, whereas smaller models do not.

Among all these QE models, LLMs such as FT-Yi-34B and FT-Deepseek-67B are more likely to produce increased scores when the translation quality is improved, like the cases in M2G1 and M2G2, since more than half of the instances experienced a score increase. This is consistent with the results from Table 6, which suggest that LLMs are prone to change their score prediction when the input has been changed. LLMs with large size outperform other QE models in two ways: they better reflect improvements in machine translation quality, and they maintain consistent scores when original homophone slang in the source text is replaced with generated alternatives.

5.3 Discussion

We observe that although our LLM-based self-information method lags behind human evaluation, it is much better than the existing percentile score method for automatically generating Chinese homophone words. Due to the context-dependent nature of the Chinese language, correlation scores to human evaluation with context can be lower than those of without context. More experiments and examples are needed for the validation of this point.

When assessing the robustness of QE models, we find that LLM-based QE models are more likely to change their prediction scores when the input is changed. When the translation quality is improved, they are more likely to produce increased scores than fine-tuned COMETKIWI or TransQuest models or MTL models. However, when the original homophone words are replaced with our generated ones (for which human evaluation indicates they are acceptable), LLM-based models are more likely to change their predicted scores as well. LLMs with a larger size such as DeepSeek-67B and its fine-tuned versions achieved a good balance between producing consistent scores to generated homophone words and increased scores to improved translations, exhibiting great stability and robustness to our perturbations in all groups.

6 Conclusion and Future Work

This paper investigates how robust emotion-related QE systems are towards emotion-loaded homophone words. For this purpose, we proposed to use self-information to automatically generate and select Chinese homophone words that frequently cause translation errors. We evaluated the efficacy of our method based on human evaluation and compared it with the baseline, percentile score. We find that our method can achieve higher correlation with human evaluation than the baseline. We picked 5 generated homophone words and replaced the original homophones with our generated ones in the source as perturbations to test the robustness of the QE systems trained by Qian et al. (2024c,b), including fine-tuned COMETKIWI, TransQuest and MTL models as well as LLMs. At the same time, we replaced the MT output with improved translations to test how robust QE systems are towards improved translations. Our results indicate that LLMs with a larger size such as DeepSeek-67B exhibited great stability and robustness to all our perturbation groups. For future work, we plan to generate homophones at a larger scale and invite more linguists to evaluate their usefulness in real-world scenarios on social media.

7 Limitations and Ethical Considerations

Due to the size of the HADQAET dataset, only 167 samples that contain 5 most frequent words causing translation errors were selected in the paper. This size of test set is comparatively smaller than other robustness tests. We will generate more homophone words for testing in our future work.

The experiments in the paper were conducted using publicly available datasets. New data were created based on those publicly available datasets using computer algorithms. No ethical approval was required. The use of all data in this paper follows the licenses in (Qian et al., 2023).

References

Yingchi Chu and Horst Ruthrof. 2017. The social semiotic of homophone phrase substitution in Chinese netizen discourse. *Social Semiotics*, 27:640–655.

Alexis Conneau, Kartikay Khandelwal, Naman Goyal, Vishrav Chaudhary, Guillaume Wenzek, Francisco Guzmán, Edouard Grave, Myle Ott, Luke Zettlemoyer, and Veselin Stoyanov. 2020. Unsupervised cross-lingual representation learning at scale. In *Proceedings of the 58th Annual Meeting of the Association for Computational Linguistics*, pages 8440–8451, Online. Association for Computational Linguistics.

Yiming Cui, Wanxiang Che, Ting Liu, Bing Qin, Shijin Wang, and Guoping Hu. 2020. Revisiting pre-trained models for Chinese natural language processing. In *Findings of the Association for Computational Linguistics: EMNLP 2020*, pages 657–668, Online. Association for Computational Linguistics.

Tim Dettmers, Artidoro Pagnoni, Ari Holtzman, and Luke Zettlemoyer. 2023. QLoRA: Efficient Finetuning of Quantized LLMs. In *Advances in Neural Information Processing Systems*, volume 36, pages 10088–10115. Curran Associates, Inc.

A. Di Sciullo and E. Williams. 1987. *On the Definition of Word*. Cambridge, MA: MIT Press.

Xianwei Guo, Hua Lai, Yan Xiang, Zhengtao Yu, and Yuxin Huang. 2021. Emotion Classification of COVID-19 Chinese Microblogs based on the Emotion Category Description. In *Proceedings of the 20th China National Conference on Computational Linguistics*, pages 916–927. Chinese Information Processing Society of China.

Hany Hassan, Anthony Aue, Chang Chen, Vishal Chowdhary, Jonathan Clark, Christian Federmann, Xuedong Huang, Marcin Junczys-Dowmunt, William Lewis, Mu Li, Shujie Liu, Tie-Yan Liu, Renqian Luo, Arul Menezes, Tao Qin, Frank Seide, Xu Tan, Fei Tian, Lijun Wu, Shuangzhi Wu, Yingce Xia, Dongdong Zhang, Zhirui Zhang, and Ming Zhou. 2018. Achieving human parity on automatic chinese to english news translation. *arXive preprint*.

Chaya Hiruncharoenvate, Zhiyuan Lin, and Eric Gilbert. 2015. Algorithmically bypassing censorship on sina weibo with nondeterministic homophone substitutions. *Proceedings of the International AAAI Conference on Web and Social Media*, 9(1):150–158.

Albert Q. Jiang, Alexandre Sablayrolles, Antoine Roux, Arthur Mensch, Blanche Savary, Chris Bamford, Devendra Singh Chaplot, Diego de las Casas, Emma Bou Hanna, Florian Bressand, Gianna Lengyel, Guillaume Bour, Guillaume Lample, Lélio Renard Lavaud, Lucile Saulnier, Marie-Anne Lachaux, Pierre Stock, Sandeep Subramanian, Sophia Yang, Szymon Antoniak, Teven Le Scao, Théophile Gervet, Thibaut Lavril, Thomas Wang, Timothée Lacroix, and William El Sayed. 2024. Mixtral of experts.

Irena Kałużyńska. 2018. Substitution by homophones in chinese and changes to old street names in beijing after 1949. *Onomastica*, No 62:273–280.

Davis Liang, Hila Gonen, Yuning Mao, Rui Hou, Naman Goyal, Marjan Ghazvininejad, Luke Zettlemoyer, and Madian Khabsa. 2023. XLM-V: Overcoming the vocabulary bottleneck in multilingual masked language models. *arXive preprint*.

Arle Richard Lommel, Aljoscha Burchardt, and Hans Uszkoreit. 2014. Multidimensional Quality Metrics: A Flexible System for Assessing Translation Quality. *Tradumàtica: tecnologies de la traducció*, 0:455–463.

Bingchun Meng. 2011. From Steamed Bun to Grass Mud Horse: E Gao as alternative political discourse on the Chinese Internet. *Global Media and Communication*, 7:33–51.

Aviv Navon, Aviv Shamsian, Idan Achituve, Haggai Maron, Kenji Kawaguchi, Gal Chechik, and Ethan Fetaya. 2022. Multi-task learning as a bargaining game. In *Proceedings of the 39th International Conference on Machine Learning*, volume 162 of *Proceedings of Machine Learning Research*, pages 16428–16446. PMLR.

Jerome L. Packard. 2000. *The Morphology of Chinese : A Linguistic and Cognitive Approach*. Cambridge University Press.

Kishore Papineni, Salim Roukos, Todd Ward, and Wei-Jing Zhu. 2002. Bleu: a method for automatic evaluation of machine translation. In *Proceedings of the 40th Annual Meeting of the Association for Computational Linguistics*, pages 311–318, Philadelphia, Pennsylvania, USA. Association for Computational Linguistics.

Shenbin Qian, Constantin Orasan, Felix Do Carmo, Qiuliang Li, and Diptesh Kanojia. 2023. Evaluation of Chinese-English machine translation of emotion-loaded microblog texts: A human annotated dataset for the quality assessment of emotion translation. In *Proceedings of the 24th Annual Conference of the European Association for Machine Translation*, pages 125–135, Tampere, Finland. European Association for Machine Translation.

Shenbin Qian, Constantin Orasan, Félix Do Carmo, and Diptesh Kanojia. 2024a. Evaluating machine translation for emotion-loaded user generated content (TransEval4Emo-UGC). In *Proceedings of the 25th Annual Conference of the European Association for Machine Translation (Volume 2)*, pages 43–44, Sheffield, UK. European Association for Machine Translation (EAMT).

Shenbin Qian, Constantin Orasan, Diptesh Kanojia, and Félix Do Carmo. 2024b. Are large language models state-of-the-art quality estimators for machine translation of user-generated content? In *Proceedings of the Eleventh Workshop on Asian Translation (WAT 2024)*, pages 45–55, Miami, Florida, USA. Association for Computational Linguistics.

Shenbin Qian, Constantin Orasan, Diptesh Kanojia, and Félix Do Carmo. 2024c. A multi-task learning framework for evaluating machine translation of emotion-loaded user-generated content. In *Proceedings of the Ninth Conference on Machine Translation*, pages 1140–1154, Miami, Florida, USA. Association for Computational Linguistics.

Qwen Team. 2024. Introducing qwen1.5.

Tharindu Ranasinghe, Constantin Orasan, and Ruslan Mitkov. 2020. TransQuest: Translation quality estimation with cross-lingual transformers. In *Proceedings of the 28th International Conference on Computational Linguistics*, pages 5070–5081, Barcelona, Spain (Online). International Committee on Computational Linguistics.

Ricardo Rei, Craig Stewart, Ana C Farinha, and Alon Lavie. 2020. COMET: A neural framework for MT evaluation. In *Proceedings of the 2020 Conference on Empirical Methods in Natural Language Processing (EMNLP)*, pages 2685–2702, Online. Association for Computational Linguistics.

Ricardo Rei, Marcos Treviso, Nuno M. Guerreiro, Chrysoula Zerva, Ana C Farinha, Christine Maroti, José G. C. de Souza, Taisiya Glushkova, Duarte Alves, Luisa Coheur, Alon Lavie, and André F. T. Martins. 2022. CometKiwi: IST-unbabel 2022 submission for the quality estimation shared task. In *Proceedings of the Seventh Conference on Machine Translation (WMT)*, pages 634–645, Abu Dhabi, United Arab Emirates (Hybrid). Association for Computational Linguistics.

Hadeel Saadany, Constantin Orăsan, Emad Mohamed, and Ashraf Tantavy. 2021. Sentiment-aware measure (SAM) for evaluating sentiment transfer by machine translation systems. In *Proceedings of the International Conference on Recent Advances in Natural Language Processing (RANLP 2021)*, pages 1217–1226, Held Online. INCOMA Ltd.

Hadeel Saadany, Constantin Orasan, Rocio Caro Quintana, Felix Do Carmo, and Leonardo Zilio. 2023. Analysing mistranslation of emotions in multilingual tweets by online MT tools. In *Proceedings of the 24th Annual Conference of the European Association for Machine Translation*, pages 275–284, Tampere, Finland. European Association for Machine Translation.

Thibault Sellam, Dipanjan Das, and Ankur Parikh. 2020. BLEURT: Learning robust metrics for text generation. In *Proceedings of the 58th Annual Meeting of the Association for Computational Linguistics*, pages 7881–7892, Online. Association for Computational Linguistics.

D. Senushkin, N. Patakin, A. Kuznetsov, and A. Konushin. 2023. Independent component alignment for multi-task learning. In *2023 IEEE/CVF Conference on Computer Vision and Pattern Recognition (CVPR)*, pages 20083–20093, Los Alamitos, CA, USA. IEEE Computer Society.

Claude. E. Shannon. 1948. A mathematical theory of communication. *The Bell System Technical Journal*.

Charles Spearman. 1904. The proof and measurement of association between two things. *The American Journal of Psychology*, 15:72–101.

Lucia Specia, Carolina Scarton, and Gustavo Henrique Paetzold. 2018. *Quality Estimation for Machine Translation*. Spinger, Cham, Germany.

William Stallings. 1975. The morphology of chinese characters: A survey of models and applications. *Computers and the Humanities*, 9(1):13–24.

Craig Stewart, Ricardo Rei, Catarina Farinha, and Alon Lavie. 2020. COMET - deploying a new state-of-the-art MT evaluation metric in production. In *Proceedings of the 14th Conference of the Association for Machine Translation in the Americas (Volume 2: User Track)*, pages 78–109, Virtual. Association for Machine Translation in the Americas.

Andy Sun. 2013. Jieba. `https://github.com/fxsjy/jieba`.

Tianyi Zhang, Varsha Kishore, Felix Wu, Kilian Q. Weinberger, and Yoav Artzi. 2019. Bertscore: Evaluating text generation with bert.

A Appendix

Original	Generated	Avg Score
尼玛	你妈	5.00
	尼妈	3.75
	泥马	3.50
	尼马	2.75
	泥玛	2.50
特么	他妈	5.00
	她妈	5.00
	它妈	4.00
	踏妈	3.50
	他玛	1.50
卧槽	我操	5.00
	我艹	5.00
	窝艹	3.75
	窝操	3.25
	我草	3.25
劳资	老子	5.00
	老资	3.50
	老自	2.00
	劳子	1.75
	劳自	1.50
草泥马	艹泥马	5.00
	操你妈	4.50
	艹你妈	4.50
	草你妈	3.75
	草尼妈	3.75

Table 8: Original vs our generated top 5 homophone words and their average human evaluation scores (Avg Score) with and without context.

Groups	FT-COMETKIWI		FT-TransQuest		CFT-TransQuest		MTL-XLM-V$_{base}$		MTL-XLM-R$_{large}$	
	ρ	r	ρ	r	ρ	r	ρ	r	ρ	r
G0	0.2617	0.3211	0.2518	0.2954	0.2853	0.3219	0.2179	0.2139	0.1958	0.1841
M1G1	0.2523	0.3014	0.2664	0.3028	0.2609	0.2987	0.2139	0.2247	0.1913	0.0076
M1G2	0.2604	0.3081	0.2725	0.3144	0.2709	0.3061	0.2475	0.2358	0.1904	0.1419
M1G3	0.2694	0.3276	0.2537	0.3019	0.2583	0.3013	0.2207	0.2070	0.1848	0.1865
M1G4	0.2770	0.3315	0.2698	0.3238	0.2380	0.2788	0.2439	0.2284	0.1915	0.1861
M1G5	0.2652	0.3100	0.2770	0.3183	0.2451	0.2806	0.2181	0.2239	0.1974	0.0935

Table 9: Original Spearman ρ and Pearson's r correlation scores of the perturbation groups in Method 1 on fine-tuned COMETKIWI (FT-COMETKIWI), TransQuest (FT-TransQuest) and continued fine-tuned TransQuest (CFT-TransQuest) models and multi-task learning (MTL) models based on XLM-V$_{base}$ and XLM-R$_{large}$.

Groups	Mixtral 8x7B		Deepseek-67B		FT-Yi-34B		FT-Deepseek-67B	
	ρ	r	ρ	r	ρ	r	ρ	r
G0	0.1886	0.1984	0.2073	0.1338	0.3413	0.3485	0.2802	0.2469
M1G1	0.0910	-0.0625	0.1899	0.0878	0.4133	0.4223	0.2320	0.2756
M1G2	0.0755	-0.0625	0.1533	0.0609	0.2620	0.2689	0.2678	0.2444
M1G3	0.0538	0.0817	0.1977	0.1441	0.2919	0.3049	0.2619	0.2780
M1G4	0.0751	0.0310	0.0905	0.0047	0.2838	0.2825	0.3528	0.3833
M1G5	0.1218	-0.0624	0.1289	0.1342	0.1880	0.2216	0.2962	0.3305

Table 10: Original Spearman ρ and Pearson's r correlation scores of the perturbation groups in Method 1 on **LLMs** and **fine-tuned (FT) LLMs** as listed in Section 4.3.

Multi-BERT: Leveraging Adapters for Low-Resource Multi-Domain Adaptation

Parham Abed Azad
Department of Computer Engineering
Sharif University of Technology
Tehran, Iran
parhamabedazad@sharif.edu

Hamid Beigy
Department of Computer Engineering
Sharif University of Technology
Tehran, Iran
beigy@sharif.edu

Abstract

Multi-domain text analysis presents significant challenges, particularly in Persian name entity recognition (NER). Using a single model for multiple domains often fails to capture the specific features of different domains. That is why many scientists have focused on prompting chatbots for this issue. However, studies show that these models do not achieve remarkable results in NER tasks without proper fine-tuning while training and storing a chatbot is extremely costly. This paper presents a new approach using one core model with various sets of domain-specific parameters. By using techniques like LoRAs and pre-fix tuning, along with extra layers, we train each set of trainable parameters for a specific domain. This allows the model to perform as well as individual models for each domain. Tests on various formal and informal datasets show that by using these added parameters, the proposed model performs much better than existing practical models. The model needs only one instance for storage but achieves excellent results across all domains. This paper also examines each adaptation strategy, outlining its strengths, weaknesses, and the best settings and hyperparameters for Persian NER. Lastly, this study introduces a new document-based domain detection system for situations where text domains are unknown. This novel pipeline enhances the adaptability and practicality of the proposed approach for real-world applications.

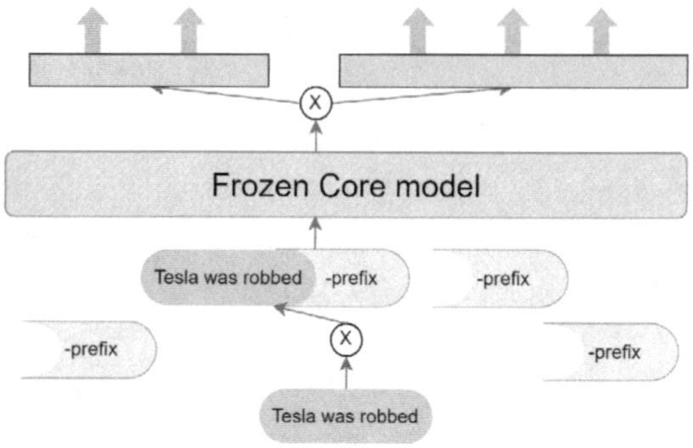

Figure 1: Each set of parameters belongs to exactly one domain but layers are often shared by a couple of domains.

1 Introduction

Named entity recognition (NER) is an essential part of natural language processing (NLP) that helps in many tasks like information extraction or question answering. Recently, NER has become even more important, thanks to the increased interest in NLP, which gave birth to many new challenges. One of the most pressing challenges is the adaptation of NER models to the ever-expanding text domains. This task becomes particularly difficult as model sizes and inference times increase. The dynamic nature of natural languages coupled with the diverse topics and contexts, presents a formidable challenge. Especially, for languages like Persian since there is a huge difference between texts found on formally written sites like Wikipedia and informally written texts from social media posts, even when those posts are made from official pages like universities. When we look closer, it becomes evident that models trained within a specific textual domain often achieve worse results when confronted with data from other domains. This performance gap shows that many sentences require different entity labels based on their specific context. For instance, consider the sentence "Tesla was robbed": in a scientific or historical context, "Tesla" would likely be tagged as a person, whereas in discussions related to business or economics, or within the context of a casual tweet, "Tesla" would be categorized as an organization. This ambiguity poses one of the primary challenges in accurately identifying entities, particularly within specialized fields such as medicine (Kundeti et al., 2016).

Traditionally, the preferred approach was to train a single transformer model for all domains. The model would be trained in a way that performs

Proceedings of the Tenth Workshop on Noisy and User-generated Text, pages 108–116
May 3, 2025

well in all domains. However, while we praise these models for performing well without knowing the text domain, these models tend to perform worse than models trained on a single domain. This problem has stimulated the exploration of different strategies to overcome the barriers posed by adapting to multiple domains in NER. An additional challenge associated with this approach arises from the limitation of a single model to produce outputs in only one format. Certain domains may require different sets of labels, leading to the necessity for varied output formats tailored to each domain's needs. The adoption of multiple models to accommodate various domains introduces significant drawbacks, including resource-intensive requirements such as extensive RAM and storage constraints, as well as the time-consuming process of training each instance. Moreover, training a model for one task should inherently contribute to the understanding and performance improvement of another.

To deal with these challenges many have turned to prompt engineering of generative models such as OpenAI's ChatGPT. However, studies show that without fine-tuning, these models underperform fine-tuned models by a large margin in many NLP tasks such as NER (Abaskohi et al., 2024). Furthermore, training these models requires a lot of computational resources. and a huge sum of data to train the model. This problem is extremely exacerbated when we look at the languages that are suffering from a lack of well-labeled and clean data such as the Persian language. We delve deeper into the details of these models in section 2.

Therefore, a novel approach is proposed. This model offers an innovative solution to address these challenges by leveraging adapters. We incorporate specific parameters for each domain and create individual output layers to produce distinct outputs for each domain. Subsequently, the added parameters and the output layers are trained for each domain. Therefore, each set of these parameters and layers is only used for certain domains. This allows the model to perform perfectly in all domains. Given access to a robust pre-trained model, the core model is frozen; however, it can also be trained during the training process if a pre-trained model is unavailable, the layers are shared between multiple domains, and the adapters are each only used for a single domain. Remarkably, even when facing limited data availability, we observe a significant performance boost compared to other models. Finally, we introduce an innovative approach for situations where the domain is unknown.

The rest of this paper is organized as follows: section 2 gives a brief overview of the related projects that try to solve these issues. Thereafter, section 3 explains the proposed architecture of the multi-Bert model and the model will be thoroughly evaluated in section 4. Moreover, section 5 will propose a novel pipeline that deals with the issues that arise from not knowing the exact domain of the texts, while section 6 concludes the paper and section 7 talks about the future possibilities.

2 Related work

Named entity recognition has always been a popular task in NLP. Many new papers like PUnifiedNER advocate for customizing and training a generative LLM model capable of understanding diverse text domains and label sets (Lu et al., 2023). By incorporating a lot of information into prompts and leveraging extensive training data, this model demonstrates a remarkable capability to label various data types with diverse labels. However, other papers focus on the development of template-free models utilizing few-shot learning. These studies introduced models that, with a minimal set of labeled examples (typically 16, 32, or 64), can adeptly label texts (Wang et al., 2022; Lu et al., 2023; He et al., 2023; Ma et al., 2022). However, these papers still fine-tuned the model. In fact, it is shown that for some NLP tasks like NER fine-tuning the model is a crucial step and solely relying on prompt engineering results in subpar results (Li et al., 2023). Furthermore, Our experiments with ChatGPT on Arman and ParsTwiNER datasets have resulted in much worse performance compared to Bert models. This is in line with other scientific research done with LLMs like Abaskohi's benchmarking of ChatGPT which achieved decent results on tasks like question answering while getting extremely low results on token classification tasks. (Abaskohi et al., 2024).

At the forefront of Persian NER, current state-of-the-art models include BeheshtiNER (Taher et al., 2020) and ParsBERT (Farahani et al., 2021). a BERT model fine-tuned for NER tasks. Recent advancements in Persian NER have predominantly focused on fine-tuning models to cater to diverse domains. Outstanding examples of this strategy include ParsTwiNER (Aghajani et al., 2021), a BERT model fine-tuned for informal and formal texts.

However, as seen in this paper, while the model outperforms the original ParsBert on informal text, it underperforms on the formal dataset, Arman. Another example is Hengam, a BERT model tailored for token classification in the tagging of formal and informal texts. As seen, these models exhibit notable drawbacks, such as prolonged training times and diminished performance in previous domains when adapting to new ones. The need for more efficient and adaptable models remains an ongoing concern within the landscape of Persian NER research.

3 The proposed method

To mitigate the challenges posed by time and size constraints inherent in employing multiple models, a model called multi-Bert is presented. In multi-Bert, a single pre-trained model is completely frozen, while multiple sets of additional parameters and layers are integrated into the model. This configuration allows for the generation of diverse results from a single model. Moreover, this design facilitates training for specific tasks without modifying the underlying base model, thereby safeguarding the performance of one task from affecting another. However, while the domain-specific parameters are completely separate from each other, we use pre-training for each set of parameters on other sets of data. This approach allows us to leverage any correlating information that can aid the model's performance. As seen in figure 1, the model allows the selection of task-specific parameters during inference, tailoring the model's behavior to the requirements of each individual task.

A significant advantage of multi-Bert is its efficient use of adapters compared to traditional fine-tuning methods. Adapters accelerate the training process (He et al., 2021), reducing the time required for each epoch and enabling model convergence in fewer than 10 epochs. This efficiency allows us to employ a two-step training approach: first, pre-training one set of parameters on all available data, and then fine-tuning a copy of these parameters for each specific task of interest. By leveraging task-specific data, we can effectively utilize cross-task information during fine-tuning.

To incorporate these parameters we utilize adapters. After exploring various methods and adapters the most effective techniques were selected. The first chosen adapter is Prefix-tuning (Li and Liang, 2021). Prefix tuning is a technique where a small set of learnable parameters, known as a prefix, is embedded directly into the input of all layers of a pre-trained language model. This allows the model to rapidly adapt to task-specific information without the need to fine-tune all the model parameters. The prefix acts as a continuous task-specific vector that can influence the behavior of the model across all layers, providing a lightweight and efficient way to customize large language models for specific tasks. It has been shown to achieve comparable performance to full model fine-tuning while requiring the tuning of only a tiny fraction of the parameters By leveraging the structured nature of prompts, this approach facilitates prompt-driven learning, a crucial aspect in multi-domain scenarios. On the other hand, for adapters, we employ the well-known Low-rank adaptation method, also known as LoRA (Hu et al., 2022). This method yields comparable results by incorporating learnable parameters into the model layers. LoRA focuses on preserving adaptability without compromising the integrity of the base model. By adding parameters to each layer without introducing new ones, LoRAs have emerged as highly reliable adapters. Their efficiency lies in seamlessly integrating new parameters into existing layers, yielding impressive results within a short time frame, and facilitating straightforward merging of the new parameters with the existing layers.

Additionally, a classification layer is introduced based on the required number of classes. In cases where tasks share the same output structure, both the size of output and the specific labels, this layer can be shared among them. Conversely, for tasks with differing output structures, we accommodate multiple final layers tailored to each task's unique requirements. This streamlined approach not only addresses the challenges associated with multiple models but also provides flexibility in adapting to diverse task requirements. The effectiveness of multi-Bert is validated through comprehensive evaluations utilizing various parameter addition methods and task-specific classification layers.

We use a fine-tuned core model, ParsBert which is arguably the best pre-trained Bert model. There are a lot of different models pre-trained for the Persian language and each one can be used. However, based on our calculations ParsBert performs the best for the NER tasks. Therefore, ParsBert was used in this study and due to the high performance of this model, it was frozen throughout the training

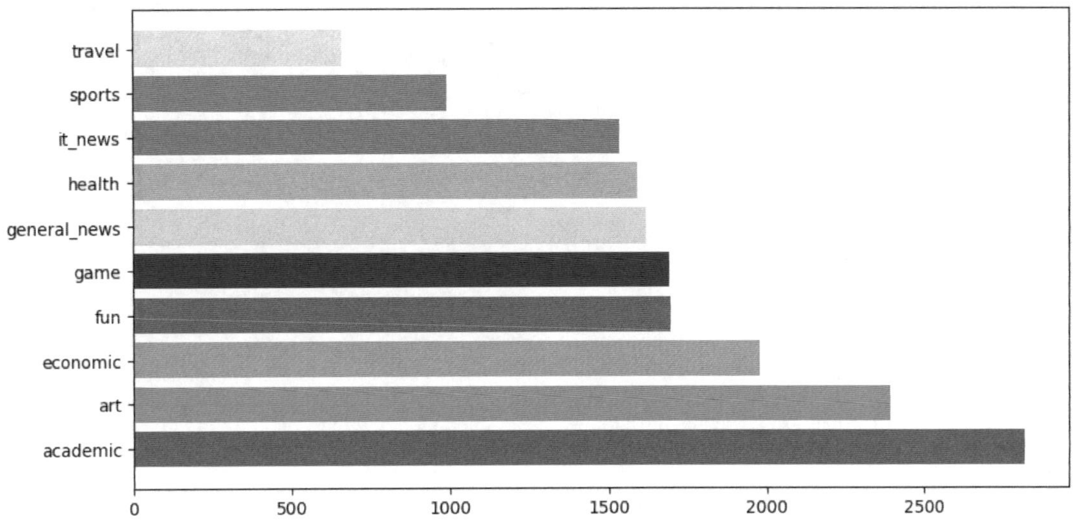

Figure 2: The size of the data in each domain of text greatly differs from one another, which results in massive challenges.

steps of the multi-Bert model.

There are a few steps to train the model, firstly, for each domain, exactly one adapter is introduced, and for each set of adapters, that have the same output template, a classifier header is included. Initially, one adapter is trained on all available data associated with that classifier excluding the domain of interest for a couple of epochs to ensure the adapters have all the correlating knowledge from other domains and the classifier is properly tuned. Subsequently, this adapter is replicated across all other adapters of the same classifier and fine-tuned on each domain separately, until convergence and before over fitting.

The classifier is only trained when the adapter is being pre-trained since this step includes all of the data associated with that particular output scheme. Furthermore, this layer is frozen during the fine-tuning of the adapters this helps make the overall training to be shorter and helps preserve the knowledge of the adapters from inference. After the training process is complete, there is only one core model with multiple headers and many domain-specific parameters. Therefore, we have multiple models each tailored for a single domain that can perform separately while they share much of their architecture. The subsequent section outlines the implementation and workflow of the proposed model, showing its efficiency and adaptability in handling multi-domain NER tasks.

4 Evaluation and Results

The proposed model is evaluated by using three different distinct datasets, each chosen to represent diverse unique challenges in the realm of NER and to test the performance of our model in dealing when faced with different challenges. We also introduce important baselines to show the effectiveness of our model. Finally, we compare the results of all the models and discuss the hyperparameters and advantages of prefix-tuning and LoRAs.

4.1 Datasets

To evaluate the aforementioned strategy the models are tested on three distinct datasets. For the first two datasets, we focus on the classic formal versus informal NER tasks, we utilize the Arman dataset for formal entities, and ParstwiNER (Aghajani et al., 2021), for the informal ones. This dataset serves as a benchmark for the adaptability of our model across standard formal and informal contexts characterized by minimal noise. This is very important since in many datasets all the text does fall into these domains. For instance, if we have a close look at the data on Twitter's more established accounts we see that many tweets are written perfectly and cleanly whether in a formal language or an informal one. However, these two datasets are extremely standard, they are both based on the CONLL format, have 21 entity types, and lack considerable errors or use of niche grammar which makes them very similar to the majority of the text the core model is trained on. Hence, the results on

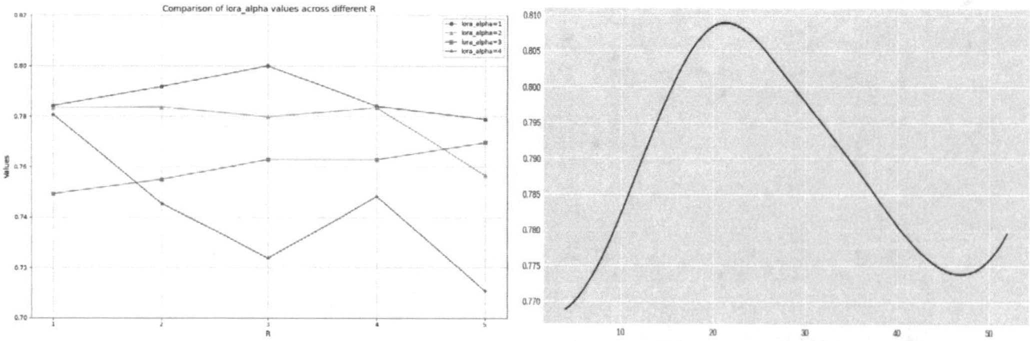

(a) The best score is from the blue line

(b) F1 peaks at 22 and 23 and falls after that.

Figure 3: All values are F1 scores of training a pre-trained model with the adapter for 2 epochs.

these two datasets differ from when datasets with noisy data taken from sites like Twitter are used.

That's where the third dataset, ParsNER (Asgari, 2021), comes in, ParsNER, This dataset consists of a huge amount of noise, whether it is words that are tagged inconsistently or general script errors. More importantly, the labels of this model are different from the previous datasets with only nine tags and a "MISC" tag that is supposed to represent any other tag, and probably any other dataset, since it's not based on a standard. The data is taken from posts on Twitter pages reflecting different topics. Thus, the data is clustered and grouped in different domains. These domains are extremely different from each other and as we mentioned at the start of the paper, the tagging will be greatly influenced by the topic at hand as a word like "Iran" is probably a "loc" when we are talking about travel and an "org" when we are talking about economics. This feature turns the differences in domain huge as we will see in later results that models that are specialized in the domain greatly outperform general models.

Moreover, the number of entries in each domain differ from one another you can see the number of entries in each domain in the figure 2. Normally, we would not be able to share one model for this dataset with the previous ones due to these huge differences. Still, with multi-Bert, we will use our model to achieve state-of-the-art results across all of our domains and datasets to show that this model can truly be a solution fit for all problems. Therefore, we have two sets of data with different outputs each one has other domains that we need to focus on and we will show that one instance of our model can give state-of-the-art results across all of these domains and datasets.

4.2 Baselines

For the baseline, we introduce two models that we expect our model to perform between them. Firstly, our lower bound baseline is a general model that is trained on all of the domains however since a model cannot give outputs in two different formats like our multi-Bert we train two general models one for the first two datasets and another for all the domains in the ParsNER dataset. These general models are trained by fine-tuning our pre-trained core model on the concatenation of all domains. However, we also design an upper-bound baseline. We fine-tune the core model on all of our data and fine-tune it on a single domain, we do this twelve times for each single domain. This is an extremely time-consuming experiment and the result is twelve huge models that are not a feasible solution. However, this does give us the best possible solution. Furthermore, ChatGPT is used to tag the sentences in the formal and informal datasets. However, a simple prompt is used that gives the model the desired tags and asks the model to tag each word. Using approaches like few-shot learning or training the model might achieve greater results but those require a huge sum of data and computational power, that the abstinence of it, is the main problem we are trying to solve.

4.3 Hyper-parameters setting

One of the main challenges of using adapters in general is the complex parameters. In this paper, we used an approach that closely resembles grid-search. Firstly we set all parameters to every number that is apart from each other eight(4, 12, 20, e.g) after finding the best performing sets of parameters, we adapt the model to all possible parameters in the range. After many experiments on our different

Model	Domains									
	acad	art	econ	fun	game	news	med	it	sport	travel
Gen-Bert-9	82%	66%	70%	69%	78%	79%	83%	86%	81%	76%
Spec-Bert	86%	**87%**	**93%**	90%	**96%**	93%	**95%**	93%	**95%**	90%
Multi-lr	70%	78%	80%	86%	90%	87%	86%	83%	92%	87%
Multi-pre	**90%**	**87%**	86%	**92%**	91%	**97%**	93%	**94%**	93%	**95%**

Table 1: The F1 Scores of the general Bert is overshadowed in any domain but the difference is much more visible in smaller domains

datasets, we came to the final conclusion that the best number of tokens to add to our prompt is 22. Adding fewer tokens to each input layer results in worse performance while adding more tokens leads to no positive change in the model performance, if not worse, and only leads to much longer training time. For the LoRA model, we also did the same thing but the only difference is that there are two parameters and the result is dependent on their combinations. Thus, Moreover, we use a batch size of 16 with a learning rate of 0.0001 as it has proven to give the best results.

As we see in the figure 3 the performance of the model rises up to the 18 parameters and starts falling significantly which makes choosing the 22 an easy choice. However, it's a little more complicated for the LoRA model since the results of the model for each value of R or alpha are dependent on the value of the other one. We came to the conclusion that for our named entity recognition task the best combination is LoRA alpha and r of 1 and 3 respectively. With these hyperparameters, the prefix model adds 468,490 parameters, and the LoRA model adds 136,714 parameters to the model, which constitute 0.38% and 0.11% of the model parameters, respectively. Since the base model has 124 million parameters, the added parameters are less than 1% of the model parameters, and having a few of these adapters is very low-cost.

Model	parameters	Save/trainable
Bert-21	117,722K	100%
Multi-Bert-lr	118,070K	0.294%
Multi-Bert-pre	119,522K	1.503%
ChatGPT	175B	100%

Table 2: Only a small percent of the parameters are trained and saved for Multi-Bert

4.4 Training details

In this section we will discuss the details of the models and the training procedure. The table 2 shows the number of parameters. The models were trained on a t4x2 for 30 epochs and saved the best model.

4.5 Results

As we see in the final results at table 3 and table 1 the general model under-performs in every domain. It is clear that the general model performs better at Formal v. Informal task compared to the 10-domain task for multiple reasons. Firstly, the data between the two classes are more even, we see that in the second general model, the domains with much smaller datasets are clearly forgotten for the sake of the bigger domains. Secondly, the more the number of our domains is, the harder it becomes for the model to adapt to all of them. We see that in the results of the domains that have much less data compared to their competitors, the model gets over-fixated on the other domains and greatly under-performs in these domains while doing relatively well in the domains with more data. When we look at the F1 score of the specialized models we see that even though each one of them is trained on all of the data and specialized on a single domain they do not outperform our model by a huge margin, in fact, the multi-Bert with prompt-tuning outperforms fine-tuning a model on multiple instances by a small margin. Another important observation is that prompt-tuning outperforms LoRA and is championed as the best way to create this model. This is due to the problem of limited data. Adapters require more data to train effectively. For this simple reason, we see that LoRA gives us results close to the fine-tuned ones, but is greatly overshadowed by prompt-tuning for the domains with much smaller datasets.

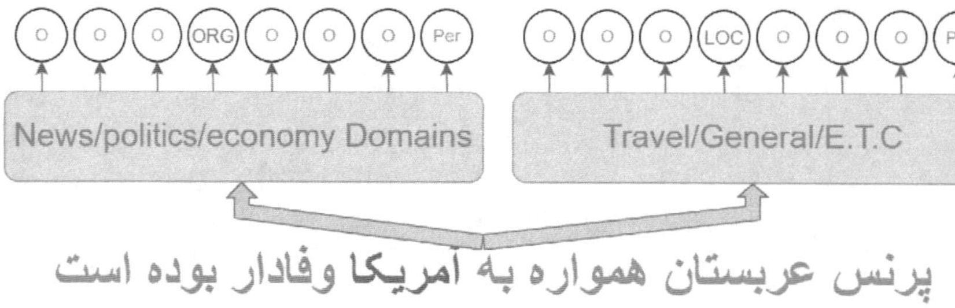

Figure 4: The models specialized on News, politics and economy get the tag of US right. Text from the political domain of ParsNER. Text translation: The Saudi prince proved to be a loyal ally to the United States.

Model	Arman	ParstwiNER
General-Bert-21	95.2%	75.4%
Spec Bert	**99.6%**	81.7%
Multi-Bert-lr	99.4%	80.8%
Multi-Bert-pre	99.3%	**83.1%**
ChatGPT	67.8%	55.7%

Table 3: Multi-Bert achieves similar results to a whole specialized Bert.

4.6 Discussion

So the model is getting better results, but why and where are these improvements? To answer these essential questions in this section the domain models are tested on a particular example from the ParsNER dataset in the general news section. The translation of the sentence goes "The Saudi prince proved to be a loyal ally to the United States". The word United States has a huge ambiguity here, if the loyalty is to the land of the country it needs to be labeled as "LOC", however, if the point is to be loyal to the government of the country the label would be "ORG". To us, humans, labeling this sentence might not be that hard, after all from the tone and the context we might be able to understand that the context of the sentence is politics. But this sentence proves to be exceptionally hard for the model, as seen in the figure 4 not only do the travel domains get this answer wrong but general models and others such as the ones designed for IT news also get this sentence wrong while the models that know the context of politics, economics or even general news get it right. This also outlines that a small boost goes a long way as seen in some specialized models.

5 Document-based classifier pipeline

In this section, we address the challenges posed by the absence of domain knowledge and propose an innovative solution to overcome this obstacle. Fortunately, determining the domain of a given text becomes relatively straightforward when the text is sufficiently long or when multiple samples are available. Nevertheless, feeding multiple samples simultaneously to a model is impractical, as it may lead to unwanted interference among distinct entries. To tackle this issue, we introduce a new pipeline by fine-tuning a new set of parameters to our core model.

To achieve this objective, we aggregate every set of elements (for example 8 elements) and assign them a label representing the domain of the data. Subsequently, we shuffle the data from all domains and train a new adapter for the model with the additional parameters tailored for a text classification task. Upon completion of the training process, we construct our pipeline as seen in the figure 5. When employing the model for inference—whether it involves tagging a series of comments on a website, tweets within a Twitter thread, or processing a lengthy book—we provide 512 tokens from the text to the model to find the domain and based on the identified domain, we apply the respective parameters from the core model to obtain the final results.

It is important to note that since we utilize the core model already employed in our token classification tasks and entirely freeze the core model during the classifier training, this pipeline does not adversely impact the main token classification models. To train, we concatenate each 8 input rows as one input. However, we only concatenate up to a length of 512. Therefore, if the sum size of 5 elements exceeds 512 we only concatenate 5 elements

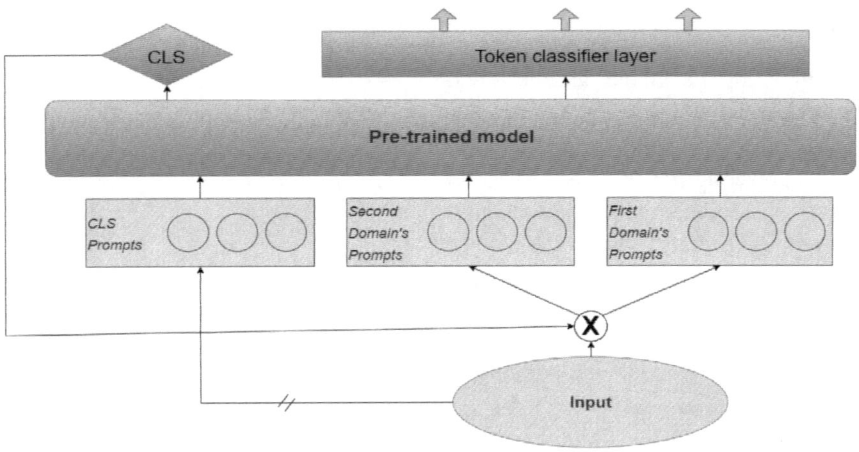

Figure 5: One forward pass determines the domain of a set which then can be used for each single input.

and cut the first 512 tokens of it. Consequently, each group of inputs turns into one input with the label of the dataset they are picked from. Then, we mix and shuffle all of the data and train and evaluate the model on all the data.

For the formal and the informal datasets, we get an accuracy of 100%. This is reasonable considering the distinctions between these two datasets. However, when we look at the ParsNER dataset we get an accuracy of 97% which is decent since we have 8 different classes. Moreover, even if this model fails to predict the right domain of the text, it does not guarantee a wrong final output as the chosen version may generate correct results. In fact, the decided domain is probably extremely close for this mix-up to happen. Hence we can use this pipeline to use the collection of texts to decide on their context and then process them normally one by one.

6 Conclusions

This paper proposed the multi-Bert model. This model is designed to perform well for all domains with any set of outputs. This is thanks to the deliberate design of this model by adding parameters for each domain and output layers for different sets of outputs coupled with the faster training time. This design allowed the model to perform the task on all domains perfectly. Moreover, this paper evaluated the proposed model on Arman (a formal dataset), ParstwiNER (an informal dataset), and the ParsNER, a collection of ten datasets from different contexts with large amounts of noise. The results proved that this model performs as well as the state-of-the-are for each domain, if not better. In addition, we also proposed a pipeline that can decide the domain of the data when a small set of sentences are available. We observed that if we use the model for sets of 8, it could understand the formality of the inputs completely with a 100% accuracy and can classify the exact domain of the news with an astonishing accuracy of 97% for the ParsNER dataset.

7 Future works

There is much to do in the future as this paper is only one step toward dealing with multi-domain problems. Firstly, creating a Multi-Bert with the newer proposed ModernBERT might achieve greater results (Warner et al., 2024). Secondly, the effectiveness of chatbots should be tested in multi-domain settings with fine-tuning. Due to limited computational resources, we only tested prompt engineering for generative LLMs but as seen in other papers generative LLMs do not have satisfying performance without proper fine-tuning (Abaskohi et al., 2024). While no one has actually fine-tuned these models for NER, fine-tuning these models will probably give us better results compared to smaller models like BERT. However, this task needs a huge amount of computational power. Last but not least, the proposed method approach should be tested for other low-resource NLP tasks such as question answering. Domain knowledge becomes even more important in generative tasks such as translation and question answering since the generated text also needs to be in the domain of the incoming text. However, in such research, using BART or generative LLMs such as LLAMA might give better results.

Limitations

This work is limited by the smaller architectures of the Bert model. While the smaller size and parameter count helps us fine-tune the model with low computation power it limits the results we are able to get compared to huge generative models. Moreover, the proposed approach is only tested for the Persian language and only for the NER task. Furthermore, the tests on ChatGPT are done with a simple prompt, while our results are in line with some of the found research in this field engineering greater prompts or using few-shot approaches might result in a higher F1 score. However, due to the huge difference in performance compared to the fine-tuned models used in this paper it is extremely likely that any prompt would achieve a accuracy close to the trained Bert models.

References

Amirhossein Abaskohi, Sara Baruni, Mostafa Masoudi, Nesa Abbasi, Mohammad Hadi Babalou, Ali Edalat, Sepehr Kamahi, Samin Mahdizadeh Sani, Nikoo Naghavian, Danial Namazifard, et al. 2024. Benchmarking large language models for persian: A preliminary study focusing on chatgpt. *arXiv preprint arXiv:2404.02403*.

MohammadMahdi Aghajani, AliAkbar Badri, and Hamid Beigy. 2021. ParsTwiNER: A corpus for named entity recognition at informal persian. In *Proceedings of the Seventh Workshop on Noisy User-generated Text (W-NUT 2021)*, pages 131–136.

Majid Asgari. 2021. Parsner. `https://github.com/majidasgari/ParsNER`.

Mehrdad Farahani, Mohammad Gharachorloo, Marzieh Farahani, and Mohammad Manthouri. 2021. Pars-Bert: Transformer-based model for Persian language understanding. *Neural Processing Letters*, 53:3831–3847.

Kai He, Rui Mao, Yucheng Huang, Tieliang Gong, Chen Li, and Erik Cambria. 2023. Template-free prompting for few-shot named entity recognition via semantic-enhanced contrastive learning. *IEEE Transactions on Neural Networks and Learning Systems*, pages 1–13.

Ruidan He, Linlin Liu, Hai Ye, Qingyu Tan, Bosheng Ding, Liying Cheng, Jia-Wei Low, Lidong Bing, and Luo Si. 2021. On the effectiveness of adapter-based tuning for pretrained language model adaptation. *arXiv preprint arXiv:2106.03164*.

Edward J Hu, Yelong Shen, Phillip Wallis, Zeyuan Allen-Zhu, Yuanzhi Li, Shean Wang, Lu Wang, and Weizhu Chen. 2022. LoRA: Low-Rank adaptation of large language models. In *International Conference on Learning Representations*.

Srinivasa Rao Kundeti, J Vijayananda, Srikanth Mujjiga, and M Kalyan. 2016. Clinical named entity recognition: Challenges and opportunities. In *Proceedings of IEEE International Conference on Big Data*, pages 1937–1945.

Xiang Lisa Li and Percy Liang. 2021. Prefix-tuning: Optimizing continuous prompts for generation. *arXiv preprint arXiv:2101.00190*.

Zongxi Li, Xianming Li, Yuzhang Liu, Haoran Xie, Jing Li, Fu-lee Wang, Qing Li, and Xiaoqin Zhong. 2023. Label supervised llama finetuning. *arXiv preprint arXiv:2310.01208*.

Jinghui Lu, Rui Zhao, Brian Mac Namee, and Fei Tan. 2023. PUnifiedNER: A prompting-based unified ner system for diverse datasets. In *Proceedings of the AAAI Conference on Artificial Intelligence*, volume 37, pages 13327–13335.

Ruotian Ma, Xin Zhou, Tao Gui, Yiding Tan, Linyang Li, Qi Zhang, and Xuanjing Huang. 2022. Template-free prompt tuning for few-shot NER. In *Proceedings of the 2022 Conference of the North American Chapter of the Association for Computational Linguistics: Human Language Technologies*, pages 5721–5732.

Ehsan Taher, Seyed Abbas Hoseini, and Mehrnoush Shamsfard. 2020. Beheshti-NER: Persian named entity recognition using BERT. *arXiv preprint arXiv:2003.08875*.

Liwen Wang, Rumei Li, Yang Yan, Yuanmeng Yan, Sirui Wang, Wei Wu, and Weiran Xu. 2022. InstructionNER: A multi-task instruction-based generative framework for few-shot ner. *arXiv preprint arXiv:2203.03903*.

Benjamin Warner, Antoine Chaffin, Benjamin Clavié, Orion Weller, Oskar Hallström, Said Taghadouini, Alexis Gallagher, Raja Biswas, Faisal Ladhak, Tom Aarsen, et al. 2024. Smarter, better, faster, longer: A modern bidirectional encoder for fast, memory efficient, and long context finetuning and inference. *arXiv preprint arXiv:2412.13663*.

Enhancing NER Performance in Low-Resource Pakistani Languages using Cross-Lingual Data Augmentation

Toqeer Ehsan, Thamar Solorio
Department of Natural Language Processing,
Mohamed Bin Zayed University of Artificial Intelligence (MBZUAI),
Abu Dhabi, United Arab Emirates
{toqeer.ehsan, thamar.solorio}@mbzuai.ac.ae

Abstract

Named Entity Recognition (NER), a fundamental task in Natural Language Processing (NLP), has shown significant advancements for high-resource languages. However, due to a lack of annotated datasets and limited representation in Pre-trained Language Models (PLMs), it remains understudied and challenging for low-resource languages. To address these challenges, we propose a data augmentation technique that generates culturally plausible sentences and experiments on four low-resource Pakistani languages; Urdu, Shahmukhi, Sindhi, and Pashto. By fine-tuning multilingual masked Large Language Models (LLMs), our approach demonstrates significant improvements in NER performance for Shahmukhi and Pashto. We further explore the capability of generative LLMs for NER and data augmentation using few-shot learning.

1 Introduction

The performance of Named Entity Recognition (NER) in low-resource languages faces challenges due to the scarcity of annotated datasets and insufficient coverage in masked Large Language Models (LLMs) (Subedi et al., 2024). Causal LLMs, on the other hand, demonstrate their performance by achieving moderate scores for NER (Chen et al., 2023; Ye et al., 2023). These challenges make it difficult to develop effective NLP applications and highlight the need of focused effort to improve the applicability of these models on available datasets for low-resource languages.

Data augmentation approaches could be effective to enhance the NER datasets for low-resource languages. One such approach is the Easy Data Augmentation (EDA) (Wei and Zou, 2019), that offers simple and effective techniques, including synonym replacement, random insertion, random swap, and random deletion (Khalid et al., 2023; Liu and Cui, 2023; Litake et al., 2024). However, EDA can produce linguistically implausible text lacking verbal agreement based on gender and number. Additionally, EDA may produce out-of-context or offensive data for culturally sensitive content. This can affect the generalizability and learning of NER models. We aim to enhance NER performance for Pakistani low-resource languages by employing effective data augmentation as shown in Figure 1.

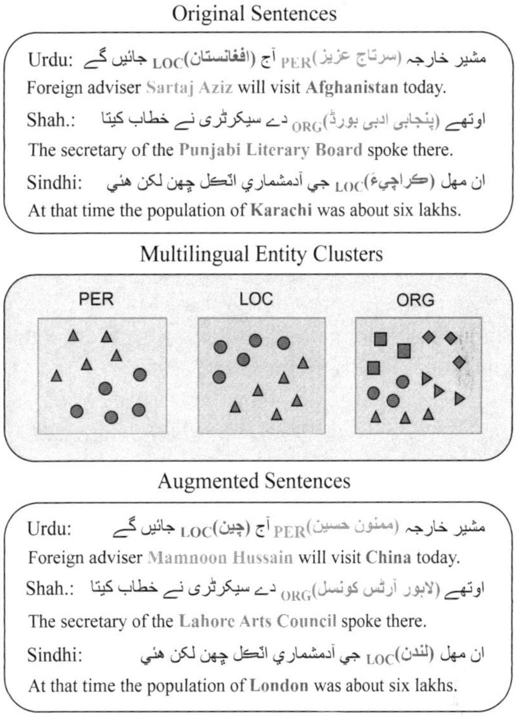

Figure 1: Examples of clustering-based data augmentation applied to three sample sentences. Entity mentions are represented in orange, blue and green colors.

Four Urdu sentences are shown in Figure 2, illustrating the problem of implausibility. Urdu, Shahmukhi and Sindhi require verbal agreements, and augmenting entities from

Proceedings of the Tenth Workshop on Noisy and User-generated Text, pages 117–132
May 3, 2025 ©2025 Association for Computational Linguistics

1- **(مومنہ)**$_{PER}$ گورنمنٹ گرلز ہائی سکول میں پڑھتی ہے۔

(Momina)$_{PER}$ studies in Government Girls High School.

2- **(چوہدری محمد سرور)**$_{PER}$ آج صبح لاہور پہنچ گئے ہیں۔

(Chaudhry Muhammad Sarwar)$_{PER}$ has reached Lahore this morning.

3- **(تحریک منہاج القرآن)**$_{ORG}$ کا سالانہ عالمی مذہبی اجتماع کل ہو گا۔

The annual global religious gathering of **(Minhaj-ul-Quran Movement)**$_{ORG}$ will be held tomorrow.

4- کل **(لاہور آرٹس کونسل)**$_{ORG}$ نے انٹرنیشنل ڈانس ڈے کا پروگرام منعقد کیا

(Lahore Arts Council)$_{ORG}$ organized the program of International Dance Day yesterday.

Figure 2: Sample Urdu sentences for the analysis of EDA. Named entities are highlighted in bold.

the sentences 1 and 2, could result in disagreements. *Momina* (Nom.Fem.Sg) is a feminine name that has agreement with the verb *paRHtI* (study.Hab.Fem.Sg), while *Chaudhry Muhammad Sarwar* (Nom.Masc.Sg) is a masculine name that agrees with the verb *gaE* (go.Past.Masc.Sg.Hon). Replacing these named entities can produce implausible text; for instance, the sentence *Chaudhry Muhammad Sarwar studies in Government Girls High School* would violate the verbal agreement rules of the language. The named entities in the last two sentences are considered opposites within the community, and replacing such named entities can produce text that is very offensive to the native community. The generated sentences remain grammatically correct but create contextual ambiguity.

We propose a cross-lingual data augmentation technique by clustering named entities as shown in Figure 1. This technique improves the quality of culturally sensitive content and grammar of the augmented text. We performed unsupervised entity clustering and entity replacement by aligning clusters for the source and candidate named entities of each type. NER experiments were conducted for low-resource settings as well as for entire datasets. We compared the results with EDA-based and generative augmentation methods for mono- and multilingual settings by fine-tuning the Glot500 (Imani et al., 2023) and XLM-RoBERTa (Conneau et al., 2019) models. Shahmukhi and Pashto datasets demonstrated significant improvements, producing F_1 scores of 88.06 and 88.29 with increases of 5.53 and 1.81 points, respectively.

Zero- or few-shot learning is relevant in low-resource scenarios where even augmented datasets are limited in size. We explore the capabilities of causal LLMs to perform NER and data augmentation for our low-resource languages using few-shot learning. The key contributions of this paper are as follows:

- We propose a novel cross-lingual augmentation technique that uses cluster dictionaries to produce culturally and linguistically plausible augmentations.
- We demonstrate the effectiveness of the proposed technique in multilingual NER experiments by utilizing cross-lingual representations.
- We provide insights into the potential of causal LLMs to perform NER and data augmentation for low-resource languages using few-shot learning.

2 Related Work

Manually annotated corpora are crucial for achieving state-of-the-art results in NER (Mayhew et al., 2023). Cross-lingual transfer also supports generalization and enhances the performance of models (Ding et al., 2024; Mo et al., 2024; Cotterell and Duh, 2024; Le et al., 2024; Hu et al., 2020). Data augmentation techniques enhance the size and learning capabilities of datasets for low-resource languages (Litake et al., 2024; Ye et al., 2024; Lancheros et al., 2024). For the task of NER, three data augmentation methods are mainly used; Easy Data Augmentation (EDA) (Wei and Zou, 2019) and its variants, translation-based methods and generative LLMs. EDA-based techniques demonstrate enhanced NER performance for low-resource languages (Litake et al., 2024). The data augmentation quality can be enhanced by using contextualized word embeddings (Torres et al., 2024) and cosine similarity (Bartolini et al., 2022).

Data augmentation based on back-translation has shown improvements for code-switched NER (Sabty et al., 2021). The translation-based data augmentation technique that performs cross-lingual entity augmentation also improves the performance of NER models (Liu et al., 2021; Lancheros et al., 2024; Chen et al., 2022).

The capabilities of causal LLMs are being explored for data augmentation (Evuru et al., 2024; Ye et al., 2024) and underlying NLP tasks such as NER (Naguib et al., 2024; Villena et al., 2024; Lu et al., 2024). Generative data augmentation techniques have demonstrated improvements (Evuru et al., 2024; Liu et al., 2022; Ye et al., 2024).

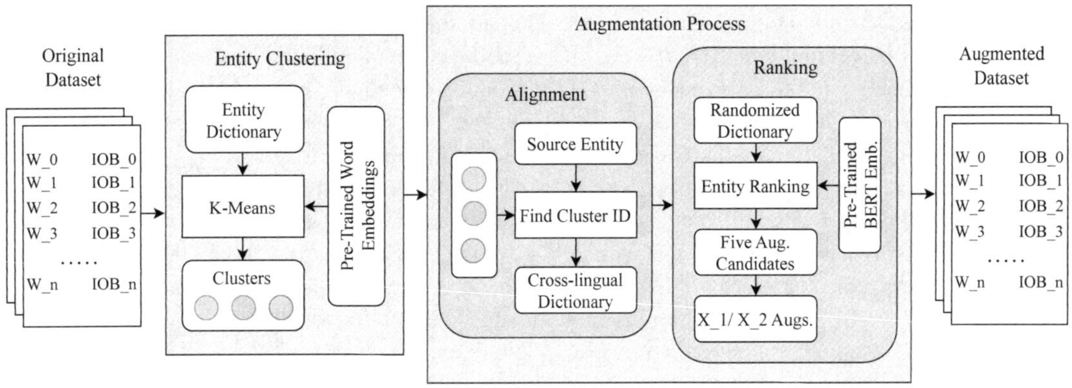

Figure 3: Cluster-based data augmentation process, which contains three phases. The entity clustering phase extracts unsupervised clusters for each entity type, alignment phase aligns cluster dictionaries with respect to the source (original) entities and the final phase ranks the source entity mentions with the best candidate. The original dataset corresponds to the manually annotated dataset, while the augmented dataset is the updated version obtained through the augmentation process.

Masking-based generative methods have produced better NER results by generating more plausible data augmentations (Song et al., 2024).

Causal LLMs are further employed to perform NER with zero- and few-shot learning (Naguib et al., 2024; Villena et al., 2024) as an alternative approach to data augmentation. These models are also progressing in various text domains (Lu et al., 2024; Monajatipoor et al., 2024). These advancements highlight the need to investigate the capabilities of these models for low-resource languages.

3 Cross-Lingual Data Augmentation

The languages selected in this work are topologically related and culturally similar. In terms of named entities, they share similar names, locations and organizations. Given these similarities, cross-lingual representation could be helpful in improving the performance of NER for the regional languages. Additionally, data augmentation techniques have shown improvements for low-resource languages, but EDA-based methods are blunt and may produce culturally offensive and/or ungrammatical sentences by replacing entities with the other entities of the same type without any additional semantic information. Out of 100 randomly selected sentences, 32 instances of verbal disagreements and three of sensitive religious named entities were found. These percentages estimate the occurrence of such issues in the augmented data. To address these issues, we propose a data augmentation technique that generates more sensible sentences and produces competitive NER performance for the selected low-resource languages. The next section describes our proposed technique, followed by descriptions of EDA-based random replacement and generative approaches.

3.1 Cluster-based$_{\text{Aug.}}$

We propose a hybrid data augmentation technique inspired by EDA, combined with the application of unsupervised entity clustering. The technique consists of three phases; entity clustering, alignment, and ranking as illustrated by Figure 3.

Entity Clustering Named entities were clustered using context-free word embeddings from pre-trained models (Grave et al., 2018; Tehseen et al., 2023), where each word has a single embedding regardless of its context which are helpful in clustering process. We employed the K-Means clustering algorithm to cluster entities based on their embeddings and cosine similarity. While clustering is an unsupervised method, we interpreted these clustering representing specific categories for each entity type. To evaluate the effectiveness of the approach, we manually assessed the unsupervised clustering of 200 entities for each entity type in Urdu. The person and location types were categorized into two clusters; masculine and feminine for persons, and country/continent and city/places for locations. In contrast, named entities from the organization type were grouped into ten clusters; entertainment, financial, health/education, justice/govt, news, politics, religious, water/electricity, abbreviations and miscellaneous. The accuracies for correctly clustered named entities were 86.0% for persons, 87.5% for locations, and 84.5% for organizations, as determined through manual evaluation. The K-means clustering approach was implemented using NLTK's *KMeansClusterer* to categorize named entity embeddings into distinct groups. The clustering process utilized cosine distance as the similarity metric, ensuring that entities with similar vector representations were grouped together effectively. To enhance the stability and robustness of the clustering process, we performed 25 repetitions. For clustering, separate dictionaries of unique named entities were created based on the splits of annotated training sets.

We achieve a single feature vector by averaging the vectors for each token in an entity of the location and organization types. However, person names have a specific pattern in Pakistani culture. The first name usually belongs to the individual, followed by a family name. A feminine first name is typically followed by a masculine name, that could be the name of the father, tribe, caste, or creed. For instance, in the entity mention *Madiha Khalid*, *Madiha* is the feminine name followed by the masculine name *Khalid*. Similarly, many names, particularly masculine names, begin with a title representing a designation, tribe, caste, or creed. We prepared a list of these titles to filter them out and used first names to obtain feature vectors. This approach improved the performance of clustering.

Alignment The prepared clusters are aligned between the source and candidate entity mentions. The source entity refers to the original entity mention in the dataset, while the candidate entity is the one selected to replace the source entity. In the alignment phase, the cluster ID of the source entity is determined by looking it up in the manually identified clusters. A dictionary containing unique named entities from the corresponding cluster is then passed to the next phase.

Ranking The ranking procedure is performed in two steps. In the first step, an entity is selected from a randomized cluster dictionary by computing highest cosine similarity with respect to the source entity mention. Unlike the clustering process, contextualized word embeddings from Glot500-base, which has data coverage of all our selected languages, are used to select similar candidate entities. This step generates five augmented sentences for each original sentence. In the second step, micro F_1 score is computed for augmented sentences to assess their plausibility, using Glot500-base model fine-tuned on multilingual datasets. This pretrained model automatically validates each generated candidate. The tokens of each augmented sentence are fed into the model to predict the named entities. The sentence with the highest F_1 score is selected to be a part of the augmented dataset. The F_1 score is computed by treating the model output as the predicted annotation, while the manually annotated named entities in the augmented sentence serve as a reference in the process. We further prepared multiple augmented datasets by including one sentence with the highest score (X_1), two sentences with top two scores (X_2) and all augmented sentences with an F_1 score of 1.0.

3.2 Random Replacement (EDA-RR$_{\text{Aug.}}$)

The random replacement data augmentation is a straightforward approach which is based on EDA methods (Wei and Zou, 2019). The augmentation process has two steps; 1) take all sentences in the training data with labeled named entities, 2) for each entity mention in a sentence, replace it with a named entity of the same type. The second step continues until all entity mentions in a sentence are replaced randomly. As a result, a new augmented dataset is produced, which is added to the training set to enhance its size and diversity. This method is simple and efficient to implement, but it may produce contextually implausible text that could be incorrect or offensive to the community.

3.3 Generative$_{\text{Aug.}}$

To add the contextual information in the data augmentation, we performed generative data augmentation using LLaMA3 (Touvron et al., 2023) with few-shot learning. The approach is similar to the entity-level augmentation proposed by Ye et al. (2024). We employed instruction-finetuned version of LLaMA3 (LLaMA3-8B-Instruct). We selected LLaMA3 due to its open-access nature and strong few-shot learning capabilities. LLaMA3 has been trained on a diverse multilingual corpus, but its direct exposure to Pakistani languages is limited. However, Urdu is a widely spoken language with significant online resources, LLaMA3 demonstrates moderate performance in generating Urdu text. We constructed a prompt by providing three examples containing each entity type and instructed the model to replace entity mentions with similar entities. The augmentation was performed for low-resource training sets due to time and resource constraints. The prompt that we used for data augmentation is given below:

You are an expert in augmenting data for named entities for Urdu language. The input contains the ORIGINAL TEXT followed by the AUGMENTED TEXT. Perform augmentation by replacing named entities with new entities of the same type and return the AUGMENTED TEXT. Three examples are given for your reference:
EXAMPLE 1:
ORIGINAL TEXT:
AUGMENTED TEXT:

4 Languages and Datasets

Pakistan is home to many widely spoken languages, each with unique linguistic characteristics and cultural significance. Urdu is the national language of Pakistan that has 232 million speakers worldwide. Shahmukhi (Punjabi), Sindhi, and Pashto have 67, 30 and 40 million speakers, respectively (Eberhard and Fennig, 2024). These languages pose several challenges for the task of NER, such as absence of capitalization, contextual ambiguity, flexible word-order, and agglutinating nature (Khalid et al., 2023; Ehsan and Hussain, 2021; Ahmed et al., 2024). The statistics of the selected datasets are shown in Table 1. Despite the larger sample sizes in Shahmukhi, Sindhi, and Urdu datasets, they face limited domain coverage, incomplete NER labels, low sentence-to-entity ratio, and noisy annotations, underscoring their low-resource status. The MK-PUCIT, Shahmukhi and SiNER datasets were released without validation sets; therefore, we used 10% of the train sets for validation.

Lang./Dataset	Type	Train	Test	Val.
Urdu / Urdu-Wikiann	PER	6,839	363	340
	LOC	6,891	334	352
	LOC	6,891	334	352
	ORG	6,759	323	327
	# Sents.	20,000	1,000	1,000
Urdu / MK-PUCIT	PER	11,965	5,215	–
	LOC	23,880	8,380	–
	ORG	8,665	3,014	–
	# Sents.	24,080	16,609	–
Punjabi / Shahmukhi	PER	4,655	1,957	–
	LOC	1,855	648	–
	ORG	538	236	–
	# Sents.	13,547	5,821	–
Sindhi / SiNER	PER	12,894	5,564	–
	LOC	2,769	630	–
	ORG	1,331	891	–
	# Sents.	31,870	7,418	–
Pashto / Pashto-Wikiann	PER	32	28	39
	LOC	37	45	45
	ORG	43	38	33
	# Sents.	100	100	100

Table 1: Type-wise statistics of the datasets for Urdu, Shahmukhi, Sindhi and Pashto.

Urdu: Being in the *Vital* category (Eberhard and Fennig, 2024), Urdu is relatively resource-rich compared to the regional languages. Several NER datasets are available for Urdu with different data annotations and sizes (Khana et al., 2016; Hussain, 2008; Jahangir et al., 2012; Malik, 2017). However, we experimented with Urdu-Wikiann (Rahimi et al., 2019; Lovenia et al., 2024) and MK-PUCIT (Kanwal et al., 2019), which are larger datasets annotated with coarse-grained named entities; person, location and organization.

Shahmukhi: There is only one NER dataset available for Shahmukhi, which has been annotated using person, location, and organization types (Ahmad et al., 2020). The quality of the dataset was further enhanced by using the BIO annotation scheme (Tehseen et al., 2023). The dataset contained some annotation inconsistencies. To ensure the validity of our NER results, we manually reviewed and corrected the annotations in one thousand sentences from the test set. While this review process was conducted to enhance the reliability of our evaluation.

Sindhi: Ali et al. (2020) released the first large annotated dataset for the Sindhi language called SiNER. We experimented with three coarse-grained entity types to make it compatible with the other datasets.

Pashto: Pashto lacks in fundamental language processing tools (Eberhard and Fennig, 2024). We used the Pashto dataset from Wikiann (Rahimi et al., 2019) that contains 100 sentences for train, test and validation sets. Since the dataset was automatically annotated and exhibited some annotation inconsistencies, we reviewed the test set manually to ensure valid NER results.

5 Experimental Setup

We conducted NER experiments designed to improve performance for low-resource languages, where supervised models often struggle due to limited annotated datasets. This research addresses three key questions; 1) How effective are data augmentation techniques to enhance NER for low-resource languages? 2) Do cross-lingual data representations improve NER performance in multilingual settings? 3) How does few-shot learning compare to fully supervised models as an alternative to data augmentation? We hypothesize that cross-lingual representations, combined with multilingual datasets improve NER results for topologically related and culturally similar languages.

5.1 NER Models and Architectures

For our NER experiments, we employed two pre-trained multilingual masked language models: Glot500-base (Imani et al., 2023) and XLM-RoBERTa-large (Conneau et al., 2019).

- Glot500-base supports over 500 languages and is based on RoBERTa's (Conneau et al., 2019) architecture. It uses transformer-based contextualized token embeddings and is particularly designed for low-resource languages like Urdu, Shahmukhi, Sindhi, and Pashto.
- XLM-RoBERTa-large is another transformer-based multilingual models that supports 100 languages, including Urdu, Sindhi, and Pashto. It is pre-trained on massive multilingual text corpora using masked language modeling (MLM) objectives.

To fine-tune these models for NER, we added a token classification layer on the top of the final transformer layer which receives the hidden states from the last layer of the model and computes the multi-class probability distribution over the entity classes for each token. This setup classifies tokens into person, location and organization categories.

We fine-tuned both models on mono- and multilingual datasets to investigate their performance for NER for low-resource setting by including 100, 200, 500 and 1000 train samples. Additionally, we experimented with the data augmentation techniques to further improve NER performance for low-resource languages.

5.2 Few-Shot Learning with Causal Models

While the primary focus of this paper is on data augmentation techniques to enhance NER performance in low-resource languages, we also explore few-shot learning as an alternative approach. Although various causal LLMs have recently been evaluated for the task of NER, they still struggle to compete with state-of-the-art supervised models (Naguib et al., 2024; Villena et al., 2024; Lu et al., 2024). This raises a research question; how well do these models perform in low-resource languages?

We performed NER by using a few-shot learning approach by prompting LLaMA3-8B-Instruct[1] and Mistral-7B-Instruct-v0.3[2] which are instruction tuned. LLaMA3-8B is trained on 15 trillion tokens with a context length of 8K. Mistral-7B also has the same context length but its training size is not disclosed. We created a prompt, similar to $\text{Generative}_{\text{Aug.}}$, describing details of the task by providing three examples for each language (Appendix E). The inputs and outputs were formatted as sequences of texts and NER labels. For erroneous outputs, the number of labels matching the number of tokens in the input was selected for evaluation. We evaluated the performance of both causal models on 1,000 sentences from each dataset.

6 Results and Discussion

We use micro F-scores to ensure a balanced evaluation of NER performance across all entity types. Table 2 presents Micro-F_1 score for low-resource NER experiments using monolingual and multilingual data settings. The training sets contain 100, 200, 500 and 1,000 samples for each dataset. In the multilingual settings, we combined training samples from all selected languages (Urdu, Shahmukhi, Sindhi, and Pashto). To maintain balanced representation, we ensured that each language contributed an equal number of samples in low-resource scenarios. The results are presented from fine-tuned Glot500-base and XLM-RoBERTa-large models. Similarly, Table 3 shows NER results for the entire datasets. The training samples in all augmented datasets were doubled in one iteration, and the NER results are presented after this iteration. Further analysis from multiple iterations is presented in the Appendix C.

Our data augmentation technique improved NER results for low-resource languages by reducing the generation of grammatically implausible and culturally offensive content. The augmentation technique helps maintain semantics and cultural appropriateness, that highly impacted the model performance. The model trained on the augmented datasets demonstrated higher generalizability due to less exposure to the contextually implausible in-

[1] https://huggingface.co/meta-llama/Meta-Llama-3-8B-Instruct

[2] https://huggingface.co/mistralai/Mistral-7B-v0.3

Monolingual Settings		Glot500-base				XLM-RoBERTa-large			
Dataset	**Augmentation**	**100**	**200**	**500**	**1000**	**100**	**200**	**500**	**1000**
Urdu-Wikiann	Original dataset	70.93	77.23	83.51	80.24	72.77	71.21	84.21	**87.21**
	Generative$_{\text{Aug.}}$	**77.13**	79.29	84.24	**86.81**	**79.66**	**83.85**	**85.01**	85.50
	EDA-RR$_{\text{Aug.}}$	74.87	77.42	**84.57**	85.87	71.75	80.27	82.79	85.84
	Cluster-based$_{\text{Aug.}}$	76.62	**81.00**	83.78	85.31	75.24	80.79	84.30	85.97
Shahmukhi	Original dataset	59.62	65.27	71.92	75.44	53.67	59.44	70.65	75.58
	Generative$_{\text{Aug.}}$	53.83	62.45	69.85	74.89	58.81	58.64	66.96	74.68
	EDA-RR$_{\text{Aug.}}$	58.44	63.98	70.34	73.87	51.95	64.75	72.40	75.32
	Cluster-based$_{\text{Aug.}}$	**60.78**	**68.03**	**73.17**	**77.11**	**59.61**	**65.89**	**74.19**	**77.40**
SiNER	Original dataset	62.25	69.61	75.82	**80.27**	73.63	**78.16**	81.22	82.80
	Generative$_{\text{Aug.}}$	53.76	60.64	69.09	73.76	64.12	71.58	73.81	77.09
	EDA-RR$_{\text{Aug.}}$	64.69	**72.29**	73.50	72.65	**75.40**	75.22	80.01	83.00
	Cluster-based$_{\text{Aug.}}$	**65.64**	71.17	**76.88**	79.46	74.27	75.96	**81.60**	**84.48**
Pashto-Wikiann	Original dataset	32.86	–	–	–	44.24	–	–	–
	Generative$_{\text{Aug.}}$	45.66	–	–	–	45.26	–	–	–
	EDA-RR$_{\text{Aug.}}$	45.75	–	–	–	48.92	–	–	–
	Cluster-based$_{\text{Aug.}}$	**48.54**	–	–	–	**50.00**	–	–	–
Multilingual Settings		**Glot500-base**				**XLM-RoBERTa-large**			
Dataset	**Augmentation**	**100**	**200**	**500**	**1000**	**100**	**200**	**500**	**1000**
Urdu-Wikiann	Original dataset	73.12	74.82	**84.45**	84.90	63.32	78.25	**82.33**	80.97
	Generative$_{\text{Aug.}}$	**78.92**	79.67	84.16	**85.77**	77.78	**80.93**	82.07	**85.43**
	EDA-RR$_{\text{Aug.}}$	72.75	77.43	83.04	83.98	**79.13**	78.70	81.10	82.02
	Cluster-based$_{\text{Aug.}}$	76.83	**82.25**	84.35	85.34	78.60	79.49	81.14	83.21
Shahmukhi	Original dataset	65.33	69.21	75.84	79.38	56.87	67.85	72.27	76.66
	Generative$_{\text{Aug.}}$	64.32	68.45	74.46	77.45	65.69	69.23	74.68	78.21
	EDA-RR$_{\text{Aug.}}$	66.23	69.34	74.48	78.32	65.90	69.44	**75.86**	77.26
	Cluster-based$_{\text{Aug.}}$	**68.88**	**73.47**	**77.51**	**80.01**	**67.83**	**71.38**	73.79	**78.90**
SiNER	Original dataset	62.35	67.78	73.85	78.83	67.37	74.02	76.42	79.23
	Generative$_{\text{Aug.}}$	58.53	65.30	71.78	73.59	56.76	68.78	75.19	76.96
	EDA-RR$_{\text{Aug.}}$	64.72	69.71	74.30	77.84	69.79	74.48	76.06	79.77
	Cluster-based$_{\text{Aug.}}$	**66.76**	**73.22**	**76.26**	**79.61**	**71.99**	**75.24**	**78.40**	**80.45**
Pashto-Wikiann	Original dataset	62.26	67.68	73.68	78.58	67.01	73.79	76.22	78.96
	Generative$_{\text{Aug.}}$	58.51	65.19	71.62	73.43	65.68	68.66	74.98	76.73
	EDA-RR$_{\text{Aug.}}$	64.66	69.53	74.12	77.59	69.60	74.32	75.86	79.53
	Cluster-based$_{\text{Aug.}}$	**66.63**	**73.12**	**76.05**	**79.35**	**71.78**	**74.98**	**78.17**	**80.21**

Table 2: Micro-F_1 scores of fine-tuned multilingual Glot500-base and XLM-RoBERTa-large models for NER in low-resource settings. The results of the cluster-based augmentation are compared against the original training set, generative augmentation from LLaMa3 (Generative$_{\text{Aug.}}$) and EDA - Random Replacement (EDA-RR$_{\text{Aug.}}$).

formation. This confirms that grammatically and contextually inappropriate data can degrade the model performance by introducing noise and reducing its ability to generalize effectively. The following paragraphs present a comparison of data augmentation techniques for each dataset.

Urdu-Wikiann The Urdu-Wikiann dataset demonstrates inconsistent performance for different augmentation techniques, which is caused by three main reasons. First, Urdu is a resource-rich language compared to the other three regional languages and fine-tuning using cross-lingual data augmentation enhances its diversity, but does not significantly impact NER results due to the large size of the dataset. Second, causal LLMs, such as LLaMA3 have better support for Urdu compared to the other three languages as Urdu dataset shows improvements using Generative$_{\text{Aug.}}$ method. Third, the Urdu-Wikiann dataset is an automatically annotated dataset that may have some inconsistencies (Mayhew et al., 2023) which can limit the effectiveness of cross-lingual augmentation.

Shahmukhi The Shahmukhi dataset demonstrates consistent performance with cluster-based data augmentation as the proposed method generates plausible augmentations that leads to improved results. The fine-tuned XLM model produced a state-of-the-art F_1 score of 88.06 in multilingual settings using the BIO annotation scheme, which outperforms the previous best score of 75.55 (Tehseen et al., 2023).

However, Generative$_{\text{Aug.}}$ decreased NER performance for Shahmukhi. The causal model produced various augmentations that violated entity types, resulting in incorrect labeling. The low scores in-

Monolingual Settings		Glot500-base			XLM-RoBERTa-large		
Dataset	**Augmentation**	**Precision**	**Recall**	**F_1 Score**	**Precision**	**Recall**	**F_1 Score**
Urdu-Wikiann	Original dataset	95.46	95.86	**95.66**	95.80	96.75	**96.28**
	EDA-$RR_{Aug.}$	94.89	96.38	95.63	96.08	96.08	96.08
	Cluster-$based_{Aug.}$	94.51	94.61	94.56	93.97	94.34	94.16
Shahmukhi	Original dataset	79.12	73.92	76.44	80.77	73.40	76.91
	EDA-$RR_{Aug.}$	85.58	76.96	81.04	85.55	79.76	**82.55**
	Cluster-$based_{Aug.}$	84.04	82.23	**83.13**	86.52	78.71	82.43
SiNER	Original dataset	90.50	85.69	88.03	88.78	89.12	88.95
	EDA-$RR_{Aug.}$	88.66	87.88	**88.27**	88.14	90.10	**89.11**
	Cluster-$based_{Aug.}$	87.49	88.82	88.15	87.50	89.68	88.58
Pashto-Wikiann	Original dataset	51.55	32.29	39.71	49.74	38.86	43.63
	EDA-$RR_{Aug.}$	46.45	47.77	**47.10**	48.19	53.45	**50.68**
	Cluster-$based_{Aug.}$	43.93	46.96	45.40	54.23	46.54	50.09
Multilingual Settings		**Glot500-base**			**XLM-RoBERTa-large**		
Dataset	**Augmentation**	**Precision**	**Recall**	**F_1 Score**	**Precision**	**Recall**	**F_1 Score**
Urdu-Wikiann	Original dataset	95.93	96.38	96.16	96.09	96.43	**96.26**
	EDA-$RR_{Aug.}$	96.10	96.75	**96.42**	95.02	95.58	95.30
	Cluster-$based_{Aug.}$	96.07	96.18	96.12	96.23	96.28	96.25
Shahmukhi	Original dataset	83.63	80.70	82.14	83.36	81.71	82.53
	EDA-$RR_{Aug.}$	87.98	83.43	85.64	88.51	83.62	86.00
	Cluster-$based_{Aug.}$	89.03	85.50	**87.22**	89.29	86.85	**88.06**
SiNER	Original dataset	87.99	84.82	86.37	87.12	86.35	86.73
	EDA-$RR_{Aug.}$	88.01	86.91	87.46	90.52	86.33	88.38
	Cluster-$based_{Aug.}$	89.19	86.69	**87.92**	89.33	87.80	**88.56**
Pashto-Wikiann	Original dataset	87.78	84.63	86.18	86.77	86.18	86.48
	EDA-$RR_{Aug.}$	87.51	86.72	87.12	90.15	85.94	88.00
	Cluster-$based_{Aug.}$	89.00	86.29	**87.62**	89.14	87.45	**88.29**

Table 3: Micro-F_1 scores of fine-tuned multilingual Glot500-base and XLM-RoBERTa-large models for complete datasets. The results of the cluster-based augmentation are compared against the original training sets and EDA - Random Replacement (EDA-$RR_{Aug.}$). Improved scores are highlighted in bold.

dicate that multilingual causal LLMs have limited support for low-resource languages. The cluster-based data augmentation technique outperformed other two augmentation methods in both monolingual and multilingual experiments.

SiNER For the Sindhi dataset, the cluster-based cross-lingual augmentation improved NER results in a multilingual setting by utilizing cross-lingual representations. This approach introduced linguistic variation and diversity that enhanced the models' ability to generalize. For the entire dataset, EDA-$RR_{Aug.}$ demonstrated improved results by adding cross-lingual entities that enriched the training set, making it a suitable augmentation technique for Sindhi in a monolingual training setup. However, $Generative_{Aug.}$ had a negative impact on all low-resource training sets, highlighting limited capabilities of causal LLMs for low-resource languages. Sindhi's use of Arabic script with additional unique letters, unlike Urdu, Shahmukhi, and Pashto, may negatively impact multilingual fine-tuning

Pashto-Wikiann The Pashto-Wikiann dataset demonstrates significant improvements with data augmentation techniques, especially in a multilingual setup, except for $Generative_{Aug.}$. The best reported F_1 score for Pashto is 82.0 achieved from an HMM-based tagger (Momand et al., 2020). By using cluster-based augmentation, the multilingual fine-tuned Glot500 and XLM models produced F_1 scores of 87.62 and 88.29, respectively. However, these findings should be interpreted with caution due to the small size of the training and evaluation sets, which may limit the generalizability of the results.

Few-Shot Learning Table 4 presents NER results obtained from causal LLMs using few-shot learning. The performance of both LLaMA-3-8B and Mistral-7B on low-resource languages is not remarkable. LLaMa-3 performed better for Shahmukhi; however, its performance on Urdu, a relatively high-resource language, is quite low. The few-shot NER results indicate that causal LLMs are still far behind in NER for low-resource languages.

6.1 Limitations

Despite demonstrating significant advantages in the application of cross-lingual data augmentation, this study has a few limitations. The Shahmukhi, SiNER and MK-PUCIT datasets contain some an-

LLaMA-3-8B-Instruct			
Dataset	**Precision**	**Recall**	**F_1 Score**
Urdu-Wikiann	20.13	24.26	22.00
Shahmukhi	74.63	72.06	73.32
SiNER	39.98	48.66	43.89
Pashto-Wikiann	48.46	56.76	52.28
Mistral-7B-Instruct-v0.3			
Dataset	**Precision**	**Recall**	**F_1 Score**
Urdu-Wikiann	42.54	45.29	43.87
Shahmukhi	41.49	47.13	44.13
SiNER	27.02	38.40	31.72
Pashto-Wikiann	47.29	54.95	50.83

Table 4: Micro-F_1 scores by few-shot learning NER from LLaMA3-8B-Insruct and Mistral-7B-Instruct-v0.3. Both models have been evaluated for 1,000 sentences from each dataset except Pashto-Wikiann that has only 100 samples.

notation inconsistencies and errors that affect the overall performance of the models. Furthermore, the cluster-based data augmentation technique used entity clusters by employing an unsupervised clustering algorithm. The accuracy of the clustering process poses a limitation on the quality of the augmentation. Future work should focus on improving the annotation quality and consistency of such datasets.

7 Conclusion

This study explored various data augmentation techniques and their effect on the task of NER for low-resource languages. We used pre-trained LLMs on mono- and multilingual setups. Our findings highlight that cluster-based data augmentation improves NER performance for Shahmukhi, Sindhi and Pashto datasets by incorporating linguistically plausible text and cross-lingual diversity. Urdu-Wikiann, an automatically annotated dataset, does not take advantage of cross-lingual augmentations. Generative augmentation shows improved results on Urdu, while have a negative impact on the other three regional languages. Few-shot learning with causal models reveal their current limitations for low-resource languages when used for data augmentation and NER. Overall, the research emphasizes the potential of hybrid data augmentation techniques to enhance NER performance for low-resource languages.

References

Muhammad Tayyab Ahmad, Muhammad Kamran Malik, Khurram Shahzad, Faisal Aslam, Asif Iqbal, Zubair Nawaz, and Faisal Bukhari. 2020. Named Entity Recognition and Classification for Punjabi Shahmukhi. *ACM Transactions on Asian and Low-Resource Language Information Processing (TALLIP)*, 19(4):1–13.

Anil Ahmed, Degen Huang, Syed Yasser Arafat, and Imran Hameed. 2024. Enriching Urdu Ner with BERT Embedding, Data Augmentation, and Hybrid Encoder-CNN Architecture. *ACM Transactions on Asian and Low-Resource Language Information Processing*, 23(4):1–38.

Wazir Ali, Junyu Lu, and Zenglin Xu. 2020. SiNER: A Large Dataset for Sindhi Named Entity Recognition. In *Proceedings of the Twelfth Language Resources and Evaluation Conference*, pages 2953–2961.

Ilaria Bartolini, Vincenzo Moscato, Marco Postiglione, Giancarlo Sperlì, and Andrea Vignali. 2022. COSINER: COntext SImilarity data augmentation for Named Entity Recognition. In *International Conference on Similarity Search and Applications*, pages 11–24. Springer.

Xuanting Chen, Junjie Ye, Can Zu, Nuo Xu, Rui Zheng, Minlong Peng, Jie Zhou, Tao Gui, Qi Zhang, and Xuanjing Huang. 2023. How Robust is GPT-3.5 to Predecessors? A Comprehensive Study on Language Understanding Tasks. *arXiv preprint arXiv:2303.00293*.

Yang Chen, Chao Jiang, Alan Ritter, and Wei Xu. 2022. Frustratingly Easy Label Projection for Cross-lingual Transfer. *arXiv preprint arXiv:2211.15613*.

Alexis Conneau, Kartikay Khandelwal, Naman Goyal, Vishrav Chaudhary, Guillaume Wenzek, Francisco Guzmán, Edouard Grave, Myle Ott, Luke Zettlemoyer, and Veselin Stoyanov. 2019. Unsupervised Cross-lingual Representation Learning at Scale. *CoRR*, abs/1911.02116.

Ryan Cotterell and Kevin Duh. 2024. Low-Resource Named Entity Recognition with Cross-Lingual, Character-level Neural Conditional Random Fields. *arXiv preprint arXiv:2404.09383*.

Zhuojun Ding, Wei Wei, Xiaoye Qu, and Dangyang Chen. 2024. Improving Pseudo Labels with Global-Local Denoising Framework for Cross-lingual Named Entity Recognition. *arXiv preprint arXiv:2406.01213*.

Gary F. Simons Eberhard, David M. and Charles D. Fennig. 2024. Ethnologue: Languages of the world. *SIL International*, 27.

Toqeer Ehsan and Sarmad Hussain. 2021. Development and Evaluation of an Urdu Treebank (CLE-UTB) and a Statistical Parser. *Language Resources and Evaluation*, 55(2):287–326.

Chandra Kiran Reddy Evuru, Sreyan Ghosh, Sonal Kumar, Utkarsh Tyagi, Dinesh Manocha, et al. 2024. CoDa: Constrained Generation based Data Augmentation for Low-Resource NLP. *arXiv preprint arXiv:2404.00415*.

Edouard Grave, Piotr Bojanowski, Prakhar Gupta, Armand Joulin, and Tomas Mikolov. 2018. Learning Word Vectors for 157 Languages. In *Proceedings of the International Conference on Language Resources and Evaluation (LREC 2018)*.

Junjie Hu, Sebastian Ruder, Aditya Siddhant, Graham Neubig, Orhan Firat, and Melvin Johnson. 2020. XTREME: A massively multilingual multitask benchmark for evaluating cross-lingual generalisation. In *Proceedings of the 37th International Conference on Machine Learning*, volume 119 of *Proceedings of Machine Learning Research*, pages 4411–4421. PMLR.

Sarmad Hussain. 2008. Resources for Urdu language processing. In *Proceedings of the 6th workshop on Asian Language Resources*.

Ayyoob Imani, Peiqin Lin, Amir Hossein Kargaran, Silvia Severini, Masoud Jalili Sabet, Nora Kassner, Chunlan Ma, Helmut Schmid, André FT Martins, François Yvon, et al. 2023. Glot500: Scaling Multilingual Corpora and Language Models to 500 Languages. *arXiv preprint arXiv:2305.12182*.

Faryal Jahangir, Waqas Anwar, Usama Ijaz Bajwa, and Xuan Wang. 2012. N-gram and Gazetteer List based Named Entity Recognition for Urdu: A Scarce Resourced Language. In *Proceedings of the 10th Workshop on Asian Language Resources*, pages 95–104.

Safia Kanwal, Kamran Malik, Khurram Shahzad, Faisal Aslam, and Zubair Nawaz. 2019. Urdu Named Entity Recognition: Corpus Generation and Deep Learning Applications. *ACM Transactions on Asian and Low-Resource Language Information Processing (TALLIP)*, 19(1):1–13.

Hamza Khalid, Ghulam Murtaza, and Qaiser Abbas. 2023. Using Data Augmentation and Bidirectional Encoder Representations from Transformers for Improving Punjabi Named Entity Recognition. *ACM Transactions on Asian and Low-Resource Language Information Processing*, 22(6):1–13.

Wahab Khana, Ali Daudb, Jamal A Nasira, and Tehmina Amjada. 2016. Named Entity Dataset for Urdu Named Entity Recognition Task. *Language & Technology*, 51.

Brayan Stiven Lancheros, Gloria Corpas Pastor, and Ruslan Mitkov. 2024. Data Augmentation and Transfer Learning for Cross-lingual Named Entity Recognition in the Biomedical Domain. *Language Resources and Evaluation*, pages 1–20.

Duong Minh Le, Yang Chen, Alan Ritter, and Wei Xu. 2024. Constrained Decoding for Cross-lingual Label Projection. *arXiv preprint arXiv:2402.03131*.

Onkar Litake, Niraj Yagnik, and Shreyas Labhsetwar. 2024. IndiText Boost: Text Augmentation for Low Resource India Languages. *arXiv preprint arXiv:2401.13085*.

Jian Liu, Yufeng Chen, and Jinan Xu. 2022. Low-Resource NER by Data Augmentation With Prompting. In *IJCAI*, pages 4252–4258.

Linlin Liu, Bosheng Ding, Lidong Bing, Shafiq Joty, Luo Si, and Chunyan Miao. 2021. MulDA: A Multilingual Data Augmentation Framework for Low-Resource Cross-Lingual NER. In *Proceedings of the 59th Annual Meeting of the Association for Computational Linguistics and the 11th International Joint Conference on Natural Language Processing (Volume 1: Long Papers)*, pages 5834–5846.

Wenzhong Liu and Xiaohui Cui. 2023. Improving Named Entity Recognition for Social Media with Data Augmentation. *Applied Sciences*, 13(9):5360.

Holy Lovenia, Rahmad Mahendra, Salsabil Maulana Akbar, Lester James V. Miranda, Jennifer Santoso, Elyanah Aco, Akhdan Fadhilah, Jonibek Mansurov, Joseph Marvin Imperial, Onno P. Kampman, Joel Ruben Antony Moniz, and Others. 2024. SEACrowd: A Multilingual Multimodal Data Hub and Benchmark Suite for Southeast Asian Languages. *arXiv preprint arXiv: 2406.10118*.

Qiuhao Lu, Rui Li, Andrew Wen, Jinlian Wang, Liwei Wang, and Hongfang Liu. 2024. Large Language Models Struggle in Token-Level Clinical Named Entity Recognition. *arXiv preprint arXiv:2407.00731*.

Muhammad Kamran Malik. 2017. Urdu Named Entity Recognition and Classification System using Artificial Neural Network. *ACM Transactions on Asian and Low-Resource Language Information Processing (TALLIP)*, 17(1):1–13.

Stephen Mayhew, Terra Blevins, Shuheng Liu, Marek Šuppa, Hila Gonen, Joseph Marvin Imperial, Börje F Karlsson, Peiqin Lin, Nikola Ljubešić, Lester James Miranda, et al. 2023. Universal NER: A Gold-Standard Multilingual Named Entity Recognition Benchmark. *arXiv preprint arXiv:2311.09122*.

Ying Mo, Jian Yang, Jiahao Liu, Qifan Wang, Ruoyu Chen, Jingang Wang, and Zhoujun Li. 2024. MCL-NER: Cross-Lingual Named Entity Recognition via Multi-View Contrastive Learning. In *Proceedings of the AAAI Conference on Artificial Intelligence*, volume 38, pages 18789–18797.

Rafiullah Momand, Shakirullah Waseeb, and Ahmad Masood Latif Rai. 2020. A Comparative Study of Dictionary-based and Machine Learning-based Named Entity Recognition in Pashto. In *Proceedings of the 4th International Conference on Natural Language Processing and Information Retrieval*, pages 96–101.

Masoud Monajatipoor, Jiaxin Yang, Joel Stremmel, Melika Emami, Fazlolah Mohaghegh, Mozhdeh Rouhsedaghat, and Kai-Wei Chang. 2024. LLMs in Biomedicine: A Study on Clinical Named Entity Recognition. *arXiv preprint arXiv:2404.07376*.

Marco Naguib, Xavier Tannier, and Aurélie Névéol. 2024. Few Shot Clinical Entity Recognition in Three Languages: Masked Language Models Outperform LLM Prompting. *arXiv preprint arXiv:2402.12801*.

Afshin Rahimi, Yuan Li, and Trevor Cohn. 2019. Massively Multilingual Transfer for NER. In *Proceedings of the 57th Annual Meeting of the Association for Computational Linguistics*, pages 151–164, Florence, Italy. Association for Computational Linguistics.

Caroline Sabty, Islam Omar, Fady Wasfalla, Mohamed Islam, and Slim Abdennadher. 2021. Data Augmentation Techniques on Arabic Data for Named Entity Recognition. *Procedia Computer Science*, 189:292–299.

Sihan Song, Furao Shen, and Jian Zhao. 2024. RoPDA: Robust Prompt-Based Data Augmentation for Low-Resource Named Entity Recognition. In *Proceedings of the AAAI Conference on Artificial Intelligence*, volume 38, pages 19017–19025.

Bipesh Subedi, Sunil Regmi, Bal Krishna Bal, and Praveen Acharya. 2024. Exploring the Potential of Large Language Models (LLMs) for Low-resource Languages: A study on Named-Entity Recognition (NER) and Part-Of-Speech (POS) Tagging for Nepali Language. In *Proceedings of the 2024 Joint International Conference on Computational Linguistics, Language Resources and Evaluation (LREC-COLING 2024)*, pages 6974–6979.

Amina Tehseen, Toqeer Ehsan, Hannan Bin Liaqat, Xiangjie Kong, Amjad Ali, and Ala Al-Fuqaha. 2023. Shahmukhi Named Entity Recognition by using Contextualized Word Embeddings. *Expert Systems with Applications*, 229:120489.

Arthur Elwing Torres, Edleno Silva de Moura, Altigran Soares da Silva, Mario A Nascimento, and Filipe Mesquita. 2024. An Experimental Study on Data Augmentation Techniques for Named Entity Recognition on Low-Resource Domains.

Hugo Touvron, Thibaut Lavril, Gautier Izacard, Xavier Martinet, Marie-Anne Lachaux, Timothée Lacroix, Baptiste Rozière, Naman Goyal, Eric Hambro, Faisal Azhar, et al. 2023. LLaMA: Open and Efficient Foundation Language Models. *arXiv preprint arXiv:2302.13971*.

Fabián Villena, Luis Miranda, and Claudio Aracena. 2024. llmNER:(Zero| Few)-Shot Named Entity Recognition, Exploiting the Power of Large Language Models. *arXiv preprint arXiv:2406.04528*.

Jason Wei and Kai Zou. 2019. EDA: Easy Data Augmentation Techniques for Boosting Performance on Text Classification Tasks. *arXiv preprint arXiv:1901.11196*.

Junjie Ye, Xuanting Chen, Nuo Xu, Can Zu, Zekai Shao, Shichun Liu, Yuhan Cui, Zeyang Zhou, Chao Gong, Yang Shen, et al. 2023. A Comprehensive Capability Analysis of GPT-3 and GPT-3.5 Series Models. *arXiv preprint arXiv:2303.10420*.

Junjie Ye, Nuo Xu, Yikun Wang, Jie Zhou, Qi Zhang, Tao Gui, and Xuanjing Huang. 2024. LLM-DAA: Data Augmentation via Large Language Models for Few-Shot Named Entity Recognition. *arXiv preprint arXiv:2402.14568*.

A MK-PUCIT Dataset

The MK-PUCIT dataset was released with IO (Inside-Outside) annotation that has some annotation inconsistencies and errors. We converted it to the BIO (Begin-Inside-Outside) scheme automatically. For missing annotations, we extracted dictionaries with unique entities for each entity type from the training set and mapped the missing annotations throughout the dataset. After the mapping process, there was an overall increase of 19.9% in entity mentions for the train set and an increase of 13.8% for the test set. This highlights a significant number of missing annotations. Table 1 presents the updated statistics of the MK-PUCIT dataset.

We performed NER experiments by fine-tuning the Glot500 model and compared the results with different versions of the dataset in mono- and multilingual settings. Table 5 shows NER results for the MK-PUCIT. The original dataset, after conversion from IO to BIO scheme, performs with a micro F_1 score of 68.47. By performing the entity mapping for missing annotations, its performance was enhanced by 8.69 points, which is a significant improvement. Its performance remains in the same range in a multilingual setup. F_1 scores for the other three languages are lower compared to Urdu-Wikiann, therefore, we selected the Urdu-Wikiann dataset for multilingual NER experiments in this study.

Monolingual NER			
Dataset	**Precision**	**Recall**	**F_1 Score**
MK-PUCIT$_{Original}$	74.27	63.51	68.47
MK-PUCIT$_{Mapped}$	81.14	73.56	77.16
MK-PUCIT$_{Combined}$	83.26	72.27	77.37
Shahmukhi	81.89	74.75	78.15
SiNER	81.44	79.76	80.59
Pashto-Wikiann	81.32	79.62	80.46

Table 5: NER results by fine-tuning Glot500-base on the MK-PUCIT dataset. The fine-tuned model has been trained on; 1) original dataset after conversion from IO scheme to BIO, 2) with entity mapping for missing annotations, 3) multilingual setup by combining datasets of four languages.

B Dataset Analysis

To investigate the capability of pre-trained models to generalize cross-lingual entity representations, we analyzed the ratio of named entities which are common in both training and test sets. The main objective of this analysis is to determine whether the models are only memorizing seen examples or if they are improving generalization in multilingual training setup?. Table 6 shows type-wise presence of entity mentions from the test sets in the training sets. The analysis is given for both, mono- and multilingual datasets. All four datasets demonstrate a minor increase in seen examples from monolingual to multilingual datasets. The small increase in the ratio of seen entities is evident that the models enhance their learning by generalization and produce better NER results in multilingual setups.

C Augmentation Analysis

The cluster-based data augmentation has been performed to produce enhanced datasets with multiple iterations. The X_1 iteration shows a single pass of augmentation, X_2 iteration depicts two passes, and so on. In this section, we present an experimental analysis of the cluster-based augmentation with respect to different augmentation iterations.

Table 7 presents the NER results from the fine-tuned Glot500 model with mono- and multilingual low-resource data settings. The micro F_1 scores are compared against one and two iterations. The Urdu-Wikiann dataset demonstrates some improvements for X_2 in the monolingual setup using 100 and 200 samples. However, there is a decrease in the performance in multilingual experiments for all the other training sets. Similarly, Shahmukhi shows improved performance in monolingual setup and performance degradation in multilingual training. The SiNER and Pashto-Wikiann datasets also follow the similar trend for low-resource training splits.

Table 8 further shows NER results after fine-tuning on the entire datasets. In monolingual experiments, SiNER shows a subtle increase in scores with X_2 iterations in both mono- and multilingual setups. However, all the other datasets demonstrate performance degradation with the increase of iterations of data augmentations. Based on these NER results, we presented results and comparisons against one iteration of data augmentation in the results section of the paper.

Additionally, we compared the data augmentation method by selecting all correct sentences from the top five candidates with one and two iterations. Table 9 shows the comparison for low-resource settings. In the low-resource datasets, Urdu-Wikiann and Shahmukhi datasets perform better for only 100 samples for both mono- and mul-

	Monolingual Datasets			
	Urdu-Wikiann	Shahmukhi	SiNER	Pashto-Wikiann
PER	254, 82.2%	482, 48.59%	555, 32.04%	3, 10.71%
LOC	102, 30.82%	140, 52.83%	115, 28.97%	5, 12.5%
ORG	234, 77.74%	66, 42.86%	57, 22.62%	8, 23.53%
Total	590, 62.69%	688, 48.75%	727, 30.53%	16, 15.68%
	Multilingual Datasets			
	Urdu-Wikiann	Shahmukhi	SiNER	Pashto-Wikiann
PER	255, 82.52%	507, 51.11%	559, 32.27%	6 21.43%
LOC	106, 32.02%	151, 56.98%	116, 29.22%	11 27.5%
ORG	234, 77.74%	69, 44.81%	57, 22.62%	9 26.47%
Total	595, 63.23%	727, 51.52%	732, 30.74%	26, 25.49%

Table 6: Analysis of presence of named entities of test sets in monolingual and multilingual training sets.

Monolingual Setup	100		200		500		1000	
Datasets	X_1	X_2	X_1	X_2	X_1	X_2	X_1	X_2
Urdu-Wikiann	76.62	76.48	81.00	82.32	83.78	83.13	85.31	84.73
Shahmukhi	60.78	62.24	68.03	68.79	73.17	73.03	77.11	78.15
SiNER	65.64	65.66	71.17	70.84	76.90	78.67	79.46	79.77
Pashto-Wikiann	48.54	48.51	–	–	–	–	–	–
Multilingual Setup	**100**		**200**		**500**		**1000**	
Datasets	**X_1**	**X_2**	**X_1**	**X_2**	**X_1**	**X_2**	**X_1**	**X_2**
Urdu-Wikkiann	76.83	70.81	82.25	74.75	84.35	81.79	85.34	84.27
Shahmukhi (1k)	68.88	65.55	73.47	70.59	77.51	75.56	80.01	79.52
Sindhi	66.76	68.77	73.22	71.72	76.26	75.89	79.61	79.01
Pashto	66.63	68.67	73.12	71.60	76.05	75.68	79.35	78.81

Table 7: Micro-F_1 scores by fine-tuning Glot500-base on low-resource multilingual datasets by using data augmentation with one (X_1) and two (X_2) iterations.

tilingual experiments. The other data splits start performance degradation. SiNER demonstrates some improvements for 1,000 sentences in monolingual experiment and for 100 train samples for multilingual setup. The performance degradation is observed for all the other training sets. Pashto-Wikian is a smaller dataset that contains only 100 sentences and it shows improvements by learning cross-lingual representations in multilingual setup.

We further compared the results by selecting all correct sentences for entire datasets as shown in Table 10. The F_1 score for Urdu-Wikiann remains in the same range for monolingual training but deceases significantly in the multilingual training setup. However, F_1 scores for Shahmukhi and Sindhi are quite low compared to X_1 and X_2 iterations. Pashto-Wikiann shows the similar behaviour.

The Shahmukhi and SiNER datasets were further analyzed for one, two and three augmentation iterations for low-resource monolingual settings as shown in Table 11. Shahmukhi shows improvements by training with three iterations. However, in the multilingual setup, it shows performance degradation when adding more augmented sentences (Table 10). On the other hand, SiNER performs with mixed results but it also demonstrates decreased performance in multilingual training setup with increased data augmentation iterations. Based on these analysis, augmentation with one iteration produces optimal performance for Urdu-Wikiann, Shahmukhi, SiNER and Pashto-Wikiann datasets. Therefore, in the main paper, we presented the results achieved by using one iteration of the cluster- and EDA-based data augmentation methods for all the selected datasets.

Table 12 presents the F_1 scores for Shahmukhi and SiNER Few-Shot experiments with five different randomly selected training sets to analyze the variation in scores across datasets. Pashto-Wikiann is a small dataset with only 100 instances, and our data augmentation technique does not perform well on Urdu-Wikiann; therefore, we experimented only on the Shahmukhi and SiNER datasets. Shahmukhi exhibits a consistent trend across all Few-Shot settings, with a mean score closely aligning with the actual scores. However, SiNER, on the other hand, demonstrates higher variance for to the smaller number of examples.

D Hyperparameters

In the fine-tuning process, the learning rate of 2e-5 was used along with the AdamW optimizer. The batch size was set to 8, which helped to maintain

Monolingual Setup		X_1			X_2	
Datasets	**Precision**	**Recall**	**F_1**	**Precision**	**Recall**	**F_1**
Urdu-Wikiann	94.51	94.61	94.56	93.75	94.14	93.94
Shahmukhi	84.04	82.23	83.13	82.33	82.20	82.27
SiNER	87.49	88.82	88.15	88.91	88.01	88.48
Pashto-Wikiann	52.08	45.45	48.54	58.46	41.45	48.51
Multilingual Setup		**X_1**			**X_2**	
Datasets	**Precision**	**Recall**	**F_1**	**Precision**	**Recall**	**F_1**
Urdu-Wikiann	96.07	96.18	96.12	94.76	95.70	95.23
Shahmukhi	89.03	85.50	87.22	86.83	86.08	86.45
SiNER	89.19	86.69	87.92	88.16	88.01	88.08
Pashto-Wikiann	89.00	86.29	87.62	87.85	87.54	87.69

Table 8: Micro-F_1 scores by fine-tuning Glot500-base on multilingual setting for the entire datasets by using data augmentation with one (X_1) and two (X_2) iterations.

Train Size	Iteration	Urdu-Wikiann	Shahmukhi	SiNER	Pashto-Wikiann
		Monolingual Setup			
100	**X_1**	76.62	60.78	65.64	48.54
	X_2	76.48	62.25	65.66	48.51
	All correct	72.31	64.39	65.27	49.78
200	**X_1**	81.00	68.03	71.17	–
	X_2	82.32	68.79	70.84	–
	All correct	81.18	67.85	71.46	–
500	**X_1**	83.78	73.17	76.88	–
	X_2	83.13	73.03	78.67	–
	All correct	84.57	73.87	76.00	–
1000	**X_1**	85.31	77.11	79.46	–
	X_2	84.73	78.15	79.77	–
	All correct	81.76	77.16	80.98	–
		Multilingual Setup			
100	**X_1**	76.83	66.88	66.76	66.63
	X_2	70.81	65.55	68.77	68.67
	All correct	79.10	67.85	64.89	64.84
200	**X_1**	82.25	73.47	73.22	73.12
	X_2	74.75	70.59	71.72	71.60
	All correct	79.58	71.55	72.84	72.70
500	**X_1**	84.35	77.51	76.26	76.05
	X_2	81.79	75.56	75.89	75.68
	All correct	81.49	76.00	77.03	76.86
1000	**X_1**	85.34	80.01	79.61	79.35
	X_2	84.27	79.52	79.01	78.81
	All correct	85.03	79.13	79.18	79.53

Table 9: Micro-F_1 scores by fine-tuning Glot500-base on monolingual and multilingual low-resource datasets by using data augmentation with one (X_1) and two (X_2) iterations and all correct from top five augmentations.

Monolingual Setup			
Dataset	**X_1**	**X_2**	**All correct**
Urdu-Wikiann	94.56	93.94	94.58
Shahmukhi	83.13	82.27	81.79
SiNER	88.15	88.48	86.84
Pashto-Wikiann	48.54	48.51	49.78
Multilingual Setup			
Urdu-Wikiann	96.12	95.23	91.82
Shahmukhi	87.22	86.45	83.42
SiNER	87.92	88.08	84.82
Pashto-Wikiann	87.62	87.69	84.52

Table 10: Micro-F_1 scores by fine-tuning Glot500-base on monolingual low-resource datasets by using data augmentation with one (X_1) and two (X_2) iterations and all correct from top five augmentations.

Train Size	Iteration	Shahmukhi	SiNER
100	**X_1**	60.78	65.64
	X_2	62.25	65.66
	X_3	61.85	65.03
200	**X_1**	68.03	71.17
	X_2	68.79	70.84
	X_3	70.35	70.38
500	**X_1**	73.17	76.88
	X_2	73.03	78.67
	X_3	73.89	75.98
1000	**X_1**	77.11	79.46
	X_2	78.15	79.77
	X_3	77.68	80.53

Table 11: Micro-F_1 scores by fine-tuning Glot500-base on monolingual low-resource datasets by using data augmentation with one (X_1), two (X_2) and three (X_3) iterations.

memory and training efficiency. The models were fine-tuned by setting various number of epochs for low-resource datasets depending on the training samples. Early stopping was further implemented based on the micro F_1 score on the validation set. The maximum sequence length was set to 100 tokens. These hyperparameters ensured optimal performance of the models.

E Few-Shot NER - Prompt

You are an expert in identifying named entities for language. The INPUT contains text followed by an OUTPUT sequence of BIO labels. Perform named entity recognition and return the labels. Three examples are provided for your reference:
EXAMPLE 1:
INPUT: Foreign advisor Sartaj Aziz will visit Afghanistan today.
OUTPUT: O O B-PER I-PER O O B-LOC O.

Shahmukhi				
RUNs	**100**	**200**	**500**	**1000**
Run 1	62.12	66.04	72.05	76.69
Run 2	60.77	67.00	71.47	75.45
Run 3	60.49	65.86	72.62	77.15
Run 4	61.81	64.85	73.36	77.23
Run 5	62.58	67.33	72.05	74.98
Mean	61.55	66.22	72.31	76.30
Variance	0.7963	0.9698	0.5098	1.0511
Standard Deviation	0.8924	0.9848	0.7140	1.0252
SiNER				
RUNs	**100**	**200**	**500**	**1000**
Run 1	64.81	70.40	75.83	77.78
Run 2	60.54	66.62	75.21	79.32
Run 3	63.40	65.89	74.94	76.81
Run 4	63.67	69.44	74.57	78.74
Run 5	64.65	69.86	73.55	79.45
Mean	63.41	68.44	74.82	78.42
Variance	2.9505	4.1682	0.7155	1.2437
Standard Deviation	1.7177	2.0416	0.8458	1.1152

Table 12: Mean, variance, and standard deviation by fine-tuning Glot500-base for Shamukhi and SiNER Few-Shot settings on five randomly selected train sets.

Wikipedia is Not a Dictionary, Delete! Text Classification as a Proxy for Analysing Wiki Deletion Discussions

Hsuvas Borkakoty[1] and Luis Espinosa-Anke[1,2]
[1]Cardiff NLP, School of Computer Science and Informatics, Cardiff University, UK
[2]AMPLYFI, UK
{borkakotyh,espinosa-ankel}@cardiff.ac.uk

Abstract

Automated content moderation for collaborative knowledge hubs like Wikipedia or Wikidata is an important yet challenging task due to multiple factors. In this paper, we construct a database of discussions happening around *articles marked for deletion* in several Wikis and in three languages, which we then use to evaluate a range of LMs on different tasks (from predicting the outcome of the discussion to identifying the implicit policy an individual comment might be pointing to). Our results reveal, among others, that discussions leading to deletion are easier to predict, and that, surprisingly, self-produced tags (keep, delete or redirect) don't always help guiding the classifiers, presumably because of users' hesitation or deliberation within comments[1].

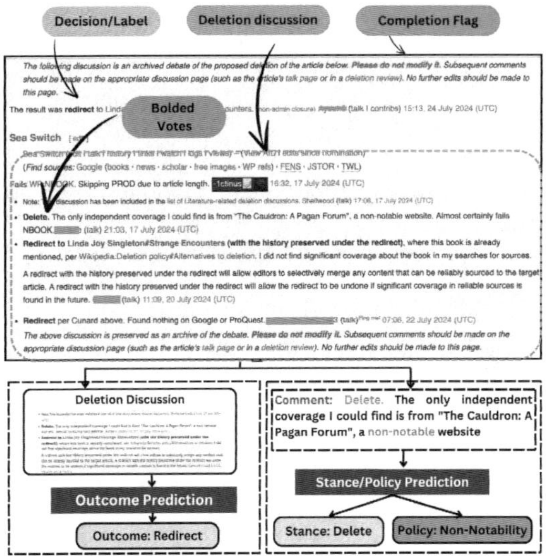

Figure 1: Example of a Deletion Discussion in English Wikipedia

1 Introduction

Wikipedia and its sister Wikis play an indispensable role as a collaborative knowledge source, and are widely used by students (Selwyn and Gorard, 2016) and the general public (Singer et al., 2017; Lemmerich et al., 2019) alike. They fulfill use cases that range from core knowledge *go-tos*, as well as "free" supporting documentation for content providers and search engines (e.g., Google[2] or YouTube[3]). However, due to their size and, most importantly, their collaborative nature, ensuring high quality in these platforms is challenging, especially given the need to "map" content to existing policies at least semi-automatically (Ribeiro et al., 2022). This is particularly relevant in the GenAI era, as AI-generated content has proliferated throughout the Internet (Brooks et al., 2024).

More generally, content moderation in online platforms is often the outcome of group coordination and communication (Chidambaram and Tung, 2005; Jensen and Scacchi, 2005; Butler et al., 2008). Unsurprisingly, NLP plays an important role in automating this process. For example, Singhal et al. (2023) defined a framework for social media moderation as a function of community guidelines, policy enforcement and violation detection. Some prominent examples of works connected with such a framework are: policy based content moderation in Facebook (Sablosky, 2021), rule-breaking behavior analysis on Reddit (Chandrasekharan et al., 2018), and topic based content moderation discourse on X (Alizadeh et al., 2022). In the case of Wikis, both the guidelines and the rules that govern the quality of their content are maintained by contributions from the community (Seering, 2020), where discussion-based approaches towards content moderation are the norm.

[1]Dataset available at: https://huggingface.co/datasets/hsuvaskakoty/wider.

[2]https://en.wikipedia.org/wiki/Relationship_between_Google_and_Wikipedia

[3]https://support.google.com/youtube/answer/7630512?hl=en

Proceedings of the Tenth Workshop on Noisy and User-generated Text, pages 133–142
May 3, 2025 ©2025 Association for Computational Linguistics

Task	Lang.	Platform	Label Set
Outcome Prediction	En	Wikipedia	delete, keep, redirect, no-consensus, merge, speedy keep, speedy delete, withdrawn
		Wikidata-ent.	delete, keep, merge, redirect, no-consensus, comment
		Wikidata-pr.	delete, keep, no-consensus
		Wikiquote	delete, keep, redirect, merge, no-consensus
		Wikinews	delete, keep, speedy delete, comment
	Es	Wikipedia	borrar (delete), mantener (keep), fusionar (merge), otros (others)
	Gr	Wikipedia	Διαγραφή (delete), Διατήρηση (keep), Δεν υπάρχει συναίνεση (no-consensus)
Stance Detection	En	Wikipedia	delete, keep, merge, comment
Policy Prediction	En	Wikipedia	Wikipedia:Notability, Wikipedia:What Wikipedia is not, Wikipedia:No original research, Wikipedia:Verifiability, Wikipedia:Arguments to avoid in deletion discussions, Wikipedia:Biographies of living persons, Wikipedia:Criteria for speedy deletion, Wikipedia:Articles for deletion, Wikipedia:Wikipedia is not a dictionary, Wikipedia:Deletion policy

Table 1: Label set for the different tasks and datasets we consider in this paper (Outcome, Stance, and Policy), for three languages (English: En, Spanish: Es, and Greek: Gr) and five (4+1) platforms (Wikipedia, Wikidata-Entity (ent.) and Property (pr.), Wikinews, and Wikiquote).

The way this generally works is that, given an article flagged by a community member, users justify their stance towards it and its adherence to the policies, and then editors act. However, manual efforts to clear the backlog are insufficient. Therefore, NLP techniques for predicting the outcome of a deletion discussion, or for capturing a user's stance towards a specific article are critical (Mayfield and Black, 2019b; Kaffee et al., 2023). Despite this need, there is a surprising lack of work beyond Wikipedia, and there is almost no published work that looks at non-English languages (with the exception of Kaffee et al. (2023)). Moreover, in-depth comparative analyses of parameter-efficient techniques have also been so far largely unexplored.

We therefore aim to address all of the above with an analysis on a novel collection of deletion discussions, in three languages and four platforms. These discussions come, if resolved, alongside the discussion outcomes (generally speaking, suggesting to `keep` or `delete` the article, although the actual outcome tags are more fine grained than this), with individual comments having their own stance and referring to specific policies Kaffee et al. (2023). Our classification experiments set strong baseline results for the community to build upon, and provide insights into these community-led activities.

2 Tasks and dataset Construction

We consider three tasks, namely (1) **Outcome prediction** - given a full discussion around an article marked for deletion, predict the final decision; (2) **Stance detection**, i.e. given an individual comment, determine its stance towards the decision to be made for that article; and (3) **Policy prediction**, where again, given one single comment, we want to determine the policy that comment is most likely be referring to (Figure 1 shows an exmaple). We build a novel dataset for outcome prediction, while for the other two tasks we largely rely on the dataset from Kaffee et al. (2023) (although with some important modifications to enable the goal of this paper, namely an in-depth analysis). We provide more detail about these datasets in the following subsections.

Language	Platform	Total
en	Wikipedia	18,528
	Wikidata-entities	355,428
	Wikidata-properties	498
	Wikinews	91
	Wikiquote	695
es	Wikipedia	3,274
gr	Wikipedia	392

Table 2: Overall number of deletion discussions per language and platform in the outcome prediction dataset.

2.1 Outcome Prediction

We retrieve and clean deletion discussions programmatically[4] for three different languages and four

[4]We use the WIDE-ANALYSIS toolkit: https://pypi.org/project/wide-analysis/ (Borkakoty and

Platform	Language	Example title	Discussion (truncated)	Outcome
Wikipedia	en	Beast Poetry	Editor 1: Keep in one form or another. Editor 2: One option could be to re-frame the article to be about the book.	Keep
Wikidata-Ent	en	Q28090948	Editor 1: no description : Vandalism.	Delete
Wikidata-Prop	en	JMdict sequence number (P11700)	Editor 1: Deleted - ( ) Support I assume no comments have been made because this is a clear case to delete...	Delete
Wikinews	en	Mugalkhod Jeedga Mutta organizes mass marriage in Belgaum, India	Editor 1: There is no further meaningful work on the article. Editor 2: All advice ignored, kill it with cleansing fire and stop wasting time.	Speedy delete
Wikiquote	en	3rd Rock From The Sun	Editor 1: Two reasons to delete this: - It is a copy of about half of quotes on IMDB - 3rd Rock from the Sun is a different article. Editor 2: Merge, perhaps with some trimming.	Merge
Wikipedia-Es	es	Héroes: El legado de la Evolución	Editor 1: Bórrese Irrelevante enciclopédico. Editor 2: Bórrese Irrelevante.	Borrar
Wikipedia-gr	gr	Μουσείο Μιχάλη Τσαρτσίδη	Editor 1: Σχόλιο Διαφωνώ έντονα με την λογική/φράση «Απλώς ένα από τα πολλά ανά την Ελλάδα μουσε... Editor 2: Ο μόνος λόγος διαγραφής μπορεί να είναι η παραβίαση πνευματικών.	διαγραφή

Table 3: Examples for different platforms and languages, alongside outcome labels.

platforms (with Wikidata being split in two: properties and entities, as their discussions happen separately). In terms of coverage, for small platforms with less activity such as Wikinews or Wikiquote[5], we consider all data available in their website at the time of scraping, whereas for larger and more active platforms like Wikidata, we consider the last 4 full years (from 2021 to 2024, both inclusive). Label sets per task are provided in Table 1, whereas statistics in terms of raw size can be found in Table 2.

2.2 Dataset for Stance Detection and Policy Prediction

For stance detection and policy prediction we use the existing WIKI-STANCE dataset (Kaffee et al., 2023). We keep the stance detection dataset as-is, including their original label set. However, for policy prediction, we consider a reduced label set in order to perform error analysis, and so keep only the top 10 most frequent labels (as opposed to the 92 contained in the original dataset). This change, however, has a small effect on the overall dataset size, as retaining only these labels still results in roughly 80% of the original dataset. As an example, policy labels contained in the original dataset like `Wikipedia: Userfication`, `Wikipedia: Record charts` or `Wikipedia: Attack page` account for only 106, 105 and 102 instances, respectively (out of 437,770, which means a negligible percentage, around 0.02%).

3 Experiments

With these datasets in place, we proceed to run classification experiments.

3.1 Outcome Prediction

While previous works (Mayfield and Black, 2019a) cast outcome prediction as binary classification (`Delete` and `Keep`), we follow Wikipedia's official guidelines[6] and propose a more nuanced scheme (again, c.f. Table 1) and re-cast it as a multi-class classification. Following Mayfield and Black (2019b), we have two set ups: *Masked*, where labels are redacted from the comments, and *Full-text* where classifiers see the full dataset, including the self-assigned labels (which in theory act as extremely informative features about the stance of each comment and therefore good predictors of the final outcome of the discussion - however, as we will see, this is not always the case). We evaluate BERT (Devlin et al., 2018), RoBERTa (Liu et al., 2019), DistilBERT (Sanh et al., 2020) (all in Base and Large), and Twitter-RoBERTa-Base (Barbieri

Espinosa-Anke, 2024).

[5]According to Wikimedia Statistics, in 2024 Wikipedia and Wikidata received 130 Billion and 3 Billion pageviews, whereas Wikinews and Wikiquote received 77 Million and 179 Million respectively.

[6]`https://en.wikipedia.org/wiki/Wikipedia:Guide_to_deletion`

Input Type	Model	Wikip.	Wikid.-ent	Wikid.-pr	Wikin.	Wikiq.
Fulltext	RoBERTa-B	0.56	0.61	0.56	0.4	0.71
	RoBERTa-L	**0.58**	**0.63**	**0.62**	**0.47**	**0.76**
	BERT-B	0.56	0.57	0.54	0.4	0.7
	BERT-L	**0.58**	0.62	0.61	**0.47**	0.73
	DistilBERT	0.55	0.56	0.5	0.39	0.57
	Tw.-RoBERTa-B	0.49	0.6	0.55	0.4	0.7
Masked	RoBERTa-B	0.49	0.51	0.56	0.36	0.62
	RoBERTa-L	**0.52**	**0.61**	0.56	**0.42**	0.65
	BERT-B	0.49	0.57	0.56	0.33	0.7
	BERT-L	0.5	0.62	**0.6**	0.36	**0.72**
	DistilBERT	0.43	0.56	0.5	0.27	0.32
	Tw-RoBERTa-B	0.46	0.52	0.42	0.3	0.38

Table 4: F1 Scores for fine-tuned models in Wikipedia (Wikip.), Wikid.-end (Wikidata, entities subset), Wikid.-pr (Wikidata, entities subset), and Wikiq. (Wikiquote), both for (a) full text and (b) masked text inputs. Models are identified by their versions: Tw (Twitter), B (Base) and L (Large).

et al., 2020) (in order to explore the effect of models tailored to user-generated content). Information about training, validation and tests splits, and implementation details, are provided in Appendices A (Table 10) and B, respectively. Furthermore, we divide our set of experiments in three scenarios: in-platform, cross-platform and multilingual.

3.1.1 In-platform

We train each model with platform-specific training sets under both masked and full text settings, and report F1 results in Table 4. As expected, we can see that hiding the self-reported tags generally causes a drop in performance across the board, most noticeable in the X (Twitter)-specific model. We can also see that RoBERTa large is always the best model in full text, while this is more inconsistent in the masked setup. Further per-label analysis of the difference between the full text and masked settings for RoBERTa large (the best performing model) is provided in Figure 2, which shows confusion matrices for the Wikipedia-en dataset. The performance drop for 'keep', 'merge' and 'withdrawn' suggests that editors are more decisive about deletion of the article than keeping it. It also shows that full text is almost always useful, but interestingly, `merge` decisions benefit less from seeing these tags, likely because merging discussions are often less explicit and drift more between deletion and keep. Another interesting finding (which is consistent across both platforms) is that the `withdrawn` outcome often gets confused with keep, again reinforcing this idea of more ambiguity when the decision is *not* leading towards deletion. Next, `no consensus` outputs seem very hard to predict, with an almost even split

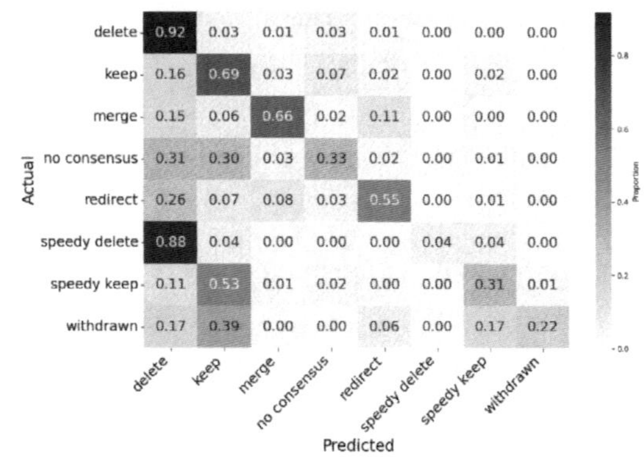

(a) Fulltext Setting

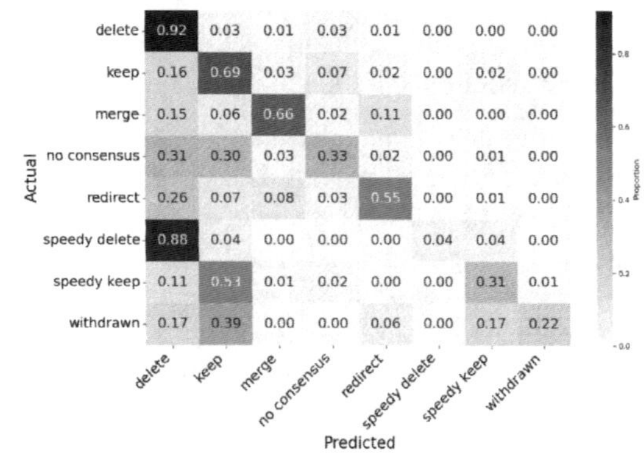

(b) Masked Setting

Figure 2: Confusion Matrix for RoBERTa-Large model in Outcome Prediction Task.

between predictions spread among the correct class (no consensus), delete and keep. And finally, a striking result is the massive confusion between speedy delete and delete in the masked setting. This suggests that, in practice, there virtually no difference in how editors *talk about* deleting articles, but they are however implicitly opinionated about how urgently the decisions needs to happen.

Another interesting perspective on this experiment is the option to explore more efficient approaches than simply fine-tuning an arguably large model, especially given that the size of the datasets is very varied. To test our hypothesis that simpler approaches could be beneficial, we evaluate a SetFit (Sentence-transformer Fine-tuning) model (Tunstall et al., 2022). SetFit is a simple yet powerful technique that fine-tunes a sentence transformers model[7] by artificially sampling training pairs for a contrastive learning stage, and uses the fine-tuned embeddings as feature vectors for a logistic regression classifier. Note that, in SetFit, in the embedding fine-tuning stage a large number of document pairs can be generated, specifically $K(K-1)/2$, where K is the number of labeled examples (i.e., the original training set). Therefore, we subsample the original training sets into a smaller stratified training set of 100 labeled examples. We found a striking boost in performance with this model, especially for smaller datasets (like Wikinews), which suggestst that, in production environments, SetFit could be an efficient and highly performing option. We show a SetFit vs best model comparison in Table 5.

Platform	Setting	Model	F1
Wikipedia	Fulltext	RoBERTa-L	0.60
	Masked	RoBERTa-L	0.52
	Fulltext	SetFit	**0.65**
	Masked	SetFit	0.57
Wikidata-ent	Fulltext	RoBERTa-L	0.63
	Masked	RoBERTa-L	0.61
	Fulltext	SetFit	**0.88**
	Masked	SetFit	0.87
Wikidata-pr	Fulltext	RoBERTa-L	0.62
	Masked	BERT-L	0.60
	Fulltext	SetFit	0.61
	Masked	SetFit	**0.70**
Wikinews	Fulltext	RoBERTa-L	0.47
	Masked	RoBERTa-L	0.42
	Fulltext	SetFit	**0.57**
	Masked	SetFit	0.44
Wikiquote	Fulltext	RoBERTa-L	0.76
	Masked	BERT-L	0.72
	Fulltext	SetFit	**0.87**
	Masked	SetFit	0.44

Table 5: Best model vs. SetFit results.

3.1.2 Cross-platform

In previous training experiments, we observe that models struggle to perform well in smaller datasets, likely due to the lack of training data (like Wikinews, where the performance was lowest on average for all models, with some cases up to 30% drop - as in the case of the Twitter-specialized model). This motivates us to explore the potential of a cross-platform training regime, under the hypothesis that many features in deletion discussions might be similar across Wiki-platforms. We therefore perform an experiment where, for each model and training set, we evaluate on the test set of all the Wiki-platforms. Due to the variation in label sets, we simplify this experiment and map all the labels of each dataset to only keep and delete, the two common labels in all the datasets. We test the models in the fulltext setting.

The expectation from the results listed in Table 6 would be to have a bold diagonal, i.e., a model trained on dataset X would be expected to be the best on the test set for X. While this is primarily the case, we find a comparable performance in other datasets, indicating a subtle but prominent generalization of the models across the platforms. The outlier in this trend is Wikinews, where we see both Wikipedia and Wikidata Entity-derived models performing better than the in-domain model. This can be attributed to the size of Wikinews dataset, which may not be enough for the models learn platform specific patterns. In fact, for this case, training on the most general dataset (i.e., Wikipedia) yields the best performance, specifically a non-negligible 11% increase in F-1. The performances of Wikidata-entity and property across all other platform is also quite similar, despite of the large difference in data instances between them, further signaling the similarity in contents between the two important components of the same platform. However, there is an important difference, it seems that Wikidata properties transfers well into Wikidata entities (with only a 2% drop in F1), however this

[7]We used BAAI/bge-base-en-v1.5 (Xiao et al., 2023), a model roughly 3 times smaller than our best performing fine-tuned models.

	Wikip.	Wikid.-ent	Wikid.-pr	Wikin.	Wikiq.
Wikip.	**0.76**	0.63	0.67	0.55	0.14
Wikid.-ent	0.43	**0.89**	0.87	0.33	0.63
Wikid.-pr	0.61	0.71	**0.83**	0.04	0.1
Wikin.	**0.44**	0.42	0.39	0.35	0.04
Wikiq.	0.07	0.04	0.05	0.01	**0.94**

Table 6: Results of F1 scores of model performance on different test sets (columns represent the data models were trained on and rows represent the data model is tested on.).

Language	Model	F1 (FT)	F1 (M)
gr	XLM-R-Base	0.47	0.38
	XLM-R-Large	0.59	0.49
	MBERT	0.59	0.40
	Tw.-XLM-R	0.44	0.40
	SetFit	**0.81**	**0.60**
es	XLM-R-Base	0.66	0.47
	XLM-R-Large	0.88	**0.85**
	MBERT	0.70	0.67
	Tw.-XLM-R	0.56	0.46
	SetFit	**0.90**	0.61

Table 7: F1 score for Fulltext (FT) and Masked (M) settings for multilingual models in Spanish (es) and Greek (gr).

is not the case vice versa, as a Wikidata entities-trained model falls short by 12% vs the in-domain model (trained on Wikidata properties).

Amongst all the similar performances from the models, an obvious outlier is Wikiquote, which fails to perform well on the other datasets, and all of the other models also fail to perform on the Wikiquote dataset, clearly showing the distinctive nature of Wikiquote discussions. However, it should be noted that compared to other popular platforms like Wikipedia, Wikiquote has a smaller editor base[8], which could cause a lack of diversity, consistency and overall quality, such as unmoderated discussions or inconsistencies between outcomes.

3.1.3 Multilingual

For multilingual datasets (Wikipedia-es and Wikipedia-gr), we experiment with XLM-R (Conneau, 2019) (Base and Large, XLM-R-Base and XLM-R-Large), Multilingual BERT (MBERT) (Devlin et al., 2018), and Twitter-XLM-R (Tw.-XLM-R) (Barbieri et al., 2020) (to explore if a model specialized on Twitter, another instance of user-generated content, could give advantages). We also introduced SetFit in this experiment, on top of a multilingual embedding model[9]. Due to the large data difference between the languages we consider (c.f. Table 2), as well as them having a different set of outcome labels, a cross language comparison is perhaps not appropriate, and therefore we discuss classification results on both languages separately.

Table 7 shows results following a similar performance pattern as the English experiment, with a significant difference between fulltext and masked setups. However, it is worth noting that XLM-R-Large and MBERT trained and tested on masked data in Spanish were able to come very close to the fulltext variant. This clearly points to Spanish editors using more explicit language when discussing whether an article should be deleted, giving a stronger signal to a classifier even after masking these self-assigned labels. This can be further verified in confusion matrices (on the fulltext setting, Figure 4), where the Greek model struggles to distinguish between `delete` and `no consensus`, which is certainly not the case in Spanish. Concerning the SetFit results, these are, again, surprisingly good, being the best model on the same test sets over fully fine-tuned models, with the exception only of the masked experiment, where it is outperformed by XLM-R-Large and MBERT. We attribute this to a potential mismatch of the style/topics/theme of the subsampled dataset and the training set. We leave for future work performing multiple runs to evalute the robustness of SetFit (or other approaches based on synthetic data generation) when datasets are varied.

Finally, we asked ourselves the question of why a strong multilingual model (XLM-R) further specialized on multilingual data from social media (Tw.-XLM-R) model would perform so poorly on another instance of user-generated texts which, as we can see from the examples in Tables 3 and 8, are not so different from well-formed tweets (note that in the original sampling from Barbieri et al. (2020) a few heuristics were put in place to filter out pure noise like all-emoji tweets). One approach to gain further insights is by computing pseudo (log) likelihood (Salazar et al., 2019) over sequences in the dataset from different models by taking a sample of the data, masking the actual (sub)word one at a time, and compute the loss of the models, and averaging over the whole sequence. Higher likelihood

[8]According to Wikiquote's official Wikipedia page, it only has 474 active editors as compared to Wikipedia's 126,324 (in other words, Wikiquote has only 0.004% of the editors of Wikipedia).

[9]Specifically, `paraphrase-multilingual-MiniLM-L12-v2`.

Policy	Example	Instances
Wikipedia:Notability	[WP:N] Fails and with only routine coverage.	232,422 (70.22%)
Wikipedia:What Wikipedia is not	If there are sources linking this to the attack.	34,559 (10.44%)
Wikipedia:No original research	"WP:OR, . Mishmash of random trivia.	13,583 (4.10%)
Wikipedia:Verifiability	I'm leaning delete per as this is completely unverified.	12,531 (3.78%)
Wikipedia:Arguments to avoid in deletion discussions	Her own work is admittedly ordinary, even run-of-the-mill.	8,105 (2.44%)
Wikipedia:Biographies of living persons	Because of BLP requirements, it needs to be rewritten.	7,346 (2.21%)
Wikipedia:Criteria for speedy deletion	In regards to the above comment about speedy deletion.	5,833 (1.77%)
Wikipedia:Articles for deletion	What searches did you do to establish notability?	5,758 (1.75%)
Wikipedia:Wikipedia is not a dictionary	Clearly a lexical entry and in violation of policies.	5,474 (1.65%)
Wikipedia:Deletion policy	In this case, I don't see the point of a redirect.	5,332 (1.61%)

Table 8: Top 10 Policies of policy prediction task dataset with examples and number of instances (with percentage of the complete dataset).

typically points to a model with a "good grasp" of the presented data (domain, style, themes, etc), as shown, e.g., in the context of temporal adaptation (Loureiro et al., 2022). To this end, we computed pseudo log likelihood over a sample of 1,000 Greek Wikipedia articles. We find the distribution in Figure 3, which, instead of a curve-shaped distribution (which would be the ideal), has two clear spikes, which suggests that this particular Twitter model might struggle to generalize (very low likelihood scores). Further analysis into the role of tokenization is left for future work.

3.2 Stance and Policy prediction

Stance detection classifies a moderator's opinion towards the article using stance labels (keep, delete, merge, comment), while policy prediction identifies an explicitly or implicitly mentioned Wikimedia policy (refer to Table 8 for illustrative examples). Both are comment level tasks. We experiment with the same base models from the Outcome Prediction task. We report our results in Table

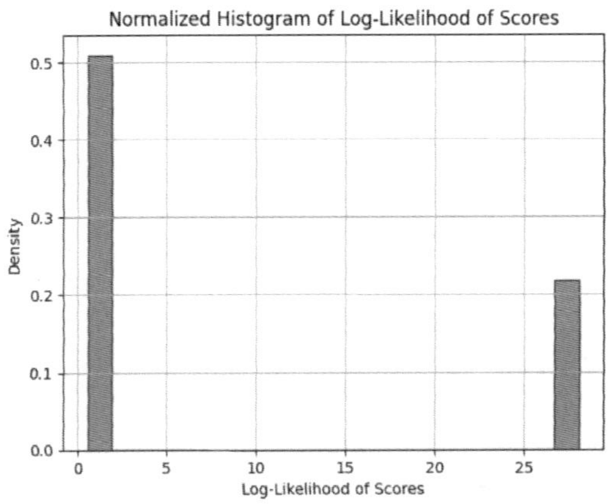

Figure 3: Normalized perplexity distribution for Twitter-XLM-Roberta in a sample of the Greek Wikipedia.

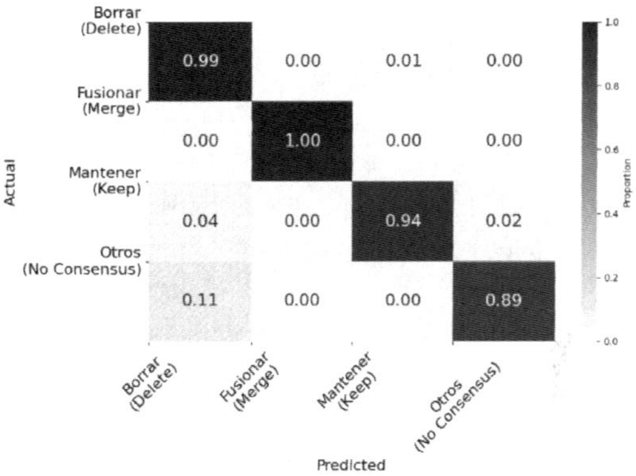

(a) Wikipedia-Es

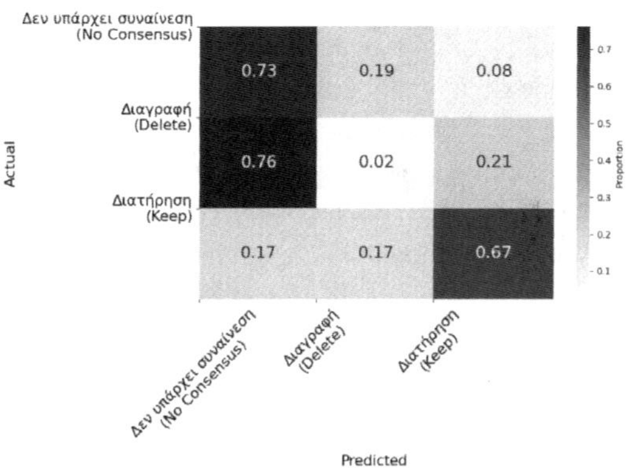

(b) Wikipedia-Gr

Figure 4: Confusion Matrix for XLM-RoBERTa-Large model in Outcome Prediction Task for Spanish and Greek Wikipedia.

9, which shows results for both tasks according to weighted F1-score. We are interested primarily in this metric to understand the benefit of such models for the platform as a whole, rather than investigating nuances in individual categories which account, in practice, for a very small proportion of the dataset. We still perform per-label analysis,

	Stance				Policy			
	Acc,	Prec.	Rec.	F1	Acc,	Prec.	Rec.	F1
RoBERTa-B	0.90	0.83	0.78	0.81	0.83	0.70	0.56	0.61
RoBERTa-L	0.94	0.85	0.81	**0.83**	0.86	0.74	0.62	**0.67**
BERT-B	0.89	0.81	0.80	0.80	0.81	0.65	0.49	0.55
BERT-L	0.91	0.84	0.82	**0.83**	0.84	0.71	0.59	0.63
DistilBERT-B	0.90	0.83	0.74	0.78	0.80	0.69	0.46	0.50
Tw.-RoBERTa-B	0.88	0.80	0.66	0.70	0.81	0.68	0.53	0.58
SetFit	0.83	0.81	0.82	0.82	0.66	0.68	0.67	**0.67**

Table 9: Stance and policy prediction results (with Weighted-F1 scores).

but we believe weighted F1 in this scenario sends a clearer takeaway message to those interested in automating content moderation in these platforms in production environments.

3.2.1 Stance Detection

Similar to Kaffee et al. (2023) we pose our stance detection task as a 4-class classification with the labels `delete`, `keep`, `merge` and `comment`, where the first three labels carry the same meaning as the outcome prediction task, and `comment` means the discussion goes on. Our stance detection results are comparable to the ones reported in Kaffee et al. (2023), which in fact points to their strong and robust model, since their reported results were in macro F1, and are only slightly lower than ours (80% macro F1, vs our 83% weighted F1). In terms of analysis, we do not find any major differences between RoBERTa-Large and BERT-Large, although as is the norm in this paper, Tw.-RoBERTa-B does not perform well. Following from our previous experiments, we also test the ability of SetFit in these tasks. In this case, we also downsample the training and validation sets, in this case, from the original to 1,000 (train) and 300 (validation) stratified samples, with the test set staying the same for enabling a comparison. While not clearly outperforming the other models, as it was the case in previous experiments, it turned out to be an extremely competitive option, rivaling fully fine-tuned PLMs.

3.2.2 Policy Prediction

We modify the policy prediction task into a 10-label setup and follow a similar experimental setup as in previous sections. Our results show that with this task formulation works quite well, with 0.67 F1 for the best model (RoBERTa-Large) as shown in Table 9. In terms of comparison with previous works, Kaffee et al. (2023) reported Accuracy figures about 0.75 on the original dataset (90+ labels), whereas we achieve about 10 points more in a trimmed down version. This suggests that the very long tail of about 80 infrequent labels and

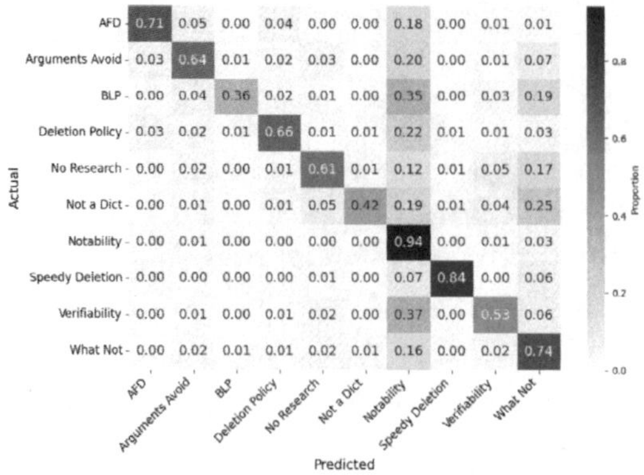

Figure 5: Confusion Matrix for RoBERTa-Large in Policy Prediction.

the likely under-performance on them does not impact the overall picture, and we can conclude that both their models and ours would behave similarly if deployed. The most interesting part of this experiment, however, is again looking at sources of confusion in the test set. In Figure 5 we see, for RoBERTa-Large, a well formed diagonal showing the correlation between actual and predicted labels. However, two major confounding sources emerge: 'Notability' and 'What Not' (shortened for 'What Wikipedia is Not'). Notability is less surprising as this is the most frequent category, but 'What Not' seems to be an overly generic category acting as a superset of other finer grained policies like 'Not a Dict' (Wikipedia is Not a Dictionary). It would be interesting to explore the actual differences in comments pointing to these arguably interrelated policies, which could perhaps lead to merging them or further splitting 'What Not' into others.

4 Conclusion

Automated Content moderation is a challenging yet important part of maintaining healthy content in community driven Wiki-platforms. Through this work, we analyze four different Wiki-platforms and three languages to give an all-round understanding of automated content moderation scenarios in these Wikis. Our analysis shows that these community based platforms can highly benefit from the usage of PLM based content moderation strategies, and to that end, we contribute a dataset and a range of strong baseline results from different PLMs for the community to build on.

Limitations

Our work does not extensively explore all deletion discussions obtainable from Wikipedia (throughout the years), even though it can be obtained using our package. We also do not explore any other LMs except BERT-family of models, and due to lack of domain data for sentiment analysis and offensive language detection, we do not train our own models for those tasks. Finally, the tool we propose here can be made better with integration of more analytical tasks and capabilities of model based activities, such as fine-tuning.

Ethics statement

We believe that enhancing quality control for Wikipedia and other sibling Wiki platforms, which is the most popular online encyclopedia through content moderation is always of utmost importance. There is importance of Wikipedia as a viable knowledge source for users, and a data source for today's NLP research is undeniable. This calls for the necessity of tools that enable automated content moderation, so that the discussions that happens behind the curtain of Wikipedia articles regarding its reliability should maintain its standard, while providing resolution for the disputed ones.

References

Meysam Alizadeh, Fabrizio Gilardi, Emma Hoes, K Jonathan Klüser, Mael Kubli, and Nahema Marchal. 2022. Content moderation as a political issue: The twitter discourse around trump's ban. *Journal of Quantitative Description: Digital Media*, 2.

Francesco Barbieri, Jose Camacho-Collados, Luis Espinosa Anke, and Leonardo Neves. 2020. Tweeteval: Unified benchmark and comparative evaluation for tweet classification. In *Findings of the Association for Computational Linguistics: EMNLP 2020*, pages 1644–1650.

Hsuvas Borkakoty and Luis Espinosa-Anke. 2024. Wide-analysis: Enabling one-click content moderation analysis on wikipedia's articles for deletion. *arXiv preprint arXiv:2408.05655*.

Creston Brooks, Samuel Eggert, and Denis Peskoff. 2024. The rise of ai-generated content in wikipedia. *arXiv preprint arXiv:2410.08044*.

Brian Butler, Elisabeth Joyce, and Jacqueline Pike. 2008. Don't look now, but we've created a bureaucracy: the nature and roles of policies and rules in wikipedia. In *Proceedings of the SIGCHI conference on human factors in computing systems*, pages 1101–1110.

Eshwar Chandrasekharan, Mattia Samory, Shagun Jhaver, Hunter Charvat, Amy Bruckman, Cliff Lampe, Jacob Eisenstein, and Eric Gilbert. 2018. The internet's hidden rules: An empirical study of reddit norm violations at micro, meso, and macro scales. *Proc. ACM Hum.-Comput. Interact.*, 2(CSCW).

Laku Chidambaram and Lai Lai Tung. 2005. Is out of sight, out of mind? an empirical study of social loafing in technology-supported groups. *Information systems research*, 16(2):149–168.

A Conneau. 2019. Unsupervised cross-lingual representation learning at scale. *arXiv preprint arXiv:1911.02116*.

Jacob Devlin, Ming-Wei Chang, Kenton Lee, and Kristina Toutanova. 2018. Bert: Pre-training of deep bidirectional transformers for language understanding. *arXiv preprint arXiv:1810.04805*.

Chris Jensen and Walt Scacchi. 2005. Collaboration, leadership, control, and conflict negotiation and the netbeans. org open source software development community. In *Proceedings of the 38th Annual Hawaii International Conference on System Sciences*, pages 196b–196b. IEEE.

Lucie-Aimée Kaffee, Arnav Arora, and Isabelle Augenstein. 2023. Why should this article be deleted? transparent stance detection in multilingual wikipedia editor discussions. In *Proceedings of the 2023 Conference on Empirical Methods in Natural Language Processing*, pages 5891–5909.

Florian Lemmerich, Diego Sáez-Trumper, Robert West, and Leila Zia. 2019. Why the world reads wikipedia: Beyond english speakers. In *Proceedings of the twelfth ACM international conference on web search and data mining*, pages 618–626.

Yinhan Liu, Myle Ott, Naman Goyal, Jingfei Du, Mandar Joshi, Danqi Chen, Omer Levy, Mike Lewis, Luke Zettlemoyer, and Veselin Stoyanov. 2019. Roberta: A robustly optimized bert pretraining approach. *Preprint*, arXiv:1907.11692.

Daniel Loureiro, Francesco Barbieri, Leonardo Neves, Luis Espinosa Anke, and Jose Camacho-Collados. 2022. Timelms: Diachronic language models from twitter. *arXiv preprint arXiv:2202.03829*.

Elijah Mayfield and Alan W Black. 2019a. Analyzing wikipedia deletion debates with a group decision-making forecast model. *Proceedings of the ACM on Human-Computer Interaction*, 3(CSCW):1–26.

Elijah Mayfield and Alan W Black. 2019b. Stance classification, outcome prediction, and impact assessment: Nlp tasks for studying group decision-making. In *Proceedings of the Third Workshop on Natural Language Processing and Computational Social Science*, pages 65–77.

Manoel Horta Ribeiro, Justin Cheng, and Robert West. 2022. Automated content moderation increases adherence to community guidelines. *arXiv preprint arXiv:2210.10454*.

Jeffrey Sablosky. 2021. Dangerous organizations: Facebook's content moderation decisions and ethnic visibility in myanmar. *Media, culture & society*, 43(6):1017–1042.

Julian Salazar, Davis Liang, Toan Q Nguyen, and Katrin Kirchhoff. 2019. Masked language model scoring. *arXiv preprint arXiv:1910.14659*.

Victor Sanh, Lysandre Debut, Julien Chaumond, and Thomas Wolf. 2020. Distilbert, a distilled version of bert: smaller, faster, cheaper and lighter. *Preprint*, arXiv:1910.01108.

Joseph Seering. 2020. Reconsidering self-moderation: the role of research in supporting community-based models for online content moderation. *Proceedings of the ACM on Human-Computer Interaction*, 4(CSCW2):1–28.

Neil Selwyn and Stephen Gorard. 2016. Students' use of wikipedia as an academic resource—patterns of use and perceptions of usefulness. *The Internet and Higher Education*, 28:28–34.

Philipp Singer, Florian Lemmerich, Robert West, Leila Zia, Ellery Wulczyn, Markus Strohmaier, and Jure Leskovec. 2017. Why we read wikipedia. In *Proceedings of the 26th international conference on world wide web*, pages 1591–1600.

Mohit Singhal, Chen Ling, Pujan Paudel, Poojitha Thota, Nihal Kumarswamy, Gianluca Stringhini, and Shirin Nilizadeh. 2023. Sok: Content moderation in social media, from guidelines to enforcement, and research to practice. In *2023 IEEE 8th European Symposium on Security and Privacy (EuroS&P)*, pages 868–895. IEEE.

Lewis Tunstall, Nils Reimers, Unso Eun Seo Jo, Luke Bates, Daniel Korat, Moshe Wasserblat, and Oren Pereg. 2022. Efficient few-shot learning without prompts. *arXiv preprint arXiv:2209.11055*.

Shitao Xiao, Zheng Liu, Peitian Zhang, and Niklas Muennighoff. 2023. C-pack: Packaged resources to advance general chinese embedding. *Preprint*, arXiv:2309.07597.

A Train/Validation/Test Splits

The data splits with number of instances used in this paper are described in Table 10.

B Training details and results for Outcome Prediction

Following are the details of different hyperparameters we use in our experiments, which as can be seen vary across datasets due mostly to dataset size.

Lang.	Platform	Data	Rows	Total
en	Wikipedia	Train	12,963	18,528
		Val	1,856	
		Test	3,709	
	Wikidata-ent	Train	248,871	355,428
		Val	35,558	
		Test	70,999	
	Wikidata-pr	Train	349	498
		Val	52	
		Test	97	
	Wikinews	Train	63	91
		Val	9	
		Test	19	
	Wikiquote	Train	484	695
		Val	69	
		Test	142	
es	Wikipedia	Train	2,291	3,274
		Val	294	
		Test	689	
gr	Wikipedia	Train	274	392
		Val	35	
		Test	83	
en	Stance	Train	372,033	437,770
		Val	21,961	
		Test	43,776	
en	Policy	Train	274,867	341,337
		Val	30,540	
		Test	35,930	

Table 10: Data distribution statistics, divided in 3 blocks: English Outcome Prediction (top), Multilingual Outcome Prediction (middle), and (English) Stance and Policy Prediction (bottom).

- Number of epochs: 20 (Outcome Prediction)/ 5 (Stance/Policy detection)
- Learning rate: 1e-5 (Outcome Prediction)/ 2e-6 (Stance/Policy detection)
- Batch size: 4
- Optimizer: Adam
- Resource used: NVIDIA RTX 4090

From Conversational Speech to Readable Text: Post-Processing Noisy Transcripts in a Low-Resource Setting

Arturs Znotins
IMCS, University of Latvia
arturs.znotins@lumii.lv

Normunds Gruzitis
University of Latvia
normunds.gruzitis@lu.lv

Roberts Dargis
RGP, Latvia
Viroling Technology, Latvia

Abstract

We present ongoing research on automatic post-processing approaches to enhance the readability of noisy speech transcripts in low-resource languages, with a focus on conversational speech in Latvian. We compare transformer-based sequence-labeling models and large language models (LLMs) for the standard punctuation and capitalization restoration task, while also considering automatic correction of mispronounced words and disfluency, and partial inverse text normalization. Our results show that very small LLMs (approx. 2B parameters), fine-tuned on a modest text corpus, can achieve near state-of-the-art performance, rivaling orders of magnitude larger LLMs. Additionally, we demonstrate that a fine-tuned Whisper model, leveraging acoustic cues, outperforms text-only systems on challenging conversational data, even for a low-resource language. Error analysis reveals recurring pitfalls in sentence boundary determination and disfluency handling, emphasizing the importance of consistent annotation and domain adaptation for robust post-processing. Our findings highlight the feasibility of developing efficient post-processing solutions that significantly refine ASR output in low-resource settings, while opening new possibilities for editing and formatting speech transcripts beyond mere restoration of punctuation and capitalization.

1 Introduction

Automatic punctuation and capitalization restoration has been widely studied as a post-processing step for automatic speech recognition (ASR) systems, aiming to improve transcript readability and facilitating downstream NLP tasks such as machine translation, named entity recognition, etc.

Early methods leveraged statistical approaches, such as n-gram language modeling and prosodic cues (Stolcke et al., 1998; Beeferman et al., 1998), as well as sequence labeling techniques like Conditional Random Fields (CRFs) (Lu and Ng, 2010; Wang et al., 2012) and Maximum Entropy models. With the advent of deep learning, recurrent neural networks (RNNs) and long short-term memory (LSTM) models proved to be more efficient in modeling sequential dependencies (Tilk and Alumäe, 2015). Bidirectional RNNs and transformer-based architectures further enhanced accuracy by using richer contextual representations (Yi and Tao, 2019; Nguyen and Salazar, 2019).

Recent work has demonstrated that transformer-based models outperform previous neural approaches. BERT-based models, such as RoBERTa and ELECTRA, have achieved state-of-the-art results on punctuation restoration by leveraging large-scale pretraining (Devlin et al., 2018; Poláček et al., 2023). Other studies have explored multilingual transformer models such as XLM-RoBERTa (Conneau et al., 2020) to address punctuation restoration across multiple languages.

End-to-end ASR models, such as OpenAI's Whisper (Radford et al., 2023), directly generate transcriptions with punctuation and capitalization. Whisper is trained on large-scale weakly supervised data, allowing it to outperform conventional ASR models that require separate punctuation restoration modules.

Recent advances in large-scale auto-regressive large language models (LLMs), such as GPT-4 (OpenAI et al., 2024), have introduced new paradigms for punctuation restoration. Unlike conventional sequence labeling approaches, GPT-style models perform text infilling and editing, enabling them to restore punctuation in a generative manner. Recent developments in open-source multilingual LLMs have led to the creation of smaller models that effectively support low-resource languages (Dargis et al., 2024).

Developing robust punctuation restoration models relies on sufficiently large and representative annotated corpora. Europarl (Koehn, 2005) and TED-LIUM (Rousseau et al., 2014) have been widely

Proceedings of the Tenth Workshop on Noisy and User-generated Text, pages 143–148
May 3, 2025 ©2025 Association for Computational Linguistics

used, but they often lack domain-specific noise typical of real-world ASR. Fu et al. (2021) demonstrated that domain-adaptive fine-tuning with n-gram similarity-based data sampling can improve model robustness. Data augmentation methods that simulate ASR errors have also been shown to yield significant performance gains (Alam et al., 2020).

For Latvian (approx. 1.5M native speakers), relevant work on punctuation restoration includes (Salimbajevs, 2016; Vāravs and Salimbajevs, 2018), which focus on bidirectional models and sequence labeling for punctuation and capitalization. One publicly available resource is a proprietary on-line service that allows users to correct the punctuation and formatting of a text, where the underlying model, likely an encoder-decoder, is trained on academic texts[1]. Another publicly available resource is an open-source punctuation model based on XLM-RoBERTa[2] (Guhr et al., 2021), trained on Europarl data. The best available end-to-end Latvian ASR models that include text formatting are *whisper-large-v3* and *whisper-large-v3-lv*, the latter being fine-tuned on the dataset described in Section 2 as well as on the Common Voice 19.0 dataset[3] (Dargis et al., 2024).

Our contributions in this study are as follows:

- We demonstrate that even the smallest generative LLMs (i.e., in the 2B parameter range) can be fine-tuned on a relatively small text corpus to achieve near state-of-the-art results, bridging the gap between reference text formatting and noisy ASR output.

- We present a thorough error analysis highlighting common pitfalls, such as mispunctuation, ambiguous sentence boundaries, and speaker disfluencies.

- Beyond punctuation and capitalization, we show that LLMs can partially learn error correction and inverse text normalization from limited data, underlining their potential to further refine ASR outputs in low-resource settings.

[1] https://salieckomatus.lv

[2] https://huggingface.co/1-800-BAD-CODE/xlm-roberta_punctuation_fullstop_truecase

[3] https://huggingface.co/AiLab-IMCS-UL/whisper-large-v3-lv-late-cv19

2 Dataset

We use the LATE-Media corpus[4] (Auzina et al., 2024a,c), which comprises approximately 70 hours of conversational Latvian speech from broadcast recordings, sourced from public media. The data includes both spontaneous and prepared speech (but not read speech) from more than 250 speakers, offering a diverse range of speaking styles and topics.

Transcriptions are provided in standard Latvian orthography, with additional punctuation and grammar rules applied. When necessary, annotations in square brackets capture non-standard pronunciation (e.g., "lasām [lasam]") and foreign words (e.g., "Rail [reil] Baltica [boltik]"). The corpus also documents the reading of numbers, accounting for syntactic agreement in context (e.g., *nominative* vs. *dative* forms). This rich annotation scheme ensures that spontaneous variations – such as word repetitions, truncated words, and different realizations of abbreviations – are properly represented.

To simplify the punctuation restoration task, we unify several less frequent or inconsistently annotated marks by replacing them with periods. Specifically, we map exclamation marks, ellipses, and em dashes to periods. We also ignore seldom-used marks such as colons and semicolons, which tend to be subjectively annotated. These steps reduce annotation noise and help stabilize model performance in subsequent training and evaluation.

The dataset statistics, including the distribution of punctuation, capitalization types, average sentence length, and correction annotations, are presented in Table 1.

	Train	Dev	Test
Comma	56268	1624	1595
Period	49599	2363	2389
Question	3454	409	419
Title	73675	3172	3257
Upper	3528	87	78
Avg Sent Len	10.3	7.6	7.2
Corrections	4541	80	85

Table 1: Dataset statistics for punctuation, capitalization and sentence lengths.

[4] https://korpuss.lv/en/id/LATE-mediji

3 Experimental Setup

In our experiments, we address the following key research questions:

- How do small generative models compare to larger models in punctuation and capitalization restoration tasks for a low resource language, and how does their performance degrade on ASR-generated transcripts?
- To what extent are models capable of correcting transcript text without introducing unnecessary modifications?
- What are the predominant error types?

We evaluate two distinct scenarios: formatting ASR-generated transcripts and formatting manually transcribed reference text. This setup allows us to assess how models handle noisy ASR outputs and whether they can refine reference transcripts without unnecessary modifications. The evaluation of ASR-generated transcripts is conducted on the outputs of *whisper-large-v3-lv*, currently the strongest open-source Latvian ASR model. We use publicly available *salieckomatus.lv* and XLM-RoBERTa (Guhr et al., 2021) as baselines. Additionally, we evaluate the performance of *whisper-large-v3* and *whisper-large-v3-lv*.

Performance is measured using F1-score (F1) for punctuation restoration and capitalization. To ensure that models do not introduce unnecessary modifications, we also compute the word error rate (WER) on the normalized formatted transcript. A heuristic fuzzy alignment method is used to align incorrectly recognized words and words that differ in spoken and written forms, such as number expressions, acronyms, and abbreviations.

For LLMs, we employ the following task-specific prompt:

> *"You are a skilled editor specializing in Latvian transcripts. Your task is to format this short (under 30 seconds) ASR-produced transcript by adding punctuation (use only commas, periods, and question marks), capitalization, and making minimal edits for readability. Correct grammar, mispronounced words, and abbreviations as needed. Convert numbers into their written form. Do not alter the sentence structure or meaning – only refine specific words, punctuation, and formatting while keeping it as close to the original as possible."*

For fine-tuned models, we use a shorter prompt, observing no noticeable drop in performance:

> *"Proofread the provided Latvian transcript by inserting appropriate punctuation and applying proper capitalization."*

Models are fine-tuned exclusively on the training split, without incorporating any external data. The fine-tuning uses a linearly decreasing learning rate of 2e-5, a warm-up ratio of 0.1, a batch size of 32, and runs for 3 epochs.

4 Results

The results of our experiments are presented in Table 2. Generative models, such as GPT-4o and GPT-4o *mini*, demonstrate strong capabilities for Latvian punctuation and capitalization tasks. However, they also introduce unintended transcript modifications, reflected in elevated WER – an issue which can potentially be mitigated with more extensive prompt optimization.

Fine-tuned (FT) models show significant gains in consistency, with GPT-4o FT achieving the highest overall performance (F1 scores of 81.5 for punctuation and 84.4 for capitalization). Notably, smaller fine-tuned models (e.g., Gemma-2B, EuroLLM-1.7B) perform at levels comparable to GPT-4o *mini*, suggesting that the model size alone does not dictate effectiveness for this task.

Table 3 highlights a key limitation of generative models if compared to BERT-based models – unintended alterations to the transcripts. This issue is especially pronounced in the case of non-fine-tuned models. GPT-4o, for example, often attempts to enhance fluency by removing words deemed superfluous (e.g., "*And my*" → "*My*") or by adding implied speech elements (e.g., "*tea, coffee*" → "*tea or coffee*"). The most frequently observed and potentially the most influential errors are word substitutions that alter the meaning or introduce syntactic agreement errors. Although prompt optimization can partially address these issues, they remain challenging to be completely eliminated without highly descriptive prompting and provision of examples for in-context learning.

Smaller generative models like GPT-4o *mini* can introduce more pronounced substitutions (e.g., "*bračka*" (brother) → "*brāķa*" (defect)) as well as occasionally produce non-existent words (e.g.,

Model	Punctuation				Capitalization			WER
	Comma	Period	Question	Total	Title	Upper	Total	
whisper-large-v3	64.1	73.0	63.3	68.4	72.2	41.7	72.0	31.3
whisper-large-v3-lv	77.5	79.9	72.1	78.3	81.9	53.3	81.8	12.7
ASR Output								
XLM-RoBERTa	74.7	78.8	57.5	75.1	79.0	46.2	78.9	12.7
salieckomatus.lv	74.9	75.9	40.7	73.1	77.6	22.2	77.4	13.1
GPT-4o	78.1	80.8	62.6	78.2	81.4	36.4	81.3	13.2
GPT-4o FT	**81.2**	**84.0**	**68.9**	**81.5**	**84.6**	38.5	**84.4**	**12.5**
GPT-4o mini	74.4	80.0	57.5	75.8	79.8	36.4	79.7	15.2
GPT-4o mini FT	79.3	82.0	64.2	79.3	82.5	41.7	82.4	12.7
EuroLLM-1.7B-Instruct FT	78.8	82.5	60.1	79.0	82.8	**53.8**	82.7	12.8
gemma-2-2b-it FT	79.5	81.5	63.2	79.1	82.0	41.7	81.9	12.7
Reference Transcripts								
XLM-RoBERTa	77.9	79.7	62.4	77.4	84.3	72.7	84.3	0.0
salieckomatus.lv	77.6	76.7	43.2	74.8	81.6	43.5	81.4	1.4
GPT-4o	80.9	82.4	67.6	80.5	86.6	48.3	86.4	3.0
GPT-4o FT	**85.9**	**86.0**	**76.5**	**85.1**	**91.8**	83.9	**91.8**	0.4
GPT-4o mini	76.7	81.5	63.2	78.0	84.9	58.3	84.8	4.7
GPT-4o mini FT	83.1	84.0	70.0	82.4	89.7	80.0	89.6	0.3
EuroLLM-1.7B-Instruct FT	83.2	84.9	69.1	82.8	89.6	**90.3**	89.6	0.4
gemma-2-2b-it FT	82.7	83.1	68.1	81.6	88.3	75.0	88.3	0.4

Table 2: Results on test split: F1 scores for punctuation and capitalization, and WER.

"*paliec*" (stay) → "*paliķ*" (∅), "*filmēs*" (will shoot) → "*filmes*" (∅)).

Overall, fine-tuning reduces unintended text changes by an order of magnitude for all model sizes. While fine-tuned models in the two billion parameter range rarely alter transcripts, the errors they produce typically manifest as ungrammatical forms rather than semantic substitutions.

The Whisper model fine-tuned for Latvian (i.e., *whisper-large-v3-lv*) achieves WER of 12.7, significantly outperforming the base Whisper *large-v3* model while maintaining strong punctuation and capitalization scores.

Models generally perform better on reference transcripts than on ASR outputs, which is expected since ASR-generated text contains recognition errors that interfere with punctuation and capitalization. Similarly, fine-tuned LLMs outperform their non-fine-tuned counterparts when applied to ASR outputs.

We manually annotated 100 samples to analyze errors made by the various models. In the cases of mismatched predictions, we categorized errors as follows:

- Actual errors: incorrect punctuation placement, capitalization mistakes, or misinterpretation of sentence boundaries (57 cases).
- Alternative formatting choices: instances where a model's output differs from the reference but remains grammatically valid (43 cases).

For 21 of the cases, we had to listen to the audio to apply a correct markup, highlighting the importance of audio features, for example, "*Labi. Sakratīts ir.*" ('*Well. Shaken [it] is.*') vs. "*Labi sakratīts ir.*" ('*Well shaken [it] is.*'). This also explains the better question mark performance for *whisper-large-v3-lv* without any extra processing.

We further evaluated model performance in correcting mispronounced words: by using annotated mispronunciations, number expressions, and generally acceptable written forms annotated in the dataset. Approximately 50% of these cases were correctly replaced by LLMs, suggesting a potential for these models to learn error correction and inverse text normalization tasks for the low-resource Latvian from relatively small datasets. However, further investigation is needed, since the current test set is too small for a reliable evaluation.

We have also evaluated a broader set of punctuation marks. However, because of their low fre-

Model	Changed Utt.	Substitute	Inflect	Delete	Insert
XLM-RoBERTa	0.0				
salieckomatus.lv	10.0	58	16	16	11
GPT-4o	16.4	42	21	29	8
GPT-4o FT	**1.4**	79	14	0	7
GPT-4o mini	24.6	41	24	28	7
GPT-4o mini FT	1.5	67	25	8	0
EuroLLM-1.7B-Instruct FT	2.7	69	8	15	8
gemma-2-2b-it FT	1.7	47	27	20	7

Table 3: Error analysis of changed utterances by error type, based on a manual review of a sample of 100 utterances (or fewer if fewer were found) in each model's test split. All values are percentages.

quency beyond commas, periods, and question marks, these results can currently only be considered preliminary and are not yet reliable. Moreover, their usage in conversational ASR transcripts is often subjective, justified by increased inter-annotator disagreement.

5 Conclusion and Further Work

End-to-end ASR systems, such as Whisper fine-tuned for Latvian (using a relatively small amount of data), already provide reasonably well-formatted transcripts for general-domain speech by leveraging acoustic features that are unavailable in text-only approaches. However, even without acoustic cues, formatting performance can be improved with LLMs using a prompt-based approach. Further task-specific fine-tuning yields the best and most stable results, and it is feasible even with smaller LLMs in the 2B parameter range on a small dataset. Larger models often provide higher accuracy but come with increased computational costs and deployment complexity.

Audio features (pauses, intonation) remain a crucial signal for punctuation restoration. Sentence boundaries in speech are often ambiguous, with multiple valid interpretations, and better annotation guidelines could improve consistency. One major challenge in training ASR models for Latvian and other low-resource languages is the lack of datasets that include both conversational speech and formatted transcriptions. LLMs enable transcript transformations such as inverse text normalization and error correction by leveraging their built-in language knowledge, even when trained on relatively small datasets. Thus, fine-tuned LLMs can expedite the addition of such formatting to existing orthographically transcribed datasets, for instance, the LATE-Conversational speech corpus (Auzina et al., 2024b) which comprises 35 hours of informal conversations in Latvian – this is currently a work in progress, to be followed by human verification and evaluation.

6 Limitations

Our models are evaluated on a single dataset for Latvian, limiting generalizability to other domains or languages. Future research should extend these evaluations to multiple datasets.

ASR errors significantly impact formatting performance. Introducing ASR-like noise or synthetic errors during training could improve robustness but risks unintended meaning changes if not done carefully.

In fields like law or medicine, over-corrections can subtly alter meaning. Generative and punctuation models may introduce edits beyond basic formatting, risking inaccuracies in sensitive transcripts. Hence, they should be used cautiously when exact fidelity to the original speech is required.

Acknowledgments

This work was funded by the European Union Recovery and Resilience Facility projects "Language Technology Initiative" (2.3.1.1.i.0/1/22/I/CFLA/002) and "Competence Centre of Information and Communication Technologies" (5.1.1.2.i.0/1/22/A/CFLA/008).

References

Tanvirul Alam, Akib Khan, and Firoj Alam. 2020. Punctuation restoration using transformer models for high- and low-resource languages. In *Proceedings of the Sixth Workshop on Noisy User-generated Text (W-NUT)*, pages 132–142.

Ilze Auzina, Roberts Dargis, Kristine Levane-Petrova, Arta Auzina, Baiba Saulite, Ilze Laksa-Timinska, Elina Gailite, Gunta Nespore-Berzkalne, Guna Rabante-Busa, Kristine Pokratniece, and Agute Klints. 2024a. LATE Media Speech Corpus V1 (LATE-mediji). CLARIN-LV digital library at IMCS, University of Latvia.

Ilze Auzina, Roberts Dargis, Guna Rabante-Busa, Ilze Timinska-Laksa, Elina Gailite, and Arta Auzina. 2024b. LATE Conversational Speech Corpus V1 (LATE-sarunas). CLARIN-LV digital library at IMCS, University of Latvia.

Ilze Auzina, Normunds Gruzitis, Roberts Dargis, Guna Rabante-Busa, Didzis Gosko, Janis Vempers, Raivis Kivkucans, and Arturs Znotins. 2024c. Recent Latvian Speech Corpora for Linguistic Research and Technology Development. *Baltic Journal of Modern Computing*, 12(4):646–658.

Doug Beeferman, Adam Berger, and John Lafferty. 1998. Cyberpunc: A lightweight punctuation annotation system for speech. In *Proceedings of the IEEE International Conference on Acoustics, Speech and Signal Processing (ICASSP)*, volume 2, pages 689–692.

Alexis Conneau, Kartikay Khandelwal, Naman Goyal, Vishrav Chaudhary, Guillaume Wenzek, Francisco Guzmán, Edouard Grave, Myle Ott, Luke Zettlemoyer, and Veselin Stoyanov. 2020. Unsupervised Cross-lingual Representation Learning at Scale. In *Proceedings of the 58th Annual Meeting of the Association for Computational Linguistics*, pages 8440–8451.

Roberts Dargis, Arturs Znotins, Ilze Auzina, Baiba Saulite, Sanita Reinsone, Raivis Dejus, Antra Klavinska, and Normunds Gruzitis. 2024. BalsuTalka.lv – Boosting the Common Voice Corpus for Low-Resource Languages. In *Joint International Conference on Computational Linguistics, Language Resources and Evaluation (LREC-COLING)*, pages 2080–2085.

Jacob Devlin, Ming-Wei Chang, Kenton Lee, and Kristina Toutanova. 2018. BERT: Pre-training of Deep Bidirectional Transformers for Language Understanding. *arXiv:1810.04805*.

Xue-Yong Fu, Cheng Chen, Md Tahmid Rahman Laskar, Shashi Bhushan TN, and Simon Corston-Oliver. 2021. Improving punctuation restoration for speech transcripts via external data. *arXiv:2110.00560*.

Oliver Guhr, Anne-Kathrin Schumann, Frank Bahrmann, and Hans Joachim Böhme. 2021. FullStop: Multilingual Deep Models for Punctuation Prediction. In *Proceedings of the Swiss Text Analytics Conference*. CEUR Workshop Proceedings.

Philipp Koehn. 2005. Europarl: A parallel corpus for statistical machine translation. In *Proceedings of Machine Translation Summit X*, pages 79–86.

Wei Lu and Hwee Tou Ng. 2010. Better punctuation prediction with dynamic conditional random fields. In *Proceedings of the Conference on Empirical Methods in Natural Language Processing (EMNLP)*, pages 177–186.

Toan Q Nguyen and Julian Salazar. 2019. Transformers without tears: Improving the normalization of self-attention. *arXiv:1910.05895*.

OpenAI, Josh Achiam, Steven Adler, Sandhini Agarwal, Lama Ahmad, Ilge Akkaya, Florencia Leoni Aleman, Diogo Almeida, Janko Altenschmidt, Sam Altman, Shyamal Anadkat, Red Avila, Igor Babuschkin, Suchir Balaji, Valerie Balcom, Paul Baltescu, Haiming Bao, Mohammad Bavarian, Jeff Belgum, et al. 2024. GPT-4 Technical Report. *arXiv:2303.08774*.

Martin Poláček, Petr Červa, Jindřich Žd'ánský, and Lenka Weingartová. 2023. Online Punctuation Restoration using ELECTRA Model for streaming ASR Systems. In *Interspeech*, pages 446–450.

Alec Radford, Jong Wook Kim, Tao Xu, Greg Brockman, Christine McLeavey, and Ilya Sutskever. 2023. Robust speech recognition via large-scale weak supervision. In *International Conference on Machine Learning*, pages 28492–28518.

Anthony Rousseau, Paul Deléglise, Yannick Esteve, et al. 2014. Enhancing the TED-LIUM corpus with selected data for language modeling and more TED talks. In *LREC*, pages 3935–3939.

Askars Salimbajevs. 2016. Bidirectional LSTM for automatic punctuation restoration. In *Human Language Technologies – The Baltic Perspective*, pages 59–65. IOS Press.

Andreas Stolcke, Elizabeth Shriberg, Rebecca A Bates, Mari Ostendorf, Dilek Zeynep Hakkani, Madelaine Plauche, Gökhan Tür, and Yu Lu. 1998. Automatic detection of sentence boundaries and disfluencies based on recognized words. In *ICSLP*, volume 2, pages 2247–2250.

Ottokar Tilk and Tanel Alumäe. 2015. LSTM for punctuation restoration in speech transcripts. In *Interspeech*, pages 683–687.

Andris Vāravs and Askars Salimbajevs. 2018. Restoring punctuation and capitalization using transformer models. In *6th International Conference on Statistical Language and Speech Processing (SLSP)*, pages 91–102.

Xuancong Wang, Hwee Tou Ng, and Khe Chai Sim. 2012. Dynamic conditional random fields for joint sentence boundary and punctuation prediction. In *Interspeech*, pages 1384–1387.

Jiangyan Yi and Jianhua Tao. 2019. Self-attention based model for punctuation prediction using word and speech embeddings. In *IEEE International Conference on Acoustics, Speech and Signal Processing (ICASSP)*, pages 7270–7274.

Text Normalization for Sentiment Analysis in Japanese Social Media

Risa Kondo[†] **Ayu Teramen**[†] **Reon Kajikawa**[†] **Koki Horiguchi**[†] **Tomoyuki Kajiwara**[†‡]
Takashi Ninomiya[†] **Hideaki Hayashi**[‡] **Yuta Nakashima**[‡] **Hajime Nagahara**[‡]
[†]Ehime University [‡]Osaka University
{kondo@ai., teramen@ai., reon@ai., horiguchi@ai., kajiwara@}cs.ehime-u.ac.jp
ninomiya.takashi.mk@ehime-u.ac.jp
{hayashi, n-yuta, nagahara}@ids.osaka-u.ac.jp

Abstract

We manually normalize noisy Japanese expressions on social networking services (SNS) to improve the performance of sentiment polarity classification. Despite advances in pre-trained language models, informal expressions found in social media still plague natural language processing. In this study, we analyzed 6,000 posts from a sentiment analysis corpus for Japanese SNS text, and constructed a text normalization taxonomy consisting of 33 types of editing operations. Text normalization according to our taxonomy significantly improved the performance of BERT-based sentiment analysis in Japanese. Detailed analysis reveals that most types of editing operations each contribute to improve the performance of sentiment analysis.

1 Introduction

For research and development of sentiment analysis models, datasets with sentiment labels for text on social networking services (SNS) are available (Mohammad and Bravo-Marquez, 2017; Mohammad et al., 2018; Plaza del Arco et al., 2020; Bostan et al., 2020). In Japanese, sentiment analysis datasets for SNS posts such as WRIME[1] (Kajiwara et al., 2021; Suzuki et al., 2022) are available. Text from social media often contains informal Japanese expressions such as misspellings and Internet slang. These noisy texts may degrade the performance of natural language processing, including sentiment analysis.

In this study, to improve the performance of sentiment analysis in Japanese, various noisy expressions in SNS texts were manually normalized. We performed text normalization on 6,000 posts from the WRIME dataset, and organized the editing operations contained therein into 6 major categories and 33 subcategories. Then, our detailed analysis based on this Japanese text normalization taxonomy revealed which type of normalization contributes to improved performance of sentiment analysis in Japanese.

Experimental results showed that our text normalization improved the performance of sentiment analysis in Japanese. Furthermore, our detailed analysis reveals that most types of normalization contribute to improved performance in sentiment analysis. Among them, there were notable improvements due to the normalization of *casual/formal sentence endings*, *missing symbols*, *abbreviations*, and inconsistencies in *hiragana, katakana, and kanji*.[2] In contrast, since the normalization of *pronunciation variations* worsened the performance of sentiment analysis, the *pronunciation variations* may express the writer's emotions. We plan to release[1] our 6,000 normalized post pairs with our Japanese text normalization taxonomy.

2 Related Work

Noisy expressions found in social media deteriorate the performance of various natural language processing such as word segmentation and sentiment analysis. To address this issue, text normalization has been studied. Text normalization corpora have been developed for various languages, including English (Liu et al., 2011; Han and Baldwin, 2011; Yang and Eisenstein, 2013; Baldwin et al., 2015), German (Sidarenka et al., 2013), Spanish (Alegria et al., 2013, 2015), Turkish (Çolakoğlu et al., 2019), Danish (Plank et al., 2020), Italian (van der Goot et al., 2020), Thai (Limkonchotiwat et al., 2021), and Vietnamese (Nguyen et al., 2024), to facilitate the development of data-driven approaches for text normalization. For text normalization in Japanese, approaches to sequence labeling (Sasaki et al., 2013; Osaki et al., 2017) and sequence-to-sequence generation (Ikeda et al., 2016; Saito et al.,

[1]https://github.com/ids-cv/wrime

[2]Japanese text can be written in three types of letters: hiragana, katakana, and kanji.

Proceedings of the Tenth Workshop on Noisy and User-generated Text, pages 149–157
May 3, 2025

2017) have been proposed. However, these previous studies are based on small parallel corpora of about 1,000 sentence pairs (Sasaki et al., 2013; Kaji and Kitsuregawa, 2014; Osaki et al., 2017; Higashiyama et al., 2021), automatically generated corpus (Ikeda et al., 2016), and non-public corpora (Saito et al., 2013, 2017). Therefore, a larger-scale parallel corpus that is freely available for Japanese text normalization is desired.

3 Japanese Text Normalization for Sentiment Analysis in Social Media

This section describes what types of text normalization are covered in this study and how we perform text normalization.

3.1 Japanese Text Normalization Taxonomy

Combining the 14 types of Japanese text normalization employed in previous studies (Saito et al., 2013; Sasano et al., 2013; Osaki et al., 2017; Higashiyama et al., 2021) and the 19 new types of normalization that we found by analyzing Japanese SNS texts in WRIME, we define a Japanese text normalization taxonomy consisting of 6 major categories and 33 subcategories.[3] Table 1 lists the taxonomy and its examples.

Typos and Misspellings As in the previous study (Saito et al., 2013), we define misspellings as separate subcategories of *misuse* of kanji and *typos*. We also employ the *missing characters* that have been employed in the previous study (Osaki et al., 2017). In addition, since *conjugation errors* were frequently observed, this is newly added as an independent category.

Even minor changes such as the presence or absence of punctuation can affect the performance of sentiment analysis. We therefore introduce a new subcategory, *missing symbols*. This type of normalization not only completes punctuation but also encloses proper nouns in parentheses.

Dialect In addition to characteristic expressions such as *Internet slang* and *censored words*, SNS texts frequently contain expressions that reflect the writer's personality, such as *regional dialect* and *unique sentence endings* that are rarely seen in normal written language. As in previous studies (Saito et al., 2013; Osaki et al., 2017), we employ these types of normalization.

Also, casual and formal forms are made consistent. Because of the frequency of each, this study divides the subcategories according to whether the editing point is sentence-ending or not, thus providing subcategories for *casual/formal sentence endings* and *casual/formal functional expressions*.

Alternative Spellings Alternative spellings, which have been employed in previous studies (Saito et al., 2013; Osaki et al., 2017; Higashiyama et al., 2021), are often found on SNS text. Since abbreviations are often used due to character count constraints, we use the category of *abbreviations* independently of changes in character types: *hiragana, katakana, and kanji*.

Along with *pronunciation variations*, *homophones*, and *small/large characters* employed in many previous studies (Saito et al., 2013; Sasano et al., 2013; Osaki et al., 2017; Higashiyama et al., 2021), we also employ *synonyms* (Sasano et al., 2013) and *loanwords* (Higashiyama et al., 2021). Considering compatibility with pre-trained language models, *synonyms* are paraphrased into the most frequent expressions, and *loanwords* are translated or transliterated into hiragana or kanji.

There was also variation in the use of parentheses and other symbols. Therefore, we also add the category of *symbol conversion*.

Emphasis Expressions *Inserted sounds*, *inserted symbols*, and *repetition* of characters and symbols, which have been employed in the previous study (Osaki et al., 2017), are also frequently used in social media for the purpose of emphasis. To eliminate redundancy and to make these expressions consistent across the corpus, they are also normalized in this study.

Some posts list parallel items with *bullet points* or *word order changes* to uncommon or unreadable sentences. We newly normalize and edit them into fluent and complete sentences.

Simplification As a new major category, we introduce a new category of "simplification" to paraphrase complex expressions or to complement missing information. We employ five types of subcategories: *lexical/phrasal simplification* to paraphrase complex expressions and SNS-specific expressions such as neologisms and coined words, *completion*

[3]The "similar forms" employed by previous studies (Saito et al., 2013; Sasano et al., 2013) were not employed in this study because they did not appear in our analysis. For example, this category includes ネ申 → 神, うれUい → うれしい, etc. Our analysis covers 6,000 posts from the WRIME dataset, which consists of SNS texts posted from 2010 to 2020.

1. Typos and Misspellings	Example
Missing Symbols	暑い→ 暑い。, 天地明察を見たい→ 『天地明察』を見たい
Missing Characters‡	みんな起きている→ みんなが起きている, とこ→ ところ
Conjugation Errors	見てたら→ 見ていたら, 起きれて→ 起きられて
Typos*‡§	腸がが→ 腸が, きます！れ→ きます!!
Misuse*	以外に少ない→ 意外に少ない
2. Dialect	Example
Casual/Formal Sentence Endings	～だ。→ ～です。, 食いたい。→ 食べたいです。
Casual/Formal Functional Expressions	っていう話→ という話, 奪われるから→ 奪われるので
Internet Slang*‡	ワロタでした→ 笑いました , ググったら→ 検索すると
Regional Dialect*‡	やん→ でしょうね, おめんど→ あなたたち
Unique Sentence Endings	ますわよ→ ますよ, っす→ です
Censored Words*	N__K → NHK
3. Alternative Spellings	Example
Hiragana/Katakana/Kanji*‡§	欲しい→ ほしい, スカート＋ヒール→ スカートとヒール
Abbreviations*‡	ネット→ インターネット, コロナ→ 新型コロナウイルス感染症
Pronunciation Variations*†‡	いくん→ いくの, こりゃ→ これは
Synonyms	本日→ 今日, お菓子→ 菓子
Symbol Conversion	「悪の教典」→ 『悪の教典』,。。。 → …。
Loanwords§	good night → おやすみなさい, オーダー→ 注文
Homophones*†‡	行けそーな→ 行けそうな, °C → 度
Small/Large Characters*†‡§	まぁまぁ→ まあまあ, ﾜｨｬﾚｽ→ ワイヤレス
4. Emphasis Expressions	Example
Inserted Sounds*†‡§	よーし→ よし, 雨かあ→ 雨か
Inserted Symbols‡	"一般的な人" → 一般的な人
Word Order Changes	そのまま私が食べるパンを→ 私が食べるパンをそのまま
Repetition‡	え??????? → え??, いやいやいやいや→ いやいや
Bullet Points	結論: → 結論として言えるのは、
5. Simplification	Example
Completion	撮ればよかったな→ 撮ればよかったなと後悔しています
Lexical/Phrasal Simplification	カットに行く→ 美容院に行く, ノミの心臓→ 臆病
Deletion	男（ひと）→ 男, せいで(おかげで) → おかげで
Fusion	今朝方のツイート。酔っていた→ 今朝方のツイートは酔っていた
Splitting	買い物に行き、買った服を→ 買い物に行きました。買った服を
6. Emotional Expressions	Example
Numerical Expressions	21時→ <num>時, ひとつ→ <num>つ, 数回→ <num>回
Emotional Symbols	(笑) → <joy>, (怒) → <anger>
Emoticons	(●´ з ` ●) → <joy>, orz → <sadness>
Emojis	☆→ <joy>, ♪♪ → <joy><joy>

Table 1: Japanese text normalization taxonomy as defined in this study and examples for each subcategory. The symbols in the subcategory represent the type of normalization employed in previous studies, where ∗ is (Saito et al., 2013), † is (Sasano et al., 2013), ‡ is (Osaki et al., 2017), and § is (Higashiyama et al., 2021), respectively.

of missing information, *deletion* of redundant information, *splitting* and *fusion* of sentences to improve readability across sentences.

Emotional Expressions In SNS text, emoticons and emojis are frequently used to express the writer's emotions. While these can be valuable cues for sentiment analysis, there are diverse expressions, for example, "（笑）" and "www" to express feelings of joy. Therefore, to effectively utilize these for sentiment analysis, a new major category of "emotional expressions" is defined. This type of normalization groups *emoticons*, *emojis*, and *emotional symbols* such as "（笑）" into Plutchik's basic eight emotions (Plutchik, 1980) and replaces them with special tokens such as <joy> and <sudness> that are assigned to each emotion. In addition, *numerical expressions* are also replaced with the special token <num>.

3.2 Details of Our Text Normalization

This section provides details on text normalization methods for each major category. Note that, as shown in Figure 1, multiple parts of a post may be normalized at the same time, and that multiple types of normalization may be applied to one expression.

Typos and Misspellings All errors are revised to the correct wording. In addition, missing punctuation should be completed, and proper nouns, including the titles of books and movies, should be consistently enclosed in parentheses with 『』.

Dialect Styles of sentence endings and functional expressions consistently transfer from casual to formal. Other types of dialects are normalized while using web searches as much as the annotator can detect.

Alternative Spellings Pronunciation variations, homophones, and small/large characters are revised to the correct wording. For symbol conversion, a sequence of punctuations is replaced by an ellipsis, and a comma at the end of a sentence is replaced by a period. Here, parentheses are consistently used with a single 「」 for utterances and a double 『』 for proper nouns.

Loanwords written in alphabetic or katakana characters are replaced with their Japanese counterparts when fluency can be improved by translation or transliteration. In addition, hiragana/katakana/kanji, abbreviations, and synonyms are replaced with high-frequency words. Here, word frequencies are counted from the Japanese edition of the CC-100[4] (Wenzek et al., 2020), a large-scale Web corpus, by word segmentation[5] (Kudo et al., 2004) of the text. Note that we therefore do not replace high-frequency abbreviations. For example, common abbreviations, such as "TV", are left as abbreviations because they are more frequent than the formal name of "television". However, proper nouns are not abbreviated regardless of their frequency.

[4]https://data.statmt.org/cc-100/
[5]https://github.com/neologd/mecab-ipadic-neologd

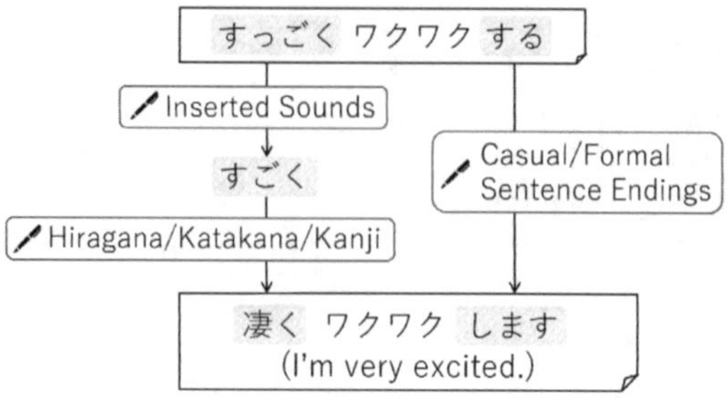

Figure 1: Example of our text normalization.

Emphasis Expressions Repetition of symbols, characters, words, or phrases should be limited to two times following the previous study (Osaki et al., 2017). Redundant sounds and symbols are also removed. Bullet points are expanded into sentences and word order is reformatted to improve fluency.

Simplification To improve readability, long compound sentences that should be expressed in multiple sentences are split, while short multiple sentences that should be expressed in one sentence are fused. Missing information should be completed if it can be inferred by the annotator, while redundant information should be deleted for simplicity. We paraphrase technical terms, low-frequency words, onomatopoeia, and other difficult-to-understand expressions into general and objective expressions.

Emotional Expressions Emojis, emoticons, and other emotional symbols are replaced with following special tokens according to Plutchik's basic eight emotions (Plutchik, 1980): <anger>, <disgust>, <fear>, <joy>, <sadness>, <surprise>, <trust>, and <anticipation>. Annotators choose which of the special tokens to replace the emotional symbols with, based on the context. We replace all numbers with the special token <num>, without regard to how large or small the numerical expressions are. However, we do not edit numerical expressions that are part of idioms, because replacing them would change their meaning.

4 Experiment

Our experiments evaluate the performance of sentiment polarity classification on sentences with individual or all normalizations, and assess the effectiveness of preprocessing with text normalization.

4.1 Settings

Task We evaluate the performance of Japanese sentiment polarity classification on the WRIME dataset (Kajiwara et al., 2021; Suzuki et al., 2022). This is a dataset of Japanese SNS posts labeled with five levels of sentiment polarity (-2, -1, 0, 1, 2) by the text writer. We used quadratic weighted kappa (QWK) (Cohen, 1968) as our evaluation metric.

Annotation For this experiment, we manually performed the text normalization described in the previous section on a total of 6,000 posts from WRIME, consisting of 5,000 posts from the training set and 500 posts each from the validation and evaluation sets. Annotations of text normalization were performed by three of the authors. First, one of the authors performed text normalization on the original posts. Then, another one of the authors evaluated the acceptability of their normalization and modified them as necessary. Finally, the remaining one author categorized each text normalization example based on our taxonomy.

Model Our sentiment analysis models were built by fine-tuning pre-trained Japanese BERT (Devlin et al., 2019) on the training set described above. For fine-tuning, AdamW (Loshchilov and Hutter, 2019) was used for optimization, the batch size was set to 64, and training was terminated when the QWK in the validation set stopped improving by 3 epochs. The learning rate was chosen from $\{1, 2, 3, 4, 5\} \times 10^{-5}$ to achieve the highest QWK in the validation set. We used two types of BERT, a base[6] model and a large[7] model, and added nine types of special tokens to the vocabulary for *emotional* and *numerical expressions*. In the following sections, we report the average score of 5 experiments conducted while changing the random seed.

4.2 Result

Table 2 shows the experimental results. The "Manual" columns that we trained and evaluated using our normalized dataset perform better in sentiment analysis than the "Baseline" columns that we trained and evaluated using the dataset without normalization. The performance improvement in sentiment analysis by text normalization is consistent for the two types of BERT models. These experimental results show that the text normalization based on our taxonomy is effective for sentiment analysis in Japanese.

	Baseline	Manual	Automatic
BERT-base	0.506	0.582	0.517
BERT-large	0.511	0.589	0.522

Table 2: Evaluation of sentiment polarity classification by quadratic weighted kappa. "Baseline" is the performance for text without normalization, "Manual" is for manually normalized text, and "Automatic" is for automatically normalized text, respectively.

4.3 Analysis: Evaluation by Subcategory

To clarify which type of text normalization contributes to improved performance in sentiment analysis, Table 3 shows the results of training and evaluating the BERT-large model with datasets normalized to each subcategory exclusively. The other experimental settings are the same as in Section 4.1.

For most subcategories, our text normalization improved the performance of sentiment analysis. The worse performance of sentiment analysis when only *pronunciation variations* were normalized suggests that changes in pronunciation are more likely to express the writer's emotions.

Text normalization for the four categories of *casual/formal sentence endings*, *missing symbols*, *hiragana/katakana/kanji* variations, and *abbreviations* achieved significant performance improvements of more than 3 points each. The diversity of texts, including these spelling inconsistencies, is a factor that hinders the training of sentiment analysis models.

4.4 Analysis: Automatic Text Normalization

We tried automatic text normalization by fine-tuning BART[8] (Lewis et al., 2020), a pre-trained sequence-to-sequence model, using our text normalization dataset. In fine-tuning, we applied vocabulary expansion as in BERT in Section 4.1, used AdamW (Loshchilov and Hutter, 2019) for optimization, set the batch size to 8, and terminated training when the cross-entropy loss on the validation set stopped improving by 3 epochs.

The performance of text normalization was evaluated by BLEU (Papineni et al., 2002) on the evaluation set, and the results showed a significant improvement from BLEU=47.4 without normaliza-

[6]https://huggingface.co/tohoku-nlp/bert-base-japanese-whole-word-masking

[7]https://huggingface.co/tohoku-nlp/bert-large-japanese

[8]https://huggingface.co/ku-nlp/bart-large-japanese

Category	Subcategory	#	QWK
	Baseline (w/o normalization)		0.511
	Apply all types of normalization		**0.589**
Typos and Misspellings	Missing Symbols	4,453	**0.555**
	Missing Characters	3,604	**0.529**
	Conjugation Errors	1,328	**0.526**
	Typos	55	**0.538**
	Misuse	45	**0.513**
Dialect	Casual/Formal Sentence Endings	5,321	**0.559**
	Casual/Formal Functional Expressions	1,923	0.511
	Internet Slang	539	**0.515**
	Regional Dialect	319	**0.522**
	Unique Sentence Endings	128	**0.523**
	Censored Words	16	**0.527**
Alternative Spellings	Hiragana/Katakana/Kanji	2,480	**0.550**
	Abbreviations	1,262	**0.541**
	Pronunciation Variations	1,031	0.509
	Synonyms	886	**0.525**
	Symbol Conversion	461	**0.537**
	Loanwords	273	**0.518**
	Homophones	132	**0.532**
	Small/Large Characters	63	**0.514**
Emphasis Expressions	Inserted Sounds	963	**0.518**
	Inserted Symbols	331	**0.538**
	Word Order Changes	293	**0.538**
	Repetition	288	**0.525**
	Bullet Points	43	**0.525**
Simplification	Completion	918	**0.520**
	Lexical/Phrasal Simplification	771	**0.530**
	Deletion	220	**0.518**
	Fusion	105	**0.517**
	Splitting	38	**0.531**
Emotional Expressions	Numerical Expressions	968	**0.533**
	Emotional Symbols	259	**0.535**
	Emoticons	180	**0.515**
	Emojis	47	**0.521**

Table 3: Performance of sentiment polarity classification by BERT-large evaluated with quadratic weighted kappa (QWK) when only the subcategories in each row are normalized. If that normalization improves performance over the baseline, the values in the QWK column are highlighted in bold. The # column shows the number of normalizations that fall into each subcategory out of the 6,000 posts we analyzed.

tion to BLEU=62.0, indicating the effectiveness of automatic text normalization. The "Automatic" column in Table 2 shows the performance of sentiment analysis trained and evaluated using an automatically normalized dataset. Not surprisingly, automatic text normalization did not contribute to the improved performance of sentiment analysis as much as its manual counterpart. Nevertheless, consistent performance improvements were achieved for both types of BERT models. More training data would improve the performance of automatic text normalization, but that is left as our future work.

	Text	Label
Original post	しもんぬきゃわ	Negative
Automatic normalization	仕事に行きません。	Very Negative
Manual normalization	下野紘が可愛いです。	Very Positive
Reference	Hiro Shimono is cute.	Very Positive
Original post	ふふってなった	Negative
Automatic normalization	ふふっていました。	Negative
Manual normalization	ふふっとなりました。	Neutral
Reference	It made me smile.	Positive
Original post	あたまもおなかもいたい。どっちかにしてほしい	Neutral
Automatic normalization	あたまもお腹も痛いです。どっちかにしてほしいです。	Negative
Manual normalization	頭もお腹も痛いです。どちらかにしてほしいです。	Negative
Reference	I have a headache and a stomachache. Pick a side!	Negative
Original post	私３Ｆ3列26	Positive
Automatic normalization	私は列です	Positive
Manual normalization	私は**<num>**階の**<num>**列**<num>**番の席です。	Neutral
Reference	I am on the third floor, row 3, seat 26.	Very Negative

Table 4: Examples of text normalization and its sentiment analysis. Reference rows are the English translation of the normalized text and the correct emotional polarity label annotated by the writer who posted the original text.

4.5 Qualitative Evaluation

Table 4 shows examples of text normalization and the results of its sentiment analysis. As in these examples, sentences consisting only of hiragana characters deteriorate the performance of sentiment analysis. Conversely, sentences that do not contain hiragana characters, as in the bottom example, are also difficult. If these can be properly normalized, expressions such as "可愛い (cute)" and "痛い (ache)" appear as cues to positive or negative emotions, contributing to improved performance of sentiment analysis. In the bottom example, the numerical expression represents the negative emotion of distant, but normalization of the numerical expression has made it difficult to read that emotion. Although the normalization of numerical expressions contributes to sentiment analysis on average, it can also have a negative impact, as in this example. In some cases, automatic text normalization almost works, as in the second and third examples, but in others, as in the first example, it generates text that is off the mark.

5 Conclusion

In this study, we worked on text normalization as a preprocessing to improve the performance of sentiment analysis for Japanese SNS texts. We defined a Japanese text normalization taxonomy consisting of 33 types of editing operations and manually normalized 6,000 posts. Experimental results showed that both automatic and manual text normalization consistently improved the performance of sentiment analysis. In manual text normalization, most types of normalization improved the performance of sentiment analysis, respectively. Our detailed analysis reveals that *pronunciation variations* should not be edited, and are a useful linguistic phenomenon for sentiment analysis.

Limitations

We released a dataset of manually normalized Japanese text from 6,000 posts (about 11,000 sentences) on social media. Our corpus is larger, considering that the Japanese text normalization corpora available in previous studies are about 1,000 sentence pairs. However, it is an insufficient size compared to corpora available for other text-to-text generation tasks such as machine translation, grammatical error correction, and text simplification.

Acknowledgments

This work was supported by Innovation Platform for Society 5.0 from Japan Ministry of Education, Culture, Sports, Science and Technology (JPMXP0518071489).

References

Iñaki Alegria, Nora Aranberri, Pere R. Comas, Víctor Fresno, Pablo Gamallo, Lluis Padró, Iñaki San Vicente, Jordi Turmo, and Arkaitz Zubiaga. 2015. TweetNorm: A Benchmark for Lexical Normalization of Spanish Tweets. *Language Resources and Evaluation*, 49(4):883–905.

Iñaki Alegria, Nora Aranberri, Víctor Fresno, Pablo Gamallo, Lluís Padró, Iñaki San Vicente, Jordi Turmo, and Arkaitz Zubiaga. 2013. Introducción a la Tarea Compartida Tweet-Norm 2013: Normalización Léxica de Tuits en Español. In *Proceedings of the Tweet Normalization Workshop co-located with 29th Conference of the Spanish Society for Natural Language Processing*, pages 1–9.

Timothy Baldwin, Marie Catherine de Marneffe, Bo Han, Young-Bum Kim, Alan Ritter, and Wei Xu. 2015. Shared Tasks of the 2015 Workshop on Noisy User-generated Text: Twitter Lexical Normalization and Named Entity Recognition. In *Proceedings of the Workshop on Noisy User-generated Text*, pages 126–135.

Laura Ana Maria Bostan, Evgeny Kim, and Roman Klinger. 2020. GoodNewsEveryone: A Corpus of News Headlines Annotated with Emotions, Semantic Roles, and Reader Perception. In *Proceedings of the Twelfth Language Resources and Evaluation Conference*, pages 1554–1566.

Jacob Cohen. 1968. Weighted Kappa: Nominal Scale Agreement Provision for Scaled Disagreement or Partial Credit. *Psychological Bulletin*, 70(4):213–220.

Talha Çolakoğlu, Umut Sulubacak, and Ahmet Cüneyd Tantuğ. 2019. Normalizing Non-canonical Turkish Texts Using Machine Translation Approaches. In *Proceedings of the 57th Annual Meeting of the Association for Computational Linguistics: Student Research Workshop*, pages 267–272.

Jacob Devlin, Ming-Wei Chang, Kenton Lee, and Kristina Toutanova. 2019. BERT: Pre-training of Deep Bidirectional Transformers for Language Understanding. In *Proceedings of the 2019 Conference of the North American Chapter of the Association for Computational Linguistics: Human Language Technologies*, pages 4171–4186.

Bo Han and Timothy Baldwin. 2011. Lexical Normalisation of Short Text Messages: Makn Sens a #twitter. In *Proceedings of the 49th Annual Meeting of the Association for Computational Linguistics: Human Language Technologies*, pages 368–378.

Shohei Higashiyama, Masao Utiyama, Taro Watanabe, and Eiichiro Sumita. 2021. User-Generated Text Corpus for Evaluating Japanese Morphological Analysis and Lexical Normalization. In *Proceedings of the 2021 Conference of the North American Chapter of the Association for Computational Linguistics: Human Language Technologies*, pages 5532–5541.

Taishi Ikeda, Hiroyuki Shindo, and Yuji Matsumoto. 2016. Japanese Text Normalization with Encoder-Decoder Model. In *Proceedings of the 2nd Workshop on Noisy User-generated Text*, pages 129–137.

Nobuhiro Kaji and Masaru Kitsuregawa. 2014. Accurate Word Segmentation and POS Tagging for Japanese Microblogs: Corpus Annotation and Joint Modeling with Lexical Normalization. In *Proceedings of the 2014 Conference on Empirical Methods in Natural Language Processing*, pages 99–109.

Tomoyuki Kajiwara, Chenhui Chu, Noriko Takemura, Yuta Nakashima, and Hajime Nagahara. 2021. WRIME: A New Dataset for Emotional Intensity Estimation with Subjective and Objective Annotations. In *Proceedings of the 2021 Conference of the North American Chapter of the Association for Computational Linguistics: Human Language Technologies*, pages 2095–2104.

Taku Kudo, Kaoru Yamamoto, and Yuji Matsumoto. 2004. Applying Conditional Random Fields to Japanese Morphological Analysis. In *Proceedings of the 2004 Conference on Empirical Methods in Natural Language Processing*, pages 230–237.

Mike Lewis, Yinhan Liu, Naman Goyal, Marjan Ghazvininejad, Abdelrahman Mohamed, Omer Levy, Veselin Stoyanov, and Luke Zettlemoyer. 2020. BART: Denoising Sequence-to-Sequence Pre-training for Natural Language Generation, Translation, and Comprehension. In *Proceedings of the 58th Annual Meeting of the Association for Computational Linguistics*, pages 7871–7880.

Peerat Limkonchotiwat, Wannaphong Phatthiyaphaibun, Raheem Sarwar, Ekapol Chuangsuwanich, and Sarana Nutanong. 2021. Handling Cross- and Out-of-Domain Samples in Thai Word Segmentation. In *Findings of the Association for Computational Linguistics: ACL-IJCNLP 2021*, pages 1003–1016.

Fei Liu, Fuliang Weng, Bingqing Wang, and Yang Liu. 2011. Insertion, Deletion, or Substitution? Normalizing Text Messages without Pre-categorization nor Supervision. In *Proceedings of the 49th Annual Meeting of the Association for Computational Linguistics: Human Language Technologies*, pages 71–76.

Ilya Loshchilov and Frank Hutter. 2019. Decoupled Weight Decay Regularization. In *Proceedings of the Seventh International Conference on Learning Representations*.

Saif Mohammad and Felipe Bravo-Marquez. 2017. WASSA-2017 Shared Task on Emotion Intensity. In *Proceedings of the 8th Workshop on Computational Approaches to Subjectivity, Sentiment and Social Media Analysis*, pages 34–49.

Saif Mohammad, Felipe Bravo-Marquez, Mohammad Salameh, and Svetlana Kiritchenko. 2018. SemEval-2018 Task 1: Affect in Tweets. In *Proceedings of the 12th International Workshop on Semantic Evaluation*, pages 1–17.

Thanh-Nhi Nguyen, Thanh-Phong Le, and Kiet Nguyen. 2024. ViLexNorm: A Lexical Normalization Corpus for Vietnamese Social Media Text. In *Proceedings of the 18th Conference of the European Chapter of the Association for Computational Linguistics*, pages 1421–1437.

Ayaha Osaki, Yoshiaki Kitagawa, and Mamoru Komachi. 2017. Nihongo Twitter bunsho wo taishou to shita keiretsu labeling ni yoru hyouki seikika. *IPSJ SIG Technical Report*, 2017-NL-231(12):1–6. (In Japanese).

Kishore Papineni, Salim Roukos, Todd Ward, and Wei-Jing Zhu. 2002. BLEU: a Method for Automatic Evaluation of Machine Translation. In *Proceedings of the 40th Annual Meeting of the Association for Computational Linguistics*, pages 311–318.

Barbara Plank, Kristian Nørgaard Jensen, and Rob van der Goot. 2020. DaN+: Danish Nested Named Entities and Lexical Normalization. In *Proceedings of the 28th International Conference on Computational Linguistics*, pages 6649–6662.

Flor Miriam Plaza del Arco, Carlo Strapparava, L. Alfonso Urena Lopez, and Maite Martin. 2020. EmoEvent: A Multilingual Emotion Corpus based on different Events. In *Proceedings of the Twelfth Language Resources and Evaluation Conference*, pages 1492–1498.

Robert Plutchik. 1980. A General Psychoevolutionary Theory of Emotion. *Theories of Emotion*, 1:3–31.

Itsumi Saito, Kugatsu Sadamitsu, Hisako Asano, and Yoshihiro Matsuo. 2013. Extracting Derivational Patterns based on the Alignment of a Standard Form and its Variant towards the Japanese Morphological Analysis for Noisy Text. *IPSJ SIG Technical Report*, 2013-NL-214(5):1–9. (In Japanese).

Itsumi Saito, Jun Suzuki, Kyosuke Nishida, Kugatsu Sadamitsu, Satoshi Kobashikawa, Ryo Masumura, Yuji Matsumoto, and Junji Tomita. 2017. Improving Neural Text Normalization with Data Augmentation at Character- and Morphological Levels. In *Proceedings of the Eighth International Joint Conference on Natural Language Processing*, pages 257–262.

Akira Sasaki, Junta Mizuno, Naoaki Okazaki, and Kentaro Inui. 2013. Normalization of Text in Microblogging Based on Machine Learning. In *Proceedings of the 27th Annual Conference of the Japanese Society for Artificial Intelligence*. (In Japanese).

Ryohei Sasano, Sadao Kurohashi, and Manabu Okumura. 2013. A Simple Approach to Unknown Word Processing in Japanese Morphological Analysis. In *Proceedings of the Sixth International Joint Conference on Natural Language Processing*, pages 162–170.

Uladzimir Sidarenka, Tatjana Scheffler, and Manfred Stede. 2013. Rule-based Normalization of German Twitter Messages. In *Proceedings of the International Conference of the German Society for Computational Linguistics and Language Technology*.

Haruya Suzuki, Yuto Miyauchi, Kazuki Akiyama, Tomoyuki Kajiwara, Takashi Ninomiya, Noriko Takemura, Yuta Nakashima, and Hajime Nagahara. 2022. A Japanese Dataset for Subjective and Objective Sentiment Polarity Classification in Micro Blog Domain. In *Proceedings of the Thirteenth Language Resources and Evaluation Conference*, pages 7022–7028.

Rob van der Goot, Alan Ramponi, Tommaso Caselli, Michele Cafagna, and Lorenzo De Mattei. 2020. Norm It! Lexical Normalization for Italian and Its Downstream Effects for Dependency Parsing. In *Proceedings of the Twelfth Language Resources and Evaluation Conference*, pages 6272–6278.

Guillaume Wenzek, Marie-Anne Lachaux, Alexis Conneau, Vishrav Chaudhary, Francisco Guzmán, Armand Joulin, and Edouard Grave. 2020. CCNet: Extracting High Quality Monolingual Datasets from Web Crawl Data. In *Proceedings of the Twelfth Language Resources and Evaluation Conference*, pages 4003–4012.

Yi Yang and Jacob Eisenstein. 2013. A Log-Linear Model for Unsupervised Text Normalization. In *Proceedings of the 2013 Conference on Empirical Methods in Natural Language Processing*, pages 61–72.

Author Index